In P
Divi
Ruchira Avatar
Adi Da Samraj

I t is obvious, from all sorts of subtle details, that he knows what IT's all about . . . a rare being.

ALAN WATTS
author, *The Way of Zen* and *The Wisdom of Insecurity*

I regard Adi Da Samraj as one of the greatest teachers in the Western world today.

IRINA TWEEDIE
Sufi teacher; author, *Chasm of Fire*

I recognize the God-Presence Incarnate in Adi Da Samraj as whole and full and complete.

BARBARA MARX HUBBARD
author, *Conscious Evolution* and *The Revelation;*
president, The Foundation for Conscious Evolution

A di Da Samraj has created virtually the entire basis for a culture founded in love and wisdom. The magnitude of such an undertaking— let alone the accomplishment of it—cannot be overstated.

JOHN WHITE
author, *Frontiers of Consciousness,*
and *The Meeting of Science and Spirit*

A di Da Samraj is a man who has truly walked in Spirit and given true enlightenment to many.

SUN BEAR
founder, the Bear Tribe Medicine Society

T he life and teaching of Avatar Adi Da Samraj are of profound and deci- sive spiritual significance at this critical moment in history.

BRYAN DESCHAMP
Senior Adviser at the United Nations
High Commission for Refugees;
former Dean of the Carmelite House of Studies, Australia;
former Dean of Trinity College, University of Melbourne

A great teacher with the dynamic ability to awaken in his listeners something of the Divine Reality in which he is grounded, with which he is identified, and which, in fact, he is.

ISRAEL REGARDIE
author, *The Golden Dawn*

A di Da Samraj has spoken directly to the heart of our human situation—the shocking gravity of our brief and unbidden lives. Through his words I have experienced a glimmering of eternal life, and view my own existence as timeless and spaceless in a way that I never have before.

RICHARD GROSSINGER
author, *Planet Medicine*

A vatar Adi Da is the greatest Spiritual Master ever to walk the earth. He is the God-Man. He reveals the ultimate truth residing in the human heart.

THE REVEREND THOMAS E. AHLBURN
Senior Minister, First Unitarian Church
Providence, Rhode Island

M y relationship with Adi Da Samraj over many years has only confirmed His Realization and the Truth of His impeccable Teaching. He is much more than simply an inspiration of my music, but is really a living demonstration that perfect transcendence is actually possible. This is both a great relief and a great challenge. If you thirst for truth, here is a rare opportunity to drink.

RAY LYNCH
composer and musician, *Deep Breakfast*;
The Sky of Mind; and *Ray Lynch, Best Of*

A di Da Samraj and his unique body of teaching work offer a rare and extraordinary opportunity for those courageous students who are ready to move beyond ego and take the plunge into deepest communion with the Absolute. Importantly, the teaching is grounded in explicit discussion of necessary psychospiritual evolution and guides the student to self-responsibility and self-awareness.

ELISABETH TARG, M.D.
University of California, San Francisco,
School of Medicine;
director, Complementary Medicine Research Institute,
California Pacific Medical Center

That God can, among other things, actually incarnate in human form once seemed unbelievable to me. But reading the books of Avatar Adi Da obliterated all doubt about the existence of God right now, here on Earth in human form.

CHARMIAN ANDERSON, PH.D.
psychologist; author, *Bridging Heaven and Earth*
and *The Heart of Success*

Fly to the side of this God-Man. His Divine Transmission works miracles of change not possible by any other Spiritual means.

LEE SANNELLA
author, *The Kundalini Experience*

When I first read the Word of Avatar Adi Da Samraj, I was immediately transported into a state of wonderment and awe. Could it be? Could the Divine Person be here now, in this time and place? It didn't take long for my heart to answer a resounding "Yes". May the whole world be restored to Faith, Love, and Understanding by the Mystery of Real God, here and Incarnate as Avatar Adi Da Samraj.

ED KOWALCZYK
lead singer and songwriter of the rock band, *Live*

I regard the work of Adi Da and his devotees as one of the most penetrating spiritual and social experiments happening on the planet in our era.

JEFFREY MISHLOVE, PH.D.
host, PBS television series, *Thinking Allowed*;
author, *The Roots of Consciousness*

Adi Da's Teachings have tremendous significance for humanity. . . .
He represents a foundation and a structure for sanity.

ROBERT K. HALL, M.D.
psychiatrist; author, *Out of Nowhere*;
co-founder, The Lomi School and Lomi Clinic

The Divine World-Teacher,
RUCHIRA AVATAR ADI DA SAMRAJ
The Mountain Of Attention, 2000

THE
SEVEN STAGES
OF LIFE

THE SEVENTEEN COMPANIONS
OF THE TRUE DAWN HORSE

BOOK TEN

Transcending The Six Stages Of egoic Life, and Realizing The ego-Transcending Seventh Stage Of Life, In The Divine Way Of Adidam

By
The Divine World-Teacher,

RUCHIRA AVATAR
ADI DA SAMRAJ

THE DAWN HORSE PRESS
MIDDLETOWN, CALIFORNIA

NOTE TO THE READER

All who study the Way of Adidam or take up its practice should remember that they are responding to a Call to become responsible for themselves. They should understand that they, not Avatar Adi Da Samraj or others, are responsible for any decision they make or action they take in the course of their lives of study or practice.

The devotional, Spiritual, functional, practical, relational, cultural, and formal community practices and disciplines referred to in this book are appropriate and natural practices that are voluntarily and progressively adopted by members of the four congregations of Adidam (as applicable for each of the congregations and as appropriate to the personal circumstance of each individual). Although anyone may find these practices useful and beneficial, they are not presented as advice or recommendations to the general reader or to anyone who is not a member of one of the four congregations of Adidam. And nothing in this book is intended as a diagnosis, prescription, or recommended treatment or cure for any specific "problem", whether medical, emotional, psychological, social, or Spiritual. One should apply a particular program of treatment, prevention, cure, or general health only in consultation with a licensed physician or other qualified professional.

The Seven Stages Of Life is formally authorized for publication by the Ruchira Sannyasin Order of the Tantric Renunciates of Adidam, as part of the Standard Edition of the Divine "Source-Texts" of the Divine World-Teacher, Ruchira Avatar Adi Da Samraj. (The Ruchira Sannyasin Order of the Tantric Renunciates of Adidam is the senior Spiritual and Cultural Authority within the formal gathering of formally acknowledged devotees of the Divine World-Teacher, Ruchira Avatar Adi Da Samraj.)

NOTE TO BIBLIOGRAPHERS: The correct form for citing Ruchira Avatar Adi Da Samraj's Name (in any form of alphabetized listing) is:

Adi Da Samraj, Ruchira Avatar

COVER: Both the central photograph and the border photograph are by Avatar Adi Da Samraj. Please see "Camera Illuminata: The 'Bright'-Field Photography of Avatar Adi Da Samraj", pp. 39-41.

Printed in the United States of America

Produced by the Eleutherian Pan-Communion of Adidam
in cooperation with the Dawn Horse Press

International Standard Book Number: 1-57097-105-6
Library of Congress Catalog Card Number: 00-107308

CONTENTS

THE SEVEN STAGES OF LIFE

FIRST WORD:

Do Not Misunderstand <u>Me</u>—
I Am <u>Not</u> "Within" <u>you</u>, but you <u>Are</u> In <u>Me</u>,
and I Am <u>Not</u> a Mere "Man" in the "Middle" of Mankind,
but All of Mankind Is Surrounded, and Pervaded,
and Blessed By <u>Me</u>

51

PROLOGUE:
My Divine Disclosure

73

PART ONE:
Tat Sundaram!—
All Of This Is <u>Sacred</u>, All Of This Is <u>Beautiful</u>!
(The Essence of the Message of Adidam
and of the One and Entire Great Tradition of Mankind)

87

PART FIVE:
The Heart-Summary Of Adidam
335

EPILOGUE:
I _Am_ The Perfectly Subjective Divine Person,
Self-Manifested _As_ The Ruchira Avatar—
Who _Is_ The First, The Last, and The Only
Adept-Realizer, Adept-Revealer, and
Adept-Revelation of The Seventh Stage of Life
341

RUCHIRA AVATAR ADI DA SAMRAJ
The Mountain Of Attention, 2000

Introduction

This book is an invitation to enter a different world. A world that is completely <u>real</u>, in the largest possible sense of that word. A world in which none of the sufferings and difficulties of life are ignored or denied—but also a world in which yearnings for truth, wisdom, happiness, and love are addressed at an extraordinary depth. A world in which there is real, trustable guidance through the "maze" of life's confusions and crises. A world that vastly exceeds all limited notions of what is "real". A world of deep, abiding joy.

People from all walks of life have felt this world open up to them when they read the books of the Divine World-Teacher, Ruchira Avatar Adi Da Samraj. Those of us who have done so have felt our deepest questions answered, our most profound heart-longings satisfied. We have treasured His Instruction about the real issues everyone faces: death, sex, intimacy, emotional maturity, community life, and many more. We have marveled at His precise "map" of the entire course of Spiritual life, and at His description of the nature of reality in all its dimensions. We have been sobered by His criticism of the universal human bondage to the self-centered desires and purposes of the ego. And, altogether, through His words, we have felt His Divine Spiritual Blessing deeply affecting our lives.

Those of us who have been drawn to Avatar Adi Da have discovered that the impact of His Truth (and the Blessing it conveys) is so great in our lives, so far beyond anything else we have known, that a truly amazing recognition began to grow in our hearts and minds: Avatar Adi Da Samraj is not merely a great human being who speaks profound Truth—He is the Divine Reality Itself, Appearing in a human body in order to Offer His Revelation of Truth directly to all of humankind.

Often, this awakened recognition of Him—as the Divine Reality Present in human Form—comes as a complete surprise. In this age of skepticism, many regard the idea of a Divine Incarnation as strictly mythological. But Avatar Adi Da Samraj is not a myth— He is an intensely real living being. He is an utterly spontaneous and free manifestation, moved (by overwhelming love) to serve the Happiness and Liberation of beings everywhere, and to bring our global home out of this time of potential political and ecological disaster.

However, no one is asked to "believe" that Avatar Adi Da is the Divine. He has even said, "You must not believe in Me." Why? Because mere belief is not transformative. Only what is revealed in one's real experience—of body, heart, and mind altogether, rather than mind only—can transform the being. Therefore, Avatar Adi Da does not offer you a set of beliefs, or even a set of Spiritual techniques. He simply offers you His Revelation of Truth as a free gift, to respond to as you will. And, if you are moved to take up His Way, He invites you to enter into a direct Spiritual relationship with Him. Those of us who have taken this step have found the Spiritual relationship to Avatar Adi Da Samraj to be a supremely precious gift, a literally miraculous blessing, the answer to our deepest longings—greatly surpassing anything we have ever experienced or even imagined to be possible. Indeed, we have found Avatar Adi Da's Revelation of Truth to be so all-encompassing and His Spiritual Power and Love to be so overwhelming that we recognize Him as the Promised God-Man—the One capable of fulfilling the yearnings of people everywhere, the One Whose Appearance has been foreshadowed by prophecies in many religious traditions.

Avatar Adi Da began Teaching formally in 1972. In the years since then, He has communicated a vast store of Wisdom. But He has also done far more than that: He has created a whole new Way of life, a new religion, which is now practiced by people of different cultures in many parts of the world.

Just as the religions of Christianity and Buddhism are named after their founders, the religion founded by Avatar Adi Da is named after Him—it is called "Adidam" (AH-dee-DAHM). Adidam is an all-embracing practice that takes every aspect of human life—the "lowest" as well as the "highest"—into account (see pp. 364-65). The foundation of Adidam is the response of heart-felt devotion to Avatar Adi Da Samraj, in loving gratitude for His Gifts of Wisdom and Spiritual Blessing.

Avatar Adi Da's books are full of ecstatic proclamations of His Divinity—and there is a secret to understanding these proclamations fully. The secret is this: Avatar Adi Da is not speaking as a separate being who presumes himself to be irreducibly "different" from every other being. No, He is speaking as the Divine Heart of every being. Therefore, His most fundamental message may be summarized as follows:

> There is no ultimate "difference" between you and the Divine.
> There is only the Divine.
> Everything that exists is a "modification" of the One Divine Reality.

However, even though it may be true that there is only the Divine, this is not, in fact, our common daily experience. Far from it! Our usual daily life is full of events and people (including ourselves!) that we experience as distinctly un-Divine.

Therefore, Avatar Adi Da is humanly present in the world in order to Reveal the Divine Condition, and to make it possible for human beings to Realize that that Condition is our True Nature. That this is so is the deep heart-certainty of Avatar Adi Da's devotees—after many years of studying His Teaching, hearing His Discourses, enjoying His Company in all kinds of circumstances, and knowing the profound Ecstasy, Joy, and Peace of His Spiritual Transmission.

Thus, when Avatar Adi Da Samraj says "I Am the One to be Realized" or "I Am the Very Divine Person" or "I Am the Divine Heart Itself" (and many other variations), He is confessing that He is, paradoxically, the Divine Condition of everyone and everything—seeming to be a separate being, in order to offer us the Way to Realize our Inherent Condition. And it is our confession to you, as those who have become His devotees, that to behold Him with an open heart is to fall into an indescribable Love, Bliss, and Happiness that is self-evidently the deepest Truth of one's own heart and the Very Heart of Existence.

As Avatar Adi Da Samraj says, with great passion and emphasis:

Beloved, Even I Am Only You (As You Are).

This is the great mystery that you are invited to discover for yourself.

A vatar Adi Da Samraj's Name is composed of four Sanskrit words.

His principal Name is "Adi Da". "Avatar" and "Samraj" are sacred Titles, used in association with His Name.

"Adi" (AH-dee) means "Original" (or "Primordial"), and "Da" means "the Divine Giver". Thus, "Adi Da" means "the Original Divine Giver".

"Avatar" means "a 'Crossing Down' of the Divine Being into the world" (or, in other words, "an Appearance of the Divine in conditionally manifested form").

"Samraj" (sahm-RAHJ) means "universal Lord".

In fuller forms of reference, Adi Da Samraj is called "the Ruchira (roo-CHIH-rah) Avatar", meaning "the Avatar of Infinite Brightness".

Avatar Adi Da Samraj:
His Life and Teaching

The Three Great Purposes
of Avatar Adi Da Samraj:
Learning Man, Teaching Man,
and Blessing Man

From the moment of His Birth (in New York, on November 3, 1939), Adi Da Samraj was Consciously Aware of His Native Divine Condition. As soon as He became able to use language, He gave this Condition a simple but very expressive Name—"the 'Bright'".* But then, at the age of two years, Avatar Adi Da made a profound spontaneous choice. He chose to relinquish His constant Enjoyment of the "Bright"—out of what He Describes as a "painful loving", a sympathy for the suffering and ignorance of human beings. Avatar Adi Da Confesses that He chose to "Learn Man"—to enter into everything that humankind feels and suffers, and also to experience all the various levels of Spiritual Realization known to humanity—in order to discover how to Draw human beings into the "Bright" Divine Condition that He knew as His own True State and the True State of everyone.

This utter Submission to all aspects of human life was the first Purpose of Adi Da's Incarnation. In His Spiritual Autobiography, *The Knee Of Listening*, Avatar Adi Da recounts this amazing and heroic Ordeal, which lasted for the first thirty years of His Life.

*For definitions of terms and names, please see the Glossary (pp. 400-37).

In 1970, Avatar Adi Da finally Re-Awakened permanently to the "Bright", and embarked upon the second great Purpose of His Incarnation—the Process of "Teaching Man".

When He began to Teach others, Avatar Adi Da Samraj simply made Himself available to all who were willing to enter into the living Process of Real-God-Realization in His Company—a Process Which He summarized as the relation-

Los Angeles, 1972

ship to Him, rather than any method or technique of Spiritual attainment. Through that relationship—an extraordinary human and Spiritual intimacy—Avatar Adi Da Samraj perfectly embraced

The Mountain Of Attention Sanctuary, 1974

each of His devotees, using every kind of skillful means to Awaken them to the Truth that the separate, un-Enlightened self—with all its fear, anxieties, and fruitless seeking for Happiness— is self-imposed suffering, a contraction of the being (which He calls "the self-contraction").

Happiness, He Revealed, cannot be attained through any kind of search, because It is "Always Already the Case". And He Offered the practice of heart-Communion with Him as the means of going beyond the self-contraction and thereby Realizing Real Happiness.

I have Come to Live (now, and forever hereafter) with those who love Me with ego-overwhelming love, and I have Come to Love them likewise Overwhelmingly. . . .

Until you fall in love, love is what you <u>fear</u> to do. When you have fallen in love, and you <u>are</u> (thus) always already in love, then you cease to fear to love . . . . Those who fall in love with Me, Fall into Me. Those whose hearts are given, in love, to Me, Fall into My Heart. [*"What Will You Do If You Love Me?", from* Da Love-Ananda Gita]

In 1986, an Event occurred that marked the beginning of a great change in Avatar Adi Da's Work in the world. In this Great Event, a profound Yogic Swoon (taking the form of His apparent near-death) overwhelmed His body-mind, and Avatar Adi Da Samraj spontaneously began the process of relinquishing His Ordeal of Learning and Teaching Man. In the wake of that great Swoon, He simply Radiated His Divinity as never before. This was the beginning of what He calls His "Divine Self-'Emergence'". From that moment, Adi Da Samraj has devoted

The Mountain Of Attention, 1986

Himself increasingly to the third and eternal Purpose of His Avataric Incarnation—that of "Blessing Man" (and even all beings).

The Way of Adidam

Even after the Great Event in 1986, Avatar Adi Da continued to Work to ensure that His Revelation of the Way of Adidam was fully and firmly founded in the world. It was not until February 1999 that Avatar Adi Da Samraj declared that all the foundation Work of His Incarnation had been completely and finally Done. Everything necessary for the understanding and right practice of the real religious process, culminating in Divine Enlightenment, has been Said and Done by Him. The summary of His Wisdom-Teaching is preserved for all time in a series of twenty-three "Source-Texts" (described on pp. 27-38). And the Way of Adidam is fully established. This monumental Work has been accomplished by Avatar Adi Da in a little over a quarter of a century—twenty-seven years of ceaseless Instruction, in constant interaction with His devotees.

Avatar Adi Da's Full Revelation of Truth and His Work to establish the Way of Adidam required an immense struggle. The reason that struggle was inevitable is that human beings—especially in this time when the "individual" is regarded to be the supreme measure of value—have enormous resistance to any process that requires them to go beyond ego. Throughout history, people have tended to prefer forms of religion based on a system of beliefs and a code of moral and social behavior. But this kind of religion, as Avatar Adi Da has always pointed out, does not go to the core, to the root-suffering of human beings. This is because ordinary religion, rather than going beyond the ego-principle, is actually based on it: the ego-self stands at the center, and the Divine is sought and appealed to as the great Power that is going to save and satisfy the individual self. Avatar Adi Da Describes such religion as "client-centered".

In contrast to conventional religion, there is the process that Avatar Adi Da calls "true religion", religion that is centered in the Divine, in response to a true Spiritual Master who has (to at least some significant degree) Realized God (as opposed to merely offering teachings about God). Thus, true religion does not revolve around the individual's desire for any kind of "spiritual" consolations or experience—it is ego-transcending, rather than ego-serving. True religion based on ego-surrendering devotion to a Spiritual Master has existed for thousands of years, but the ecstatic confession of Avatar Adi Da's devotees is that now the Very Divine Itself is directly Present, Functioning as Divine Heart-Master, Alive in the human form of Avatar Adi Da Samraj.

All religions are historical forms of the Single and Ancient Way of Distracted love for the Divine Person, especially as Revealed in the Life and in the Company and in the Person of Incarnate Adepts (or Realizers) in their various degrees and stages of Realization. This is the Great Secret. [*"What Will You Do If You Love Me?"*, *from* Da Love-Ananda Gita]

[E]goity is the "disease" that <u>*all*</u> *the true Spiritual Masters of religion come here to cure.* Unfortunately, . . . *religious and Spiritual institutions tend to develop along lines that serve, accommodate, and represent the common egoity—and this is why the esoteric true Teachings of true Spiritual Masters tend to be bypassed, and even suppressed, in the drive to develop the exoteric cult of any particular Spiritual Master.*

The relationship to Me . . . is a profound esoteric discipline, <u>*necessarily*</u> *associated with real and serious and mature . . . practice of the "radical" Way (or root-Process) of Realizing* <u>*Real*</u> *God (Which* <u>*Is*</u> *Reality and Truth).*

The Way of Adidam is the . . . Way to live in <u>*Freedom*</u>—*not to be bound by separate and separative self, or by conditional Nature as a whole. Therefore, the ego-transcending devotional relationship to Me is the Context and the Means of Free Divine Self-Realization.* [*"Beyond the Cultic Tendency in Religion and Spirituality, and in Secular Society"*, *from* Ruchira Avatara Gita]

Standing Free of the Common Egoity

In His Spiritual Work with His devotees and the world, Avatar Adi Da Samraj has confronted the realities of egoity in a completely direct and unflinching manner. In His years of "Teaching Man", He did not hesitate in the slightest to grapple with the ego as it might be manifested in any moment by an individual devotee or a group of devotees—for the sake of helping His devotees understand and go beyond their ego-possessed disposition and activity.

However, even in the midst of that compassionate struggle with the forces of egoity, Avatar Adi Da has always Stood utterly Free of the ego-world. And, especially since the late 1970s, that Free Stand more and more took the form of His living in an essentially private circumstance, at one of the Hermitages established for Him (at secluded locations in California, Hawaii, and Fiji—see p. 373). In His Hermitage sphere, Avatar Adi Da is served by an intimate group of renunciate devotees, with whom He does particularly intensive Spiritual Work. And it is in the set-apart domain of His Hermitages (rather than in some kind of more public setting) that Avatar Adi Da receives His devotees in general (and, on rare occasions, specially invited members of the public), to Grant them His Spiritual Blessing.

The reasons why Avatar Adi Da maintains a Hermitage life are profound. The purpose of His Existence is to Reveal the Divine Reality—in other words, to Manifest the Freedom, Purity, and unbounded Blissfulness of His own Divine Nature, to Exist simply as He Is, without having to make compromises or adjustments in order to "fit in" to the ordinary ego-patterned world. Therefore, it is essential that He live in a sacred domain that conforms to Him and to the nature of His Spiritual Work, where He can remain independent of (but not disconnected from) the common world, even the daily world of the practical functioning of His community of devotees. Indeed, it is essential that He be free of institutional or organizational responsibilities relative to the gathering of His own devotees—because any such level of functioning would be a limitation on His Spiritual Work, an impingement on His Freedom to Manifest His own True Nature in the fullest and most pristine manner.

As He has commented many times, His Hermitage life is a life of seclusion, but not of isolation. His secluded Hermitage life is what allows His Divine Blessing to Flow into the world with the greatest possible force and effectiveness—it is what allows His Spiritual connection to all beings to be as strong as possible.

The "Problem" Is ego— Not Anything Else

For more than a quarter of a century, during His years of Teaching and Revelation (from 1972 to 1999), Avatar Adi Da undertook a vast, in-life "consideration" with His devotees of everything related to Spiritual life—from the most rudimentary matters to the most esoteric. One extremely important area of "consideration" was how to rightly relate to the most basic urges and activities of human life—what Avatar Adi Da describes as the realm of "money, food, and sex". (By "money", Avatar Adi Da means not only the earning and use of money itself, but the exercising of life-energy in general.)

In most religious traditions, an ascetical approach to these primal urges is recommended—in other words, desires related to "money, food, and sex" are to be minimized or denied. Avatar Adi Da took a different approach. When they are rightly engaged, ordinary human enjoyments are not a problem, not "sinful" or "anti-spiritual" in and of themselves. Thus, the root-problem of human beings is not any particular activity or desire of the body-mind, but the ego itself—the governing presumption that one is a separate and independent entity, threatened by the inevitable prospect of death. Therefore, in living dialogue and experimentation with His devotees, Avatar Adi Da brought to light, in detail, exactly how the human functions of money (or life-energy), food, and sex can be rightly engaged, in a truly ego-transcending manner—an entirely life-positive and non-suppressive manner that is both pleasurable and supportive of the Spiritual process in His Company.

The transcending of egoic involvement with "money, food, and sex" is a matter that relates to the beginnings of (or preparation for) real Spiritual practice. But the necessity for ego-transcendence does not end there. In His years of Teaching and Revelation, Avatar Adi Da Revealed that the ego is still present, in one form or another, in all the possible varieties of Spiritual attainment short of Most Perfect Divine Enlightenment. The word "Enlightenment" is used by different people and in different traditions with various different meanings. In Avatar Adi Da's language, "Enlightenment" (which He sometimes modifies, for the sake of clarifying His meaning, as "Most Perfect Divine Enlightenment", and which is synonymous with "Divine Self-Realization", "Real-God-Realization", and "seventh stage Realization") specifically means that the process of ego-transcendence has been entirely completed, relative to all the dimensions of the being. In other words, the ego has been transcended in three distinct phases—first at the physical (or gross) level (the level of "money, food, and sex"), then at the subtle level (the level of internal visions, auditions, and all kinds of mystical experience), and finally at the causal level (the root-level of conscious existence, wherein the sense of "I" and "other", or the subject-object dichotomy, seems to arise in Consciousness).

The complete process of ego-transcendence is extraordinarily profound and can only proceed on the basis of all the foundation disciplines and an ever-increasing heart-surrender to the Blessing-Transmission of Adi Da Samraj. Then, progressively, there is a transformation of view, a "positive disillusionment" (in Adi Da's Words) with each phase of egoity—until there is Most Perfect Divine Enlightenment (or "Open Eyes"), the Realization of Consciousness Itself as the Single Love-Blissful Reality and Source of existence.

Thus, the Way of Adidam truly represents an extraordinary and unique Offering to humankind. It is the Way Given by the Primal Divine Realizer and Revealer of Most Perfect Divine Enlightenment. He Transmits the Divinely Enlightened State, and He has the Power to Draw His devotees into that Perfectly Love-Blissful State. Such great statements about Avatar Adi Da Samraj are not something to be either accepted or rejected as a matter of belief. Rather, they are His Free Self-Confession to you—and His invitation to you to fall into His Divine Embrace.

A Testimony of Spiritual Practice

The process of the Way of Adidam unfolds by Avatar Adi Da's Grace, according to the depth of surrender and response in each devotee. One of the most extraordinary living testimonies to the Greatness and Truth of the Way of Adidam is one of Avatar Adi Da's longtime devotees, whose renunciate name is Ruchira Adidama Sukha Sundari Naitauba. Adidama Sukha Sundari has totally consecrated herself to Avatar Adi Da and lives always in His Sphere, in a relationship of unique intimacy and service. By her profound love of, and most exemplary surrender to, her Divine Heart-Master, she has become combined with Him at a unique depth. She manifests the signs of deep and constant immersion in His Divine Being, both in meditation and daily life. Adidama Sukha Sundari is a member of the Ruchira Sannyasin Order (the senior cultural authority within the gathering of Avatar Adi Da's devotees), practicing in the ultimate stages of the Way of Adidam.

Through a process of more than twenty years of intense testing, Avatar Adi Da has been able to lead Adidama Sukha Sundari to the threshold of Divine Enlightenment. The profound and ecstatic relationship with Avatar Adi Da that Adidama Sukha Sundari has come to know can be felt in this intimate letter of devotional confession to Him:

RUCHIRA ADIDAMA SUKHA SUNDARI:
Bhagavan Love-Ananda, Supreme and
Divine Person, Real-God-Body of Love,

I rest in Your Constant and Perfect
Love-Embrace, with no need but to for-
ever worship You. Suddenly in love,
Mastered at heart, always with my head
at Your Supreme and Holy Feet, I am
beholding and recognizing Your "Bright"
Divine Person. My Beloved, You so
"Brightly" Descend and utterly Convert
this heart, mind, body, and breath, from
separate self to the "Bhava" of Your Love-Bliss-Happiness.

Ruchira Adidama Sukha Sundari
Naitauba with Ruchira Avatar
Adi Da Samraj, 1999

Supreme Lord Ruchira, the abandonment of the contracted personality, the relinquishment of ego-bondage to the world, and the profound purification and release of ego-limitations—all brought about by Your Grace, throughout the years since I first came to You—has culminated in a great comprehensive force of one-pointed devotion to You and a great certainty in the Inherent Sufficiency of Realization Itself. The essence of my practice is to always remain freely submitted and centralized in You—the Condition Prior to all bondage, all modification, and all illusion.

My Beloved Lord Ruchira, You have Moved me to renounce all egoic "bonding" with conditionally manifested others, conditionally manifested worlds, and conditionally manifested self, to enter into the depths of this "in-love" and utter devotion to You. Finding You has led to a deep urge to abandon all superficiality and to simply luxuriate in Your Divine Body and Person. All separation is shattered in Your Divine Love-Bliss-"Bhava". Your Infusion is Utter. I feel You everywhere.

I am Drawn, by Grace of Your Spiritual Presence, into profound meditative Contemplation of Your Divine State. Sometimes, when I am entering into these deep states of meditation, I remain vaguely aware of the body, and particularly of the breath and the heartbeat. I feel the heart and lungs slow down. Then I am sometimes aware of my breath and heartbeat being suspended in a state of Yogic sublimity. Then there is no awareness of body, no awareness of mind, no perceptual awareness, and no conceptual awareness. There is only abiding in Contemplation of You in Your Domain of Consciousness Itself. And, when I resume association with the body and begin once again to hear my breath and heartbeat, I feel the remarkable Power of Your Great Samadhi. I feel no necessity for anything, and I feel Your Capability to Bless and Change and Meditate all. I can feel how this entrance into objectless worship of You as Consciousness Itself (allowing this Abiding to deepen ever so profoundly, by utter submission of separate self to You) establishes me in a different relationship to everything that arises.

My Beloved Bhagavan, Love-Ananda, I have Found You. Now, by Your Grace, I am able to behold You and live in this constant Embrace. This is my Joy and Happiness and the Yoga of ego-renunciation I engage. [October 11, 1997]

Inherent in this confession is the certainty that lasting happiness cannot be found in the things of the world, all of which change and die. This is a crucial understanding—which is at the foundation of real religious life, and which grows over time as one advances in the Spiritual process.

AVATAR ADI DA SAMRAJ: Absolutely NOTHING conditional is satisfactory. Everything conditional disappears—everything. This fact should move the heart to cling to Me, to resort to Me, to take refuge in Me. This is why people become devotees of Mine. This is the reason for the religious life. The unsatisfactoriness of conditional existence requires resort to the Divine Source, and the Realization of the Divine Source-Condition. [August 9, 1997]

Finding Real Happiness

This book is Avatar Adi Da's invitation to you to come to know Him—by freely considering His words, and feeling their impact on your life and heart. Avatar Adi Da Himself has never been satisfied with anything conditional. He has never been satisfied with anything less than Real, Permanent, Absolute Happiness—even in the midst of the inevitable sufferings of life. And that Happiness is What He is Offering to you.

The heart has a question.
The heart must be Satisfied.
Without that Satisfaction—Which is necessarily Spiritual in Nature—there is no Real Happiness.

The contraction of the heart is what you are suffering.
It is the ego.
The egoic life is a search—founded upon (and initiated by) the self-contraction of the total body-mind.
The egoic life is a self-caused search to be relieved of the distress of self-reduced, self-diminished, even utterly self-destroyed Love-Bliss.

Love-Bliss gone, non-existent, unknown—just this pumping, agitated, psycho-physical thing.

The ego-"I" does not know What It Is That Is Happening.
You are just "hanging out" for a while, until "it" drops dead.
It is not good enough.
Therefore, I Advise you to begin to be profoundly religious, and not waste any time about it.

You must Realize the Spiritual Condition of Existence Itself . . . .
You cannot be sane if you think there is only flesh, only materiality, only grossness.
Such thinking is not fully "natural", not enough.
There is "Something" you are not accounting for.
Be open to "Whatever" That Is.
You must look into this. [Hridaya Rosary]

Avatar Adi Da Samraj's Teaching-Word: The "Source-Texts" of Adidam

For twenty-seven years (from 1972 to 1999), Avatar Adi Da Samraj devoted Himself tirelessly to Teaching those who came to Him. Even before He formally began to Teach in 1972, He had already written the earliest versions of two of His primary Texts—His "liturgical drama" (*The Mummery*) and His Spiritual Autobiography (*The Knee Of Listening*). Then, when He opened the doors of His first Ashram in Hollywood (on April 25, 1972), He initiated a vast twenty-seven-year "conversation" with the thousands of people who approached Him during that period of time—a "conversation" that included thousands of hours of sublime and impassioned Discourse and thousands of pages of profound and exquisite Writing. And the purpose of that "conversation" was to fully communicate the Truth for Real.

Both His Speech and His Writing were conducted as a kind of living "laboratory". He was constantly asking to hear His devotees' questions and their responses to His Written and Spoken Word. He was constantly calling His devotees to live what He was Teaching and discover its Truth in their own experience—not merely to passively accept it as dogma. He was constantly testing whether His communication on any particular subject was complete and detailed enough or whether He needed to say more. And everything He said and wrote was a spontaneous expression of His own direct Awareness of Reality—never a merely theoretical or speculative proposition, never a statement merely inherited from traditional sources.

This immense outpouring of Revelation and Instruction came to completion in the years 1997-1999. During that period, Avatar

Adi Da Samraj created a series of twenty-three books that He designated as the "Source-Texts" of Adidam. He incorporated into
these books His most essential Writings and Discourses from all
the preceding years, as well as many new Writings and Discourses
that had never been published previously. His magnificent
"Source-Texts" are thus His Eternal Message to all. They contain
His complete Revelation of Truth, and (together with the
"Supportive Texts", in which Avatar Adi Da Gives further detailed
Instruction relative to the functional, practical, relational, and cultural disciplines of the Way of Adidam) they give His fully detailed
description of the entire process of Awakening, culminating in
Divine Enlightenment.

Avatar Adi Da's twenty-three "Source-Texts" are not simply a
series of books each of which is entirely distinct from all the others. Rather, they form an intricately interwoven fabric. Each book
contains some material found in no other "Source-Text", some
material shared with certain other "Source-Texts", and some material included in all twenty-three of the "Source-Texts". (The three
Texts shared by all twenty-three books are "Do Not Misunderstand
Me", "My Divine Disclosure", and "The Heart-Summary Of Adidam".
Each of these Texts has a particular function and message that is
essential to every one of the books.) Thus, to read Avatar Adi Da's
"Source-Texts" is to engage a special kind of study (similar to the
practice of repeating a mantra), in which certain Texts are repeatedly read, such that they penetrate one's being even more profoundly and take on deeper significance by being read in a variety
of different contexts. Furthermore, each of the "Source-Texts" of
Adidam is thereby a complete and self-contained Argument.
Altogether, to study Avatar Adi Da's "Source-Texts" is to enter into
an "eternal conversation" with Him, in which different meanings
emerge at different times—always appropriate to the current
moment in one's life and experience.

At the conclusion of His paramount "Source-Text", *The Dawn
Horse Testament*, Avatar Adi Da Samraj makes His own passionate
Confession of the Impulse that led Him to create His twenty-three
"Source-Texts".

Now I Have, By All My "Crazy" Means, Revealed My One and Many Divine Secrets As The Great Person Of The Heart. For Your Sake, I Made My Every Work and Word. And Now, By Every Work and Word I Made, I Have Entirely Confessed (and Showed) Myself—and Always Freely, and Even As A Free Man, In The "Esoteric" Language Of Intimacy and Ecstasy, Openly Worded To You (and To all). Even Now (and Always), By This (My Avatarically Self-Revealed Divine Word Of Heart), I Address every Seeming Separate being (and each one As The Heart Itself), Because It Is Necessary That all beings, Even The Entire Cosmic Domain Of Seeming Separate beings, Be (In all times and places) Called To Wisdom and The Heart.

Capitalization and Punctuation in the "Source-Texts" of Avatar Adi Da Samraj

Speaking and Writing in the twentieth and twenty-first centuries, Avatar Adi Da Samraj has used the English language as the medium for His Communication. Over the years of His Teaching-Work, Avatar Adi Da developed a thoroughly original manner of employing English as a sacred language. (He also includes some Sanskrit terminology in His Teaching vocabulary, in order to supplement the relatively undeveloped sacred vocabulary of English.)

Avatar Adi Da's unique use of English is evident not only with respect to vocabulary, but also with respect to capitalization and punctuation.

Vocabulary. A glossary is included at the end of this book (pp. 400-37), where specialized terms (both English terms and terms derived from Sanskrit) are defined.

Capitalization. Avatar Adi Da frequently capitalizes words that would not ordinarily be capitalized in English—and such capitalized words include not only nouns, but also pronouns, verbs, adjectives, adverbs, and even articles and prepositions. By such capitalization, He is indicating that the word refers (either inherently, or by virtue of the context) to the Unconditional Divine Reality, rather than the conditional (or worldly) reality. For example:

If there is no escape from (or no Way out of) the corner (or the "centered" trap) of ego-"I"—the heart goes mad, and the body-mind becomes more and more "dark" (bereft of the Indivisible and Inherently Free Light of the Self-Evident, and Self-Evidently Divine, Love-Bliss That Is Reality Itself). ["Do Not Misunderstand Me"]

Avatar Adi Da's chosen conventions of capitalization vary in different "Source-Texts" and in different sections of a given "Source-Text". In certain "Source-Texts" (notably *The Dawn Horse Testament Of The Ruchira Avatar, The Heart Of The Dawn Horse Testament Of The Ruchira Avatar,* and the various Parts of the other "Source-Texts" that are excerpted from *The Dawn Horse Testament Of The Ruchira Avatar*), Avatar Adi Da employs a highly unusual convention of capitalization, in which the overwhelming majority of all words are capitalized, and only those words that indicate the egoic (or dualistic) point of view are left lower-cased. This capitalization convention (which Avatar Adi Da has worked out to an extraordinarily subtle degree—in ways that are often startling) is in itself a Teaching device, intended to communicate His fundamental Revelation that "There Is Only Real God", and that only the ego (or the dualistic or separative point of view) prevents us from living and Realizing that Truth. For example:

Therefore, For My Every Devotee, all conditions Must Be Aligned and Yielded In Love With Me—or Else any object or any other Will Be The Cause Of Heart-Stress, self-Contraction, Dissociation, Clinging, Boredom, Doubt, The Progressive Discomfort Of Diminished Love-Bliss, and All The Forgetfulness Of Grace and Truth and Happiness Itself. [Ruchira Avatara Hridaya-Tantra Yoga]

Note that "and" and "or" are lower-cased—because these conjunctions are (here, and in most contexts) primal expressions of the point of view of duality. Also note that "all conditions", "any object", "<u>any</u> other", and "self-" are lower-cased, while "Heart-Stress", "Contraction", "Dissociation", "Clinging," "Boredom", "Doubt", "Discomfort", "Diminished", and "Forgetfulness" are capitalized. Avatar Adi Da is telling us that unpleasant or apparently "negative" states are not inherently egoic. It is only the presumption of duality and separateness—as expressed by such words as "conditions", "object", "other", and "self"—that is egoic.

Punctuation. Because of the inevitable complexity of much of His Communication, Avatar Adi Da has developed the conventions of punctuation (commas, dashes, and parentheses) to an extraordinary degree. This allows Him to clearly articulate complex sentences in such a way that His intended meaning can be expressed with utmost precision—free of vagueness, ambiguity, or unclarity. Many of His sentences contain parenthetical definitions or modifying phrases as a way of achieving unmistakable clarity of meaning. For example:

The Apparently individual (or Separate) self Is Not a "spark" (or an Eternal fraction) Of Self-Radiant Divinity, and Somehow Complete (or Whole) In itself. [<u>Real</u> God <u>Is</u> The Indivisible Oneness Of Unbroken Light]

Another punctuation convention relates to the use of quotation marks. Avatar Adi Da sometimes uses quotation marks in accordance with standard convention, to indicate the sense of "so to speak":

Make the contact with Me that gets you to "stick" to Me like glue. Your "sticking" to Me is what must happen. [Hridaya Rosary]

In other instances, He uses quotation marks to indicate that a word or phrase is being used with a particular technical meaning that differs from common usage:

During <u>all</u> of My present Lifetime (of Avataric Divine Incarnation), the "<u>Bright</u>" has <u>always</u> been My Realization—and the "<u>Thumbs</u>" and My own "Radical" Understanding have <u>always</u> been My Way in the "Bright".

"Bright", "Thumbs" (referring to a specific form of the Infusion of Avatar Adi Da's Divine Spirit-Current in the body-mind), and "Radical" are all used with specific technical meanings here (as defined in the Glossary).

Finally, Avatar Adi Da also makes extensive use of underlining to indicate special emphasis on certain words (or phrases, or even entire sentences):

> The <u>only</u> true religion is the religion that <u>Realizes</u> Truth. The <u>only</u> true science is the science that <u>Knows</u> Truth. The <u>only</u> true man or woman (or being of any kind) is one that <u>Surrenders</u> to Truth. The only true world is one that <u>Embodies</u> Truth. And the only True (and <u>Real</u>) God Is the One Reality (or Condition of Being) That <u>Is</u> Truth. ["Do Not Misunderstand <u>Me</u>"]

The True Dawn Horse

The Seven Stages Of Life is Book Ten of *The Seventeen Companions Of The True Dawn Horse*. The "True Dawn Horse" is a reference to *The Dawn Horse Testament Of The Ruchira Avatar*, the final book among Avatar Adi Da's "Source-Texts". In *The Dawn Horse Testament*, Avatar Adi Da describes the entire Process of Real-God-Realization in detail. Each of *The Seventeen Companions Of The True Dawn Horse* is a "Companion" to *The Dawn Horse Testament* in the sense that it is an elaboration of a major theme (or themes) from *The Dawn Horse Testament*. And in many of the "Seventeen Companions", an excerpt from *The Dawn Horse Testament* forms the principal Part, around which the other Parts of the book revolve. (In *The Seven Stages Of Life*, the principal Part—Part Two—comprises chapter sixteen of *The Dawn Horse Testament*.)

The Sacred Image of the Dawn Horse (which appears above) derives from a vision that Avatar Adi Da Samraj had one night during the spring of 1970, a few months before His Divine Re-Awakening (on September 10, 1970). As His physical body lay sleeping, Avatar Adi Da wandered in subtle form into an open hall, where a great Adept was seated on a throne. The Adept's disciples were lined up in rows in front of him. A pathway bounded on both sides by the disciples led to the throne. Avatar Adi Da was Himself standing at the end of a row a few rows away from the Adept's chair.

The disciples were apparently assembled to learn the miraculous Yogic power of materializing something from nothing. They waited respectfully for the lesson to begin.

The Adept then initiated the process of materialization. A brief while later, the disciples got up and left the room, satisfied that the materialization had been accomplished, although nothing had appeared yet. The Adept remained sitting in his chair, and Avatar Adi Da remained standing before him, attentive to the process at hand.

A vaporous mass gradually took shape in the space between Avatar Adi Da and the Adept. At first it was not clearly defined, but Avatar Adi Da recognized it as it began to take on the features of a horse. Gradually, the vapor coalesced into a living, breathing brown horse. Its features were as fine as a thoroughbred's, but it was quite small, perhaps three feet tall. The horse stood alert, motionless, facing away from the Adept's chair.

At this point in the dream vision, Avatar Adi Da returned to physical consciousness and the waking state.

It was many years later, at the time when Avatar Adi Da was starting to write *The Dawn Horse Testament*, that He Revealed the identity of the Adept He had visited in that vision:

AVATAR ADI DA SAMRAJ: I was at once the Adept who performed the miracle of manifesting the horse, and also the one who was party to the observation of it and its result. And I did not have any feeling of being different from the horse itself. I was <u>making</u> the horse, I was <u>observing</u> the horse, and I was <u>being</u> the horse. [October 18, 1984]

The Dawn Horse is, therefore, a symbol for Avatar Adi Da Samraj Himself—and *The Dawn Horse Testament* is His Personal

Testament to all beings. Avatar Adi Da has commented that He refers to Himself and to His principal "Source-Text" as the "True Dawn Horse" because the effects of His Liberating Work in the world will appear only gradually—just as, in the vision, the horse gradually became visible after the Adept had initiated its materialization.

In creating the Sacred Image of the Dawn Horse, Avatar Adi Da transformed His original vision of a small brown horse, with all four hooves planted on the ground, into a winged white stallion, rearing up nearly vertically:

AVATAR ADI DA SAMRAJ: The horse's pose is majestic and intended to show great strength. White was chosen for its obvious association with Light, or Consciousness Itself. The Image is not precisely associated with the vision of 1970. It is visual language, intended to communicate the full meaning of My Dawn Horse Vision, rather than to be a realistic presentation of it.

The Titles and Subtitles of The Twenty-Three "Source-Texts" of Avatar Adi Da Samraj

The twenty-three "Source-Texts" of Avatar Adi Da Samraj include:

(1) an opening series of five books on the fundamentals of the Way of Adidam (*The Five Books Of The Heart Of The Adidam Revelation*)

(2) an extended series of seventeen books covering the principal aspects of the Way of Adidam in detail (*The Seventeen Companions Of The True Dawn Horse*)

(3) Avatar Adi Da's paramount "Source-Text" summarizing the entire course of the Way of Adidam (*The Dawn Horse Testament*)

The basic content of each "Source-Text" is summarily described by Avatar Adi Da in the title and subtitle of each book. Thus, the following list of titles and subtitles indicates the vast scope and the artful interconnectedness of His twenty-three "Source-Texts". (For brief descriptions of each "Source-Text", please see "The Sacred Literature of Ruchira Avatar Adi Da Samraj", pp. 438-47.)

The Five Books Of The Heart Of The Adidam Revelation

BOOK ONE
Aham Da Asmi
(Beloved, I Am Da)
The "Late-Time" Avataric Revelation Of The True and Spiritual Divine Person (The egoless Personal Presence Of Reality and Truth, Which Is The Only Real God)

BOOK TWO
Ruchira Avatara Gita
(The Way Of The Divine Heart-Master)
The "Late-Time" Avataric Revelation Of The Great Secret Of The Divinely Self-Revealed Way That Most Perfectly Realizes The True and Spiritual Divine Person (The egoless Personal Presence Of Reality and Truth, Which Is The Only Real God)

BOOK THREE
Da Love-Ananda Gita
(The Free Gift Of The Divine Love-Bliss)
The "Late-Time" Avataric Revelation Of The Great Means To Worship and To Realize The True and Spiritual Divine Person (The egoless Personal Presence Of Reality and Truth, Which Is The Only Real God)

BOOK FOUR
Hridaya Rosary
(Four Thorns Of Heart-Instruction)
The "Late-Time" Avataric Revelation Of The Universally Tangible Divine Spiritual Body, Which Is The Supreme Agent Of The Great Means To Worship and To Realize The True and Spiritual Divine Person (The egoless Personal Presence Of Reality and Truth, Which Is The Only Real God)

BOOK FIVE
Eleutherios
(The <u>Only</u> Truth That Sets The Heart Free)

The "Late-Time" Avataric Revelation Of The "Perfect Practice"
Of The Great Means To Worship and To Realize The True and
Spiritual Divine Person (The egoless Personal Presence Of
Reality and Truth, Which <u>Is</u> The Only <u>Real</u> God)

◆ ◆ ◆

*The Seventeen Companions
Of The True Dawn Horse*

BOOK ONE
<u>Real</u> God <u>Is</u> The Indivisible Oneness
Of Unbroken Light

Reality, Truth, and The "Non-Creator" God
In The True World-Religion Of Adidam

BOOK TWO
The Truly Human New World-Culture
Of <u>Unbroken</u> Real-God-Man

The <u>Eastern</u> Versus The <u>Western</u> Traditional Cultures
Of Mankind, and The Unique New <u>Non-Dual</u> Culture
Of The True World-Religion Of Adidam

BOOK THREE
The <u>Only</u> Complete Way To Realize
The Unbroken Light Of <u>Real</u> God

An Introductory Overview Of The "Radical" Divine Way
Of The True World-Religion Of Adidam

BOOK FOUR
The Knee Of Listening

The Early-Life Ordeal and The "Radical"
Spiritual Realization Of The Ruchira Avatar

B O O K F I V E

The Divine Siddha-Method Of The Ruchira Avatar

The Divine Way Of Adidam Is An ego-Transcending
<u>Relationship</u>, Not An ego-Centric Technique

B O O K S I X

The Mummery

A Parable Of The Divine True Love

B O O K S E V E N

He-<u>and</u>-She <u>Is</u> Me

The Indivisibility Of Consciousness and Light
In The Divine Body Of The Ruchira Avatar

B O O K E I G H T

Ruchira Avatara Hridaya-Siddha Yoga

The <u>Divine</u> (and Not Merely <u>Cosmic</u>) Spiritual Baptism
In The Divine Way Of Adidam

B O O K N I N E

Ruchira Avatara Hridaya-Tantra Yoga

The Physical-Spiritual (and Truly Religious) Method
Of Mental, Emotional, Sexual, and <u>Whole</u> <u>Bodily</u> <u>Health</u>
<u>and</u> <u>Enlightenment</u> In The Divine Way Of Adidam

B O O K T E N

The Seven Stages Of Life

Transcending The Six Stages Of egoic Life,
and Realizing The ego-Transcending Seventh Stage Of Life,
In The Divine Way Of Adidam

B O O K E L E V E N

The <u>All-Completing</u> and <u>Final</u>
Divine Revelation To Mankind

A Summary Description Of The Supreme Yoga
Of The Seventh Stage Of Life In The Divine Way Of Adidam

BOOK TWELVE
The Heart Of The Dawn Horse Testament Of The Ruchira Avatar
The Epitome Of The "Testament Of Secrets" Of The Divine
World-Teacher, Ruchira Avatar Adi Da Samraj

BOOK THIRTEEN
What, Where, When, How, Why, and Who To Remember To Be Happy
A Simple Explanation Of The Divine Way Of Adidam
(For Children, and Everyone Else)

BOOK FOURTEEN
Santosha Adidam
The Essential Summary Of The Divine Way Of Adidam

BOOK FIFTEEN
The Lion Sutra
The "Perfect Practice" Teachings In The Divine Way Of Adidam

BOOK SIXTEEN
The Overnight Revelation Of Conscious Light
The "My House" Discourses
On The Indivisible Tantra Of Adidam

BOOK SEVENTEEN
The Basket Of Tolerance
The Perfect Guide To Perfectly Unified Understanding
Of The One and Great Tradition Of Mankind,
and Of The Divine Way Of Adidam As The Perfect Completing
Of The One and Great Tradition Of Mankind

❖ ❖ ❖

The Dawn Horse Testament Of The Ruchira Avatar

The Dawn Horse Testament Of The Ruchira Avatar
The "Testament Of Secrets" Of The Divine World-Teacher,
Ruchira Avatar Adi Da Samraj

Camera Illuminata

The "Bright"-Field Photography of Avatar Adi Da Samraj

At the same time that He was completing His Work to create a complete verbal Teaching in His "Source-Texts", Avatar Adi Da Samraj started taking black-and-white photographs as another potent means of communicating His message about Reality. He calls the collected body of His photographic work His "Camera Illuminata" collection, and He has selected a photograph from this collection for the cover of each of His twenty-three "Source-Texts". "Camera Illuminata" means "Bright Room", in contrast to the traditional term "camera obscura" (which literally means "dark room"). Thus, instead of representing the world from the "dark" point of view (or the presumption that dying matter is all there is to reality), the Camera Illuminata of Adi Da Samraj Reveals the world as a "Bright" (or Divinely Self-Radiant) Field.

Avatar Adi Da's "Bright"-Field photographic images are one of His means for conveying His Spiritual Transmission and Blessing—for the subject of Avatar Adi Da's photography is not the world as we see it, but the world as the "Bright" Field of Reality that He sees. His photography would transport us beyond our ordinary habits of thinking and perceiving into the Divine Light, in Which there is no sense of separation, otherness, or limitation.

AVATAR ADI DA SAMRAJ: From the conventional point of view, a photographer only makes pictures of conventional reality, of light falling on objects, as if the solid reality were the only reality. But neither the fixed separate point of view nor the apparently solid objective world is the Fundamental Reality. The Divine Conscious Light Is the Fundamental Reality of Existence.

Avatar Adi Da's photographic images communicate the non-dual perception of Reality via a unique process, which He describes as His "inherently egoless participatory relationship" with the subjects of His photographs (both human and non-human). Thus, His photography transcends the conventions of "self" and "other", or "subject" and "object".

AVATAR ADI DA SAMRAJ: Out of this process, images can be made that Reveal Reality, rather than merely communicating the conventions of "ego" and "other".

Therefore, even the viewing of Adi Da's Camera Illuminata images is an inherently participatory event. That is to say, His photographs, like all great art, place a demand upon us to go beyond the ordinary fixed point of view. They are a call to go beyond our ordinary limits—for each of His images is a communication of the Divine "Brightness", transforming our ordinary perception of the world into sacred occasion.

Avatar Adi Da Samraj photographing in the California redwoods

When viewed in its entirety, Avatar Adi Da's Camera Illuminata collection is an ecstatic Revelation-Transmission of the Divine Truth that He has Come to Reveal and Teach to humankind. There is extraordinary beauty to be appreciated in Avatar Adi Da's photographs, but the real purpose of His artistry is to bring Light into our lives, to literally En-Light-en us—to Liberate us from the un-Illumined and mortal vision of egoity. By offering us His Camera Illuminata, Adi Da Samraj would have us discover that "Bright-Field", that Non-separate Reality, in Which the ever-changing dualities of light and darkness rise and fall.

AVATAR ADI DA SAMRAJ: In My approach to making photographic images, I want to convey the Truth of Reality—the Truth of the Inherently egoless, Non-dual Subjective Light. I am trying to convey My own Revelation of the Nature of Reality through the artifice of visual images.

The border photograph on the cover of this book is also from Avatar Adi Da's Camera Illuminata collection. He refers to this photograph as an image of "True Water", which is one of His poetic descriptions for Consciousness Itself as the "Medium" in which all phenomena arise (and of which they are all modifications).

An Overview of
The Seven Stages
Of Life

The Divine World-Teacher, Ruchira Avatar Adi Da Samraj, has Revealed a brilliant map of the full spectrum of human adaptation and growth—seven distinct stages of life, from birth to the Most Perfect Realization of Real God. Most Perfect Real-God-Realization (or Divine Self-Realization, or Divine En-Light-enment) is the Realization and Demonstration of the inherently egoless seventh stage of life—which had never been Realized previous to Avatar Adi Da's Divine Re-Awakening in 1970. Now, by virtue of Avatar Adi Da's Revelation of the Way of Adidam and His Free Gift of His Divinely Awakening Power, the seventh stage Realization is the (present and future) potential of all beings.

Briefly described, the first three (or foundation) stages of life constitute the ordinary course of human adaptation—bodily, emotional, and mental growth from birth to nominal adulthood. The fourth and fifth (or advanced) stages of life are characterized by the Awakening to Spirit, or the Spiritualizing of the body-mind and higher psyche. The sixth and seventh (or ultimate) stages of life are based upon an Awakening to Identification with Consciousness, prior to the body-mind and all the planes of possibility high and low.

In the sixth stage of life, the Realizer first Awakens to Identification with Consciousness in its Function as the "Witness" of arising phenomena. That original sixth stage Realization progressively deepens until it becomes a profound state of meditative ecstasy wherein all awareness of phenomena is excluded in Perfect (sixth stage) Identification with Consciousness <u>Itself</u>. In fact, the highest Realization previous to Avatar Adi Da's Appearance here, was this (sixth stage) Identification with Consciousness Itself Realized so profoundly that even if phenomena were then allowed to arise, It was not forgotten. But Avatar

Adi Da Reveals that this Realization, although extraordinary by any possible measure, is yet incomplete—there remains a very subtle contraction of the being in its implicit dissociation from conditional existence, a refusal of Reality in its totality.

Only the seventh stage of life (or the Realization of "Open Eyes") transcends this last limit on Most Perfect Real-God-Realization. No exclusion of, or implicit dissociation from, conditional Reality is necessary, for the world is directly Realized to be a modification of Consciousness Itself, not separate (or "different") from Consciousness at all.

The fact that there are precisely seven stages of life (and not six or eight or however many one may propose) is intimately related to the hierarchical structural anatomy of the human body-mind. That structural anatomy includes not only the fleshy dimensions of muscles, bones, and so forth, but it also includes the subtler dimensions of energy and mind and Consciousness.

In some of the most highly developed religious and Spiritual traditions of mankind, the human individual is described as comprising three "bodies".

The "gross body" is the physical body—which has typically been presumed by Western medical science to be the only human body. The "subtle body" comprises the dimensions of life-energy and emotion, mind and psyche, as well as the higher functions of intelligence and will. The "causal body" is the core of the apparently separate egoic self, the root-sense of existing as an "I". These three "bodies" are traditionally understood to form the foundation of the waking, dreaming, and deep-sleep states, respectively. Avatar Adi Da confirms that this traditional description is correct, but He goes further and describes the structural anatomy underlying these three bodies.

Avatar Adi Da describes that the hierarchical structural anatomy of the human body-mind exists in two fundamental "planes"—the vertical and the horizontal. The vertical plane is a great energy-circuit, which He calls "the Circle". The Circle runs down the front of the body from the crown of the head to the perineum, and up the back of the body along the spinal line to the crown of the head. The horizontal plane comprises the esoteric structure of the heart, which has three parts—the left side, the middle station, and the right side. Beyond the Circle and rooted in the right side of the heart stands the most esoteric of all psychophysical structures—"Amrita Nadi", or the "Current of Immortal Bliss". Amrita Nadi is rooted in the right side of the heart and rises in an S-shaped curve to the Matrix of Light, the apparently Objective Source of all forms and energies, Which lies infinitely above the crown of the head.

The left side of the heart and the frontal line of the Circle are the fundamental structures underlying the gross body—they are particularly associated with development in the first three stages of life and the beginnings of the fourth stage of life. The middle station of the heart and the spinal line of the Circle are the fundamental structures underlying the subtle body—they are particularly associated with development in the advanced fourth stage of life and in the fifth stage of life. The right side of the heart is the fundamental structure underlying the causal body—it is particularly associated with development in the sixth stage of life. Amrita Nadi, which stands prior to all these structures, is particularly associated both with the fullest Realization of the process of the sixth stage of life and with Divine Self-Realization in the seventh stage of life.

Avatar Adi Da's map of the seven stages of life is not only a powerful tool for understanding the fullest human potential—it is also the unique means by which the diverse religious and Spiritual traditions of the world can be understood to form a single (collective) Great Tradition. The various (and often contradictory) philosophies and practices recommended within the Great Tradition are—by means of Avatar Adi Da's Revelation of the seven stages of life—rightly understood as simply reflecting the different points of view of the different stages of life Realized by each particular tradition.

Avatar Adi Da has also Revealed that the seventh stage of life does not merely lie at the <u>end</u> of the developmental unfoldment of the previous six stages of life. Indeed, He Reveals that each of the first six stages of life is to be progressively dissolved in the always present Realization of the seventh stage of life. And how is that always present Realization of the seventh stage of life possible?

By virtue of Avatar Adi Da's Most Perfect Divine Self-Realization, any moment of true devotional self-surrender to Him Grants immediate access to His seventh stage Condition. That is the Great Secret of Most Perfect Real-God-Realization in the Way of Adidam. Avatar Adi Da Samraj Himself is the Great Means for the Realization of all beings.

As with each of Avatar Adi Da's "Source-Texts", *The Seven Stages Of Life* begins with His First Word, "Do Not Misunderstand Me— I Am Not 'Within' you, but you Are In Me, and I Am Not a Mere 'Man' in the 'Middle' of Mankind, but All of Mankind Is Surrounded, and Pervaded, and Blessed By Me". In this remarkable Essay, Avatar Adi Da Explains that His open Confession of Most Perfect Real-God-Realization is not to be misapprehended as a claim of the "Status" of the "Creator"-God of conventional religious belief—but, rather, His Divine Self-Confession must be understood and appreciated as a Free Demonstration of What is Realized in the Perfect Fulfillment of esoteric Spiritual practice, Which is the Most Perfectly Non-Dual Realization of Reality Itself. By virtue of His Free Demonstration, Avatar Adi Da Samraj makes clear that Most Perfect Real-God-Realization is the ultimate Potential and Destiny of all beings.

The Prologue to *The Seven Stages Of Life,* "My Divine Disclosure" (also, like "First Word", found in all twenty-three "Source-Texts"), is a poetic epitome of Avatar Adi Da's Avataric Divine Self-Revelation and His Call to all to turn to Him at heart and practice the Real-God-Realizing life of devotional self-surrender.

In Part One, "Tat Sundaram!—All Of This Is Sacred, All Of This Is Beautiful! (The Essence of the Message of Adidam and of the One and Entire Great Tradition of Mankind)", Avatar Adi Da Sings the essential Secret of the Realization of Reality, Truth, or Real God:

No matter What, Where, When, How, Why, or Who Is Reality, Truth, or Real God—Consciousness (Itself) Is (Inherently, and Necessarily, and Always Already) the Only Basis for (and the Only Substance of) your Realization of That Which Is Reality, Truth, and Real God.

In Part Two of *The Seven Stages Of Life,* Avatar Adi Da describes the progression of each of the seven stages of life. He describes how children and young people in the first three stages of life are to be served by the community of practitioners in the Way of Adidam. And He describes how the Way of Adidam is the same for those who come to Him as adults as for those who attain maturity within the Wisdom-Culture of Adidam. He then goes on to explain how the fourth, fifth, sixth, and seventh stages of life develop, and how Most Perfect Real-God-Realization is ultimately Demonstrated by the Outshining of all of conditional existence in the unspeakably Sublime Event of Divine Translation.

Part Three of *The Seven Stages Of Life* consists of seven extraordinary Essays. "'God'-Talk, Real-God-Realization, and Most Perfect Divine Awakening" contains Avatar Adi Da's explanation of the five possible worldviews, their relationship to the Great Tradition of mankind, and the nature of exoteric and esoteric religious ideas and practices. "The Servant, The 'Soul', and The Very Self: The Three Points of View of the Progressive Stages of Life" is Avatar Adi Da's commentary on the stages of life as summarized in the epilogue to *The Wisdom of Unity* (or *Manisa-Pancakam*), traditionally ascribed to the great Indian Sage Shankara. "The Cultivation of My Divine Samadhi" is Avatar Adi Da's explanation of how Divine Self-Realization can and must be the Foundation of the entire course of the Way of Adidam via the moment to moment practice of devotional Communion with Him. "The Samadhis of Earth, Moon, and Sun" is Avatar Adi Da's metaphorical description of the traditional samadhis of the first six stages of life and how they relate to the hierarchical structure of the human being and to the seventh stage Awakening in the Way of Adidam. "I Am The Only 'Room' That Is" contains Avatar Adi Da's mind-dissolving "consideration" of the "Point of View" of Totality—which "Point of View" transcends all separate points of view within space-time. In "The Only Way To My 'Room'", Avatar Adi Da describes the uniqueness of the Way of Adidam. And in "On Transcending the First Six Stages of Life" Avatar Adi Da explains how the Way of Adidam is a Process that is both progressive and instant, and how the characteristic errors of the fourth, fifth, and sixth stages of life are to be transcended.

Part Four, "I (Alone) Am The Adidam Revelation", is Avatar Adi Da's full elucidation of the uniqueness of His Revelation of the seventh stage Realization. In this unparalleled Essay, incomparable in its scope and profundity, Avatar Adi Da examines His own Course of Divine Self-Realization in order to Demonstrate how the two primary divisions of the Great Tradition—the Emanationist (or absorptive mystical) Way (associated with the first five stages of life) and the non-Emanationist (or Transcendentalist) Way (associated with the sixth stage of life)—are, in Truth, only different aspects of the great seven-stage process of Most Perfect Divine Self-Realization.

In Part Five, "The Heart-Summary of Adidam" (a brief Essay that is included in all twenty-three "Source-Texts"), Avatar Adi Da Samraj summarizes the profound implications of His Statement that the Way of Adidam is the Way of Devotion to Him "As Self-Condition, rather than As exclusively Objective Other".

In the Epilogue to this Great Scripture, Avatar Adi Da Confesses His Most Perfect Realization of Identity with the Divine Self-Condition and Source-Condition of all and All. And He Reveals His Unique Function as the Adept-Realizer, Adept-Revealer, and Adept-Revelation of the seventh stage of life.

Altogether, *The Seven Stages Of Life* is Avatar Adi Da's All-Completing, and Perfectly Clarifying, Revelation of the Ultimate Potential of a human life. In reading this Divine "Source-Text" of Adidam, you have the unparalleled opportunity not only to learn about that Ultimate Potential, but to directly taste the Radiant Divine Grace of Avatar Adi Da Samraj, which makes Most Perfect Real-God-Realization possible.

THE SEVEN STAGES
OF LIFE

RUCHIRA AVATAR ADI DA SAMRAJ
Los Angeles, 2000

Do Not Misunderstand <u>Me</u>—
I Am <u>Not</u> "Within" <u>you</u>,
but you <u>Are</u> In <u>Me</u>,
and I Am <u>Not</u> a Mere "Man"
in the "Middle" of Mankind,
but All of Mankind Is Surrounded,
and Pervaded, and Blessed By <u>Me</u>

This Essay has been written by Avatar Adi Da Samraj as His Personal Introduction to each volume of His "Source-Texts". Its purpose is to help you to understand His great Confessions rightly, and not interpret His Words from a conventional point of view, as limited cultic statements made by an ego. His Description of what "cultism" <u>really</u> is is an astounding and profound Critique of mankind's entire religious, scientific, and social search. In "Do Not Misunderstand <u>Me</u>", Avatar Adi Da is directly inviting you to inspect and relinquish the ego's motive to glorify itself and to refuse What is truly Great. Only by understanding this fundamental ego-fault can one really receive the Truth that Adi Da Samraj Reveals in this Book and in His Wisdom-Teaching altogether. And it is because this fault is so ingrained and so largely unconscious that Avatar Adi Da has placed "Do Not Misunderstand <u>Me</u>" at the beginning of each of His "Source-Texts", so that, each time you begin to read one of His twenty-three "Source-Texts", you may be refreshed and strengthened in your understanding of the right orientation and approach to Him and His Heart-Word.

Yes! There is <u>no</u> religion, <u>no</u> Way of God, <u>no</u> Way of Divine Realization, <u>no</u> Way of Enlightenment, and <u>no</u> Way of Liberation that is Higher or Greater than Truth Itself.

Indeed, there is no religion, no science, no man or woman, no conditionally manifested being of any kind, no world (any "where"), and no "God" (or "God"-Idea) that is Higher or Greater than Truth Itself.

Therefore, no ego-"I" (or presumed separate, and, necessarily, actively separative, and, at best, only Truth-seeking, being or "thing") is (itself) Higher or Greater than Truth Itself. And no ego-"I" is (itself) even Equal to Truth Itself. And no ego-"I" is (itself) even (now, or ever) Able to Realize Truth Itself—because, necessarily, Truth (Itself) Inherently Transcends (or Is That Which Is Higher and Greater than) every one (himself or herself) and every "thing" (itself). Therefore, it is only in the transcending (or the "radical" Process of Going Beyond the root, the cause, and the act) of egoity itself (or of presumed separateness, and of performed separativeness, and of even all ego-based seeking for Truth Itself) that Truth (Itself) Is Realized (As It Is, Utterly Beyond the ego-"I" itself).

Truth (Itself) Is That Which Is Always Already The Case. That Which Is The Case (Always, and Always Already) Is (necessarily) Reality. Therefore, Reality (Itself) Is Truth, and Reality (Itself) Is the Only Truth.

Reality (Itself) Is the Only, and (necessarily) Non-Separate (or All-and-all-Including, and All-and-all-Transcending) One and "What" That Is. Because It Is All and all, and because It Is (Also) That Which Transcends (or Is Higher and Greater than) All and all, Reality (Itself)—Which Is Truth (Itself), or That Which Is The Case (Always, and Always Already)—Is the One and Only Real God. Therefore, Reality (Itself) Is (necessarily) the One and Great Subject of true religion, and Reality (Itself) Is (necessarily) the One and Great Way of Real God, Real (and True) Divine Realization, Real (and, necessarily, Divine) En-Light-enment, and Real (and, necessarily, Divine) Liberation (from all egoity, all separateness, all separativeness, all fear, and all heartlessness).

The only true religion is the religion that Realizes Truth. The only true science is the science that Knows Truth. The only true man or woman (or being of any kind) is one that Surrenders to Truth. The only true world is one that Embodies Truth. And the only True (and <u>Real</u>) God Is the One Reality (or Condition of Being) That <u>Is</u> Truth. Therefore, <u>Reality</u> (Itself)—Which <u>Is</u> the One and Only Truth, and (therefore, necessarily) the One and Only Real God—<u>must</u> become (or be made) the constantly applied Measure of religion, and of science, and of the world itself, and of even <u>all</u> of the life (and <u>all</u> of the mind) of Man—or else religion, and science, and the world itself, and even any and every sign of Man <u>inevitably</u> (all, and together) become a pattern of illusions, a mere (and even terrible) "problem", the very (and even principal) cause of human seeking, and the perpetual cause of contentious human strife. Indeed, if religion, and science, and the world itself, and the total life (and the total mind) of Man are not Surrendered and Aligned to Reality (Itself), and (Thus) Submitted to be Measured (or made Lawful) by Truth (Itself), and (Thus) Given to the truly devotional (and, thereby, truly ego-transcending) Realization of <u>That</u> Which Is the <u>Only Real</u> God—then, in the presumed "knowledge" of mankind, Reality (Itself), and Truth (Itself), and <u>Real</u> God (or the One and Only Existence, or Being, or Person That <u>Is</u>) <u>ceases to Exist</u>.

Aham Da Asmi. Beloved, I <u>Am</u> Da—the One and Only Person Who <u>Is</u>, the Avatarically Self-Revealed, and Eternally Self-Existing, and Eternally Self-Radiant (or "Bright") Person of Love-Bliss, the One and Only and (Self-Evidently) Divine Self (or Inherently Non-Separate—and, therefore, Inherently egoless—Divine Self-Condition and Source-Condition) of one and of all and of All. I Am Divinely Self-Manifesting (now, and forever hereafter) <u>As</u> the Ruchira Avatar, Adi Da Samraj. I <u>Am</u> the Ruchira Avatar, Adi Da Samraj—the Avataric Divine Realizer, the Avataric Divine Revealer, the Avataric Divine Incarnation, and the Avataric Divine Self-Revelation of Reality <u>Itself</u>. I <u>Am</u> the Avatarically Incarnate Divine Realizer, the Avatarically Incarnate Divine Revealer, and the Avatarically Incarnate Divine Self-Revelation of the One and Only Reality—Which Is the One and Only Truth, and Which Is the One and Only <u>Real</u> God. I <u>Am</u> the Great Avataric Divine Realizer, Avataric Divine Revealer, and Avataric Divine Self-Revelation long-Promised (and long-Expected) for the "late-time"—<u>this</u> (now, and forever hereafter) time, the "dark" epoch of mankind's "Great

Forgetting" (and, <u>potentially</u>, the Great Epoch of mankind's Perpetual Remembering) of Reality, of Truth, of Real God (Which Is the Great, True, and Spiritual Divine Person—or the One and Non-Separate and Indivisible Divine Source-Condition and Self-Condition) of all and All.

Beloved, I <u>Am</u> Da, the Divine Giver, the Giver (of All That I <u>Am</u>) to one, and to all, and to the All of all—now, and forever here-after—here, and every "where" in the Cosmic domain. Therefore, for the Purpose of Revealing the Way of <u>Real</u> God (or of Real and True Divine Realization), and in order to Divinely En-Light-en and Divinely Liberate all and All—I Am (Uniquely, Completely, and Most Perfectly) Avatarically Revealing My Very (and Self-Evidently Divine) Person (and "Bright" Self-Condition) to all and All, by Means of My Avatarically Given Divine Self-Manifestation, <u>As</u> (and by Means of) the Ruchira Avatar, Adi Da Samraj.

In My Avatarically Given Divine Self-Manifestation As the Ruchira Avatar, Adi Da Samraj—I <u>Am</u> the Divine Secret, the Divine Self-Revelation of the <u>Esoteric</u> Truth, the Direct, and all-Completing, and all-Unifying Self-Revelation of <u>Real</u> God.

My Avatarically Given Divine Self-Confessions and My Avatarically Given Divine Teaching-Revelations Are <u>the</u> Great (Final, and all-Completing, and all-Unifying) <u>Esoteric</u> Revelation to mankind—and <u>not</u> a merely exoteric (or conventionally religious, or even ordinary Spiritual, or ego-made, or so-called "cultic") com-munication to public (or merely social) ears.

The greatest opportunity, and the greatest responsibility, of My devotees is Satsang with Me—Which is to live in the Condition of ego-surrendering, ego-forgetting, and (always more and more) ego-transcending devotional relationship to Me, and (Thus and Thereby) to Realize My Avatarically Self-Revealed (and Self-Evidently Divine) Self-Condition, Which <u>Is</u> the Self-Evidently Divine Heart (or Non-Separate Self-Condition and Non-"Different" Source-Condition) of all and All, and Which <u>Is</u> Self-Existing and Self-Radiant Consciousness Itself, but Which is <u>not</u> <u>separate</u> in or as any one (or any "thing") at all. Therefore, My essential Divine Gift to one and all is Satsang with Me. And My essential Divine Work with one and all is Satsang-Work—to Live (and to Be Merely

Present) <u>As</u> the Avatarically Self-Revealed Divine Heart among My devotees.

The only-by-Me Revealed and Given Way of Adidam (Which is the only-by-Me Revealed and Given Way of the Heart, or the only-by-Me Revealed and Given Way of "Radical" Understanding, or Ruchira Avatara Hridaya-Siddha Yoga) is the Way of Satsang with Me—the devotionally Me-recognizing and devotionally to-Me-responding practice (and ego-transcending self-discipline) of living in My constant Divine Company, such that the relationship with Me becomes the Real (and constant) Condition of life. Fundamentally, this Satsang with Me is the one thing done by My devotees. Because the only-by-Me Revealed and Given Way of Adidam is <u>always</u> (in every present-time moment) a directly ego-transcending <u>and</u> Really Me-Finding practice, the otherwise constant (and burdensome) tendency to <u>seek</u> is not exploited in this Satsang with Me. And the essential work of the community of the four formal congregations of My devotees is to make ego-transcending Satsang with Me available to all others.

<u>Everything</u> that serves the availability of Satsang with Me is (now, and forever hereafter) the responsibility of the four formal congregations of My formally practicing devotees. I am not here to <u>publicly</u> "promote" this Satsang with Me. In the intimate circumstances of their humanly expressed devotional love of Me, I Speak My Avatarically Self-Revealing Divine Word to My devotees, and <u>they</u> (because of their devotional response to Me) bring My Avatarically Self-Revealing Divine Word to <u>all</u> others. Therefore, even though I am <u>not</u> (and have never been, and never will be) a "public" Teacher (or a broadly publicly active, and conventionally socially conformed, "religious figure"), My devotees function fully and freely (<u>as</u> My devotees) in the daily public world of ordinary life.

I Always Already Stand Free. Therefore, I have always (in My Divine Avataric-Incarnation-Work) Stood Free, in the traditional "Crazy" (and non-conventional, or spontaneous and non-"public") Manner—in order to Guarantee the Freedom, the Uncompromising Rightness, and the Fundamental Integrity of My Avatarically Self-Manifested Divine Teaching (Work and Word), and in order to

Freely and Fully and Fully Effectively Perform My universal (Avatarically Self-Manifested) Divine Blessing-Work. I Am Present (now, and forever hereafter) to Divinely Serve, Divinely En-Light-en, and Divinely Liberate those who accept the Eternal Vow and all the life-responsibilities (or the full and complete practice) asso-ciated with the only-by-Me Revealed and Given Way of Adidam. Because I Am (Thus) Given to My formally and fully practicing devotees, I do not Serve a "public" role, and I do not Work in a "public" (or even a merely "institutionalized") manner. Nevertheless—now, and forever hereafter—I constantly Bless all beings, and this entire world, and the total Cosmic domain. And all who feel My Avatarically (and universally) Given Divine Blessing, and who heart-recognize Me with true devotional love, are (Thus) Called to devotionally resort to Me—but only if they approach Me in the traditional devotional manner, as responsibly practicing (and truly ego-surrendering, and rightly Me-serving) members (or, in some, unique, cases, as invited guests) of one or the other of the four formal congregations of My formally practicing devotees.

I expect this formal discipline of right devotional approach to Me to have been freely and happily embraced by every one who would enter into My physical Company. The natural human reason for this is that there is a potential liability inherent in all human associations. And the root and nature of that potential liability is the ego (or the active human presumption of separateness, and the ego-act of human separativeness). Therefore, in order that the liabilities of egoity are understood (and voluntarily and responsi-bly disciplined) by those who approach Me, I require demon-strated right devotion (based on really effective self-understanding and truly heart-felt devotional recognition-response to Me) as the basis for any one's right to enter into My physical Company. And, in this manner, not only the egoic tendency, but also the tendency toward religious "cultism", is constantly undermined in the only-by-Me Revealed and Given Way of Adidam.

Because people appear within this human condition, this simultaneously attractive and frightening "dream" world, they tend to live—and to interpret both the conditional (or cosmic and psycho-physical) reality <u>and</u> the Unconditional (or Divine) Reality—from the "point of view" of this apparent (and bewildering) mortal human condition. And, because of this universal human bewilderment (and the ongoing human reaction to the threatening force of mortal life-events), there is an even ancient ritual that <u>all</u> human beings rather unconsciously (or automatically, and without discriminative understanding) desire and tend to repeatedly (and under <u>all</u> conditions) enact. Therefore, wherever you see an association of human beings gathered for <u>any</u> purpose (or around <u>any</u> idea, or symbol, or person, or subject of any kind), the same human bewilderment-ritual is <u>tending</u> to be enacted by one and all.

Human beings <u>always</u> <u>tend</u> to encircle (and, thereby, to contain—and, ultimately, to entrap and abuse, or even to blithely ignore) the presumed "center" of their lives—a book, a person, a symbol, an idea, or whatever. They tend to encircle the "center" (or the "middle"), and they tend to seek to <u>exclusively</u> acquire all "things" (or all power of control) for the circle (or toward the "middle") of <u>themselves</u>. In this manner, the <u>group</u> becomes an <u>ego</u> ("inward"-directed, or separate and separative)—just as the individual body-mind becomes, by self-referring self-contraction, the separate and separative ego-"I" ("inward"-directed, or egocentric—and exclusively acquiring all "things", or all power of control, for itself). Thus, by <u>self-contraction</u> upon the presumed "center" of their lives—human beings, in their collective egocentricity, make "cults" (or bewildered and frightened "centers" of power, and control, and exclusion) in <u>every</u> area of life.

Anciently, the "cult"-making process was done, most especially, in the political and social sphere—and religion was, as even now, mostly an exoteric (or political and social) exercise that was <u>always</u> used to legitimize (or, otherwise, to "de-throne") political and social "authority-figures". Anciently, the cyclically (or even annually) culminating product of this exoteric religio-political "cult" was the ritual "de-throning" (or ritual deposition) of the one in the "middle" (just as, even in these times, political leaders are periodically "deposed"—by elections, by rules of term and succession, by scandal, by slander, by force, and so on).

Everywhere throughout the ancient world, traditional societies made and performed this annual (or otherwise periodic) religio-political "cult" ritual. The ritual of "en-throning" and "de-throning" was a reflection of the human observation of the annual cycle of the seasons of the natural world—and the same ritual was a reflection of the human concern and effort to <u>control</u> the signs potential in the cycle of the natural world, in order to ensure human survival (through control of weather, harvests and every kind of "fate", or even every fraction of existence upon which human beings depend for both survival and pleasure, or psycho-physical well-being). Indeed, the motive behind the ancient agrarian (and, later, urbanized, or universalized) ritual of the one in the "middle" was, essentially, the same motive that, in the modern era, takes the form of the culture of scientific materialism (and even all of the modern culture of materialistic "realism"): It is the motive to gain (and to maintain) <u>control</u>, and the effort to control even everything and everyone (via both knowledge and gross power). Thus, the ritualized, or bewildered yes/no (or desire/fear), life of mankind in the modern era is, essentially, the same as that of mankind in the ancient days.

In the ancient ritual of "en-throning" and "de-throning", the person (or subject) in the "middle" was ritually mocked, abused, deposed, and banished—and a new person (or subject) was installed in the "center" of the religio-political "cult". In the equivalent modern ritual of dramatized ambiguity relative to everything and everyone (and, perhaps especially, "authority-figures"), the person (or symbol, or idea) in the "middle" (or that which is given power by means of popular fascination) is first "cultified" (or made much of), and then (progressively) doubted, mocked, and abused—until, at last, all the negative emotions are (by culturally and socially ritualized dramatization) dissolved, the "middle" (having thus ceased to be fascinating) is abandoned, and a "new" person (or symbol, or idea) becomes the subject of popular fascination (only to be reduced, eventually, to the same "cultic" ritual, or cycle of "rise" and "fall").

Just as in <u>every</u> other area of human life, the tendency of <u>all</u> those who (in the modern era) would become involved in religious or Spiritual life is also to make a "cult", a circle that ever increases its separate and separative dimensions—beginning from the "center", surrounding it, and (perhaps) even (ultimately) controlling it (such that it altogether ceases to be effective, or even interesting). Such "cultism" is ego-based, and ego-reinforcing—and, no matter how "esoteric" it presumes itself to be, it is (as in the ancient setting) entirely exoteric, or (at least) more and more limited to (and by) merely social (and gross physical) activities and conditions.

The form that every "cult" imitates is the pattern of egoity (or the pattern that is the ego-"I") itself—the presumed "middle" of every ordinary individual life. It is the self-contraction (or the avoidance of relationship), which "creates" the fearful sense of separate mind, and all the endless habits and motives of egoic desire (or bewildered, and self-deluded, seeking). It is what is, ordinarily, called (or presumed to be) the real and necessary and only "life".

From birth, the human being (by reaction to the blows and limits of psycho-physical existence) begins to presume separate existence to be his or her very nature—and, on that basis, the human individual spends his or her entire life generating and serving a circle of ownership (or self-protecting acquisition) all around the ego-"I". The egoic motive encloses all the other beings it can acquire, all the "things" it can acquire, all the states and thoughts it can acquire—<u>all</u> the possible emblems, symbols, experiences, and sensations it can possibly acquire. Therefore, when any human being begins to involve himself or herself in some religious or Spiritual association (or, for that matter, <u>any</u> extension of his or her own subjectivity), he or she tends again to "create" that same circle about a "center".

The "cult" (whether of religion, or of politics, or of science, or of popular culture) is a dramatization of egoity, of separativeness, even of the entrapment and betrayal of the "center" (or the "middle"), by one and all. Therefore, I have always Refused to assume the role and the position of the "man in the middle"—and I have always (from the beginning of My formal Work of Teaching and Blessing) Criticized, Resisted, and Shouted About the "cultic" (or

THE SEVEN STAGES OF LIFE

ego-based, and ego-reinforcing, and merely "talking" and "believing", and not understanding and not really practicing) "school" (or tendency) of ordinary religious and Spiritual life. Indeed, true Satsang with Me (or the true devotional relationship to Me) is an always (and specifically, and intensively) anti-"cultic" (or truly non-"cultic") Process.

The true devotional relationship to Me is not separative (or merely "inward"-directed), nor is It a matter of attachment to Me as a mere (and, necessarily, limited) human being (or a "man in the middle")—for, if My devotee indulges in ego-bound (or self-referring and self-serving) attachment to Me as a mere human "other", My Divine Nature (and, therefore, the Divine Nature of Reality Itself) is <u>not</u> (as the very Basis for religious and Spiritual practice in My Company) truly devotionally recognized and rightly devotionally acknowledged. And, if such non-recognition of Me is the case, there is <u>no</u> truly ego-transcending devotional response to My Avatarically Self-Revealed (and Self-Evidently Divine) Presence and Person—and, thus, such presumed-to-be "devotion" to Me is <u>not</u> devotional heart-Communion with Me, and such presumed-to-be "devotion" to Me is <u>not</u> Divinely Liberating. Therefore, because the <u>true</u> <u>devotional</u> (and, thus, truly devotionally Me-recognizing and truly devotionally to-Me-responding) relationship to Me is <u>entirely</u> a counter-egoic (and truly and only Divine) discipline, it does not tend to become a "cult" (or, otherwise, to support the "cultic" tendency of Man).

The true devotional practice of Satsang with Me is (inherently) <u>expansive</u> (or <u>relational</u>)—and the self-contracting (or separate and separative) self-"center" is neither Its motive nor Its source. In true Satsang with Me, the egoic "center" is always already undermined as a "<u>center</u>" (or a presumed separate, and actively separative, entity). The Principle of true Satsang with Me is <u>Me</u>— Beyond (and not "within"—or, otherwise, supporting) the ego-"I".

True Satsang with Me is the true "Round Dance" of <u>Esoteric</u> Spirituality. I am not trapped in the "middle" of My devotees. I "Dance" in the "Round" with <u>each</u> and <u>every</u> one of My devotees. I "Dance" in the circle—and, therefore, I am not merely a "motionless man" in the "middle". At the <u>true</u> "Center" (or the Divine

Heart), I <u>Am</u>—Beyond definition (or separateness). I <u>Am</u> the Indivisible—or Most Perfectly Prior, Inherently Non-Separate, and Inherently egoless (or centerless, boundless, and Self-Evidently Divine)—Consciousness (Itself) <u>and</u> the Indivisible—or Most Perfectly Prior, Inherently Non-Separate, and Inherently egoless (or centerless, boundless, and Self-Evidently Divine)—Light (Itself). I <u>Am</u> the Very Being <u>and</u> the Very Presence (or Self-Radiance) of Self-Existing and Eternally Unqualified (or Non-"Different") Consciousness (Itself).

In the "Round Dance" of true Satsang with Me (or of right and true devotional relationship to Me), I (Myself) Am Communicated directly to every one who lives in heart-felt relationship with Me (insofar as each one feels—<u>Beyond</u> the ego-"I" of body-mind—to <u>Me</u>). Therefore, I am not the mere "man" (or the separate human, or psycho-physical, one), and I am not merely "in the middle" (or separated out, and limited, and confined, by egoic seekers). I <u>Am</u> the One (Avatarically Self-Revealed, and All-and-all-Transcending, and Self-Evidently Divine) Person of Reality Itself—Non-Separate, never merely at the egoic "center" (or "in the middle"—or "<u>within</u>", and "inward" to—the egoic body-mind of My any devotee), but always <u>with</u> each one (and all), and always in relationship with each one (and all), and always Beyond each one (and all).

Therefore, My devotee is not Called, by Me, merely to turn "inward" (or upon the ego-"I"), or to struggle and seek to survive merely as a self-contracted and self-referring and self-seeking and self-serving ego-"center". Instead, I Call My devotee to turn the heart (and the total body-mind) <u>toward</u> Me (all-and-All-Surrounding, and all-and-All-Pervading), <u>in</u> relationship—<u>Beyond</u> the body-mind-self of My devotee (and <u>not</u> merely "<u>within</u>"—or contained and containable "within" the separate, separative, and self-contracted domain of the body-mind-self, or the ego-"I", of My would-be devotee). I Call My devotee to function freely—My (Avatarically Self-Transmitted) Divine Light and My (Avatarically Self-Revealed) Divine Person always (and under all circumstances) presumed and experienced (and not merely sought). Therefore, true Satsang with Me is the Real Company of Truth, or of Reality Itself (Which <u>Is</u> the Only Real God). True Satsang with

Me Serves life, because I Move (or Radiate) into life. I always Contact life in relationship.

I do not Call My devotees to become absorbed into a "cultic" gang of exoteric and ego-centric religionists. I certainly Call all My devotees to cooperative community (or, otherwise, to fully cooperative collective and personal relationship) with one another—but not to do so in an egoic, separative, world-excluding, xenophobic, and intolerant manner. Rather, My devotees are Called, by Me, to transcend egoity—through right and true devotional relationship to Me, and mutually tolerant and peaceful cooperation with one another, and all-tolerating (cooperative and compassionate and all-loving and all-including) relationship with all of mankind (and with even all beings).

I Give My devotees the "Bright" Force of My own Avatarically Self-Revealed Divine Consciousness Itself, Whereby they can become capable of "Bright" life. I Call for the devotion—but also the intelligently discriminative self-understanding, the rightly and freely living self-discipline, and the full functional capability—of My devotees. I do not Call My devotees to resist or eliminate life, or to strategically escape life, or to identify with the world-excluding ego-centric impulse. I Call My devotees to live a positively functional life. I do not Call My devotees to separate themselves from vital life, from vital enjoyment, from existence in the form of human life. I Call for all the human life-functions to be really and rightly known, and to be really and rightly understood, and to be really and rightly lived (and not reduced by, or to, the inherently bewildered—and inherently "cultic", or self-centered and fearful—"point of view" of the separate and separative ego-"I"). I Call for every human life-function to be revolved away from self-contraction (or ego-"I"), and (by Means of that revolving turn) to be turned "outwardly" (or expansively, or counter-contractively) to all and All, and (thereby, and always directly, or in an all-and-All-transcending manner) to Me—rather than to be turned merely "inwardly" (or contractively, or counter-expansively), and, as a result, turned away from Me (and from all and All). Thus, I Call for every human life-function to be thoroughly (and life-positively, and in the context of a fully participatory human life) aligned and adapted to <u>Me</u>, and (Thus and Thereby) to be turned and Given to the Realization of Me (the Avataric Self-Revelation of Truth, or Reality Itself—Which <u>Is</u> the Only Real God).

Truly benign and positive life-transformations are the characteristic signs of right, true, full, and fully devotional Satsang with Me—and freely life-positive feeling-energy is the characteristic accompanying "mood" of right, true, full, and fully devotional Satsang with Me. The characteristic life-sign of right, true, full, and fully devotional Satsang with Me is the capability for ego-transcending relatedness, based on the free disposition of no-seeking and no-dilemma. Therefore, the characteristic life-sign of right, true, full, and fully devotional Satsang with Me is not the tendency to seek some "other" condition. Rather, the characteristic life-sign of right, true, full, and fully devotional Satsang with Me is freedom from the presumption of dilemma within the <u>present-time</u> condition.

One who rightly, truly, fully, and fully devotionally understands My Avatarically Given Words of Divine Self-Revelation and Divine Heart-Instruction, and whose life is lived in right, true, full, and fully devotional Satsang with Me, is not necessarily (in function or appearance) "different" from the ordinary (or natural) human being. Such a one has not, necessarily, acquired some special psychic abilities, or visionary abilities, and so on. The "radical" understanding (or root self-understanding) I Give to My devotees is not, itself, the acquisition of <u>any</u> particular "thing" of experience. My any particular devotee may, by reason of his or her developmental tendencies, experience (or precipitate) the arising of extraordinary psycho-physical abilities and extraordinary psycho-physical phenomena—but not <u>necessarily</u>. My every true devotee is simply Awakening (and always Awakened to Me) within the otherwise bewildering "dream" of <u>ordinary human</u> life.

Satsang with Me is a natural (or spontaneously, and not strategically, unfolding) Process, in Which the self-contraction that <u>is</u> each one's suffering is transcended by Means of <u>total</u> psycho-physical (or whole bodily) heart-Communion with My Avatarically Self-Revealed (and Real—and Really, and tangibly, experienced) Divine (Spiritual, and Transcendental) Presence and Person. My devotee is (as is the case with <u>any</u> and <u>every</u> ego-"I") <u>always</u> <u>tending</u> to be preoccupied with ego-based seeking—but, all the while of his or her life in <u>actively</u> ego-surrendering (and really ego-forgetting and, more and more, ego-transcending) devotional Communion with Me, I Am <u>Divinely</u> Attracting (and <u>Divinely</u> Acting upon) My true devotee's heart (and total body-mind), and (Thus and Thereby) Dissolving and Vanishing My true devotee's fundamental egoity (and even all of his or her otherwise motivating dilemma and seeking-strategy).

There are <u>two</u> principal tendencies by which I am always being confronted by My devotee. One is the tendency to <u>seek</u>— rather than to truly enjoy and to fully animate the Condition of Satsang with Me. And the other is the tendency to make a self-contracting circle around Me—and, thus, to make a "cult" of ego-"I" (and of the "man in the middle"), or to duplicate the ego-ritual of mere fascination, and of inevitable resistance, and of never-Awakening unconsciousness. Relative to these two tendencies, I Give <u>all</u> My devotees only <u>one</u> resort. It is this true Satsang—the devotionally Me-recognizing, and devotionally to-Me-responding, and always really counter-egoic devotional relationship to My Avatarically Self-Revealed (and Self-Evidently Divine) Person.

The Great Secret of My Avatarically Self-Revealed Divine Person, and of My Avatarically Self-Manifested Divine Blessing-Work (now, and forever hereafter)—and, therefore, the Great Secret of the only-by-Me Revealed and Given Way of Adidam—Is that I am <u>not</u> the "man in the middle", but I <u>Am</u> Reality Itself, I <u>Am</u> the Only <u>One</u> Who <u>Is</u>, I <u>Am</u> That Which Is Always Already The Case, I <u>Am</u> the Non-Separate (Avatarically Self-Revealed, and Self-Evidently Divine) Person (or One and Very Divine Self, or One and True Divine Self-Condition) of all and All (<u>Beyond</u> the ego-"I" of every one, and of all, and of All).

Aham Da Asmi. Beloved, I <u>Am</u> Da—the One and Only and Non-Separate and Indivisible and Self-Evidently Divine Person, the Non-Separate and Indivisible Self-Condition and Source-Condition of all and All. I <u>Am</u> the Avatarically Self-Revealed "Bright" Person, the One and Only and Self-Existing and Self-Radiant Person—Who <u>Is</u> the One and Only and Non-Separate and Indivisible and Indestructible Light of All and all. I <u>Am</u> <u>That</u> One and Only and Non-Separate <u>One</u>. And—<u>As</u> <u>That</u> <u>One</u>, and <u>Only</u> <u>As</u> <u>That</u> <u>One</u>—I Call all human beings to heart-recognize Me, and to heart-respond to Me with right, true, and full devotion (demonstrated by Means of formal practice of the only-by-Me Revealed and Given Way of Adidam—Which Is the One and Only by-Me-Revealed and by-Me-Given Way of the Heart).

I do not tolerate the so-called "cultic" (or ego-made, and ego-reinforcing) approach to Me. I do not tolerate the seeking ego's "cult" of the "man in the middle". I am not a self-deluded ego-man—making much of himself, and looking to include everyone-and-everything around himself for the sake of social and political power. To be the "man in the middle" is to be in a Man-made trap, an absurd mummery of "cultic" devices that enshrines and perpetuates the ego-"I" in one and all. Therefore, I do not make or tolerate the religion-making "cult" of ego-Man. I do not tolerate the inevitable abuses of religion, of Spirituality, of Truth Itself, and of My own Person (even in bodily human Form) that are made (in endless blows and mockeries) by ego-based mankind when the Great Esoteric Truth of devotion to the Adept-Realizer is not rightly understood and rightly practiced.

The Great Means for the Teaching, and the Blessing, and the Awakening, and the Divine Liberating of mankind (and of even all beings) Is the Adept-Realizer Who (by Virtue of True Divine Realization) Is Able to (and, indeed, cannot do otherwise than) Stand In and <u>As</u> the Divine (or Real and Inherent and One and Only) Position, and to <u>Be</u> (Thus and Thereby) the Divine Means (In Person) for the Divine Helping of one and all. This Great Means Is the Great Esoteric Principle of the collective historical Great Tradition of mankind. And Such Adept-Realizers Are (in their Exercise of the Great Esoteric Principle) the Great Revelation-Sources That Are at the Core and Origin of <u>all</u> the right and true religious and Spiritual traditions within the collective historical Great Tradition of mankind.

By Means of My (now, and forever hereafter) Divinely Descended and Divinely Self-"Emerging" Avataric Incarnation, I Am the Ruchira Avatar, Adi Da Samraj—the Divine Heart-Master, the First, the Last, and the Only Adept-Realizer of the seventh (or

Most Perfect, and all-Completing) stage of life. I <u>Am</u> the Ruchira Avatar, Adi Da Samraj, the Avataric Incarnation (and Divine World-Teacher) everywhere Promised for the "late-time" (or "dark" epoch)—which "late-time" (or "dark" epoch) is <u>now</u> upon <u>all</u> of mankind. I <u>Am</u> the Great and Only and Non-Separate and (Self-Evidently) Divine Person—Appearing in Man-Form As the Ruchira Avatar, Adi Da Samraj, in order to Teach, and to Bless, and to Awaken, and to Divinely Liberate all of mankind (and even all beings, every "where" in the Cosmic domain). Therefore, by Calling every one and all (and All) to <u>Me</u>, I Call every one and all (and All) <u>Only</u> to the Divine Person, Which <u>Is</u> My own and Very Person (or Very, and Self-Evidently Divine, Self—or Very, and Self-Evidently Divine, Self-Condition), and Which <u>Is</u> Reality Itself (or Truth Itself—the Indivisible and Indestructible Light That <u>Is</u> the Only Real God), and Which <u>Is</u> the <u>One</u> and <u>Very</u> and <u>Non-Separate</u> and <u>Only</u> Self (or Self-Condition, and Source-Condition) of all and All (Beyond the ego-"I" of every one, and of all, and of All).

The only-by-Me Revealed and Given Way of Adidam necessarily (and As a Unique Divine Gift) requires and involves devotional recognition-response to Me In and Via (and <u>As</u>) My bodily (human) Divine Avataric-Incarnation-Form. However, because I Call every one and all (and All) to Me <u>Only</u> <u>As</u> the Divine Person (or Reality Itself), the only-by-Me Revealed and Given Way of Adidam is not about ego, and egoic seeking, and the egoic (or the so-called "cultic") approach to Me (as the "man in the middle").

According to <u>all</u> the esoteric traditions within the collective historical Great Tradition of mankind, to devotionally approach <u>any</u> Adept-Realizer as if he or she is (or is limited to being, or is limited by being) a mere (or "ordinary", or even merely "extraordinary") human entity is the great "sin" (or fault), or the great error whereby the would-be devotee fails to "meet the mark". Indeed, the Single Greatest Esoteric Teaching common to <u>all</u> the esoteric religious and Spiritual traditions within the collective historical Great Tradition of mankind Is that the Adept-Realizer should <u>always</u> and <u>only</u> (and <u>only</u> devotionally) be recognized and approached <u>As</u> the Embodiment and the Real Presence of <u>That</u> (Reality, or Truth, or Real God) Which would be Realized (Thus and Thereby) by the devotee.

Therefore, <u>no</u> <u>one</u> should misunderstand <u>Me</u>. By Avatarically Revealing and Confessing My Divine Status to one and all and All, I am not indulging in self-appointment, or in illusions of grandiose Divinity. I am not claiming the "Status" of the "Creator-God" of exoteric (or public, and social, and idealistically pious) religion. Rather, by Standing Firm in the Divine Position (<u>As</u> I <u>Am</u>)—and (Thus and Thereby) <u>Refusing</u> to be approached as a mere man, or as a "cult"-figure, or as a "cult"-leader, or to be in any sense defined (and, thereby, trapped, and abused, or mocked) as the "man in the middle"—I Am Demonstrating the Most Perfect Fulfillment (and the Most Perfect Integrity, and the Most Perfect Fullness) of the Esoteric (and Most Perfectly <u>Non-Dual</u>) Realization of Reality. And, by Revealing and Giving the Way of Adidam (Which Is the Way of ego-transcending devotion to Me <u>As</u> the Avatarically Self-Revealed One and Only and Non-Separate and Self-Evidently Divine Person), I Am (with Most Perfect Integrity, and Most Perfect Fullness) Most Perfectly (and in an all-Completing and all-Unifying Manner) Fulfilling the Primary Esoteric Tradition (and the Great Esoteric Principle) of the collective historical Great Tradition of mankind—Which Primary Esoteric Tradition and Great Esoteric Principle Is the Tradition and the Principle of devotion to the Adept-Realizer <u>As</u> the Very Person and the Direct (or Personal Divine) Helping-Presence of the Eternal and Non-Separate Divine Self-Condition and Source-Condition of all and All.

Whatever (or whoever) is cornered (or trapped on all sides) bites back (and fights, or <u>seeks</u>, to break free). Whatever (or whoever) is "in the middle" (or limited and "centered" by attention) is patterned by (or conformed to) the ego-"I" (and, if objectified as "other", is forced to represent the ego-"I", and is even made a scapegoat for the pains, the sufferings, the powerless ignorance, and the abusive hostility of the ego-"I").

If there is no escape from (or no Way out of) the corner (or the "centered" trap) of ego-"I"—the heart goes mad, and the body-mind becomes more and more "dark" (bereft of the Indivisible and Inherently Free Light of the Self-Evident, and Self-Evidently Divine, Love-Bliss That <u>Is</u> Reality Itself).

I am not the "man in the middle". I do not stand here as a mere man, "middled" to the "center" (or the cornering trap) of ego-based mankind. I am not an ego-"I", or a mere "other", or the representation (and the potential scapegoat) of the ego-"I" of mankind (or of any one at all).

I Am the Indivisible and Non-Separate One, the (Avatarically Self-Revealed) One and Only and (Self-Evidently) Divine Person—the Perfectly Subjective Divine Self-Condition (and Source-Condition) That Is Perfectly centerless (and Perfectly boundless), Eternally Beyond the "middle" of all and All, and Eternally Surrounding, Pervading, and Blessing all and All.

I Am the Way Beyond the self-cornering (and "other"-cornering) trap of ego-"I".

In this "late-time" (or "dark" epoch) of worldly ego-Man, the collective of mankind is "darkened" (and cornered) by egoity. Therefore, mankind has become mad, Lightless, and, like a cornered "thing", aggressively hostile in its universally competitive fight and bite.

Therefore, I have not Come here merely to stand Manly in the "middle" of mankind—to suffer its biting abuses, or even to be coddled and ignored in a little corner of religious "cultism".

I have Come here to Divinely Liberate one and all (and All) from the "dark" culture and effect of this "late-time", and (now, and forever hereafter) to Divinely Liberate one and all (and All) from the pattern and the act of ego-"I", and (Most Ultimately) to Divinely Translate one and all (and All) Into the Indivisible, Perfectly Subjective, and Eternally Non-Separate Self-Domain of My Divine Love-Bliss-Light.

The ego-"I" is a "centered" (or separate and separative) trap, from which the heart (and even the entire body-mind) must be Retired. I Am the Way (or the Very Means) of that Retirement from egoity. I Refresh the heart (and even the entire body-mind) of My devotee, in every moment My devotee resorts to Me (by devotionally recognizing Me, and devotionally—and ecstatically, and also, often, meditatively—responding to Me) Beyond the "middle", Beyond the "centering" act (or trapping gesture) of ego-"I" (or self-contraction).

I Am the Avatarically Self-Revealed (and Perfectly Subjective, and Self-Evidently Divine) Self-Condition (and Source-Condition) of every one, and of all, and of All—but the Perfectly Subjective (and Self-Evidently Divine) Self-Condition (and Source-Condition) is not "within" the ego-"I" (or separate and separative body-mind). The Perfectly Subjective (and Self-Evidently Divine) Self-Condition (and Source-Condition) is not in the "center" (or the "middle") of Man (or of mankind). The Perfectly Subjective (and Self-Evidently Divine) Self-Condition (and Source-Condition) of one, and of all, and of All Is Inherently centerless (or Always Already Beyond the self-contracted "middle"), and to Be Found only "outside" (or by transcending) the bounds of separateness, relatedness, and "difference". Therefore, to Realize the Perfectly Subjective (and Self-Evidently Divine) Self-Condition and Source-Condition (or the Perfectly Subjective, and Self-Evidently Divine, Heart) of one, and of all, and of All (or even, in any moment, to exceed the ego-trap—and to be Refreshed at heart, and in the total body-mind), it is necessary to feel (and to, ecstatically, and even meditatively, swoon) Beyond the "center" (or Beyond the "point of view" of separate ego-"I" and separative body-mind). Indeed, Most Ultimately, it is only in self-transcendence to the degree of unqualified relatedness (and Most Perfect Divine Samadhi, or Utterly Non-Separate Enstasy) that the Inherently centerless and boundless, and Perfectly Subjective, and Self-Evidently Divine Self-Condition (and Source-Condition) Stands Obvious and Free (and Is, Thus and Thereby, Most Perfectly Realized).

It Is only by Means of devotionally Me-recognizing (and devotionally to-Me-responding) devotional meditation on Me (and otherwise ecstatic heart-Contemplation of Me), and total (and totally open, and totally ego-forgetting) psycho-physical Reception of Me, that your madness of heart (and of body-mind) is (now, and now, and now) escaped, and your "darkness" is En-Light-ened (even, at last, Most Perfectly). Therefore, be My true devotee—and, by (formally, and rightly, and truly, and fully, and fully devotionally) practicing the only-by-Me Revealed and Given Way of Adidam (Which Is the True and Complete Way of the True and Real Divine Heart), always Find Me, Beyond your self-"center", in every here and now.

Aham Da Asmi. Beloved, I <u>Am</u> Da. And, because I <u>Am</u> Infinitely and Non-Separately "Bright", all and All <u>Are</u> In My Divine Sphere of "Brightness". By feeling and surrendering Into My Infinite Sphere of My Avatarically Self-Revealed Divine Self-"Brightness", My every devotee <u>Is</u> In Me. And, Beyond his or her self-contracting and separative act of ego-"I", My every devotee (self-surrendered Into heart-Communion With Me) <u>Is</u> the One and Only and Non-Separate and Real God I Have Come to Awaken— by Means of My Avataric Divine Descent, My Avataric Divine Incarnation, and My (now, and forever hereafter) Avataric Divine Self-"Emergence" (here, and every "where" in the Cosmic domain).

RUCHIRA AVATAR ADI DA SAMRAJ
The Mountain Of Attention, 2000

PROLOGUE

My Divine Disclosure

"My Divine Disclosure" has been Freely Developed—As a Further, and All-Completing, Avataric Self-Revelation of His own Self-Evidently Divine Person—by the Ruchira Avatar, Adi Da Samraj, from selected verses of the traditional Bhagavad Gita *(2:13-17, 8:3, 8:22, 9:3, 9:11, 9:26, 15:15, 18:61-66).*

My Divine Disclosure

1.

ham Da Asmi. Beloved, I <u>Am</u> Da—The One and Only and Self-Evidently Divine Person, Avatarically Self-Revealed To You.

2.

Therefore, Listen To <u>Me</u>, and Hear <u>Me</u>, and See <u>Me</u>.

3.

This Is My Divine Heart-Secret, The Supreme Word Of My Eternal Self-Revelation.

4.

Here and Now, I Will Tell You What Will Benefit You The Most, Because I Love You <u>As</u> My Very Self and Person.

5.

I <u>Am</u> The Ruchira Avatar, The Da Avatar, The Love-Ananda Avatar, Adi Da Love-Ananda Samraj—The Avataric Incarnation, and The Self-Evidently Divine Person, Of The One True Heart (or The One, and Only, and Inherently egoless Self-Condition and Source-Condition) Of All and all.

6.

Here I <u>Am</u>, In <u>Person</u>, To Offer (To You, and To all) The Only-By-<u>Me</u> Revealed and Given True World-Religion (or Avatarically All-Completing Divine Devotional and Spiritual Way) Of Adidam, Which Is The One and Only By-<u>Me</u>-Revealed and By-<u>Me</u>-Given (and Only <u>Me</u>-Revealing) Divine Devotional and Spiritual Way Of Sri Hridayam (or The Only-By-<u>Me</u> Revealed and Given, and

Entirely <u>Me</u>-Revealing, Way Of The True Divine Heart Itself), and Which Is The One, and All-Inclusive, and All-Transcending, and Only-By-<u>Me</u> Revealed and Given (and Only <u>Me</u>-Revealing) Way Of The True Divine Heart-Master (or The Only-By-<u>Me</u> Revealed and Given, and Entirely <u>Me</u>-Revealing, Way Of Ruchira Avatara Bhakti Yoga, or Ruchira Avatara Hridaya-Siddha Yoga), and Which Is The "Radically" ego-Transcending Way Of Devotionally <u>Me</u>-Recognizing and Devotionally To-<u>Me</u>-Responding Reception Of My Avatarically Self-Manifested Divine (and Not Merely Cosmic) Hridaya-Shaktipat (or Divinely Self-Revealing Avataric Spiritual Grace).

7.

If You Surrender Your heart To <u>Me</u>, and If (By Surrendering Your ego-"I", or self-Contracted body-mind, To <u>Me</u>) You Make <u>Yourself</u> A Living Gift To <u>Me</u>, and If You (<u>Thus</u>) <u>Constantly</u> Yield Your attention To <u>Me</u> (Through True Devotional Love and Really ego-Transcending Service), Then You Will Hear <u>Me</u> (Truly), and See <u>Me</u> (Clearly), and Realize <u>Me</u> (Fully), and Come To <u>Me</u> (Eternally). I Promise You <u>This</u>, Because I Love You <u>As</u> My Very Self and Person.

8.

<u>Abandon</u> The Reactive Reflex Of self-Contraction—The Separative (or egoic) Principle In <u>all</u> Your concerns. Do Not <u>Cling</u> To <u>any</u> experience that May Be Sought (and Even Attained) As A Result Of desire (or The Presumption Of "Difference"). <u>Abandon</u> Your Search For what May Be Gotten As A Result Of the various kinds of strategic (or egoic) action.

9.

I <u>Am</u> Love-Bliss <u>Itself</u>—Now (and Forever Hereafter) "Brightly" Present here. Therefore, I Say To You: <u>Abandon</u> <u>All</u> <u>Seeking</u>— By <u>Always</u> "Locating" (and <u>Immediately</u> Finding) <u>Me</u>.

10.

Instead Of <u>Seeking</u> <u>Me</u> (As If My Divine Person Of Inherent
Love-Bliss-Happiness Were <u>Absent</u> From You), <u>Always</u> <u>Commune</u>
<u>With</u> <u>Me</u> (<u>Ever</u>-Present, <u>Never</u> Absent, and <u>Always</u> Love-Bliss-Full
and Satisfied). Thus, Your <u>Me</u>-"Locating" <u>Relinquishment</u> Of All
Seeking Is <u>Not</u>, Itself, To Be Merely Another Form Of Seeking.

11.

If You <u>Always</u> "Locate" <u>Me</u> (and, Thus, <u>Immediately</u> Find <u>Me</u>),
You Will <u>Not</u> (In <u>any</u> instance) self-Contract Into the mood and
strategy of <u>inaction</u>.

12.

You Must <u>Never</u> <u>Fail</u> To act. <u>Every</u> moment of Your life <u>Requires</u>
Your particular <u>Right</u> action. Indeed, the living body-mind <u>is</u>
(itself) action. Therefore, <u>Be</u> <u>Ordinary</u>, By Always Allowing the
body-mind its <u>Necessity</u> Of Right action (and Inevitable Change).

13.

Perform <u>every</u> act As An ego-Transcending Act Of Devotional
Love Of <u>Me</u>, In body-mind-Surrendering Love-Response To <u>Me</u>.

14.

Always Discipline <u>all</u> Your acts, By <u>Only</u> Engaging In action that
Is <u>Appropriate</u> For one who Loves <u>Me</u>, and Surrenders To <u>Me</u>, and
acts <u>Only</u> (and <u>Rightly</u>) In Accordance With My Always <u>Explicit</u>
Word Of Instruction.

15.

Therefore, Be My <u>Always</u> Listening-To-<u>Me</u> Devotee—and, Thus,
<u>Always</u> live "Right Life" (According To My Word), and (This)
<u>Always</u> By Means Of <u>active</u> Devotional Recognition-Response
To <u>Me</u>, and While <u>Always</u> Remembering and Invoking and
Contemplating <u>Me</u>. In <u>This</u> Manner, Perform <u>every</u> act As A
Form Of Direct, and Present, and Whole bodily (or Total psycho-
physical), and Really ego-Surrendering Love-Communion With <u>Me</u>.

16.

If You Love <u>Me</u>—Where <u>Is</u> doubt and anxious living? If You Love <u>Me</u> <u>Now</u>, Even anger, sorrow, and fear Are <u>Gone</u>. When You <u>Abide</u> In Devotional Love-Communion With <u>Me</u>, the natural results of Your various activities No Longer Have Power To Separate or Distract You From <u>Me</u>.

17.

The ego-"I" that is born (as a body-mind) In The Realm Of Cosmic Nature (or the conditional worlds of action and experience) Advances From childhood To adulthood, old age, and death—While Identified With the same (but Always Changing) body-mind. Then the same ego-"I" Attains another body-mind, As A <u>Result</u>. One whose heart Is (Always) Responsively Given To <u>Me</u>, Overcomes (<u>Thereby</u>) <u>Every</u> Tendency To self-Contract From This Wonderfully Ordinary Process.

18.

The Ordinary Process Of "Everything Changing" Is Simply The Natural Play Of Cosmic Life, In Which the (<u>Always</u>) <u>two</u> sides of every possibility come and go, In Cycles Of appearance and disappearance. Winter's cold alternates with summer's heat. Pain, Likewise, Follows every pleasure. <u>Every</u> appearance Is (<u>Inevitably</u>) Followed By its <u>disappearance</u>. There Is <u>No</u> <u>Permanent</u> <u>experience</u> In The Realm Of Cosmic Nature. One whose heart-Feeling Of <u>Me</u> Is <u>Steady</u> Simply <u>Allows</u> All Of This To Be <u>So</u>. Therefore, one who Truly Hears <u>Me</u> Ceases To Add self-Contraction To This Inevitable Round Of Changes.

19.

Happiness (or True Love-Bliss) <u>Is</u> Realization Of <u>That</u> Which Is <u>Always</u> <u>Already</u> The Case.

20.

I <u>Am</u> <u>That</u> Which Is <u>Always</u> <u>Already</u> The Case.

21.
Happiness <u>Is</u> Realization Of <u>Me</u>.

22.
Realization Of Me Is Possible <u>Only</u> When a living being (or body-mind-self) Has heart-Ceased To <u>React</u> To The <u>Always Changing</u> Play Of Cosmic Nature.

23.
The body-mind Of My True Devotee Is <u>Constantly</u> Steadied In <u>Me</u>, By Means Of the Feeling-heart's Always Constant Devotional Recognition-Response To <u>Me</u>.

24.
Once My True Devotee Has Truly heart-Accepted That The Alternating-Cycle Of Changes (Both Positive and Negative) Is <u>Inevitable</u> (In the body-mind, and In <u>all</u> the conditional worlds), the living body-mind-self (or ego-"I") Of My True Devotee Has Understood <u>itself</u> (and, <u>Thus</u>, Heard <u>Me</u>).

25.
The body-mind-self (Of My True <u>Me</u>-Hearing Devotee) that Constantly Understands itself (At heart) By Constantly Surrendering To <u>Me</u> (and Communing With <u>Me</u>) No Longer self-Contracts From <u>My</u> Love-Bliss-State Of <u>Inherent</u> Happiness.

26.
Those who Truly <u>Hear</u> <u>Me</u> Understand That whatever Does Not Exist Always and Already (or Eternally) <u>Only</u> Changes.

27.
Those who Truly <u>See</u> <u>Me</u> Acknowledge (By heart, and With every moment and act of body-mind) That What <u>Is</u> Always Already The Case <u>Never</u> Changes.

28.

Such True Devotees Of Mine (who Both <u>Hear</u> <u>Me</u> <u>and</u> <u>See</u> <u>Me</u>) Realize That The Entire Cosmic Realm Of Change—and Even the To-<u>Me</u>-Surrendered body-mind (itself)—Is <u>Entirely</u> Pervaded By <u>Me</u> (Always Self-Revealed <u>As</u> <u>That</u> Which <u>Is</u> Always Already The Case).

29.

Now, and Forever Hereafter, I Am Avatarically Self-Revealed, Beyond The Cosmic Play—"Bright" Behind, and Above, the To-<u>Me</u>-Surrendered body-mind Of My Every True Devotee.

30.

I <u>Am</u> The Eternally Existing, All-Pervading, Transcendental, Inherently Spiritual, Inherently egoless, Perfectly Subjective, Indivisible, Inherently Perfect, Most Perfectly Non-Separate, and Self-Evidently Divine Self-Condition and Source-Condition Of <u>all</u> Apparently Separate (or self-Deluded) selves.

31.

My Divine Heart-Power Of Avataric Self-Revelation Is (Now, and Forever Hereafter) Descending Into The Cosmic Domain (and Into the body-mind Of Every To-<u>Me</u>-True True Devotee Of Mine).

32.

I <u>Am</u> The Avatarically Self-"Emerging", Universal, All-Pervading Divine Spirit-Power and Person Of Love-Bliss (That Most Perfectly Husbands and Transcends The Primal Energy Of Cosmic Nature).

33.

I <u>Am</u> The One and Indivisibly "Bright" Divine Person.

34.

Now, and Forever Hereafter, My Ever-Descending and Ever-"Emerging" Current Of Self-Existing and Self-Radiant Love-Bliss Is Avatarically <u>Pervading</u> The Ever-Changing Realm Of Cosmic Nature.

35.

I <u>Am</u> The One, and Indivisibly "Bright", and Inherently egoless Person Of all-and-All, Within <u>Whom</u> every body-mind Is arising (as a mere, and unnecessary, and merely temporary appearance that, merely apparently, modifies <u>Me</u>).

36.

I Am To Be Realized By Means Of ego-Transcending Devotional Love—Wherein <u>every</u> action of body-mind Is Engaged As ego-Surrendering (present-time, and Direct) Communion With <u>Me</u>.

37.

Those who Do <u>Not</u> heart-Recognize <u>Me</u> and heart-Respond To <u>Me</u>—and who (Therefore) Are Without Faith In <u>Me</u>—Do <u>Not</u> (and <u>Cannot</u>) <u>Realize</u> <u>Me</u>. Therefore, they (By Means Of their own self-Contraction From <u>Me</u>) Remain ego-Bound To The Realm Of Cosmic Nature, and To The Ever-Changing Round Of conditional knowledge and temporary experience, and To The Ceaselessly Repetitive Cycles Of birth and search and loss and death.

38.

Such Faithless beings <u>Cannot</u> Be Distracted By <u>Me</u>—Because they Are Entirely Distracted By <u>themselves</u>! They Are Like Narcissus—The Myth Of ego—At His Pond. Their Merely self-Reflecting minds Are Like a mirror in a dead man's hand. Their tiny hearts Are Like a boundless desert, where the mirage of Separate self is ceaselessly admired, and The True Water Of My Constant Presence Stands Un-Noticed, In the droughty heap and countless sands of ceaseless thoughts. If Only they Would Un-think themselves In <u>Me</u>, these (Now Faithless) little hearts Could Have <u>Immediate</u> <u>Access</u> To The True Water Of My True Heart! Through Devotional Surrender Of body, emotion, mind, breath, and all of Separate self To <u>Me</u>, Even Narcissus Could Find The Way To My Oasis (In The True Heart's Room and House)—but the thinking mind of ego-"I" Is <u>Never</u> Bathed In Light (and, So, it sits, Un-Washed, Like a desert dog that wanders in a herd of flies).

39.

The "Un-Washed dog" of self-Contracted body-mind Does Not think To Notice Me—The Divine Heart-Master Of its wild heart and Wilderness.

40.

The "Wandering dog" of ego-"I" Does Not "Locate" Me In My Inherent "Bright" Perfection—The Divine Heart-Master Of Everything, The Inherently egoless Divine True Self Of all conditionally Manifested beings, and The Real Self-Condition and Source-Condition Of All-and-all.

41.

If Only "Narcissus" Will Relent, and heart-Consent To Bow and Live In Love-Communion With Me, heart-Surrendering all of body-mind To Me, By Means Of Un-Contracting Love Of Me, Then—Even If That Love Is Shown With Nothing More Than the "little gift" of ego-"I" (itself)—I Will Always Accept The Offering With Open Arms Of Love-Bliss-Love, and Offer My Own Divine Immensity In "Bright" Return.

42.

Therefore, whoever Is Given (By heart) To Me Will Be Washed, From head To toe, By All The True Water Of My Love-Bliss-Light, That Always "Crashes Down" On All and all, Below My Blessing-Feet.

43.

My Circumstance and Situation Is At the heart of all beings—where I Am (Now, and Forever Hereafter) Avatarically Self-"Emerging" As The One and All-and-all-Outshining Divine and Only Person (Avatarically Self-Manifested As The "Radically" Non-Dual "Brightness" Of All-and-all-Filling Conscious Love-Bliss-Light, Self-Existing and Self-Radiant As The Perfectly Subjective Fundamental Reality, or Inherently egoless Native Feeling, Of Merely, or Unqualifiedly, Being).

44.

The True heart-Place (Where I Am To Be "Located" By My True Devotee) Is Where The Ever-Changing Changes Of waking, dreaming, and sleeping experience Are <u>Merely</u> <u>Witnessed</u> (and <u>Not</u> Sought, or Found, or Held).

45.

Every conditional experience appears and disappears In Front Of The Witness-heart.

46.

Everything Merely Witnessed Is Spontaneously Generated By The Persistent Activity Of The Universal Cosmic Life-Energy.

47.

The self-Contracted heart of body-mind Is Fastened, <u>Help-lessly</u>, To That Perpetual-Motion Machine Of Cosmic Nature.

48.

I <u>Am</u> The Divine and One True Heart (<u>Itself</u>)—Always Already Existing <u>As</u> The Eternally Self-Evident Love-Bliss-Feeling Of Being (and Always Already Free-Standing <u>As</u> Consciousness Itself, Prior To the little heart of ego-"I" and its Seeming Help-less-ness).

49.

In Order To Restore all beings To The One True Heart Of <u>Me</u>, I Am Avatarically Born To here, <u>As</u> The "Bright" Divine Help Of conditionally Manifested beings.

50.

Therefore (Now, and Forever Hereafter), I <u>Am</u> (Always Free-Standing) <u>At</u> the To-<u>Me</u>-True heart Of You—and I <u>Am</u> (Always "Bright") Above Your body-mind and world.

51.

If You Become My True Devotee (heart-Recognizing My Avatarically Self-Manifested Divine Person, and heart-Responding—With <u>all</u> the parts of Your single body-mind—To My Avatarically Self-Revealing Divine Form and Presence and State), You Will <u>Always</u> Be Able To Feel <u>Me</u> ("Brightly-Emerging" here) Within Your Un-Contracting, In-<u>Me</u>-Falling heart—and You Will Always Be Able To "Locate" <u>Me</u>, As I "Crash Down" (All-"Bright" Upon You) From Above the worlds Of Change.

52.

The To-<u>Me</u>-Feeling (In-<u>Me</u>-Falling) heart Of My Every True Devotee <u>Is</u> (At its Root, and Base, and Highest Height) <u>My</u> Divine and One True Heart (<u>Itself</u>).

53.

Therefore, Fall Awake In <u>Me</u>.

54.

Do Not <u>Surrender</u> Your Feeling-heart Merely To experience and know the Ever-Changing world.

55.

Merely To know and experience The Cosmic Domain (Itself) Is To live As If You Were In Love With Your Own body-mind.

56.

Therefore, <u>Surrender</u> Your Feeling-heart <u>Only</u> To <u>Me</u>, The True Divine Beloved Of the body-mind.

57.

I <u>Am</u> The Truth (and The Teacher) Of the heart-Feeling body-mind.

58.

I <u>Am</u> The Divine and Eternal Master Of Your To-<u>Me</u>-Feeling heart and Your To-<u>Me</u>-Surrendering body-mind.

59.

I <u>Am</u> The Self-Existing, Self-Radiant, and Inherently Perfect Person Of Unconditional Being—Who Pervades The Machine Of Cosmic Nature <u>As</u> The "Bright" Divine Spirit-Current Of Love-Bliss, and Who Transcends All Of Cosmic Nature <u>As</u> Infinite Consciousness, The "Bright" Divine Self-Condition (and Source-Condition) Of All and all.

60.

If You Will Give (and Truly, Really, Always Give) Your Feeling-attention To My Avatarically-Born Bodily (Human) Divine Form, and If You Will (Thus, and Thereby) Yield Your body-mind Into The "Down-Crashing" Love-Bliss-Current Of My Avatarically Self-Revealed and All-Pervading Divine Spirit-Presence, and If You Will Surrender Your conditional self-Consciousness Into My Avatarically Self-Revealed and Perfectly Subjective and Self-Evidently Divine Self-Consciousness (Which <u>Is</u> The Divine True Heart Of Inherently egoless Being, Itself)—Then I Will Also Become An Offering To You.

61.

By <u>That</u> Offering Of Mine, You Will Be Given The Gift Of Perfect Peace, and An Eternal Domain For Your To-<u>Me</u>-True Feeling-heart.

62.

Now I Have Revealed To You The Divine Mystery and The Perfect Heart-Secret Of My Avataric Birth To here.

63.

"Consider" This <u>Me</u>-Revelation, <u>Fully</u>—and, Then, <u>Choose</u> What You Will Do With Your "little gift" of Feeling-heart and Your "Un-Washed dog" of body-mind.

RUCHIRA AVATAR ADI DA SAMRAJ

Tat Sundaram, 1998

Tat Sundaram!—
All Of This Is <u>Sacred</u>,
All Of This Is <u>Beautiful</u>!

(The Essence of the Message of Adidam
and of the One and Entire Great Tradition
of Mankind)

Tat Sundaram!— All Of This Is <u>Sacred</u>, All Of This Is <u>Beautiful</u>!

(The Essence of the Message of Adidam and of the One and Entire Great Tradition of Mankind)

1.

Form <u>only</u> changes.

Energy is <u>always</u> conserved.

Being only <u>Is</u>, and It is <u>never</u> negated.

2.

Perception and conception—and all their objects (or "things"), including the physical body, every thought, and all the kinds of "others"—are an immense and ultimately unfathomable and (as a whole) unknowable Process of changes. The arising of conditions is a Play of changes—and every form <u>only</u> changes (until it disappears—or, otherwise, ceases to appear as it was). The entire Process of appearances, or conditions, or forms, or changes is a Dynamic Display (or a Play of opposites). Every apparent action is always accompanied by an equal and opposite apparent reaction. Every positive becomes negative. Every negative becomes positive. Whatever arises, changes—positively and negatively— until it disappears (or even reappears—modified, or newly defined).

All appearances, conditions, forms, or changes are apparent modifications of Primal Energy (or Spirit-Power). Primal Energy is the Essence of every body-mind. Primal Energy is the Essence of all "things". Primal Energy is the Essence of all opposites and all changes. Primal Energy is the Essence of the activity of change itself. Nevertheless, Primal Energy Itself is inherently changeless. Even in all changes, Primal Energy Itself is forever conserved. Primal Energy Itself cannot be destroyed. Primal Energy Itself is a Constant and Self-Existing Shine, Merely (or Only) Self-Radiant.

Primal Energy Itself Merely (or Only) Is. Therefore, Its Totality of changes, and even every conditional form, Merely (or Only) Is. Being Is the Constant Sign, even in all changes. The Direct Intuition of Being (or of Existence Itself) Demonstrates (To and In Consciousness Itself) that non-Being (or non-Existence) is an illusion (or a myth of possibility), generated by fear (or false knowledge). And fear itself is the result of clinging to forms—without Understanding the Process of forms, and without Real (Participatory) Observation of Primal Energy, and without Perfectly Direct (or Native and Non-objective) Intuition of Being (Itself).

3.

Every conditional "thing" (or apparent "object") is only Energy (Itself).

Every conditional "self" (or apparently individual "subject") Is only Consciousness (Itself).

The Conscious conditional "self" (or apparently individual "subject") "knows" its every "object", but no "object" can "know" its "knower".

No "thing" can Contemplate Consciousness.

Therefore, Energy (Itself) cannot Contemplate (or ever "know") Consciousness (Itself).

Consciousness (Itself) only (Eternally) Contemplates Itself.

Consciousness (Itself) Is the Native and Inherently Perfect Intuition of Being (Itself).

Being (Itself) Is Self-Existing and Self-Radiant.

Consciousness (Itself) Is the Eternal Contemplation of the Self-Existing Self-Radiance (or Inherent Energy) of Being (Itself).

Therefore, Consciousness (Itself) Is the Contemplation (and Real Observation) of Energy (Itself).

Consciousness (Itself) Is Merely Being (or Existence Itself), Self-Radiant (As Primal Radiance, or Energy Itself), appearing to be modified as all forms and changes.

Consciousness (Itself) <u>Is</u> Inherently Free Radiance, or Bliss, or Happiness (Itself).

Consciousness (<u>Itself</u>)—Realized As Inherent Freedom and Self-Radiant and Self-Existing Bliss, or Happiness (Itself)—<u>Is</u> the Realization of Real God, or Truth, or Reality (<u>Itself</u>).

Therefore, Consciousness (Itself)—Self-Existing As Being (Itself), and Self-Radiant As Bliss-Energy (Itself), or Happiness (Itself)—<u>Is</u> the Divine Being, the Eternal Spirit, Forever Standing in the Midst of Life.

4.

The Divine Being Is Self-Existing Consciousness (Itself), the Unconditional Self (or Self-Condition) That inherently Transcends the separate (and always separative) heart—and, yet, <u>Is</u> the True and Non-Separate Heart—of every conditional "self".

The Divine Being Is Self-Radiant Energy, the Primal Spirit That Is Pervading all and All.

The Divine Being Is the Perfectly Subjective Source-Condition and the True (and inherently Non-Separate) Self-Condition of all and All.

There Is Always Already <u>Only</u> the One Spiritual, Transcendental, and (Self-Evidently) Divine Being.

The One Spiritual, Transcendental, and (Self-Evidently) Divine Being Is Inherently Perfect, Absolute, Un-born, Not dying or dead, Not "different"—but Self-Existing, Ever-Free, Self-Radiant, All Bliss, Only Happiness Itself, and <u>All</u> That Is <u>Only</u> Consciousness.

The One Spiritual, Transcendental, and (Self-Evidently) Divine Being Is To Be (and, indeed, Must Be) Most Perfectly Revealed to you, and Most Perfectly Offered to you, and Most Perfectly Transmitted to you, and (Thus and Thereby) progressively Activated in your own case, and (at last) Most Perfectly Awakened <u>As</u> the Very Heart (or Non-Separate and Non-"Different" Self-Condition) of your own heart (or seeming-separate "I") by the One and True Divine <u>World-Teacher</u>, the <u>Divine</u> Heart-Master, the <u>Final</u> Avatar, the Universally Promised God-Man of the "Late-Time" (or "Dark Epoch")—Ruchira Avatar Adi Da Samraj.

The Ruchira Avatar, Adi Da Samraj, Is the Complete Avataric Divine Realizer, the Complete Avataric Divine Revealer, and the Complete Avataric Divine Revelation of the One Spiritual, Transcendental, and (Self-Evidently) Divine Being.

The Divine World-Teacher, Ruchira Avatar Adi Da Samraj, Is the True Avataric-Incarnation of Reality, Truth, Happiness, Love, Bliss, and Real God.

The Divine Heart-Master, Ruchira Avatar Adi Da Samraj, Is the Last (or Final) Avatar—because the Ruchira Avatar, Adi Da Samraj, has Revealed and Given the Avataric Divine Way of the Divine-Person-Always-Already-Descended-to-here (and to every where), rather than a seeker's path that either waits for the Divine to Descend (or otherwise Appear) or strives to Ascend to the pre-sumed "somewhere else" of the Divine Domain.

The Universally Promised (or Hoped-for) God-Man (or Avataric-Incarnation of the One, and Indivisible, and Non-"Different", and Self-Evidently Divine Reality) Is here (As the Ruchira Avatar, Adi Da Samraj), Now (and Forever Hereafter) Avatarically Self-"Emerging" As the Always-Already-Present Means of Most Direct (and, Ultimately, Most Perfect) Divine Communion (and Divine Self-Realization).

Therefore, Find and Receive and Accept the Ruchira Avatar, Adi Da Samraj—That Most Perfectly Self-Revealing Avataric Person of Divine Grace.

By Means of the Most Perfectly Self-Revealing Avataric Divine Grace of the Ruchira Avatar, Adi Da Samraj—Find and Receive and Accept the Only One Who Is.

By Means of truly devotional (and really self-disciplined, ego-surrendering, ego-forgetting, and ego-transcending) Recognition-Response to the Avatarically Self-Revealed (and Self-Evidently Divine) Person of the Ruchira Avatar, Adi Da Samraj—be (more and more) purified in, of, and from the conditional (or psycho-physical) and egoic self.

By Means of counter-egoic devotional Contemplation of the Ruchira Avatar, Adi Da Samraj—always directly (and, at last, Most Perfectly) transcend the conditional (or psycho-physical) and egoic self.

Therefore, by transcending the space-time "point of view" of body and mind, in and by Means of counter-egoic Contemplation of the Ruchira Avatar, Adi Da Samraj (Who Is the Avataric Divine Self-Revelation of the Only One Who Is)—Most Perfectly Realize (and Most Perfectly Be) the Only One Who Is.

5.

Life is a Wheel that would break the separate heart in all those who do not have faith in the One, and Only, and Eternally Indivisible Heart (Itself).

Because life (or even any form of conditional existence) is a Wheel that would break the separate heart, you must always actively transcend the Wheeling Machine of life—by always actively transcending the separate (and always separative) heart (itself).

Because the separate heart must be transcended in the One, and Only, and Eternally Indivisible Heart (Itself)—an always acti-vated (or effectively counter-egoic) faith in the One, and Only, and Inherently Indivisible, and Inherently Indestructible (Spiritual, Transcendental, and Self-Evidently Divine) Being (Who Is the Non-Separate and Non-"Different" Heart Itself) Is the Great Requirement (or Heart-Law) of every conditional "self".

Therefore, have faith in the One Who Is Divinely Self-Revealed In and By and As the Ruchira Avatar, Adi Da Samraj—the Divinely Self-Revealing "Late-Time" Avataric-Incarnation of the One and Only (and Eternally Indivisible) Heart Itself.

And do not merely think that faith, but always enact it—by transcending separate self's own separative heart, in devotional Recognition-Response to the Ruchira Avatar, Adi Da Samraj (the Divinely Self-Revealing "Late-Time" Avataric-Incarnation of the One, and Only, and Eternally Indivisible Heart Itself).

And do not merely talk that religion, but always perform it—by transcending separate self's own separative heart, in devotional Recognition-Response to the Ruchira Avatar, Adi Da Samraj (the Divinely Self-Revealing "Late-Time" Avataric-Incarnation of the One, and Only, and Eternally Indivisible Heart Itself).

And do not merely want to be loved, but always do love—by transcending separative self's own separative heart, in devotional

Recognition-Response to the Ruchira Avatar, Adi Da Samraj (the Divinely Self-Revealing "Late-Time" Avataric-Incarnation of the One, and Only, and Eternally Indivisible Heart Itself).

And do not <u>cease</u> <u>to</u> <u>Out</u>-Grow the Wheeling Machine of life, but <u>always</u> actively <u>transcend</u> the Wheeling Machine of life—by always actively transcending the separate (and always separative) heart <u>itself</u>, in devotional Recognition-Response to the Ruchira Avatar, Adi Da Samraj (the Divinely Self-Revealing "Late-Time" Avataric-Incarnation of the One, and Only, and Eternally Indivisible Heart <u>Itself</u>).

6.

Do not (at any time) prevent the Process of Constant Out-Growing in the case of <u>any</u> other.

Always (at all times) serve the Process of Constant Out-Growing in the case of <u>all</u> others.

Always notice when the Process of Out-Growing has stopped—especially in your <u>own</u> case.

Always remember to re-begin the Process of Out-Growing, <u>whenever</u> It has—in your own case—stopped.

Always Grow <u>Beyond</u>—by Growing with your heart (and Into The Avatarically Self-Revealed Divine Heart of Being—Which <u>Is</u> Consciousness Itself, and Which <u>Is</u> Bliss Itself, or Happiness Itself).

Grow Beyond your own ego-self.

Grow Beyond Illusion (or the habit of thinking and feeling "two", or "otherness").

Grow Beyond all limitations, and Into the Only One (and Who) That <u>Is</u>, Such That (at last, and Most Perfectly) There Is Only the Seeing (or Realizing) of One—even if the body and the world arise, and even if they cease to arise, and even if they do not arise.

Therefore, at last, in the Divine Perfection of the Process of all your Grace-Given Out-Growing—Realize and <u>Be</u> What (by inherently Transcending the Wheeling Machine of life) <u>Is</u> Always Already Single, Whole, Only, and Complete.

Only Consciousness (Itself) Is Always Already Single, Whole, Only, and Complete.

7.

As a phenomenal function in the context of gross bodily life, Consciousness is merely the body—dependent on the body, and arising as an effect of the body, and (like the body) mortal.

As a presumption of separate personal existence, Consciousness is merely the mind—dependent on mental states, consisting <u>only</u> of mental states, and, therefore, not otherwise existing (unless mental states arise).

From the point of view of any presumed-to-be-separate-self (or ego-"I"), <u>everything</u> that arises is (always, and necessarily, and inherently) a form of <u>subjectivity</u> (or knowledge, or knowing—whether perceptual or conceptual), and <u>never</u> a totally independent "something" (<u>objectively</u> existing, in and as itself—and <u>objectively</u> appearing, as itself, independent of all experiencing, or knowing, of it).

From the point of view of any presumed-to-be-separate-self (or ego-"I"), anything and everything that arises (perceptually or conceptually) <u>is</u> a perception, or a conception—and never entirely (or even really) an object absolutely apart.

Every presumed-to-be-separate-self (or ego-"I") arises in Reality Itself, and (inherently) <u>As</u> Reality Itself—and as a Play upon (or a merely apparent modification of) Reality Itself (Wherein there may or may not be the Inherent, and Self-Evidently Divine, Self-Recognition of Reality Itself).

Conditional experience (of perception and conception) clearly (and inherently) indicates that Consciousness (Itself) <u>Is</u> Reality (Itself), and Consciousness (Itself) <u>Is</u> the One and Only Reality (Itself), and the experiential mechanisms of perception and conception are the functional means (arising in Consciousness Itself) whereby modifications of Consciousness may appear to Consciousness as a Play of objects, and the apparent "objective world" (including all the experiential mechanisms of perception and conception, and also including all the acts, results, facts, artifacts, and memories of perception and conception) is a vibratory modification of the Native Substance (or Self-Existing Self-Radiance) of Consciousness Itself.

Therefore, it is inherently, and necessarily, and Self-Evidently, and Always Already The Case that Consciousness (Itself)—or the Irreducible Conscious-Light That Is the One, and Only, and Self-Evident, and Eternally Self-Revealing, and Always Already and Unconditionally Self-Existing Reality—Is the One, and Indivisible, and Self-Existing, and Self-Radiant, and Non-dual, and Non-dependent, and Non-conditional, and Eternal Reality, Condition, Truth, and Real God of every one, and of all, and of the All of all.

What any and every presumed-to-be-separate-self (or ego-"I") requires is the truly esoteric (or yet unknown, and yet un-Realized) understanding (and the tacit—or inherent, and constant—Realization) of Reality.

8.

Consciousness (Itself)—inherently, constantly, and tacitly Realized (As It Is)—Is (Itself) the One and Only Reality.

Consciousness (Itself) Is Always Already The Case.

Consciousness (Itself) Is Not an "other".

Consciousness (Itself) Is Not one of two.

Consciousness (Itself) Is Not one half of a pair.

Consciousness (Itself) Is Not an opposite.

Consciousness (Itself) Is Not a complement.

Consciousness (Itself) Is Not related.

Consciousness (Itself) Is Not "different".

Consciousness (Itself) Is Not separate.

Consciousness (Itself) Is inherently Non-separate, and inherently Non-dual, and (therefore) inherently egoless.

Consciousness (Itself) never changes.

Consciousness (Itself) Is the Constant in all changes.

Consciousness (Itself) Is the Self-Condition and the Source-Condition of all forms.

Consciousness (Itself) Only Is (Self-Existing As Itself).

Consciousness (Itself) Is Happiness (or Bliss-Energy), Self-Radiant As Itself.

Consciousness (Itself) Is One Only.

Consciousness (Itself) Is Single, Whole, Indivisible, Indestructible, Only, and Complete.

Consciousness (Itself) Is <u>The</u> One and Only.

Everything <u>means</u> Consciousness (Itself).

Any and every thing <u>means</u> Consciousness (Itself).

This Event <u>Is</u> <u>Only</u> Consciousness—and Consciousness (Itself) Sits, Like a Fuse of Fire Within (Pre-Lit to Light the Way to end of time).

Consciousness (Itself) <u>Is</u> the Depth (or the Native State, and the Perfectly Subjective Source-Condition) of everything (and of any and every thing).

Consciousness (Itself) <u>Is</u> the Essential Substance of every experience, every perception, and every thought.

No matter what arises or does not arise in your experience and mind—now, or at any time at all—Consciousness (Itself) <u>Is</u> the <u>Only</u> Basis for (and the Only Substance of) your experience, and your perception, and your memory, and your presumed knowledge, and even any of your thinking, or even any of "you-and-yours" at all.

No matter What, Where, When, How, Why, or Who <u>Is</u> Reality, Truth, or Real God—Consciousness (Itself) <u>Is</u> (Inherently, and Necessarily, and Always Already) the <u>Only</u> Basis for (and the Only Substance of) your Realization of That Which <u>Is</u> Reality, Truth, and Real God.

That Which <u>Is</u> Always Already The Case cannot be <u>other</u> than Consciousness (Itself), or else Consciousness (Itself)—Which Is the One and Only Basis for <u>both</u> the conditional experience of Reality (or all conditional perception, and all conditional knowing, and even all mediated apprehendings of Reality) <u>and</u> the Unconditional Realization of Reality (or all unmediated appre-hendings of That Which <u>Is</u> Always Already The Case)—would not (and, indeed, could not) appear in association with either condi-tional experience or Unconditional Realization.

There are not <u>two</u> Realities (or <u>two</u> Truths, or <u>two</u> Real Gods).

There <u>Is</u> Only One Reality (Which <u>Is</u> Truth, and the <u>Only</u> Real God).

Nevertheless, the One Reality Is of Such a Nature That (Apparently) It Can <u>either</u> Be Unconditionally Realized (<u>As</u> One, and Self-Existing, and Always Already The Case) <u>or</u> conditionally experienced (as all possible perceptual and conceptual dualities, things, conditions, and states—and even all possible "differences").

In Truth (and <u>As</u> Real God), Reality must Always Already Be Unconditionally Realized—or else conditional experience is <u>always</u> (and necessarily) an incident of apparent separation (and even intentional dissociation) from the One Reality (and Truth, and Real God) Itself.

Therefore, in the context of conditional experiencing, That Which Is Always Already The Case must Always Already Be Unconditionally Realized.

You must deeply feel and "consider" (and, by means of most profound feeling-"consideration", deeply accept) that Consciousness (Itself) Is the Necessary and Irreducible Form, Presence, Substance, Nature, State, and Identity of Reality (Itself, or Unconditionally—or <u>As</u> It <u>Is</u>) <u>and</u> the Necessary and Irreducible Basis for (and the Native, or Inherent, Meaning of) all conditional experience (or all perception, and all thinking).

In the depth of feeling-acceptance of the Reality and Primacy of Consciousness (Itself), the heart is able to devotionally recognize (and, altogether, devotionally respond to) the Ruchira Avatar, Adi Da Samraj.

The mere <u>object</u> (or "thing" <u>known</u>, or "one" <u>known</u>) is unable (and uninclined) to communicate, demonstrate, or convincingly prove that Consciousness (Itself) <u>Is</u> the Great Principle of both the Realization and the experience of Reality—but <u>you</u> (or even <u>any</u> presumed-to-be-separate psycho-physical self, or person) inherently experience and tacitly know (or Always Already Realize) that Consciousness (Itself) <u>Is</u> you, and Consciousness (Itself) <u>Is</u> all and All.

9.

Make your otherwise merely objective (or externalized—and only <u>sometimes</u> you-obligating, and <u>always</u> ego-serving) religion (or idle search for Reality, Truth, and Real God) into a truly and rightly subjective (and <u>always</u> you-obligating, and <u>always</u> ego-transcending, and <u>always</u> Reality-Finding, and <u>always</u> Truth-Finding, and <u>always</u> Real-God-Finding) process.

Make your religious impulse into a process of ego-transcending devotional Recognition-Response to the Ruchira Avatar, Adi Da Samraj—the "Late-Time" Avataric-Incarnation of Consciousness (Itself), Which <u>Is</u> the One, and Only, and Eternally Indivisible Heart (Itself).

Make your body-mind into ego-surrendering, ego-forgetting, and ego-transcending Spiritual Communion with the Avatarically Self-Transmitted Divine Spiritual Presence of the Ruchira Avatar, Adi Da Samraj.

Make your life into ego-transcending Fulfillment of the Avataric Divine Way Revealed and Given by the Ruchira Avatar, Adi Da Samraj.

By Means of the Avatarically Self-Transmitted Divine Grace of the Ruchira Avatar, Adi Da Samraj—make your total body-mind (and your entire life) into a process of ego-transcending Duplication of the Divinely Spiritualized psycho-physical State of the Avatarically-Born Bodily (Human) Form (and the Divine Self-Condition of the now, and forever hereafter, Avatarically "Emerging" Divine Spiritual Presence) of the Ruchira Avatar, Adi Da Samraj.

By Means of the Avatarically Self-Transmitted Divine Grace of the Ruchira Avatar, Adi Da Samraj—Realize the Very Nature and Self-Evidently Divine Condition of Being.

By practicing (and, at last, Most Perfectly Practicing) the Way of Adidam (Which Is the One and Only Way Revealed and Given by the Ruchira Avatar, Adi Da Samraj), Realize the Inherent (or Always Already) State of Self-Existing, and Self-Radiant, and Self-Evidently Divine Being (Itself).

10.

Tat Sundaram! All of This Consciousness (Itself) Is <u>Sacred</u>! All that arises and passes In and (Necessarily) <u>As</u> Consciousness (Itself) Is <u>Beautiful</u>! Therefore, all of <u>this</u> (arising and passing of conditions, forms, and beings) Is <u>Sacred</u>!

Tat Sundaram! All of <u>this</u> (that arises and passes) Is <u>Beautiful</u>! All of <u>this</u> (arising and passing) Is <u>Self</u>-<u>Existing</u> (<u>As</u> Consciousness Itself) and <u>Self</u>-<u>Radiant</u> (<u>As</u> Primal Energy Itself, or Light Itself— Which <u>Is</u> Happiness Itself)! Therefore, <u>let</u> all of this <u>Be</u> <u>So</u>!

Tat Sundaram!

<u>All</u> Of This Is <u>Sacred</u>!

<u>All</u> Of This Is <u>Beautiful</u>!

And <u>So</u> <u>Be</u> <u>you</u>!

RUCHIRA AVATAR ADI DA SAMRAJ
Los Angeles, 2000

PART TWO

The
Seven Stages
Of Life

The
Seven Stages
Of Life

The Only-By-Me Revealed and Given Way Of The Heart (or Way Of Adidam), Developed Either In The Manner Of The Devotional Way Of Insight Or In The Manner Of The Devotional Way Of Faith, Is The Divine Way Wherein and Whereby egoity (or the Total psycho-physical self-Contraction) Is Directly, Progressively, and (Ultimately) Most Perfectly Transcended—and This By The By-My-Avataric-Divine-Grace-Given Means Of More and More Perfect Inherence In My Avatarically Self-Revealed (and Self-Existing, and Self-Radiant, and Self-Evidently Divine) Self-Condition. Therefore, The Only-By-Me Revealed and Given Way Of The Heart Is (and More and More Becomes) The Way Of Devotion (or Sacrifice) Of the conditional self To Me, Rather Than Any ego-Based Search For self-Fulfillment and self-Release.

The Only-By-Me Revealed and Given Way Of The Heart (or Way Of Adidam) Is Not A Strategic and self-Concerned Path Of self-Development (or Even Of self-Negation). The Only-By-Me Revealed and Given Way Of The Heart Is (and More and More Becomes) The ego-Surrendering, ego-Forgetting, and ego-Transcending Way Of Devotional Recognition-Response To Me (The Divine Heart-Master Of The Heart—The Avatarically Self-Revealed Transcendental, Inherently Spiritual, and Self-Evidently Divine Person Of Reality and Truth).

Practice Of The Only-By-Me Revealed and Given Way Of The Heart (or Way Of Adidam) Is An ego-Surrendering, ego-Forgetting, and ego-Transcending Devotional Ordeal That Matures In The Context (or, Otherwise, In The Transcending) Of Each Of The First Six Stages Of Life. The Full (or Most Ultimate) Maturity Of That Devotional Ordeal Is Demonstrated In The Context Of The Only-By-Me Revealed and Given Seventh Stage Of Life. The Total Devotional Ordeal Of The Only-By-Me Revealed and Given Way Of The Heart (or Way Of Adidam) Is A Great Process Of Progressive Devotional Recognition-Response To Me and Devotional Realization Of Me (The Divine Heart-Master Of The Heart). And, As (and When) My Avatarically Self-Transmitted Divine Grace Will Have It, That Process Becomes More and More Profound Devotional Recognition-Response To (and Devotional Realization Of) Me <u>As</u> The Avataric Self-Revelation Of The Spiritual, Transcendental, and Self-Evidently Divine Forms Of Real God, or Truth, or Reality.

The Foundation-Course Of The Great Ordeal Of The Only-By-Me Revealed and Given Way Of The Heart (or Way Of Adidam) Is The Progressive Process Of Listening To Me and Hearing Me. That Great Ordeal Is Based On (Progressive) Devotional Recognition-Response To Me and Devotional Realization Of Me, Through "Consideration" Of My Avatarically Self-Revealed Divine Word and My Avatarically Self-Manifested Divine Leelas, and Through Feeling-Contemplation Of (Especially) My Avatarically-Born Bodily (Human) Divine Form (and—Thus and Thereby, or Tacitly, and As My Avatarically Self-Transmitted Divine Grace Will Have It—My Avatarically Self-Revealed Spiritual, and Always Blessing, Divine Presence, and My Avatarically Self-Revealed, and Very, and Transcendental, and Perfectly Subjective, and Inherently Spiritual, and Inherently egoless, and Inherently Perfect, and Self-Evidently Divine State).

Thus, Through Effective Practice Of The Only-By-Me Revealed and Given Way Of The Heart (or Way Of Adidam) In The (General) Context Of The First Three Stages Of Life (and, More and More, In The "Original", or Beginner's, Devotional Context Of The Fourth Stage Of Life), There Is Gradual and Inevitable Release Of The Stress Of egoity (and Gradual and Inevitable Release Of the ego-Based limits on conditional energy and attention) In The Context Of the frontal personality and The Binding Patterns (or

Un-Happy Efforts) Associated With The Earliest Stages Of human Adaptation and Development. This Process Begins With Listening To Me (or The Giving Of one's Feeling-attention To My Avatarically Given Divine Sign, My Avatarically Given Divine Heart-Confessions, My Avatarically Given Divine Teaching-Arguments, My Avatarically Given Fundamental "Great Questions", and The Storied Avataric Leelas Of All My Self-Manifested Divine Work)—and (Once The Original, or Foundation, Impulse <u>Toward</u> Most Perfectly ego-Transcending Real-God-Realization Is Deeply Confirmed In Practice, and, Thereby, More and Very Fully Awakened By This Earliest "Consideration") The Process Advances (Through The Reality Process Of self-Observation and self-Understanding, and The Devotional Feeling-Process Of Effective ego-Transcendence) Toward The Realization Of True Hearing (or Most Fundamental self-Understanding).

Each Of The Stages Of Life (In The human Context) Is Associated With A Unique Form Of human Adaptation and Growth. And Each Form Of Adaptation Is Associated With a specific human organ (or Structural Pattern).*

The First Three Stages Of Life Occur Within The Context Of the lower organ functions Of human Adaptation—and, In That Context, human Development Is Associated With individuation, socialization, and integration Of The psycho-physical Patterns Of the frontal personality.

The First Stage Of Life Is The Process Of psycho-physical (and, thus, also emotional) individuation, Based On Identification With the Separate (and personal) gross physical body in the waking state. The First Stage Of Life Is Also Associated With the oral (or nutritive) function. At birth, the infant Is Separated From The Situation Of Unity With the human mother, and This Begins A Struggle With The Fact Of individual Existence. This Struggle Is Displayed In The Context Of oral Dependence On the mother as a Separate body (and Dependence On food that Must Be Acquired outside If individual bodily Existence Is To Continue). Whatever Occurs In The Drama Of breast-feeding and The Transition To food sources apart from the mother's body, human beings Tend

*See charts on pp. 386-87 and p. 390.

To Develop A Fundamental Reactive Habit (or Presumption Of Un-Happiness) At This Stage.

Un-Happy (or egoic) individuation Tends To Be Associated With A Feeling Of Separation (or Of Separating, and Of Separateness, and Of Separativeness)—and, Thus, Un-Happy (or egoic) individuation Is Also Characterized By An Only Partial (or Ambiguous) Willingness To Relinquish (or, Otherwise, Even To Accept) The Feeling Of Dependency On the mother (or On others In General). This Feeling Of Separation (or Of Separating, and Of Separateness, and Of Separativeness) Ultimately (or Primarily) Involves The Sense Of Disconnection From The Ultimate Source Of Support and Love (Which Is The Living Divine), and It Also Becomes A General Doubt (or Anxiety) About other human beings On whom one Depends For Love. Sex-Differentiation (Whereby emotional-sexual self-identity and the emotional-sexual identification of others Become Basic To Every Situation Of Relationship) Begins Even At This Stage, but all relationships are experienced from the viewpoint Of Dependency and Reluctance To Accept The Situation Of individuated Existence.

The Second Stage Of Life Is The Process Of socialization (or relationalization of the individual), Based On The Development Of emotional (or emotional-sexual) Sensitivity To the psycho-physical self, To others, and To the Natural world (including the Natural etheric energies associated with the psycho-physical self, with others, and with the entire Natural world). The Second Stage Of Life Is Also Associated With the anal (or eliminative) function and The Conflict Between Privacy (or self-Acceptance) and The Search For social Visibility (or Acceptance By others).

The anal function Begins To Develop Coincident With the oral function, but socialization itself Truly Begins Only After The Basic Struggle With individuation Has Reached A Workable (Even Though Un-Happy, or self-Contracted) Settlement. (Thus, It Can Be Said That, As A General Rule, The First Stage Of Life Involves the first seven years after birth, and The Second Stage Of Life Involves the second seven years, or The Period From early childhood Until puberty.)[*1]

Character Motivations That Are Rooted In the biology and psychology Of sex-Differentiation Are, In The Second Stage Of Life,

* Notes to the Text of *The Seven Stages Of Life* appear on pp. 391-99.

Extended and Developed In An Expanded social Context, and individuation (Including A Partial but Significantly Defined Sense Of emotional-sexual self-identity), Rather Than Ambiguously Differentiated Dependency, Becomes A Catalyst Toward social Exploration.

When individuation Has Become A Workable egoic Settlement, the individual Begins To Struggle, As an individual, With relationships (First On the intimate scale, and Then In an ever larger social sphere). The Second Stage individual Tends To Continue To function In The Context Of Dependency, but With A More Fully Developed Sense Of Separate self, Independence, and Mobility. Likewise, There Is A Gradual Discovery That There Are many kinds of relationships, and all of them Carry A Test, A Demand, and An Obstacle That Offends The Want To Be Dependent. The anal Phase Of Development Represents An Early Stage Of self-Awareness, In Which the individual's self-Esteem (or Presumed Desirability, or Presumed Lovableness) Is Apparently At Stake. Thus, Doubt Of the ego-self Appears—and, Likewise, Doubt Of The Love In others Appears. And So, The Second Stage Of Life Tends To Develop Only To The Degree Of A Tentative (or ego-Based and, Ultimately, Unsatisfactory) Resolution Of the relational and social character. Whereas The Feeling Of Separation (or Of Separating, and Of Separateness, and Of Separativeness) Characterizes The First Stage Reaction (or egoic Presumption), The Feeling Of Being Rejected (and The Felt Need To Reject or Punish others For Un-Love) Characterizes The Second Stage Reaction (or egoic and, Necessarily, Un-Happy Presumption).

The Third Stage Of Life Is The Process Of integration Of The psycho-physical Patterns (Both individual And relational) Of the frontal personality, By Means Of The Development and Application Of the functions of mind, discriminative intelligence, and the will. And This Process Is Also Associated With The genital Phase Of human Development. Genital Development and emotional-sexual gender-Differentiation Begin Even In infancy, and The emotional Trial Of The Second Stage Of Life Relates To the gender-Defined character, but The Great Struggle Of integration and self-Presentation (As a Fully Differentiated and Defined sexual, emotional-sexual, and social character) Takes Place Only After puberty.

The Third Stage Of Life Tends To Be Wasted (or Made Un-Happy) By Indulgence In Patterns That May Be Called adolescent. That Is To Say, The Third Stage Of Life Does Not Tend Toward Full (and Happy) Resolution, Because The First Two Stages Of Life (Which Are The Basis For Growth In The Third) Tend To Be Unresolved (or Patterned By Un-Happiness). As A Result, The Third Stage Of Life Becomes A Fruitless Drama Of Conflict Between Two Alternating and Contrary Impulses—The One Toward infantile and childish (or Passive and Weak-minded) Dependence, and The Other Toward willful and Rebellious (or self-Destructive and other-Destructive) Independence. The Life-Process Is Disturbed By This Un-Happy and Irresponsible Drama, and the mental faculties and the integrating function of the will Are (Thus) Impaired (or Retarded) In their Ability To Develop the True adult character—which character Is Characterized By Basic human Equanimity, Discriminative Intelligence, Responsive Heart-Feeling, and The Active Impulse (or Counter-egoic Will) To Always Continue To Grow (By ego-Transcendence—and, Necessarily, By Entering Into The Devotional and, Eventually, Spiritual Context Of The Fourth Stage Of Life).

I Have (By The Giving Of My Many Avataric Divine Gifts) Equipped The Progressive Culture Of Practitioners Of The Total Practice Of The Only-By-Me Revealed and Given Way Of The Heart (or Way Of Adidam) With Wisdom and Means Relative To Every Stage Of Life. Therefore, The Responsive Community (or Total Gathering) Of Formally Acknowledged Practitioners Of The Total Practice Of The Way Of The Heart Is (Via Its Right Use Of Those By Me Given Gifts Of Wisdom and Great Means) Empowered To Serve The Right, True, and Free Development Of children and young persons In The First Three Stages Of Life.

In The Context Of The First Three Stages Of Life, children and young people Should Be Helped To Adapt To The Requirements Of Growth In Those Stages, but In Such A Manner That The egoic (or self-Contracting) Tendencies Do Not Inhibit and Retard That Growth Through The Introduction Of infantile, childish, and adolescent Patterns Of Un-Happiness. To This End, The Responsive Community (or Total Gathering) Of True Practitioners Of The Total Practice Of The Way Of Adidam (Which Is The Only-By-Me Revealed and Given Way Of The Heart) Must Apply All Its By-Me-Given Wisdom Relative To The Development Of children and young persons In The Context Of The First Three Stages Of Life. And Part Of That Wisdom Is The Consistent Cultural Introduction Of The By-Me-Given Rudimentary (and Fundamental) Propositions and ("Original", or Beginner's) Practices Associated With The Fourth Stage Of Life (As Well As The Stages Beyond The Fourth, Including The Fundamental Disposition Of The Only-By-Me Revealed and Given Seventh, or Divinely Enlightened, Stage Of Life).

Therefore, I Have Provided Extensive Guidance[2] For Truly human (and humanizing) Growth In The Context Of The First Three Stages Of Life. In My Avataric Divine Work With children, young people, and adults, I Have Developed A Wisdom-Culture For The First Three Stages Of Life That Includes (and Rightly Guides) The physical, psychological, and social Processes Of individuation, socialization, and integration. That Wisdom-Culture (or The Only-By-Me Revealed and Given Way Of The Heart For children and young people) Also Goes Beyond the limits Of These Obligatory early-life Processes By Founding Them In The True Religion (and Mystery) Of My Avataric Divine Self-Revelation Of Real (and Really Spiritual, Transcendental, and Self-Evidently Divine) Truth. That True Religion (Of Heart-Participation In The Inherent Mystery Of Existence—By Means Of My Avatarically Self-Transmitted Divine Grace) Only Serves (and Does Not Retard) Freedom, Responsibility, and Growth. That Culture Of Devotion To Me (The Avataric Divine Revealer Of Truth and Inherent Mystery) Really Serves self-Discipline, ego-Transcendence, The Vision Of Unity, and The Realization Of Freedom, Through Real-God-Sensitive Prayer and Meditation (Even In The General, or Natural and early-life, Context Of The Spiritual, Transcendental, and Divine Reality). And That Culture Of Devotion To Me Rightly and Progressively Includes Exercises To Develop emotional and physical Sensitivity To and Responsibility For The Universal Field

Of Natural etheric energy Associated With the body-mind, Practices To Develop emotional and physical Sensitivity To (and Responsibility For) The etheric energy-Connection Between psycho-physically living beings (and Even Between psycho-physically living beings and Apparently non-living forms or things In The Cosmos Of conditional Nature), and Disciplines To Develop Sensitivity To and Responsibility For the deep psychic aspect of mind (and The psychic Connection Between psycho-physically living beings).

Without The humanizing Benefits Of Real Love (and The Learning Of ego-Transcending Love From The Example, The Help, and The Companionship Of others) In The Context Of The First Three Stages Of Life, and Without The Inspiring Benefits Of True Spiritual, Transcendental, and Divine Culture In The Context Of The First Three Stages Of Life, human beings Inevitably Tend To Develop Un-Happy Patterns (and Signs Of Failed Growth) In The Context Of The First Three Stages Of Life. Such Failures Of Love, Wisdom, and Happiness Define human Existence subhumanly and limit human Existence To the egoic model and destiny. Therefore, Relatively few adults Advance To The Fourth Stage Of Life (or, Therefrom, To Any Of The Stages Beyond The Fourth) In the most common (or Only Minimally Developed) world Of Mankind—Because the most common world Of Mankind Tends To Be limited to (and by) the egoic society Of The First Three Stages Of Life. And Religion In the most common world Of Mankind (Thus limited) Is Likewise Defined and limited By The conceptual and egoic Tendencies Of The First Three Stages Of Life. (Therefore, What Is most commonly Proposed As Religion, In The Context Of The First Three Stages Of Life, Is An ego-Serving Gloss Of Myths, Mystical Cosmology, and conventional Structures Of belief Based On The Illusions Of popular "God"-Religion and The More or Less Magical Psychology Of Seeking For Fulfillment Of desires In the conditional worlds.)

Because Of All Of This, and In Order To Love and Serve Me, The Ultimate <u>Person</u> Of Love (Avatarically Self-Revealed <u>As</u> The Inherently Perfect Self-Condition <u>and</u> Source-Condition Of Love), My Seeing Devotees (And Even All Practitioners who Embrace

The Total Practice Of The Way Of The Heart) Must (As parents, friends, educators, guides, and Loving helpers) Responsively Serve and Responsibly Perpetuate The Effective Wisdom-Culture Of early-life Practice Of The Way Of The Heart That I Have Given and Established. That practical and (In The General, or early-life Practitioner's, Sense) Devotional[3] Wisdom-Culture Must Always (Now, and Forever Hereafter) Responsively and Responsibly Incorporate All Aspects Of My Avatarically "Considered" Divine Teaching and Instruction Relative To The Practice Of The Only-By-Me Revealed and Given Way Of The Heart (or Way Of Adidam) In The Context Of The First Three Stages Of Life. Therefore, That Wisdom-Culture Must Always (Now, and Forever Hereafter) Take Into Account (As I Have Already Taken Into Account) The Truly human functional, practical, and relational Requirements Of The First Three Stages Of Life, The Truth and The (Even Earlier Stage) Callings and Requirements Of The Advanced (and The Ultimate) Stages Of Life, and The Basic Wisdom Relative To The Obligation Of ego-Transcendence. And Practice Of The Only-By-Me Revealed and Given Way Of The Heart (or Way Of Adidam) In That (early-life) Wisdom-Culture Of Listening Must Always (Now, and Forever Hereafter) Be Based Upon The (By-My-Avatarically-Revealed-Divine-Word) Rightly and Fully Instructed (and, Also, According-To-My-Avatarically-Revealed-Divine-Word, "Great-Tradition"-Informed) and, Altogether, Rightly Practiced Beginner's (early-life) Devotional Relationship To Me (As The Divine Heart-Master), Just As All adult Practitioners Of The Way Of The Heart Are Called (and Must Be Rightly Instructed—By My Avatarically Self-Revealed, and Always Me-Revealing, Divine Word, and By The Total Exemplary Culture Of Formally Acknowledged and True Practitioners Of The Total Practice Of The Only-By-Me Revealed and Given Way Of The Heart, and By The Great and Eternal and Ancient and Always New Tradition Of Devotion To The Adept Sat-Guru) To Rightly and Truly Practice Right and True Devotional Relationship To Me (The Divine Heart-Master).

Even Though they May Grow Up Under The Auspicious Circumstances Of The True Wisdom-Culture Of The Only-By-Me

Revealed and Given Way Of The Heart (or Way Of Adidam), young individuals Must Yet Grow To Understand (and Transcend) themselves As adults. If they Are, As adults, To Continue To Practice (and To Grow In) The Way Of The Heart, they Must, As adults, Devotionally Recognize Me and Devotionally Respond To Me From The Heart, and they Must, As adults, Choose The Only-By-Me Revealed and Given Way Of The Heart (or Way Of Adidam). Therefore, When they Achieve adult age (and If they, As adults, Both Respond To Me From The Heart and Choose To Practice The Way Of The Heart), all those who Have Grown Up Within The True Wisdom-Culture (Of The Formally Acknowledged Community, or Total Gathering) Of The Way Of The Heart, and (Thus) In (The early-life Practitioner's) Rightly Devotional and self-Disciplined Relationship To Me (In and Via My Avatarically Given Divine Sign, My Avatarically Self-Revealed Divine Word, and My Avatarically Self-Manifested Divine Leelas) As their Divine Heart-Master, Must (With The Continued Help Of Constant Right Guidance, Within The Formally Acknowledged Community, or Total Gathering, Of All Formally Acknowledged Practitioners Of The Total, or Full and Complete, Practice Of The Way Of The Heart) Continue (and Yet, and Truly, Complete) The Ordeal Of Listening To Me, and they Must Continue In That Listening Discipline (As Fully Responsible adult Participants In The Cooperative Culture Of All Formally Acknowledged Practitioners Of The Total Practice Of The Way Of The Heart) Until they Have (By Heart-Surrender, and Heart-Obedience, and Heart-Conformity To Me, Even To The Degree Of Hearing Me) Truly and Fully Grown Beyond the limits Of The First Three Stages Of Life.[4]

Many Practitioners Of The Way Of The Heart Come To Me At an Already adult age, and Only After infancy, childhood, and adolescence in the common world. Such Practitioners Come To Me Suffering Even Most Acutely From The egoic (or Un-Happy) Complications Of The First Three Stages Of Life. Nevertheless, The Only-By-Me Revealed and Given Way Of The Heart (or Way Of Adidam) Is The Same For all. Therefore, For Both The adult Practitioner who Has Achieved adult age In the common world and The adult Practitioner who Has Grown Up In (and, As an adult, Chooses To Practice) The Way Of The Heart, The Earliest Stage Of adult Practice Of The Way Of The Heart Involves The Listening Process Associated With Feeling-attention To Me (Always Present In The Form Of My Avatarically Given Divine Sign, and In The Form Of The Recorded Documents Of My Avatarically Self-Revealed Divine Teaching-Word, and In The Form Of The Recorded Divine Leelas Of My Avatarically Self-Manifested Teaching-Time, and In The Form Of The Recorded Divine Leelas Of All My Avatarically Self-Manifested Blessing-Work).

At The Beginning, The adult Practitioner Of The Way Of The Heart Feels (and Thereby Contemplates) My Avatarically Self-Revealed Divine Sign, Listens To My Avatarically Given Divine Self-Confessions and Teaching-Arguments and "Great Questions", Regards The Avatarically Self-Manifested Divine Leelas Of My Play Of Divine Work, and Thoroughly Observes (or Feels and, More and More, Feels Beyond) The Patterns Of his or her personal Un-Happiness (or egoity). By These Means, My Fully Practicing Listening Devotee Is (Eventually, and By Means Of My Avatarically Self-Transmitted Grace) Awakened To True (and Most Fundamental) self-Understanding. Once It Awakens, The Continued Effective Expression (or Enforcement) Of True (and Most Fundamental) self-Understanding Is The Real and Certain Process Whereby early-life Un-Happiness Is Transcended. And Such Transcendence Is The Regeneration Of The Free and Growing Movement Toward Completion Of The human Work Of individuation, socialization, and integration. Therefore, self-Observation, self-Understanding (Which Becomes Most Fundamental), and self-Transcending human (and humanizing) Growth (In The Context Of The First Three Stages Of Life) Are The Work Of The Listening and Hearing Stages Of The Only-By-Me Revealed and Given Way Of The Heart.

The Work Of The Listening Stages Of The Total Practice Of The Way Of The Heart Cannot Become Complete Until I Am Heard. And The Original Work Based On Truly Hearing Me (or The Necessary Work Of The Period Of Practice That Immediately Follows The Original Awakening Of Most Fundamental self-Understanding) In The Way Of The Heart Is Not Complete Until ordinary human Un-Happiness (or The Unfinished Effort Of The

First Three Stages Of Life) Is (In its Fundamental Aggravation) Replaced By Basic, Real, and Truly human Equanimity.

Only If The Impulse Toward Most Perfectly ego-Transcending Real-God-Realization (or Toward The Most Perfect Realization Of My Avatarically Self-Revealed, and Inherently Free, and Self-Evidently Divine, Self-Condition—Which Is The Inherent, or Native, Condition Of Being, Itself) Is Very Fully Awakened (and Activated), and Only If (On That Basis) The Process Of Thorough self-Observation, and The Reality Of Most Fundamental self-Understanding (or The Awakening Of The Directly self-Transcending Capability), and The Restoration (or Even The First Stable Achievement) Of Basic human Equanimity Are All (and Thoroughly) Established, Can the individual Continue To Grow By Entering Into The "Basic" Context Of The Fourth Stage Of Life (and, Then, Perhaps Via The "Advanced" Context Of The Fourth Stage Of Life, and Perhaps Even Via The Fifth Stage Of Life, Into The Ultimate Stages Of Life). Therefore, By Listening To Me and By Hearing Me—Grow Again, and Grow Beyond the self-Retarded limits Of The First Three Stages Of Life.

For My Truly Seeing Devotee, Listening To Me Has Become Hearing Me, and Hearing Me Has Become Seeing Me. And When Hearing Has Become Most Directly ego-Transcending Devotional Communion With Me, and When I Am Truly Seen By Means Of Such Directly ego-Transcending Devotional Communion, The Process Of Hearing Me and Seeing Me Continues To Develop Further (Via The Gift and Culture Of Satsang With Me) In The (Fullest) Devotional and (Now) Spiritual Context Of The Fully Established "Basic" Fourth Stage Of Life.

When The Process Of Listening To Me (In The Way Of The Heart) Is Complete (and I Am, Thereby, Heard), and (Thus) When the conditional self Is Understood Most Fundamentally, and When My Hearing Devotee Can (Responsibly, Directly, and Capably) Feel Beyond (and Really and Effectively Transcend) the self-Contraction, and When My Hearing Devotee Has Thereby Transcended (or Become Capably Responsible For) the Basic limits Associated With The First Three Stages Of Life, and When My Hearing Devotee Has Thus (By Means Of My Avatarically Self-

Revealed Divine Sign and My Avatarically Self-Manifested Divine Work) Realized My Avatarically Given Divine Word Of Instruction In The Form Of his or her own Real and Effective Understanding—Then My Hearing Devotee Must (By Constantly Hearing Me At Heart) Come To Me Most Fully At (and Via) The Heart, Able To Become My Devotee In Spirit.

After True Hearing Of Me Has Awakened My Hearing Devotee At The Heart, My Hearing Devotee (By Approaching Me In A Directly and Truly Hearing, or Really and Truly ego-Transcending Manner) Will (By Means Of My Avatarically Self-Transmitted Grace) Begin To (Fully, and Truly Responsibly) Heart-Recognize and Heart-Respond To My Avatarically Self-Revealed (Transcendental, Inherently Spiritual, and Self-Evidently Divine) Person. My Divine Spiritual Body Is My Avatarically Self-Revealed (and Inherently Attractive) "Bright" Divine Spirit-Presence That Draws the conditional self Beyond itself (To The Degree Of Releasing its own Contraction, In Me). When My Hearing Devotee (Now My Seeing Devotee) Awakens To My Avatarically Self-Revealed Divine Spirit-Presence At The Heart, The Process Of The Only-By-Me Revealed and Given Way Of The Heart Becomes Seeing (or Fullest emotional, and Total psycho-physical, Conversion and Infusion Via My Avatarically Self-Transmitted Divine Spirit-Baptism). And Practice Of The Only-By-Me Revealed and Given Way Of The Heart (or Way Of Adidam) Is Thereby Awakened Beyond The "Original" (or Beginner's) Context Of The Fourth Stage Of Life, and Established In The Spiritually Full (or Fully Established "Basic") Context Of The Fourth Stage Of Life.

The (Fully Established) "Basic" (or By-Me-Spiritually-Awakened) Fourth Stage Of Life (In The Way Of The Heart) Is The Process Of Spiritualization (or Spiritual Infusion) Of the psycho-physical personality Through ego-Transcending Devotional and (Directly and Fully) <u>Spiritual</u> Communion With Me. That Truly Spiritual Devotion To Me Is Expressed internally Through Heart-Feeling and Meditation, and It Is Expressed externally Through Perpetual Service To Me In all relations and circumstances. Just So, The (Total) Fourth Stage Of Life Is Associated With Progressive Awakening In The Great Organ Of The Heart.

The Region Of The Left Side Of The Heart Includes the phys-
ical and lower psychic functions Of The Heart. It Is The Ground
Of early-life Development. In The Total Context Of The Fourth
Stage Of Life, The Heart Awakens From The Left Toward The
Middle (or The subtle and higher psychic Region), Such That
Advanced (or Spiritualizing) Growth Occurs In The Domain Of
the frontal personality (Within and Beyond The Context Of The
First Three Stages Of Life). Therefore, As Devotional Heart-Feeling
and Heart-Surrender Become More and More Profound, There Is
A Growing Awareness Of the greater subtle and greater psychic
(or deep psychological) functions Of The Heart.

The "Original" Orientation (and Then The "Basic" Orientation)
Of The Fourth Stage Of Life (and Of The Way Of The Heart In The
"Original", and Then The "Basic", Context Of The Fourth Stage Of
Life, or Of The First Four Stages Of Life) Is Determined By The
Fact That The ("Original", and The "Basic", Fourth Stage) Practitioner
Is Grounded (As In The Ordinary Context Of The First Three
Stages Of Life) In The Left Side Of The Heart and, Therefore, In
The Natural Context Of the body-mind in the waking state (Rather
Than in the dreaming state or the sleeping state), and In The
Natural Context Of the world of the waking state. Naturally
Identified With the waking body-mind, The ("Original", and The
"Basic", Fourth Stage) Practitioner Of The Way Of The Heart func-
tions as the waking body-mind, To Heart-Surrender the Total
body-mind-self Through Devotional Communion With Me and
Service To Me.

In The Way Of The Heart (or Way Of Adidam), The "Original"
(and Then "Basic") Fourth Stage Practitioner Of Devotion To Me
Naturally (and By Heart) Conceives Of himself or herself As My
(Ultimately, Free) Servant, and That Service Is To Be Expressed
Through Even every form and moment of action, and Through
Constant Devotional Heart-Surrender, Heart-Obedience, and
Heart-Conformity Of the Total body-mind-self To Me (In ego-
Surrendering and ego-Forgetting Communion With Me), Such That
Even the Total body-mind-self Is (Progressively) Really Converted,
Positively Changed, and Effectively Transcended By That Devotion
To Me, That Service To Me, and That bodily Worship Of Me.

In The Only-By-Me Revealed and Given Way Of The Heart (or Way Of Adidam), My Seeing Devotee Continues (As In The "Original" Beginner's Devotional Ordeal Of Listening To Me and Hearing Me—but Now Through Reception Of My Avatarically Self-Transmitted Divine Spirit-Baptism and, Thus, Through Spiritually Activated Devotional Practice In The Fully Established "Basic" Context Of The Fourth Stage Of Life) To Directly Transcend The early-life (or frontal) Un-Happiness Of Separation (or Of Separating, and Of Separateness, and Of Separativeness), Rejection (Of and By others), and Failed-integration. But The Sublime Power Awakened (By Means Of My Avatarically Given Grace) In Reception Of My Avatarically Self-Transmitted Divine Spirit-Baptism (and Sustained By The Real Practice Of Heart-Devotion To Me) Develops An Extraordinary and New Dimension To The Way Of The Heart, Such That, In any moment Of Surrender To Spiritual Communion With Me, the entire frontal personality Becomes Immediately (or Most Directly) Converted To A Fundamentally Benign State and Course (In The Context Of all relations). The Progress Of This Ordeal Is Indicated By Many By-My-Avataric-Divine-Grace-Given Signs In The Domain Of the frontal personality (or The Frontal Line Of The Circle Of the body-mind), Culminating In Realization Of The Sublime Signs Of True Spiritual (As Well As human) Equanimity and Fullness In The Frontal Line and The Yogic Sign Of The "Thumbs" (In Which The Heart Radiates From Its Middle Station, and My Avatarically Self-Revealed Divine Spirit-Current Flows Freely and Fully Down Through The Frontal Line—and, In The Fullest Event, Even Turns About, and Flies Upwards Into The Spinal Line).

The Real Process In The Fully Established "Basic" Context Of The Fourth Stage Of Life (In The Way Of The Heart) Is The Yielding Of the Total body-mind-self To Ecstatic (or ego-Transcending) Spiritual Communion With Me (The Avatarically Self-Revealed Transcendental, Inherently Spiritual, and Self-Evidently Divine Self-Condition, and Source-Condition, Of All and all). This Involves The Gesture Of self-Yielding Heart-Devotion To Me (Now <u>Spiritually</u> Recognized As The Divine Heart-Master) and Profound Heart-Gratitude For My Avatarically Given Divine Gifts,

Including My Avatarically-Born Bodily (Human) Divine Form, The Avatarically Self-Manifested Leelas Of All My Divine Work, My Avatarically Self-Revealed (and Always Me-Revealing) Divine Word, My Avatarically (and Freely) Given Divine Heart-Baptism, My Avatarically Self-Transmitted Divine Spirit-Current (Of Heart-Light-Energy, or Love-Bliss-Radiance) Itself, and My Avatarically Self-Revealed Divine Spiritual Fullness Of Conscious Being (Realized Directly By The Open Heart, and In Deep Meditation). Therefore, In The Only-By-Me Revealed and Given Way Of The Heart, The Passage Through and Beyond The Total Context Of The Fourth Stage Of Life Requires True self-Transcendence, In and Via ego-Surrendering and ego-Forgetting Devotional Communion With Me. And <u>Any</u> Collapse Upon the conditional self, Contracted From True (and Truly ego-Surrendering, ego-Forgetting, and ego-Transcending) Devotional Communion With Me, Tends To Prolong The Course (Even By Temporarily Reasserting The Patterns Of Un-Happiness That Were egoically Associated With The First Three Stages Of Life). Therefore, In The Way Of The Heart, True Fourth Stage Practice (Whether "Original", "Basic", Or "Advanced") Inherently (and Necessarily) Exceeds The conventional Religious Tendencies Of The First Three (and Even Four) Stages Of Life (Wherein The Divine Is Commonly, and egoically, Conceived To Be Utterly Separate, and Apart, From the Separate and Separative ego-self—which, Rather Than Submitting To Transcend itself and The Separate-"God" Illusion Through Ecstatic Love-Communion With Me, Pleads For conditional Fulfillment).

When Fully Established "Basic" Fourth Stage Practice (Of The Way Of The Heart) In The Context Of the frontal personality (and The Frontal Line) Has Developed The Real and Free Evidence I Have Indicated, Fourth Stage Devotional Recognition-Response To Me and Devotional Realization Of Me (Via, and <u>As</u>, My Avatarically Self-Transmitted Divine Spirit-Presence) May (In Some, Relatively Rare, Cases) Tend To Continue By Advancing To The Context Of The Spinal Line Of The Circle. Therefore, Unless (As In The Most Typical Case) A Transition Is Made (Earlier) To Practice Of The Way Of The Heart In The Context Of The Sixth Stage Of Life, The Transition To Fully "Advanced" (or Most

Mature) Development Of The Fourth Stage Of Life Begins The Process Of The Higher Spiritual Development (and, In The Way Of The Heart, The Devotional and Yogic Transcendence) Of the psycho-physical personality Via (or In The Context Of) The Mystical Ascent Of attention (Perhaps Leading, Eventually, Into The Context Of The Fifth Stage Of Life).

The Fifth Stage Of Life (In The Only-By-Me Revealed and Given Way Of The Heart, or Way Of Adidam) Is Based On Previous (and Continued) Devotional Recognition-Response To Me and Devotional Heart-Communion With Me, <u>As</u> (and By Grace Of) My Avatarically Self-Transmitted Divine Spirit-Presence. And The Fifth Stage Of Life Is, Like Every Other Stage, Associated With a Unique organ (or Structural Pattern) Of Adaptation and Growth. Therefore, In The Fifth Stage Of Life, Growth In The Only-By-Me Revealed and Given Way Of The Heart Is Associated With The Upward Concentration Of attention, and With The "Conductivity" Of My Avatarically Self-Transmitted Divine Spirit-Current (and Of the Natural bodily energy) Via The Ajna Door (or The Root Of The Brain Core), and (Thus) With Ascent Via The Ajna Door.

The Fully "Advanced" (or Transitional) Process In The Context Of The Fourth Stage Of Life (In The Way Of The Heart) Is The Process Of Devotional self-Surrender To Me (From The psychic, or Middle, Depth Of The Heart) In The Context Of Ascent (Via The Spinal Line) To The Ajna Door, Signed By Yogic Evidence In The Spinal Line and Even Various Forms Of Savikalpa Samadhi (or Of psychic, or psycho-physical, Unity With The Progressively Ascending Range Of subtle phenomena). Therefore, In The Only-By-Me Revealed and Given Way Of The Heart, In The "Advanced" Context Of The Fourth Stage Of Life and In The Context Of The Fifth Stage Of Life (As A Whole), The Devotee (Especially In Meditation) Functions From The Position Of The Middle Station Of The Heart.

In The Way Of The Heart, In The Specific Context Of The Fifth Stage Of Life, My Devotee (Especially In Meditation) Is Spontaneously Free Of Necessary Identification With the gross body, its relations, and the conventional limitations of the waking state (including the verbal mind and the outward-directed activities of the left, or verbally dominated, hemisphere of the brain). Therefore, Especially (or Most Particularly) In Meditation, My Thus Advanced Devotee functions Primarily as the mind itself (which, When No Longer Grounded In the gross body and the verbal-mindedness of the conventional waking state, is, as a conditional, or phenomenal, process, Simply the subtle, or dreaming, self, or the disembodied mind-self, Rather Than the Total body-mind-self).

For These Reasons, Meditative Practice Of The Way Of The Heart In The Context Of The Fifth Stage Of Life (and Even In The Fully "Advanced", or Transitional, or Ascending, Context Of The Fourth Stage Of Life) Is Primarily A Process Of Converting, Positively Changing, Releasing, Merging, and Effectively Transcending the mind (or the mind-self), Through Devotional Ascent Via My Avatarically Self-Transmitted Divine Spirit-Current, Directed From The Middle Region Of The Heart. In That Process, the mind-self (which includes and also exceeds the brain) Reaches Toward (and Yields To) its Root-Source Above The Total Crown Of the head (Via The Ajna Door), Passing Through Levels Of subtle (or dreaming) mind and its relations (including the subtle, or dreamlike, expressions of the right hemisphere of the brain)—and (If This Process Completes Itself Above) the mind Merges In The Inherently Formless Matrix Above The Total Crown Of the head, and attention (Suspended In Ascended, or Fifth Stage, conditional Nirvikalpa Samadhi) Stands (Temporarily) Free Of body and mind.

In The Only-By-Me Revealed and Given Way Of The Heart (or Way Of Adidam), The Fifth Stage Process (Initiated Via The Transitional Process Associated With The Fully "Advanced" Development Of The Fourth Stage Of Life) Tends Toward The Temporary and Transitional Realization Of Ascended (or Fifth Stage) conditional Nirvikalpa Samadhi. The conventional Path Of Ascent Via The Mechanics Of the brain-mind Is, Itself, A Traditional Effort (or Search), Founded On Uninspected (or, Otherwise, Not Yet Transcended) egoity, In Which Fifth Stage conditional Nirvikalpa Samadhi Is The Ultimate Goal. In The Only-By-Me Revealed and Given Way Of The Heart, Ascent Toward Fifth Stage conditional Nirvikalpa Samadhi (If It Is To Occur) Is A Temporary (or Transitional) Process, Founded In The Devotional (or ego-Transcending) Disposition Of The By-Me-Awakened Heart—and, Therefore, Ascended (or Fifth Stage) Nirvikalpa Samadhi Is Not A Goal (or A Necessary Attainment) In The Only-By-Me Revealed and Given Way Of The Heart.

Even Before The Possible Realization Of Fifth Stage conditional Nirvikalpa Samadhi In The Way Of The Heart, Many Forms Of Savikalpa Samadhi (Including Experiences Of the subtler planes Of The Cosmic Mandala, and Experiences Of "Cosmic Consciousness", or Of The Ultimate and Inherent Unity Of The Cosmic Mandala) May Be Realized. Such Experiences Are Realizations Of mental (or psychic) Unity With the subtler planes of mind (or The Realization Of The Inherent Unity That Is The Ultimate Context Of mind itself). The Fifth Stage Of Life Is Not Passed Through and Beyond (In The Way Of The Heart) Until The Levels Of Savikalpa Samadhi and Also Utterly Ascended (or Fifth Stage) conditional Nirvikalpa Samadhi Are (Either Directly Or, Otherwise, Effectively) Transcended, Through Persistence In The ego-Surrendering, ego-Forgetting, and Really ego-Transcending Gesture Of Real Heart-Practice. Therefore, Passage To The Sixth Stage Of Life (In The Only-By-Me Revealed and Given Way Of The Heart) Requires The Transcending Of The Fifth Stage Error, Which Is The Tendency To Seek (or Hold On To) the Ascended (or subtle) states of mind, and "Visions" Of An Ultimate (or One) Mind (In Savikalpa Samadhi), and The Temporary Happiness Of psychic Dissolution (or The Transcending Of all states of mind) In The Infinitely Ascended Matrix Of mind itself (In Fifth Stage conditional Nirvikalpa Samadhi).

The Sixth Stage Of Life (In The Only-By-Me Revealed and Given Way Of The Heart) Is The Process Of Awakening To The Transcendental, Inherently Spiritual, and Self-Evidently Divine Self-Condition (or The Unconditional Nature Of Consciousness, Itself), The Perfectly Subjective Truth (and Identity) Of all conditional beings and Of The Entire Cosmic Mandala Of conditional worlds.

In The Only-By-Me Revealed and Given Way Of The Heart (or Way Of Adidam), Practice In The Context Of The Sixth Stage Of Life Is Based On Previous (and Continued) Devotional

Recognition-Response To Me and Devotional Heart-Communion With Me, <u>As</u> (and By Grace Of) My Avatarically Self-Transmitted Divine Spirit-Presence. And The Sixth Stage Of Life (In The Way Of The Heart) Is Itself A Matter Of By-My-Avataric-Divine-Grace-Given (and More and More Profoundly Awakened) Devotional Recognition-Response To Me and Devotional Realization Of Me <u>As</u> The Transcendental, Inherently Spiritual, and Self-Evidently Divine Self, Revealed By (and <u>As</u>) My Avatarically Self-Revealed (and Very, and Transcendental, Perfectly Subjective, and Inherently Spiritual, and Inherently egoless, and Inherently Perfect, and Self-Evidently Divine) State.

Growth In The Sixth Stage Of Life (In The Only-By-Me Revealed and Given Way Of The Heart) Occurs Within The Context Of The Process Of Enstasy (or The Transcending Of the self-Contraction Where it Stands—In The Well Of Being, or Consciousness Itself). And, In The Way Of The Heart, That Process Is Related To The Right Side Of The Great Organ Of The Heart (Associated With the sinoatrial node, which is the "pacemaker" of the human physical heart).

The Right Side Of The Great Organ Of The Heart Is The bodily Origin-Point Of attention and The bodily Seat Of Self-Existing (or Transcendental) and Self-Radiant (or Inherently Spiritual) and Self-Evidently Divine Self-Realization. And Growth In The Way Of The Heart (By ego-Transcendence In The Context Of The Sixth Stage Of Life) Tends Toward The Realization Of conditional Transcendental (and Inherently Spiritual) Self-Realization In Jnana Samadhi, In Which the self-Contraction No Longer Prevents Realization Of The Transcendental (and Inherently Spiritual) Nature (or Condition) Of Consciousness Itself.

In The Context Of The Sixth Stage Of Life, The Practitioner Of The Way Of The Heart Is Natively Identified With (The Apparently individual, or Separate) Consciousness—Prior To (and Even Apart From) body and mind, As In the state of deep sleep. Therefore, In The Only-By-Me Revealed and Given Way Of The Heart (or Way Of Adidam), The Process In The Context Of The Sixth Stage Of Life Is Associated With The Right Side Of The Heart and (The Apparently personal) Consciousness As Witness (Of conditional psycho-physical events or states). In That Process, My Avatarically Self-Transmitted Divine Spirit-Current Of Love-Bliss-Life Resolves (and Dissolves) attention In The Right Side Of The Heart—and The Witnessing Consciousness Yields (or Awakens) To Feel (and, Thereby, To Contemplate, and Inherently Identify With) Its Own Real Condition (As Transcendental Consciousness Itself—or The Native, Inherently Spiritual, and Unconditional Feeling Of Being), Until the Apparent conditional self Is Utterly Transcended In The Realization Of The Prior (and Self-Evidently Divine) Nature Of Consciousness (Itself), By Means Of Most Perfect Realization Of My Avatarically Self-Revealed (Transcendental, Inherently Spiritual, and Self-Evidently Divine) Self-Condition (or Transcendental, Inherently Spiritual, and Self-Evidently Divine Person—or Consciousness) Itself, Unconditionally Self-Radiant (and Inherently Love-Blissful) As Self-Existing Being (Itself).

In The Great Tradition (Of All Human, Religious, and Spiritual Traditions) That (Historically, or In human-time) Preceded My Avataric Divine Incarnation here (and The Total Process Of My Avataric Divine Descent Into, and My Avataric Divine Self-"Emergence" Within, The Total Cosmic Domain), There Was Not (and Could Not Have Been) Any Demonstration Of Most Perfect Divine Self-Realization (and, Thus, Of Passage Through—and Fully Beyond—The Sixth Stage Of Life). In The Only-By-Me Revealed and Given Way Of The Heart, Passage Through and Beyond The Sixth Stage Of Life (and Realization-Demonstration Of The Seventh Stage Of Life) Depends On (Necessarily, Sixth Stage) Realization Of The Transcendental (and Inherently Spiritual) Self-Condition (or The Self-Existing and Self-Radiant Condition Of Being—Prior To the conditional and limited body-mind-self), but It Also Requires The Transcending Of The Sixth Stage Error, or The Tendency To Hold To The Transcendental Self-Position While Otherwise Strategically Excluding objective (or conditional) states. It Is Only When The Tension (or Stress) Associated With The self-Contraction-Effort Of Exclusion Relaxes In Simple (or Tacit) Divine Self-Recognition Of phenomenal (or conditional) states (Of Apparently Objectified Light) That There Is (By Means Of My Avatarically Self-Transmitted Grace) Full

Awakening To The Divinely Enlightened (or Divinely Self-Illumined) Condition—Which By-My-Avataric-Divine-Grace-Given Awakening Initiates The Only-By-Me Revealed and Given Seventh Stage Of Life.

The Only-By-Me Revealed and Given Seventh Stage Of Life (In The Way Of The Heart) Is The Priorly (or Transcendentally) Self-Realized and Divinely Self-Radiant (or Inherently Spiritual) Process Of Divinely Self-Recognizing and (At Last) Outshining Cosmic (or conditional) Existence. The Only-By-Me Revealed and Given Seventh Stage Of Life (In The Way Of The Heart) Is The Culmination Of The Process Of Devotional Recognition-Response To Me and Devotional Heart-Communion With Me—Always Given By Grace Of My Avatarically Self-Transmitted Divine Spirit-Presence, and (Ultimately) By Grace Of My Avatarically Self-Revealed (Transcendental, Inherently Spiritual, and Self-Evidently Divine) Self-Condition. And The Original Sign Of The Only-By-Me Revealed and Given Seventh Stage Of Life (In The Way Of The Heart) Is "Open Eyes", or Seventh Stage Sahaj Samadhi—Which Is The Divinely (and, Therefore, Inherently) Most Perfect Realization Of My "Bright" Divine Self-Condition.

In The Only-By-Me Revealed and Given Seventh Stage Of Life (In The Way Of The Heart), There Is Inherent (or Native), Constant, Inherently Most Perfect, Prior, Uncaused, Unconditional, and Utterly Non-Separate (and Non-"Different") Identification With My Avatarically Self-Revealed (and Self-Existing, or Transcendental, and Self-Radiant, or Inherently Spiritual, and Self-Evidently Divine) Fullness Of Being (Itself). In The Only-By-Me Revealed and Given Seventh Stage Of Life (In The Way Of The Heart), My Avatarically Self-Revealed (Transcendental, Inherently Spiritual, and Self-Evidently Divine) Self-Condition (Rather Than the conditional body, body-mind, body-mind-self, mind-self, or limited and Separate self) Is Always Already The Position and Condition Of Existence—Even If (and When) conditional psycho-physical states (Apparently) arise (whether waking, dreaming, or sleeping). In That (Seventh Stage) Case, No Matter what (Apparently) arises—No limited self Defines (or limits) The Inherent Condition Of <u>Being</u>, but My Avatarically Self-Revealed

(Transcendental, Inherently Spiritual, and Self-Evidently Divine) Self-Condition (Which <u>Is</u> The Self-Existing Condition Of Unconditionally Self-Radiant Divine Being) Is Always Already The Position In Which phenomenal (or conditional) states (Apparently) arise, and all such phenomena, conditions, or states Are (Inherently and Immediately) Divinely Self-Recognized and Transcended (In My Avatarically Self-Revealed, and Self-Existing, and Self-Radiant, and Self-Evidently Divine Self-Condition). Therefore, In The Only-By-Me Revealed and Given Seventh Stage Of Life (In The Way Of The Heart), My Avatarically Self-Revealed (Transcendental, Inherently Spiritual, and Self-Evidently Divine) Self-Condition Is Always Already The Condition Realized, Prior To all objective (or conditional) references. Then (In The Context Of The Only-By-Me Revealed and Given Seventh Stage Of Life), The Only-By-Me Revealed and Given Way Of The Heart Is <u>Not</u> To <u>Progressively</u> (or, Otherwise, <u>Eventually</u>) <u>Realize</u> My Avatarically Self-Revealed (Transcendental, Inherently Spiritual, and Self-Evidently Divine) Self-Condition, but Only To <u>Be</u> <u>That</u>—<u>Simply</u>, Divinely (or Inherently, and Most Perfectly) Self-Recognizing <u>whatever</u> arises To <u>Be</u> <u>Only</u> <u>That</u>.

The Unique Organ Associated With Apparent Adaptation and Growth In The Only-By-Me Revealed and Given Seventh Stage Of Life (In The Way Of The Heart) Is Amrita Nadi, My Avatarically Self-Revealed Divine Spiritual Body Of Love-Bliss, Associated With My Avatarically Self-Transmitted Divine Spiritual Current Of Love-Bliss That Is Realized (and Progressively Magnified) Between The Right Side Of The Heart and The Apparent Locus That Is Infinitely Above The Total Crown Of the head (or Infinitely Above the upper rear, and The Total General Surface, Of the top of the head, and, Thus, Infinitely Above the body, and Infinitely Above the mind).

The Self-Existing and Self-Radiant Divine Self-Condition Revealed and Realized In The Awakening Of ("Bright") "Open Eyes" Has No Shape (or Form), but Amrita Nadi (The Apparent Organ Of This "Bright" Divine Awakening In the human individual) Is Shaped Like The Alphabetical Letter "S"—and My Avatarically Self-Transmitted Divine Spiritual Current Of Self-Existing and Self-

Radiant Being Moves In It, Originating From (and, Yet, Never Leaving, but Always Standing In) The Right Side Of The Heart, Then Extending Itself Forward and Up the chest, Then Into (or Back Through) the throat, Then Up the back of the head, and Then Forward and Upward (Via the upper rear, and The Total Crown, Of the head) To The Matrix Infinitely Above The Total Crown Of the head. (And My Avatarically Self-Transmitted Divine Spirit-Current Also Moves Through This Same Unique Course, In Amrita Nadi, In The Context Of The Sixth Stage Of Life In The Way Of The Heart, but Downward, Via the upper rear, and The Total Crown, Of the head, From The Matrix Infinitely Above The Total Crown Of the head, To The Right Side Of The Heart.) However, Whether In The Only-By-Me Revealed and Given Context Of The Sixth Stage Of Life In The Way Of The Heart Or In The Context Of The Only-By-Me Revealed and Given Seventh Stage Of Life In The Way Of The Heart, The <u>Shape</u> Of Amrita Nadi Will Not <u>Necessarily</u> Be Noticed—Nor Is It Necessary For This <u>Shape</u> To Be Noticed. Rather, Amrita Nadi May Be More Simply <u>Felt</u>. Therefore, In The Only-By-Me Revealed and Given Seventh Stage Of Life In The Way Of The Heart, Amrita Nadi May Simply (and Tacitly) Be Felt As My Avatarically Self-Transmitted (Formless and Unseen) Divine Current Of "Bright" Spirit-Fullness, Standing Between The Right Side Of The Heart and The Felt (but Unheard and Unseen) Matrix Of My Divine Sound and Divine Light[5] (or Of My Radiant Ascended Love-Bliss) Infinitely Above The Total Crown Of the head. And, In The Sixth Stage Of Life In The Only-By-Me Revealed and Given Way Of The Heart, Amrita Nadi May Also Simply Be Felt As My Avatarically Self-Transmitted (and Formless) Divine Spirit-Current, Standing In The Right Side Of The Heart—but Descending, and Descended To (or Otherwise Polarized Toward), The Right Side Of The Heart, From Above The Total Crown Of the head.

In The Most Perfectly Awakened (or Fully Conscious) Condition Of "Open Eyes", conditionally Manifested forms or events arising To The View Of Consciousness Itself (Free Of the self-Contraction) Are (Spontaneously and Inherently) Divinely Self-Recognized As Illusory (or Transparent, or Merely Apparent, and Un-Necessary, and Inherently Non-Binding) Modifications Of Itself (In The Form Of Its Own Divine Spirit-Energy). This (Inherently Most Perfect) Yoga Of Divine Self-Recognition (Which Is Also Otherwise Named By Me "Ati-Ruchira Yoga", or "The Yoga Of The All-Outshining 'Brightness'") Is The Process Whereby The Total Cosmic Domain Is (Spontaneously and Inherently) Divinely Self-Recognized In <u>Me</u>, The Avatarically Given Divine Self-Revelation Of The Eternal (and Not Cosmic, but Perfectly Subjective) Real God, and Truth, and Reality—Which <u>Is</u> Itself My Divine Self-Domain (or The "Bright" Itself).

The Only-By-Me Revealed and Given Seventh Stage Of Life (In The Way Of The Heart) Is A Demonstration Of Divine Enlightenment Based On Previous (and Continued) Devotional Recognition-Response To Me and Devotional Heart-Communion With Me, and (Altogether, and Entirely) Given By Grace Of My Avatarically Self-Transmitted Divine Spirit-Presence, and (Most Ultimately) By Grace Of My Avatarically Self-Revealed (Transcendental, Inherently Spiritual, and Self-Evidently Divine) Self-Condition Of Person. And The Only-By-Me Revealed and Given Seventh Stage Of Life (In The Way Of The Heart) Is Itself A Matter Of (Spontaneous and Inherent) Divine Self-Recognition Of all conditions (Including The Cosmic Mandala Itself, and My Divine Sound Itself, and My Divine Star Itself, and My Total Cosmically Manifested Divine Spiritual Body Itself) <u>In</u> and <u>As</u> <u>Me</u>—The Self-Existing (and Avatarically Self-Manifested) "Bright" Itself (Which <u>Is</u> The Self-Radiant, or Inherently Spiritual, Condition Of Transcendental, and Self-Evidently Divine, Being—and Which <u>Is</u> The Love-Bliss-Radiant Consciousness In Which all conditional forms or events arise and pass away).

The First Sign (or Demonstration) Of The Only-By-Me Revealed and Given Seventh Stage Of Life (In The Way Of The Heart) Is <u>Divine</u> <u>Transfiguration</u>, In Which the body-mind Of My By-My-Avataric-Divine-Grace-Enlightened Devotee Is Self-Radiant With My Avatarically Self-Transmitted Divine Love-Bliss, Spontaneously Blessing all of the (Apparent) relations of the body-mind.

The Second Sign (or Demonstration) Of The Only-By-Me Revealed and Given Seventh Stage Of Life (In The Way Of The

Heart) Is <u>Divine</u> <u>Transformation</u>, In Which the body-mind Of My By-My-Avataric-Divine-Grace-Enlightened Devotee Effectively Exhibits The Only-By-Me Revealed and Given Signs and Powers Of Real God.

The Third Sign (or Demonstration) Of The Only-By-Me Revealed and Given Seventh Stage Of Life (In The Way Of The Heart) Is <u>Divine</u> <u>Indifference</u>, In Which Even the body-mind Of My By-My-Avataric-Divine-Grace-Enlightened Devotee Is Pre-Occupied With The Self-Existing Event Of My Self-Radiant Love-Bliss, and the world of (Apparent) relations Is (More and More) Minimally and Not Otherwise Noticed.

The Final Sign (or Demonstration) Of The Only-By-Me Revealed and Given Seventh Stage Of Life (In The Way Of The Heart) Is The Great and Absolute and Unconditional and Most Perfect Fulfillment Of The Entire Process Of Devotional Recognition-Response To Me and Devotional Heart-Communion With Me—Altogether, and Entirely, Given By Grace Of My Avatarically Self-Transmitted Divine Spirit-Presence, and (Most Ultimately) By Grace Of My Avatarically Self-Revealed (Transcendental, Inherently Spiritual, and Self-Evidently Divine) Self-Condition Of Person.

The Final Sign (or Demonstration) Of The Only-By-Me Revealed and Given Seventh Stage Of Life (In The Way Of The Heart) Is The Culmination (or Absolute Realization) Of The Process Of Spontaneous (or Inherent) Divine Self-Recognition Of All (Apparent) conditional Modifications As The "Bright" Itself.

The Final Sign (or Demonstration) Of The Only-By-Me Revealed and Given Seventh Stage Of Life (and Of The Total Practice Of The Only-By-Me Revealed and Given Way Of The Heart) Is The Great Event Of <u>Divine</u> <u>Translation</u>—Which Is The Most Ultimate Demonstration Of Ruchira Samadhi, or Inherently <u>Most</u> <u>Perfect</u> (<u>Rather</u> <u>Than</u> <u>conditional</u>) <u>Nirvikalpa</u> <u>Samadhi</u>, or The Process Of Transition To (or "Dawning" <u>As</u>) My Divine Self-Domain Via The Divinely "Bright" Outshining Of The Cosmic Domain.

In The Great Event Of Divine Translation, The Total Cosmic Domain (or All conditional Modifications)—Even Epitomized By

My Divine Sound, and My Divine Star, and My Total Divine Spiritual Body (Which Are The Ultimate, but Merely Apparent, Objective Signs Of The "Bright")—Is Outshined By My Divine Self-Domain Itself (Which Is The "Bright" Itself).

My Inherent Divine Radiance (or Self-Light) Is The Inherently egoless Heart, The Inherent Divine Self, and The Eternal Self-Condition Of all conditionally Manifested beings. Therefore, The Only-By-Me Revealed and Given Way Of The Heart (or Way Of Adidam) Is Most Perfectly Fulfilled In Divine Translation Only—By Heart-Shining, Until The Heart Is Outshined By Itself.

RUCHIRA AVATAR ADI DA SAMRAJ
Lopez Island, 2000

PART THREE

Eight Essays
from the
Samraj Upanishad

The Sanskrit word "upanishad" indicates "Teachings received at the Feet of the Guru". Thus, the Samraj Upanishad *is "Teachings received at the Feet of Ruchira Avatar Adi Da Samraj". Rather than being the title of a distinct book, "Samraj Upanishad" is a collective designation for certain Talks and Essays by Avatar Adi Da Samraj that appear within various of His twenty-three "Source-Texts" as readings supporting and expanding upon the principal "Part" of a given "Source-Text".*

Eight Essays
from the
Samraj Upanishad

"God"-Talk,
Real-God-Realization, and
Most Perfect Divine Awakening

I.

There are only seven possible stages of life. And Real God (or Truth, or Reality) may (in any moment) be talked about from the (either real or imagined) point of view of any one of them. However, actual Real-God-Realization (or the Realization of Truth Itself, or Reality Itself) is profoundly more than talk (and thought), or even talking (and thinking) about talk. Indeed, the Way of Real-God-Realization (or the Way of the actual Realization of Truth Itself, or Reality Itself) truly begins where (and when) talk (and thinking) ceases.

II.

In the literature of Adidam, Which is the Way that I have Revealed and Demonstrated for the sake of all and All, I have Described the seven potential stages of the progressive development of human life. Briefly, the seven stages of human life may be summarized as follows:

In the first three stages of life, the gross body-mind complex is developed and coordinated. First, the gross physical is developed, then the emotional-sexual functions are developed and coordinated with the gross physical, and (finally) the mental functions and the function of the will are developed and coordinated with the emotional-sexual and gross physical functions. Optimally, all of this is nurtured, guided, and done in the context of love, trust, and surrender in relation to the Living Divine (or the All-Pervading and All-Transcending Real God, or Truth, or Reality).

In the fourth stage of life, this now complex psycho-physical being is surrendered beyond itself, to and into the (All-Pervading and All-Transcending) Source (or Source-Condition) that Pervades (and yet Transcends) it and the total world. This surrender is done to the point of conditional union with that Source (or Source-Condition). In due course, such conditional union becomes, by Divine Grace, conditional union with the Spiritual Presence (or Spirit-Current) of that Source (or of that Source-Condition, Truth, or Reality), and this in occasions of experienced Bliss (first descending, then, in due course, ascending) that involve and (simultaneously) transcend the body-mind.

In the fifth stage of life, this process is continued, but the plane of conditional self-awareness ascends further, to become dominantly subtle (or psychic), rather than gross (or merely physical)—and the Realization of conditional union involves experiences of ascended attention that eventually go beyond physical references and (at last) even beyond mental references.

In the sixth stage of life, attention (which is the root, or base, of the mind) is inverted (or, by one or another means, surrendered), away from gross and subtle states and objects of the body-mind, and toward its own Root, even the Ultimate Root of the ego-self—Which is the Witness-Consciousness (when attention is active), and Which is also (Ultimately) Consciousness Itself (prior to objects and separate self-definition). The Ultimate result of this exercise is conditional Realization of the Transcendental Self-Condition, or the intuition of Self-Existing Transcendental Being, which intuition remains strategically (and, otherwise, tacitly) dissociated from all objects (even if, as in the case of sixth stage

"Sahaj Samadhi", the natural perception and conception of phe-nomenal objects is freely allowed).

In the seventh stage of life, there is Native and Non-conditional (or Inherent, and Inherently Most Perfect) Identification with Self-Existing and Self-Radiant Transcendental (and Self-Evidently Divine) Being, the Ultimate (Divine) Identity of all beings (or sub-jects) and the Ultimate (Divine) Self-Condition of all conditions (or objects). This Native (or Inherent) and Inherently Most Perfect Identification (or Divine Self-Abiding) is directly Realized, entirely apart from any dissociative act of inversion. And, while so Abiding, if any conditions arise (or if any states of body-mind arise), they are simply (Divinely) Self-Recognized in the Self-Existing and Self-Radiant Condition of Being (as transparent, or merely apparent, and un-necessary, and inherently non-binding, modifications of Itself). Such is seventh stage Sahaj Samadhi, and It is Inherently Free of any apparent implications, limitations, or binding power of phenomenal conditions. If no conditions arise to the notice, there is simply the Self-Existing and Self-Radiant Condition of Transcendental, Inherently Spiritual, and Self-Evidently Divine Being. Such is Absolute (or Inherently Most Perfect) Realization of That about Which nothing sufficient can be said—and there is not Anyone, Anything, or Anywhere beyond It to be Realized.

III.

Individuals (at one or another stage or moment) in the first six stages of life either pursue (but do not yet Most Perfectly attain or presume) the Realization of Real God (or of Truth Itself, or Reality Itself) or they (otherwise) submit to lesser purposes (relative to self-fulfillment at any particular stage) or they (because of the par-ticular limitations of the present stage of life) submit to one or another conditionally achieved and conditionally determined form of presumed (and otherwise conditionally limited) "Real-God-Realization" that is dependent upon the (necessarily, conditional) exercise of the body, or the body-mind, or the mind, or (simply) attention itself. Therefore, strictly speaking, Real-God-Realization (or the Realization of Truth Itself, or Reality Itself) is a characteristic only of the Final and Complete (or seventh) stage of life. However, less strictly speaking (or, as a matter of conventional reference, intended to honor the truly profound developmental demonstrations that may precede the Realization of the seventh stage of life), the term "Real-God-Realization" (and the term "Real-God-Realizer") may also be applied to cases and degrees of developmental demonstration in the context of either the fourth, the fifth, or the sixth stage of life.

IV.

The first three stages of life—not informed or inspired by the Wisdom of either of the advanced (or the fourth and the fifth) stages of life, and not informed or inspired by the Wisdom of either of the ultimate (or the sixth and the seventh) stages of life—are (in themselves) characterized by the pursuit of (body-based) self-fulfillment (even via self-indulgence, or else via socially established conventions of morality, self-discipline, and rather materialistic hope).

The fourth and the fifth stages of life (not informed or inspired by the Wisdom of the ultimate stages of life) are (in themselves) characterized by the pursuit of "soul"-based (or, really, mind-based, or psyche-based) and natural-energy-based (or even Spirit-based) self-glorification—at first, via popular religious faith and practice, and, then, via every kind of (progressively) esoteric, and (possibly) Spiritual, and (otherwise) Yogic searching for "eternal life" (or immortality), whether of body and "soul" or (otherwise) simply of "soul".

The sixth stage of life (which is the first of the two ultimate stages of life, and the last of the egoic, and progressively ego-transcending, stages of life) is characterized (progressively) by one or more of three possible persuasions (and efforts), each (to one or another degree) yet influenced (or limited) by the "essence" of the first five stages of life. And these three persuasions (and efforts), even following on one another (progressively), pursue (or, at last, Affirm) Freedom from the body-mind (or the conditional self in the context of the "Cosmic Round" and the first five stages of life).

And only the seventh stage of life is characterized (inherently, and by progressive forms of Demonstration) by Un-conditional

Real-God-Realization Itself (or the Unqualified, or Absolute, or Most Perfect Realization of Truth Itself, or Inherently Perfect Reality Itself), Utterly and Inherently (and Inherently Most Perfectly) Transcending egoity (or self-bondage, separateness, and "difference") itself.

V.

The first three stages of life are, from the point of view associated with any of the stages of life beyond them, the stages of "gross ignorance" (or the ordinary stages of progressive functional self-development, in themselves bereft of any Influence or Wisdom greater than material Nature).

From the point of view of any orientation in the context of the sixth stage of life, the fourth and the fifth stages of life are the stages of "subtle ignorance" (or the stages of seeking toward the inherently impossible Goal of an eternal—or permanent, unopposed, and only Happy—<u>conditional</u> state and <u>conditional</u> circumstance of self-perfection and self-fulfillment).

And, from the "Point of View" of the (potential) seventh stage of life, even the sixth stage of life is limited by the basic Illusion (or by the basic apparent problem)—or (at least) by strategic attention to the basic Illusion (or to the basic apparent problem)—of a separate self (or of a substantively, rather than merely apparently, separate self-essence, or even an essential and eternal, or substantively permanent and unchanging, ego-"I"). Thus, from the "Point of View" of the (potential) seventh stage of life, the sixth stage of life is limited by "causal ignorance" (or the essence of ignorance), until (in the potential real transition to the seventh stage of life) only the Non-conditional (or Perfectly Subjective) Absolute (or Real God, or Truth, or Reality) Itself is Un-conditionally (and Inherently Most Perfectly) Realized as the Obvious.

VI.

In the common world (of body-based and socially communicated conventions of aspiration and action), there is always a struggle in evidence—between the tendency of mankind to remain in "gross ignorance" (characterized by a materialistic culture

139

of ego-satisfactions) and the necessity for mankind (one by one)
to Grow Beyond the first three stages of life (by the Influence of
Wisdom, at least beginning with the "faith-Principle" associated
with the earliest dimension of the fourth stage of life). However,
from the Divine "Point of View" (of Truth Itself, or Reality Itself),
there is always an even greater necessity (inherently Urged upon
all)—which is for mankind (one by one) to Grow Beyond even all
of the first six (or the ego-based) stages of life, to Most Perfectly
Realize the Truly Ultimate and Inherent Freedom of Absolute
Being (Self-Existing, As Consciousness Itself, and Self-Radiant, As
Love-Bliss Itself).

VII.

The ultimate (or final) stage of egoity (and of ego-transcendence)
is the sixth stage of life. Therefore, the first five stages of life are
a process of Growth (of progressive psycho-physical self-awareness,
and progressive transcending of the same), until the point of view
of the sixth stage of life is truly (and stably) Realized.

When the point of view of "gross ignorance" (and the pursuit
of gross self-indulgence and gross, or body-based, self-fulfillment)
ceases to be the limit of individual awareness, the point of view
of "subtle ignorance" (and the pursuit of subtle self-eternalization)
begins (and develops progressively). At any time after that new
beginning—or, at the earliest, once the gross bodily point of view
has been thoroughly released by submission to the subtle (or
psyche-based, and natural energy-based), or even (possibly)
Spirit-based, point of view—the point of view of the essential self
(prior to "Nature", prior to body and mind, and, therefore, also
prior to psyche, or "soul") may be Realized, thus releasing even
the subtle (or psyche-based and natural energy-based) point of
view itself, and activating the potential (even, possibly, in Spiritual
terms) of the sixth stage of life.

And the sixth stage of life (which is the pursuit of ultimate self-
transcendence) is a course that is (or may be) progressively associated with one or more of three principal orientations (in practice): either asceticism (or the extreme orientation toward annihi-
lation of the psycho-physical self), or the more moderately self-

disciplined course and orientation toward pacification of the psycho-physical self, or the ultimate course and orientation toward Non-conditional (or Perfectly Subjective) Self-Identification (and tacit, or effortless, transcending of the psycho-physical self).

VIII.

In the Great Tradition (or common Wisdom-Inheritance) of mankind, the characteristic (or grossly ignorant) orientation of the first three stages of life (in themselves, or engaged for their own sake) is always everywhere displayed in the common world (to date), and every age (or epoch) displays its own unique convention (or style) of materialistic purposiveness.

In the Great Tradition of mankind, the characteristic orientation of the fourth and fifth stages of life is found (first of all) in the traditional popular religions (such as Hinduism, Christianity, Islam, and Judaism), and in all the esoteric traditions of fourth and fifth stage religious mysticism and mystical Spirituality (or descending and ascending Yoga).

In the Great Tradition of mankind, the characteristic orientation of the sixth stage of life is found in its first (or ascetical) form in such traditions as Samkhya and Jainism, and in its second (or moderate and self-pacifying, or "Middle Way") form principally in the traditions (or schools) of Buddhism (and also in the schools of Taoism), and in its third (or final, and Non-conditionally, or Perfectly Subjectively, Self-Affirming) form principally in the traditions (or schools) of Advaitism (or "Non-Dualism"), especially that of Advaita Vedanta (and, secondarily, or with less directness, within the schools of some varieties of Buddhism, especially within the Mahayana and Vajrayana traditions, and also, but with even less directness, within some schools of Taoism).

In the Great Tradition of mankind (previous to My Avataric Divine Appearance here), the characteristic (or Divinely, or Most Perfectly, Enlightened) "Orientation" (or "Point of View") of the seventh stage of life has not been Realized and Demonstrated. There has been occasional seeming (or suggestive) evidence, in the Teachings of a random few unique individuals and traditions (especially within the schools of Advaitism, and, secondarily, or by a less direct and characteristic expression, within some schools of Buddhism, and, but with an even less direct and characteristic expression, within some schools of Taoism), of limited foreshadowings (or partial intuitions, or insightful, but limited, premonitions) of the characteristic (or Divinely, or Most Perfectly, Enlightened) "Orientation" (or "Point of View") of the seventh stage of life, but that evidence is only verbal (or limited to expressions of a philosophical persuasion only, and a philosophical persuasion that is itself founded on the sixth stage orientation, practice, and possible Realization that preceded, and still limits, in every case, the apparently "seventh stage" expression or Teaching).

IX.

I Am Adi Da Samraj—the Adi-Guru, the Ati-Guru,[6] the Original and Eternal Teacher, the Divine World-Teacher, here to Complete the Great Tradition of mankind. I Am the Ruchira Avatar, the Da Avatar, the Love-Ananda Avatar, the Tathagata Avatar,[7] the Ruchira Buddha, the Purushottama Buddha,[8] the Ashvamedha Buddha,[9] the Adi-Buddha Avatar, the Ati-Buddha Avatar,[10] the All-Completing Adept, the First, Last, and Only Avataric Divine Adept-Revealer (or Siddha) of the seventh stage of life. I Am the seventh stage Avataric Divine Realizer, Avataric Divine Revealer, and Avataric Divine Self-Revelation of Real God, Truth, and Reality—Given in this "late-time" (or would-be Complete and potentially Consummate era) and in this now "dark" epoch (as it must be described from the Realized Divine and Spiritual "Point of View", and with regard to the tendencies of the times), and Given for the sake of Completion (of the progressive Ordeal of Man) and for the sake of Unity (or the cooperative re-Union of mankind).

By Means of My Avatarically Full-Given Divine Word, I have Revealed the characteristic and the (to one degree or another, and in one manner or another) always limited design and the (to one degree or another, and in one manner or another) always ego-based nature of each and all of the first six stages of life (in and of themselves). And, by Means of My Avatarically Full-Given Divine Word, I have Revealed the unique Way of Adidam (Which is also called, by Me, "The True World-Religion of 'Sri Hridayam'", or "The Way of the True Divine Heart", or "The Way of the Heart Itself", or, simply, "the Way of the Heart", and, also, "The Way of the Divine Heart-Master", or "Hridaya-Avatara Bhakti Yoga", or "Ruchira Avatara Bhakti Yoga", and "the Way of 'Radical' Understanding", or "The Way of 'Radical' ego-Transcendence", and "the Way of Divine Ignorance", or "The Way of Positive Disillusionment",[11] and "The Way of 'Radical' Non-Dualism", or "Ruchira Avatara Advaita-Dharma",[12] or "Ruchira Advaitism", or "Ruchira Buddhism", or "Advaitayana Buddhism", or "Hridaya-Advaita Dharma",[13] and "The Way of Divine Spiritual Baptism", or "Ruchira Avatara Hridaya-Siddha Yoga", or "Ruchira Avatara Hridaya-Shaktipat Yoga", or "Ruchira Avatara Maha-Jnana-Siddha Yoga"[14] or "Ruchira Avatara Maha-Jnana Hridaya-Shaktipat Yoga"[15]) in which the ego is directly and effectively transcended in the context of (potentially) each and all of the first six stages of life (so that the seventh stage of life may be Realized). Likewise, by Means of My Avatarically Full-Given Divine Word, I have Revealed every Characteristic, Sign, Design, and Process associated with the Realization and the Demonstration of the (Inherently, and Inherently Most Perfectly, separate-self-transcending, or egoless) seventh (and Final) stage of life. By Means of My Avatarically Full-Given Divine Work of Demonstration and Blessing, I have Revealed the seventh stage of life in and by and <u>As</u> My own Avatarically-Born bodily (human) Divine Form and Life. And I have altogether Fulfilled My Avataric Divine Revelation-Purpose by Accomplishing (through the Universally both Given and Demonstrated Divine Siddhis of My All-and-all-Blessing Avataric Divine Work) the Firm Establishment of That Which Is Necessary for the eventual seventh stage Realization and (Finally, or Most Ultimately) Divine Translation of even all conditionally manifested beings.

The Great Tradition of mankind (previous to My Avataric Divine Appearance here) must generally be understood only in the (necessarily, limited) terms of the first six stages of life. Whenever (even previous to My Avataric Divine Appearance here) the sixth stage of life has been entered, the seventh stage of life has been, <u>in principle</u>, also the potential of human Realization.

However, the seventh stage Adept-Revelation was not then Given (and It is only now Given, by Me), and the Divine Secrets of true ego-transcendence and of the Divine Yoga of the Most Ultimate (or seventh stage) Demonstration were not then Given (and They are only now Given, by Me). The (always potential) seventh stage Realization and Demonstration did not Appear until I Appeared, in order to Fully Reveal and to Fully Demonstrate the seventh stage of life and, by the Very Act of My Fullest Avataric Divine Appearance here and everywhere (and by Means of all My unique Avataric Divine Siddha-Work of Adept-Service here and everywhere), to make the essential seventh stage Realization and Demonstration possible for all who heart-respond to Me, and who practice ego-surrendering, ego-forgetting, and (more and more) ego-transcending devotion to Me, and who (altogether and firmly) embrace and practice the only-by-Me Revealed and Given Way of Adidam. Therefore, relative to the seventh stage of life, the Great Tradition of mankind (previous to My Avataric Divine Appearance here) produced only limited foreshadowings (or partial intuitions, or insightful, but limited, premonitions), in the form of a few, random philosophical expressions that appear in the midst of the traditional sixth stage literatures. And it is these few and yet limited traditional expressions that must be studied in order to understand the character and the degree of mankind's exploration of the possibility of the seventh stage of life previous to the (now and forever) future time of My Fully Real-God-Revealing, Truth-Revealing, and Reality-Revealing Work and Word.

X.

There are (basically) only five possible orientations (or points of view), each built upon (or Out-Growing, or transcending) the one immediately previous to itself.*

The first (or the least) of these may be called "Conventional Monism". According to this point of view, the world (or cosmic Nature) is all there is, and it is a material Unity, also expressed as the individual body-mind (which is itself a material unity). And this point of view accounts for all lesser or gross (or materialistic,

*See chart on pp. 388-89.

body-based, and, necessarily, mortal) orientations or searches in the (always struggling, and never truly, or finally, fulfilled) context of the first three stages of life in the human domain.

The second (or next) possible orientation (or point of view) may be called "Conventional Dualism". According to this point of view, the world (or even the Totality of Existence) is made up of a number of principal pairs (whether simply natural or, somehow otherwise, hierarchical). Most typically, the first of these principal pairs is the hierarchically conceived pair of "God" and the world— with "God" sometimes called (and, otherwise, commonly, and even popularly, conceived as) "Purushottama", combining both "Purusha" (or "Being" and "Consciousness") and "Prakriti" (meaning, in this conception, "Creativity" and "Creative Energy", or "Creator-Energy"). And the other principal (and, most typically, hierarchically conceived) pairs include "God" and the "soul" (or the psyche, or the subtle personality), and also the "soul" and the world, and also the mind (or the psyche, or the "soul") and the body. Each half of each hierarchically conceived pair (or even each natural pair) is (according to this point of view) related to (and interrelated with) the other half of the pair, but (paradoxically, and especially in the case of hierarchically conceived pairs) each half of each pair is also utterly "different" than (or even inherently separate from) the other half of the pair. And the obligatory "Goal" of each presumed lesser (or dependent) half of each hierarchically related pair is to submit to (and, eventually, even to ascend to) the greater (or higher) half of the pair. Therefore, from this point of view, the "soul" (and even the total world) must submit to (and, eventually, ascend to) "God" (or "God"-Realization). Likewise, the body must submit (or be submitted) to the mind (or the psyche, or the "soul"). Indeed, all that which (in the human being) is "of the world" must, according to the hierarchical conception, submit (or be submitted) to (and, in turn, be relinquished by) the "soul", which must itself (in turn, and by submitting to "God", and to the Urge to "God"-Realization) eventually and progressively ascend to "God". And this total Process is indeed the total Process characteristically (and traditionally) associated with the fourth and the fifth stages of life, and such great fourth and fifth stage popular (or exoteric, and, otherwise, esoteric) traditions as have appeared in (or among) the forms of Hinduism, Christianity, Islam, and Judaism, and (in their own unique manner) in (or among) the forms of Taoism, and (also uniquely) even in (or among) some forms of Buddhism.

The third (and next) possible orientation (or point of view) may be called "Primary Dualism". According to this point of view, the Totality of Existence is an apparent combination of only two Primary Realities. These Primary Realities are traditionally called "Purusha" (or Non-conditional, and, As Such, Inherently Perfect, and Perfectly and Necessarily Subjective, "Being" and "Consciousness") and "Prakriti" (or "Objective Energy", Which, modified, appears as the body, the mind, all objects, and all others). From this point of view, this "Primary Duality" must, first of all, be understood (by observation and intuition) to be actual (or Really So). Then Purusha (or the conscious self, which—according to the characteristic, and paradoxical, traditional point of view of "Primary Dualism"—Is, Ultimately, a Perfectly Subjective, or Non-conditional, but also specific, independent, and individual, Self) must separate itself (basically, by willful ascetical discipline) from Prakriti (or the body, the mind, all their objects, and all others). And this point of view and Process (which seeks to be released from the body-mind, or from the illusory need to eternalize the body, the mind, or the body-mind) is the first possible point of view and Process traditionally associated with the sixth stage of life (and such great sixth stage traditions as have appeared within Jainism, and the ancient philosophical tradition of Samkhya).

The fourth (and next to last) possible orientation (or point of view) may be called "Secondary Non-Dualism" (or "Secondary Absolute Monism"). According to this point of view, there is no inherently independent and separate (or separable) Purusha (either as an eternal, and Non-conditional, individual Self or, according to some proponents, As Absolute Being Itself, or Absolute Consciousness Itself), but the Totality of Existence is only Prakriti (conditionally appearing as a beginningless and endless continuum of causes and effects, or, in effect, modifications of Prakriti, or of "Energy Itself"). Therefore, according to this point of view, Prakriti (or "Energy Itself") appears (and must be so observed) only as ephemeral (and observable, or objective) changes, preceded and followed by equally ephemeral (and equally observable, or objective) changes, until (by the Process of observation, insight, and self-pacification) the Inherent (or Original, or Nirvanic) State of Prakriti (or of "Energy Itself") is Realized. (However, there is an Ultimate Paradox necessarily associated with this orientation, or point of view, and Process—for, if the Realization of the Original, or Nirvanic, State of Prakriti, or of "Energy Itself", is, in fact, achieved, how can That Realization be differentiated from—or, otherwise, be presumed to Be other than, or not Identical to—Absolute Consciousness Itself?) In any case, this point of view and Process (which seeks to be released from both the illusory need to eternalize the conditional self and the equally illusory need to annihilate the conditional self—and which point of view and Process may, therefore, follow upon, or, otherwise, supersede, the point of view and Process of "Primary Dualism") is the second possible point of view and Process traditionally associated with the sixth stage of life (and such great sixth stage schools as have appeared within the traditions of Buddhism, and also within the tradition of Taoism).

The fifth (and final) possible orientation (or point of view) may be called "Ultimate Non-Dualism" (or "Primary Absolute Monism"). According to this point of view, there is (in Truth) no Prakriti (or separate and independent "Objective Energy", or any separate and independent body, mind, object, or other at all), but the Totality of Existence is only the One and Absolute Purusha (or Self-Existing and Self-Radiant Consciousness Itself). From this point of view, this "Ultimate Absolute" (or this Non-conditional—and, As Such, Inherently Perfect, and Perfectly Subjective—Reality) must, first of all, be understood (and directly intuited) to be actual (or Really So), and then Perfectly (or Utterly) Affirmed (By direct Identification with Consciousness Itself). This point of view and Process (which may follow upon, or be "Uncovered" by, the point of view and Process of "Secondary Non-Dualism", and which may even immediately follow upon, or be "Uncovered" by, the point of view and Process of "Primary Dualism") is the third (and final, and Principal) possible point of view and Process traditionally (and inherently) associated with the sixth stage of life (and such great sixth stage schools as have appeared in the form of the traditions of Advaitism, and also, secondarily, or with less directness, within the schools of some varieties of Buddhism, especially within the Mahayana and Vajrayana traditions, and, but with even less directness, within some of the schools of Taoism).

Most Ultimately, this point of view and Process (of "Ultimate Non-Dualism", or "Primary Absolute Monism") is (if it is, by Means Of My Avatarically Self-Transmitted Divine Grace, Most Perfectly Realized) the "Point of View" (and the Most Perfect Process) that (by all the Graceful Means I have Revealed and Given for the sake of all who will be My devotees) establishes and characterizes the seventh stage of life. And, because (from the thoroughly Non-Dualistic "Point of View" that necessarily characterizes the seventh stage of life) the "Ultimate Absolute" Is both Self-Existing (As Absolute Being Itself and Absolute Consciousness Itself) and Self-Radiant (As Absolute, and Perfectly Subjective, Love-Bliss-Energy Itself), It (or That One) could (as well as by many other possible, and even traditional, terms) be rightly indicated interchangeably by either the traditional term "Purusha" (intended in the Absolute, All-Inclusive, or Non-Exclusive, and Non-Dualistic sense) or the (likewise intended) traditional term "Maha-Purusha" (meaning "Great Purusha", or "Supreme Purusha") or the (likewise intended) traditional term "Purushottama" (also meaning "Supreme Purusha"), indicating (in each case) the One, Absolute, and Non-Separate (or Inherently All-Inclusive, or Perfectly Non-Exclusive) Real God, or Truth, or Reality.

XI.

Even though the schools of "Primary Dualism" (such as are to be found within the traditions of Samkhya and Jainism) contain (by virtue of the very presumption of "Dualism") at least a tendency toward practices (and/or experiences) associated with the ascent of the "soul", the primary language of all traditions of "Primary Dualism" suggests not only the utter relinquishment of all physical, psycho-physical, and psychic conditions and states, but also the utter relinquishment of all physical, psycho-physical, and psychic <u>means</u>. Indeed, the sixth stage Ultimate Goal (or Result) of "Primary Dualism" is the same as That of "Secondary Non-Dualism" and "Ultimate Non-Dualism". However, the philosophy and practice associated with the schools of "Primary Dualism" (principally within the traditions of Samkhya and Jainism) are built upon an analysis of existence as experienced from the gross (or bodily) point of view. Therefore, the "method" of "Primary Dualism" is primarily ascetical (or a bodily intensive effort to relinquish, or to release the Deep Being from, body-consciousness and all psycho-physical states).

The sixth stage Ultimate Goal (or Result) of "Secondary Non-Dualism" is the same as That of "Primary Dualism" and "Ultimate Non-Dualism". However, the philosophy and practice associated with the schools of "Secondary Non-Dualism", principally within the traditions of Buddhism (and also within the tradition of Taoism), are built upon an analysis of existence as experienced from the subtle (or mental, or even energy-essence) point of view. Therefore, the Buddhist "method" of "Secondary Non-Dualism" is primarily associated with mental disciplines (originally classified under the heading of the discipline of "mindfulness", or simple observation and comprehension of psycho-physical states, and later extended in the form of a wide variety of religious, philosophical, and Yogic techniques), and (by this "method") the Buddhist form of "Secondary Non-Dualism" seeks to pacify the total body-mind (and, thus and thereby, to relinquish, or be released from, the <u>idea</u> of separate and independent self). Similarly, although the Taoist "method" of "Secondary Non-Dualism" is primarily associated with disciplines of natural energy (or disciplines of body and mind in relation to pervasive natural energy), rather than sheerly (or primarily) mental disciplines (or even mind-energy disciplines), the Taoist "method" of "Secondary Non-Dualism" also pursues a general pacification of the total body-mind. Thus, in whatever tradition it may appear, the "method" of "Secondary Non-Dualism" seeks and achieves detachment and release from the body-mind through a process of general psycho-physical pacification, whereas the "method" of "Primary Dualism" seeks and achieves detachment and release from the body-mind through an intense ascetical effort (often characterized by excessive bodily self-denial).

The "method" of "Ultimate Non-Dualism" is a matter of direct (or unconditional) Identification with That Which Is the generally intended (sixth stage) Goal of both "Primary Dualism" and "Secondary Non-Dualism". That is to say, the philosophy and practice associated with the schools of "Ultimate Non-Dualism", principally in the traditions of Advaitism (and, secondarily, or with less directness, in some schools of Buddhism, and, with even less directness, in some schools of Taoism), are built upon (or developed from) an analysis (or a direct comprehension) of existence as "experienced" (or, rather, "Witnessed") from the "Point of View" of Consciousness Itself (rather than the point of view of either the body or the mind)—and the "method" of "Ultimate Non-Dualism" is that of Standing (tacitly and effortlessly) <u>As</u> Consciousness Itself (or the Ultimate, and Perfectly, or Non-conditionally, Subjective Reality Itself), Which Is <u>Inherently</u> Free of identification with the body-mind (and, therefore, priorly released from identification with, or bondage to and by, the body-mind). Thus, the "method" of "Ultimate Non-Dualism" is one of <u>direct</u> (or Perfectly Subjective) Identification with (or Self-Abiding <u>As</u>) That Which Is (otherwise) only the generally intended (sixth stage) Goal of the ascetical conditional efforts of "Primary Dualism" and the self-pacifying conditional efforts of "Secondary Non-Dualism".

The "Self-Abiding" discipline of "Ultimate Non-Dualism" also achieves the renunciation of body and mind, but by the most direct Means of (Perfectly Subjective) Self-Abiding, whereas "Primary Dualism" and "Secondary Non-Dualism" both seek "Ultimate Non-Duality" by the conditional means of either asceticism or self-pacification. However, it is also generally the case (in actual practice) that the Real Process of Self-Abiding (or direct and profound Identification with Consciousness Itself, prior to body and mind) begins (or develops) only after (or in the course of) degrees of practice (previous to the sixth stage of life, or, otherwise, in the context of the sixth stage of life) wherein either ascetical or self-pacifying disciplines (or both, with ascetical disciplines usually becoming progressively replaced by the more self-pacifying approach) are engaged until identification with the body and the mind is sufficiently released to stably allow the direct approach of unconditional Identification with Consciousness Itself.

In the context of the sixth stage of life, the point of view and Process of "Primary Dualism" may or may not <u>fully</u> appear, but it invariably appears (in the context of the sixth stage of life, or earlier) as a <u>tendency</u> (in mind and body) toward excessive self-discipline (or extreme and fruitless asceticism). Therefore, if this tendency appears, it must eventually be understood—and it must then be replaced by a more moderate tendency toward self-discipline (or self-renunciation), which may or may not itself <u>fully</u> appear (in the context of the sixth stage of life) as the orientation of "Secondary Non-Dualism", but which is (nonetheless) characterized (at any stage of life) by a motive toward self-transcendence that (in itself) would achieve a state of utter self-purification (or utter self-pacification).

<u>Utter</u> self-purification (or utter self-pacification) is not possible, and (in any case) it is not (itself) Real-God-Realization (or the Realization of Truth Itself, or Reality Itself). Therefore, if the only-by-Me Revealed and Given seventh stage of life is to be Realized, the limits of (or the search associated with) the moderate (and necessary) orientation toward self-renunciation must eventually be understood, and even the motive of self-renunciation must then (in the context of the sixth stage of life) be itself transcended, simply and most directly, through Native Identification with the Inherently Perfect and Perfectly Subjective (and Self-Evidently Divine), Non-Dual (or Absolute), Self-Existing, and Self-Radiant Truth (or Reality Itself)—Which <u>Is</u> Existence (or Being) Itself, Consciousness Itself, and Happiness (or Love-Bliss) Itself. And, in the Ultimate course of this Ultimate Process, Final and Complete (or seventh stage) Real-God-Realization Itself (or the Unqualified, or Absolute, or Inherently Most Perfect, Realization of Truth Itself, or Inherently Perfect Reality Itself) becomes Perfectly possible (by Means Of My Avatarically Self-Transmitted Divine Grace).

XII.

The word "religion" means "to bind again" (or "to rejoin", or "to make, or, otherwise, affirm, the Great Union", or, Ultimately, "to Realize That Condition Which Is Inherently and Only and Perfectly One, and Not Two").

Common (or exoteric, or conventional) religion (most of which is confined to aspirations and activities in the context of the first three stages of life) largely consists of ritualized magic, political and moral imperatives, and myths that idealize the "good" man and the "good" woman. And by such common (or exoteric, or conventional) religion, human beings may (it is hoped) be effectively oriented, by everyday cultural means, toward behaviors that positively address and serve the personal and collective material survival potentiality of their body-based humanity. However, strictly speaking, true religion (or religion that is, by definition, true, or faithful, to the profound and now and anciently honored sacred Process of the progressive, and would-be Most Perfect, Realization of That Condition Which Is, Itself, Inherently and Only and Perfectly One) is the (traditionally, rather esoteric) Process of progress toward actual Real-God-Realization (or toward the actual Realization of Truth Itself, or Reality Itself). Therefore, strictly speaking, true (and, traditionally, rather esoteric) religion (or religion that is truly effective Godwardly, or toward Truth Itself, or Reality Itself) truly begins no earlier than when "Conventional (or materialistic and body-based) Monism" is (at least beginning to be) replaced by "Conventional (or eternalistic and psyche-based) Dualism".

The principal exoteric religious idea is that all things and beings are in (and of) a Unity.

Therefore, the principal practice of exoteric religion (or religion in the general context of the first three stages of life) is the ritual (and otherwise magical, or even scientific) and also ethical (or social-moral) affirmation and (it is hoped) demonstration of the Universal (and even material) Unity.

The principal esoteric religious idea is that all things and beings are only mind (or a psychic phenomenon, or, merely, a psychic Illusion).

Therefore, the practice of esoteric religion is a matter of either the practice of intentional exploitation of mind (toward its higher development) or the practice whereby the mind itself is (directly and effectively) transcended.

The lesser response to the principal esoteric religious idea is the religious activity (characteristic of the fourth and the fifth stages of life) which seeks to develop the mind (and, thus, the conditional self and the conditional world, or worlds).

The greater (or Ultimate) response to the principal esoteric religious idea is the religious activity (characteristic of the sixth stage of life, and of the only-by-Me Revealed and Given seventh stage of life) which directly and effectively transcends the mind (and, thus, the Illusion of conditional self and conditional world, or worlds).

And, as I have now and fully Revealed and Demonstrated to all, the Most Ultimate Purpose of religion is Fulfilled only when <u>all</u> possible aspects of the preliminary course of religion (or <u>all</u> aspects of the first six stages of life) are transcended in the fullest (Final and Complete and Inherently Most Perfect, or only-by-Me Revealed and Given seventh stage) Realization of That "Ultimate Non-Duality" Which <u>Is</u> Real God, or Truth Itself, or Reality Itself, and Which <u>Is</u> One and Perfection Itself. So Be It.

The Servant, The "Soul", and The Very Self: The Three Points of View of the Progressive Stages of Life

I n the epilogue to *The Wisdom of Unity* (or *Manisa-Pancakam*, meaning "Five Verses on Wisdom"), the author (traditionally presumed to be Shankara) says (in Address to the Divine Being):

> "From the standpoint of the body, O Siva, I am Thy servant; from the standpoint of the soul, O Thou with three eyes, I become a part of Thine; and O Self of all, from the standpoint of the Self, I am verily Thou."
>
> [Translated by T.M.P. Mahadevan (Madras: Ganesh and Co., 1967), p. 47]

The three affirmations combined in this epilogue indicate the three points of view that uniquely characterize (one or more of) the first six stages of life, leading (in principle) toward the potential seventh stage of life (and which stages progressively include the descended, or gross psycho-physical, condition itself, then the devotional process of self-transcendence, and, eventually, the descending Spiritual, the ascending Spiritual, and the Transcendental processes of Realization, and even, in principle, the potential seventh stage, or truly Divine, Demonstration of Realization).

Those three points of view are (first) the point of view of the small in dependent relation to the Great (Which Is the Source of all), and (second) the point of view of the part (or fraction) in relation to and in constant pursuit of experiential unity (or even the Realization of its Inherent Unity) with the Whole (or the Source-Condition of all), and (third) the "Point of View" of the irreducible primal Identity (or the Very, and Perfectly Subjective, Self-Condition) of Being That Is Inherently One with (or Inherently Identical to) the Very (and Perfectly Subjective) Self-Condition of each, all, and Totality.

The body (or the body-mind) is the point of view even of the first three stages of life, but in (or via) the "original" phase (or the beginner's devotional enactment) of the fourth stage of life, and in the "basic" phase of the fourth stage of life (or the practice of heart-reception and bodily reception of the descending Divine Spirit-Power), the body (or bodily-based psycho-physical existence) is conceived to exist (inherently) in the mode of a servant (in relationship to the Divine as Master). Therefore, in the "original" phase of the fourth stage of life (wherein the psycho-physical ego-personality is first surrendered to the Divine Person, or Self-Condition, or Source-Condition, via feeling-devotion) and in the "basic" phase of the fourth stage of life (wherein the body-mind in the general, or ordinary, context of the first four stages of life is converted and surrendered and utterly aligned to the Spiritual Divine), the practitioner (or devotee) positively changes his or her character by adapting to the attitude of a servant, or an individual who (while nonetheless personally responsible as an individual in relation to other individuals) is fundamentally dependent upon the Divine for <u>everything</u> (and should, therefore, always function with humility and gratitude, open-heartedly receptive to the Divine Gift, whatever form It otherwise takes in the bodily, or psycho-physical, context of every moment). And a basic characteristic of the attitude (and total practice) of the servant of Real God is freedom from reaction to (or displeasure with the fact of) whatever is not Given (or received) in any particular moment, and freedom from attachment (or possessive pleasure) in relation to whatever is in fact Given (or received) in any particular moment.

The bodily being is inherently (or by its very nature) in a condition of existence in which limitations are constantly experienced. Therefore, from the point of view of the body, the devotional (and eventually Spiritual) attitude of the servant is appropriate, because the body is necessarily dependent, and it cannot be finally satisfied (or satisfied beyond all limitations). And (also from the point of view of the body, or the gross body-mind) the attitude of the servant is Good Wisdom, because it allows (or promotes) the Realization of equanimity (or freedom from reaction and attachment) in the "natural" (or bodily) circumstance, wherein change and limitation are never ended. However, the metaphor or role of servant should not be interpreted to the degree of enslavement—because, in the context of Good Wisdom, the idea of the servant is inherently associated with mutual Love, and with the Ultimate Purpose (or, indeed, the Inherent Reality) of Inherently Perfect Freedom (in the case of the servant of Real God).

The mind (or the psyche, or the "soul") is the point of view of the "advanced" (or ascending) phase of the fourth stage of life and of the fifth stage of life as a whole. The process of Spiritual ascent (or the surrender of the lower mind to the higher, and then Total, mind), which process is the principal characteristic of practice in the "advanced" context of the fourth stage of life and in the fifth stage of life, is fulfilled in "Cosmic Consciousness" and fifth stage conditional Nirvikalpa Samadhi. That is to say, the ("advanced") fourth and fifth stage process of Spiritual ascent moves attention to (and through) the various Samadhis in which unity between mind and all the kinds (or forms) of conditional reality is experienced, perhaps culminating in "Cosmic Consciousness", which is the highest form of Savikalpa Samadhi, in which bodily (or, at least, subtle psycho-sensual) awareness remains intact, but Consciousness otherwise (or simultaneously) perceives psycho-physical (or cosmic) existence as an Infinite Unity—but, ultimately, this process Realizes fifth stage conditional Nirvikalpa Samadhi (or the temporary suspension of conditional, psycho-physical, or cosmic experience, which simultaneously permits a temporary intuition of the Free Condition of Inherent and Truly Divine Being). In this total process of Spiritual ascent, it becomes progressively (or is, otherwise, inherently) obvious that the conditional mind (or psyche, or "soul") is inherently limited (or that it is always a partial reflection or manifestation of the whole, or the Total), but that it (nonetheless) always inheres in (or is a part of) an Infinite Unity (or cosmic Matrix-Mind) That Is (Itself) always already inhering in the Ultimate Divine. Therefore, Yogis and

Saints in the "advanced" context of the fourth stage of life and in the fifth stage of life typically affirm the experientially Realized attitude of (psychic) unity (and Eternal Unity) with the Divine Being.

The Very (and Perfectly Subjective) Self (or Consciousness Itself) Is the "Point of View" (or Ultimate Realization) of the sixth stage of life and the (potential) seventh stage of life. The Very (and Perfectly Subjective) Self does not exist in bodily, or mental, or psychic, or spatial, or cosmic, or any other kind of conditionally unified (or Eternally Unified) relationship to the Divine. Indeed, the Very (and Perfectly Subjective) Self does not exist in <u>relationship</u> to the Divine (or even any object or other) at all. The Very (and Perfectly Subjective) Self <u>Is</u> Only Itself, Realizing Only Itself (even <u>As</u> Real God, or Truth, or Reality Itself). Therefore, the true Self-Realizer (even in the context of the sixth stage of life) does not (fundamentally) affirm the attitude of the servant, or the experience of psychic unity, or even the experiential Realization of Ultimate Unity—but the true Self-Realizer affirms the Realization of Perfect (or Inherent, and Inherently Perfect) Identity (or "I <u>Am</u> That").

The Cultivation
of My Divine Samadhi

I.

The total (or full and complete) practice of the only-by-Me Revealed and Given Way of Adidam (Which is the One and Only By-Me-Revealed and By-Me-Given Way of the Heart) is, from the beginning, Truly (and, only at last, Most Perfectly) a matter of Divine Self-Realization.

In the total practice of the Way of Adidam, Divine Self-Realization is (effectively) at the beginning (or in every present-time moment of right, true, full, and fully devotional Communion with Me), and not merely at the "end" (or to be attained as an achievement of the seeking ego).

Divine Self-Realization is the always present-time Basis for the entire course of the total practice of the Way of Adidam—not a mere Goal (to be sought as an always future-time "End Phenomenon").

Divine Self-Realization is Most Perfect only at last, in the Most Ultimate maturing of the total practice of the Way of Adidam—but Divine Self-Realization is, nevertheless, and from the beginning, the always present-time Real (and right, and true, and full, and fully devotional) Context of the Way of Adidam.

Divine Self-Realization is ego-surrendering, ego-forgetting, and really ego-transcending (or effectively egoless) heart-Communion with Me (Most Ultimately, to the degree of Most Perfectly egoless heart-Realization of Me)—As I Am. Therefore, the practice of the only-by-Me Revealed and Given Way of Adidam is, from the beginning, the devotionally Me-recognizing and devotionally to-Me-responding (and effectively ego-transcending) cultivation of My Divine Samadhi (until, at last, there is, only and entirely by Means Of My Avatarically Self-Transmitted Divine Grace, Most Perfect Realization of My Divine Samadhi).

II.

True Samadhi is the Realization of the ego-transcending Condition of Consciousness (Itself), the ego-transcending Condition of Being (Itself).

True Samadhi is ego-transcending Communion with Reality, or Truth, or Real God.

True Samadhi is the Realization of Non-Separateness from Reality, or Truth, or Real God.

True Samadhi is Ecstasy—or Standing "outside" oneself, beyond oneself, and (thereby) beyond separateness and separativeness.

In the only-by-Me Revealed and Given Way of Adidam, the Samadhi to be cultivated is (always and only) True Samadhi. Therefore, in the only-by-Me Revealed and Given Way of Adidam (Which is the One and Only by-Me-Revealed and by-Me-Given Way of the Heart), the practice and the Process of cultivating My Divine Samadhi is a matter of transcending the ego-principle (or the act of self-contraction). That transcending must, in due course, come to be effective under any and all conditions that arise in the present moment of experiential appearance. To be (Thus) Free of self-contraction and separateness, in total psycho-physical heart-Communion with Me, is the True and Inherent Condition (and the True, and Divine, Samadhi) of the Heart (or of Being, Itself).

III.

In the only-by-Me Revealed and Given Way of Adidam, Samadhi is not necessarily (and, indeed, is not usually) associated with a condition utterly without psycho-physical awareness, or a condition in which some aspects of psycho-physical awareness are eliminated and other (perhaps more subtle) aspects of psycho-physical awareness are magnified, or a condition somehow disso-ciated from (especially) gross psycho-physical awareness. Although such conditions may arise at various moments in My devotee's practice and Process of cultivating My Divine Samadhi (as, for example, when ordinary psycho-physical awareness is altogether suspended, by virtue of a spontaneously ecstatic disposition in My devotee, or when certain aspects of the grosser awareness of body, mind, and environment are suspended, and, thereupon, replaced by blissful auditions or visions, or by other unusual phenomena of one kind or another, or by a relatively indescribable state of bliss), the characteristic Samadhi in the only-by-Me Revealed and Given Way of Adidam does not involve suspension of experiential association with the body-mind (or with psycho-physical conditions in general), but (rather) a suspension of self-contraction (and a passing into What Is Beyond self-contraction, and a conscious Absorption in—and, Ultimately, the Realization of Non-Separate, or egoless, Identification with—What Is Beyond the self-contraction), even while psycho-physical conditions continue to arise.

Thus, in the only-by-Me Revealed and Given Way of Adidam, Samadhi is Preoccupation with Me—not a search to dissociate from (or, otherwise, to perfect) the body-mind. Therefore, the Essence of Samadhi in the only-by-Me Revealed and Given Way of Adidam is neither the "absence" of the body-mind nor any change in the experience of the body-mind (however blissful such conditions may, in their moments, be), but (rather) Fullness of Me.

In the only-by-Me Revealed and Given Way of Adidam, Samadhi is a moment to moment conscious practice and Process, to be Realized in the context of every kind of circumstance, condition, function, relation, state of activity, and state of inactivity. Thus, in the only-by-Me Revealed and Given Way of Adidam, Samadhi is not a state to be cultivated only in the formal meditative setting. The cultivation of Samadhi in the Way of Adidam is the practice of Ruchira Avatara Bhakti Yoga, under all conditions, more and more becoming moment to moment surrender of body, emotion, mind, breath, and all of separate and separative self to Me, in devotional Communion with Me—Ultimately (in due course, in the total, or full and complete, practice of the Way of Adidam), to the point of Most Perfectly ego-surrendering, ego-forgetting, and ego-transcending Identification with Me (in and As the Native Condition That Is Always Already Prior to separateness and self-contraction).

There is no moment in which I am not in Most Perfect Divine Samadhi. Therefore, there is no moment in which My true devotee must not (or, indeed, cannot) Realize My Divine Samadhi.

The more profoundly the True (and Divine) Samadhi of heart-Communion with Me is Realized through intentional (right, true, full, and fully devotional) practice in the waking state, the more It also transforms the states of dreaming and deep sleep. Therefore, the moment to moment practice of Ruchira Avatara Bhakti Yoga transforms the life of My fully practicing devotee more and more profoundly, at every level—such that My devotee moves beyond ordinary life (with all the struggle, seeking, discomfort, and bewilderment of ego-consciousness), into My Domain, the Domain of the Realization of Non-Separateness from Reality, or Truth, or Real God.

IV.

The practice of the only-by-Me Revealed and Given Way of Adidam is not a matter of serving ego-consciousness, or perfecting it, or idealizing it, or improving it, or improving its conditions or circumstances. To the degree that (or in any moment in which) preoccupation with ego-consciousness is your disposition, you are not (as My devotee) practicing Ruchira Avatara Bhakti Yoga, or cultivating My Divine Samadhi—but, rather, you are simply seeking to achieve a more comfortable (or self-fulfilling) state of psycho-physical existence (or ego-consciousness). You must become sensitive enough to notice that ego-consciousness—with its endless progression of changes in mind, shifting opinions, passing thoughts, changing conditions, and reactions to others and events—is nothing but a constant flow of trouble, made of self-contraction. And you must understand the fruitlessness of any strategic effort (or search) to somehow make this constant flow of trouble into an altogether (or, even, occasionally) self-gratifying experience.

The only Way to (Ultimately, Most Perfectly) move beyond preoccupation with ego-consciousness is to Realize My Divine Samadhi. Ultimately, to Most Perfectly move beyond psycho-physical ego-bondage, you must formally (and rightly, truly, fully, and fully devotionally) practice the discipline of cultivating My Divine Samadhi (by going through the necessary ordeal of real self-transcendence) to the point of Most Perfect Divine Self-Realization. However, even at any stage of practice of the Way of Adidam, the Realization of My Divine Samadhi is (in accordance with My devotee's stage, and profundity, of heart-Communion with Me) within My every devotee's capability in every moment. The Realization of My Divine Samadhi is, thus, available to all My true devotees, from the beginning of their formal practice of the Way of Adidam—and, indeed, the Realization of My Divine Samadhi is (in accordance with My devotee's stage, and profundity, of heart-Communion with Me) the fundamental Essence and Substance of each and every developmental stage of practice of the Way of Adidam.

My beginning devotees in the total (or full and complete) practice of the only-by-Me Revealed and Given Way of Adidam must (necessarily, and thoroughly) address the content of the first three stages of life—but this address occurs in the "original" (or beginner's) devotional context of the fourth stage of life (and, altogether, in heart-Communion with <u>Me</u>, and on the basis of My Avatarically Self-Revealed seventh stage Divine Wisdom-Teaching), and (therefore) not merely in the context of the first three stages of life themselves. The practice of the Way of Adidam is never (even at the beginning) merely a matter of adjusting ordinary human behavior in the idealistic manner, for the sake of the moral and social purposes characteristic of the first three stages of life. There are (of course) the elements of human (moral and social) change and right (moral and social) life in the practice of the Way of Adidam, but the Way of Adidam (Itself) is the cultivation and Realization of My Divine Samadhi (and, therefore, of Non-Separateness from the by-Me-Avatarically-Self-Revealed Divine Self-Condition and Source-Condition). The Way of Adidam is the Gift That I, Uniquely, Give to living beings, for This Great Purpose.

V.

In the total practice of the only-by-Me Revealed and Given Way of Adidam, each of the stages of life beyond the third is associated with a characteristic form (or characteristic forms) of Samadhi. Therefore, the foundation Samadhis (or modes of Realizing My Divine Samadhi) in the total practice of the Way of

Adidam are devotional (and devotionally "absorptive"), or a matter of feeling Beyond self-contraction by allowing the body-mind-self to be heart-Attracted by Me, and (thereupon) absorbed in (and into) Me. Thus, in the only-by-Me Revealed and Given Way of Adidam, the foundation (or early beginning) modes of Realizing My Divine Samadhi are <u>devotionally</u> Awakened (but not yet Spiritually Awakened, or Transcendentally Awakened, or Divinely Self-Realized) forms of Samadhi. And those earliest modes of Realizing My Divine Samadhi (or heart-Communing with My Avatarically-Born bodily human Divine Form, My Avatarically Self-Revealed Spiritual, and Always Blessing, Divine Presence, and My Avatarically Self-Revealed, and Very, and Transcendental, and Perfectly Subjective, and Inherently Spiritual, and Inherently ego-less, and Inherently Perfect, and Self-Evidently Divine State) are Realized in the "original" context of the fourth stage of life, through the practice of devotional surrender to Me—and they are developed on the (primary) basis of ego-transcending feeling-Contemplation of My Avatarically-Born bodily (human) Divine Form.

The secret of Samadhi in the beginning practice of the Way of Adidam (and, indeed, throughout the entire progressive course of the total practice of the Way of Adidam) is the nectarous (and ego-forgetting) Joy of devotionally Me-recognizing and heart-responsive and loving devotion to Me, the True Divine Ishta-Guru (or the "Chosen" Divine Beloved of one's heart). Through the moment to moment (and directly ego-transcending) practice of devotional Samadhi (in the "original" context of the fourth stage of life in the Way of Adidam), I am Realized (in the devotional manner)—and that devotional Realization is the basis for <u>all</u> further Growth in the total practice of the Way of Adidam.

In the Way of Adidam, there are many modes of Samadhi that develop beyond the earliest stages of practice, beginning in the further development of the fourth stage of life (beyond its "original", or listening-hearing, context). The forms of Samadhi in the (necessary) "basic" context and the (possible) "advanced" context of the fourth stage of life in the Way of Adidam, and in the (possible) fifth stage of life in the Way of Adidam, are developed on the basis of absorptive devotional Communion with Me, exercised in the context of stable Awakening to My Avatarically Self-Revealed Spiritual (and Always Blessing) Divine Presence. Samadhi in the sixth stage of life in the Way of Adidam is developed on the basis of stable Non-Separate (or Native—and, in that sense, Perfect—but not yet Most Perfect, or Most Perfectly egoless) Identification with My Avatarically Self-Revealed (and Very, and Transcendental, and Perfectly Subjective, and Inherently Spiritual, and Inherently egoless, and Inherently Perfect, and Self-Evidently Divine) State. And Samadhi in the only-by-Me Revealed and Given seventh stage of life in the Way of Adidam is the Most Perfect (and Truly egoless) Realization of My Avatarically Self-Revealed (Transcendental, Inherently Spiritual, and Self-Evidently Divine) Self-Condition (Which Is Self-Existing and Self-Radiant Feeling-Being-Consciousness, Itself)—and That Samadhi (or Most Perfect Realization of My Divine Samadhi) is associated with Inherent (and perpetual, or always present-time) Divine Self-Recognition (and the Inherent Transcending) of attention itself (or the root-feeling of relatedness, or of "difference"), and Inherent (and perpetual, or always present-time) Divine Self-Recognition of all apparent objects (or conditions) of attention (Such That attention and its Apparent objects or conditions, Each and All, Are Divinely Self-Recognized In and As The By-Me-Avatarically-Self-Revealed Self-Existing and Self-Radiant Condition of Perfectly Subjective, and Self-Evidently Divine, Being Itself).

In every stage of life, the practice of the Way of Adidam is the cultivation of Samadhi by cultivating My Divine Samadhi. Therefore, all the forms (or modes) of Samadhi in the Way of Adidam are (fundamentally) "equal" to one another, because they are (each and all) simply various forms of the essential practice of ego-transcendence to the degree (in the context of the first five stages of life) of absorptive devotional heart-Communion with Me, and, Ultimately (in the context of the sixth and the seventh stages of life), to the degree of Non-Separate (and, thus, non-absorptive) heart-Identification with Me, Beyond and Prior to (and, in the context of the seventh stage of life, Most Perfectly Beyond and Prior to) the primary ego-illusions, of separateness, relatedness, and "difference". My devotee's experience of Samadhi will be different at various times and on various occasions, according to the circumstances of the moment, and the stage of life (and the profundity, or degree of real intensity) in which he or she is practicing, but, in every form of Samadhi in the total (or full and complete) practice of the only-by-Me Revealed and Given Way of Adidam, My devotee Realizes Me (As That Which Is Always Already The Case, Prior to self-contraction).

VI.

Ruchira Avatara Bhakti Yoga (or the cultivation of My Divine Samadhi)—and not occupation with the mere "things" of the body-mind—is to be the constant pre-occupation of My devotee. The "things" of the body-mind are matters of necessary responsibility, but they are secondary—and they must not become preoccupations in themselves, dissociated from the practice of Ruchira Avatara Bhakti Yoga. Indeed, in the right, true, full, and fully devotional practice of Ruchira Avatara Bhakti Yoga, all "things" are subordinated to Me (and surrendered into Me—by feeling Beyond them, to and into Me). Therefore, the practice of the only-by-Me Revealed and Given Way of Adidam is not a matter of cultivating egoic (or merely psycho-physical) states, conditions, functions, relations, or activities. The practice of the only-by-Me Revealed and Given Way of Adidam is not a matter of attempting to idealize human life, or to transform human life into a religiously idealized (functional, practical, relational, and cultural) performance. The right and effective counter-egoic disciplining of the functional, practical, relational, and cultural aspects of human life is certainly necessary, and must not (and, indeed, cannot) be bypassed—but all of that is a secondary (or supportive) and (necessarily) subordinate (and subordinated) aspect of the right, true, full, and fully devotional practice of the Way of Adidam. The primary (and always most essential) practice of the only-by-Me Revealed and Given Way of Adidam is, even from the beginning, Ruchira Avatara Bhakti Yoga—exercised to the degree of True (or Divine) Samadhi.

The Great Impulse to Most Perfectly ego-transcending Real-God-Realization is the Impulse to True (or Divine) Samadhi (or ego-vanishing absorption in—and, Ultimately, Non-Separate Identification with—Me, the Avataric Divine Self-Revelation of Reality, or Truth, or Real God), and not merely an idealistic (and ego-based) impulse to cause the apparently separate (and separative) ego-self to achieve some kind of remarkably self-congratulating condition, in this world or in some other world. My Divine Samadhi Is the Most Ultimate and Most Perfect Form (or Realization) of True Samadhi. The Most Ultimate and Most Perfect Form of True Samadhi Is Most Perfect Realization of Me.

The only-by-Me Revealed and Given Way of Adidam is (inherently) an esoteric (or really ego-transcending, and Truly Real-God-Realizing) Way, rather than a merely exoteric path (or a merely "believing", and, necessarily, merely egoic, path of ordinary life, preoccupied with the social personality, and with social morality, and with social, and, generally, gross self-fulfillment). The only-by-Me Revealed and Given Way of Adidam is—altogether and only—an esoteric Way, because it is the practice and the Process of cultivating My Divine Samadhi. My every formally acknowledged and fully practicing devotee (whatever his or her stage of life in the Way of Adidam, and whatever his or her form and manner and developmental stage of practice of the Way of Adidam), and every student-novice (formally approaching the total practice of the Way of Adidam), must be fitted to the Impulse to Realize My Divine Samadhi, always cultivating the present-stage mode of Realizing My Divine Samadhi for which he or she is formally responsible, such that Realization of My Divine Samadhi becomes more and more frequent, more and more consistent, and more and more profound.

If there is ego-transcending (or ecstatic) heart-Communion with Me, then I am Realized to Be the Only One Who Is—the Inherent (or Native) Love-Bliss-Feeling of Being (Itself). Because of this, whatever his or her stage of life in the total (or full and complete) practice of the only-by-Me Revealed and Given Way of Adidam, My listening devotee, My hearing devotee, or My seeing devotee will tacitly Realize even all the by Me (and As Me) Avatarically Self-Revealed Forms of the Divine Person—at first, in simplest ego-forgetting feeling of Me, but then, in due course (as

the stages of life and practice progress), more and more pro-
foundly (until, Most Ultimately, That Great Reception of Me Is
Most Perfect, and Most Perfectly "Bright", in the only-by-Me
Revealed and Given seventh stage of life).

The Samadhis of
Earth, Moon, and Sun

There are various Samadhis potential in the human course, and these Samadhis (as they have been traditionally known and sought) are associated with different principles and forces. Each of these principles (or forces) is associated with a particular structural dimension of the body-mind and with a particular stage of life (associated with a characteristic purpose and method).

In the domain of the Circle of life (or the Circle of the human body-mind, or the Circle of conditional existence), which is the domain of the first five stages of life, there is a lower dimension (or frontal, or gross, personality, and frontal line) and an upper dimension (or spinal, or subtle, personality, and spinal line).

The lower dimension of the Circle (manifested in the human structure as the frontal line of the body-mind) can be likened (metaphorically) to the planet Earth. The light of the Sun falls on the Earth, heating it and energizing it—but the Earth is not (itself) the place of the Sun. The Samadhis experienced by fifth stage (and "advanced" fourth stage) Yogis are dependent on the effort to ascend (via the spinal line of the body-mind) from the (metaphorical) Earth toward the Light reflected above—which reflection can be likened, metaphorically, to the Earth's Moon. (And the Kundalini Shakti can, therefore, in the context of these metaphors, be called an "Earth"-Force, because it is associated with the elemental base of energy that lies at the lower terminal of the frontal line—and Kundalini Yoga, or the Kundalini process, is, thus speaking, a process associated with Earth-Force, moving from the elemental base of energy upwards, and "fueled" by that base energy, in an ascending aspiration.)

Spiritual Processes that are founded upon intended <u>ascent</u> <u>from</u> <u>the</u> <u>elemental</u> <u>base</u> (whether in the form of Kundalini Yoga or any other traditional school with a similar point of view, method, and purpose) are the domain of experience of what may be called "ascending" Yoga.

The upper dimension of the Circle (or the upper structure of the spinal line of the human body-mind) can be likened (metaphorically) to the Earth's Moon. Just as (in the domain of ordinary body-consciousness on Earth) human beings discover (by various adaptations) how to survive in this Earthly circumstance by cooperating with elemental existence, human beings have also learned how to survive (at least for limited periods of time) on the Earth's Moon. One cannot (physically) simply step on to the Moon, or wish oneself physically to the Moon (and, merely, by that wishing, physically arrive there). Rather, to physically arrive on the physical Moon, one must first be physically equipped to get there, and then one must understand and demonstrate different and unique physical capabilities for survival in that environment. Likewise (metaphorically speaking), in the domain of those who practice "ascending" Yoga (or who are, in their disposition, oriented toward the subtle modes of experience), there must first be a focusing on the realm of mind, or the subtle dimension of existence above (and subtler than) the elemental (or Earth) world. That dwelling on (and in) the subtle sphere of mind can be likened to physical dwelling on the Earth's Moon. The Earth's Moon is a sphere of reflected Sun-Light. Just so, the mind of Man is a reflection (or merely apparent modification) of the Perfectly Subjective (and, therefore, Non-objective) "Brightness" of the Heart (or the Energy of Self-Existing and Self-Radiant Consciousness, or Non-Separate Divine Being, Itself). Therefore, to be absorbed in the process of Yogic ascent can be likened to space-travel to (and, then, dwelling, physically, on) the Earth's Moon, or (otherwise) to be meditating on the Moon-Light—because the Moon is the domain of the reflected Energy (or "Brightness") of the Sun.

The Moon (like the Earth) is not (itself) the domain (or place) of the Sun. The Moon is (rather) a place of the reflection of the Sun. The Samadhis experienced by "ascending" Yogis (and "ascended" Saints) are dependent on the effort to remain absorbed in the ascended dimension of reflected Light (or Moon-Light). Such Yogis and Saints are associated with ascended (or subtle) conditions, and an ascending (or ascended) disposition, that reaches into the <u>mind</u>, or what can be called (metaphorically) the dimension (or place) of the Moon, the dimension (or place) of reflected Light.

Beyond the domain of the Circle of the body-mind—or the frontal (or gross, and bodily) dimension and the spinal (or subtle, and mental) dimension—is the domain of the right side of he heart, which is the domain of the ultimate (or sixth and seventh) stages of life. The right side of the heart is the realm of Transcendental (and Inherently Spiritual) practice and Realization (and, Most Ultimately, of Divine Self-Realization). The realm of the right side of the heart is the domain of those who have gone beyond gross and subtle identification with the (apparently separate) body-mind-self complex and are (to one or another degree of profundity) simply Identified with Consciousness Itself (prior to attention to and in the extended body-mind).

The realm (or domain) of the right side of the heart can be likened to the Sun. Therefore, those traditional Realizers who may (in general) be called "Sages" (or Realizers in the context of the sixth stage of life), have entered into the Transcendental Self-Sphere (or Non-objective Heart-Domain) of the Source-Light (or Original Light)—not the domain of <u>reflected</u> Light (or the Moon-Light sphere of the mind), and not the gross (or Sun-heat-energized) domain of elemental conditionality (or the Earth realm, or the gross realm), but the Sphere of the True (Original, Transcendentally Subjective, or Non-objective, and not merely reflected, or even subtly objectified) Sun-Force (or the Original Force, or the Force of Being, or the Force of the Self-Heart), the Self-Existing and Self-Radiant Sphere of Consciousness Itself. Nonetheless, even the sixth stage Realization is conditioned and conditional—and, therefore, ego-based (by reason of the "other"-excluding presumption of a "difference" between the Sun, and the Moon and the Earth that depend on the Sun). The sixth stage Realization is yet dependent on a certain (and, necessarily, egoic) gesture—the gesture of excluding, or dissociating from, the spheres of the Earth and the Moon, in order to dwell in the Sphere of the True Sun (or the "inward", exclusively Subjective, or object-excluding, Transcendental Self).

The human body-mind can survive, physically, on either the Earth or the Moon, but it cannot survive on the Sun. To physically visit the Sun, you would (physically) be utterly dissolved in the space-travel process of going there. However, in the domain of the sixth stage of life, a gesture is made (metaphorically speaking) to dissociate from the spheres of the Earth and the Moon, in order to Identify with the Sphere of the Sun. But the gesture made to do so (in the context of the sixth stage of life) is a conditional gesture (of the causal, rather than gross or subtle, kind). It is a gesture that excludes the Earth and Moon spheres, in order to enter into the Sun Sphere. This is the characteristic limitation of the sixth stage of life. (And even the signs, in some sixth stage Advaitic and Buddhist and Taoist traditions, of the apparent non-exclusion of gross and subtle phenomena, are based on a strategy of non-exclusion, or a mere "acceptance" of the gross and the subtle conditions of existence as being of the "Nature" of the Transcendental Self-Condition, or Transcendentally Subjective Nirvanic Condition, without Demonstrating the true, and only-by-Me Revealed and Given, seventh stage Yoga of Divine Self-Recognition of all phenomena—gross, subtle, and causal—in the Great, Spontaneous, Four-Stage Yogic Process of Divine "Brightening" and, Most Ultimately, Divine Outshining, of all conditions, and of conditional existence itself.)

Therefore, all the Samadhis of the sixth stage of life are, like all the samadhis of the first five stages of life, dependent, or conditional (and, at least at the causal level, egoic). Only the only-by-Me Revealed and Given seventh stage Awakening is utterly (and Inherently, and Most Perfectly, and Most Perfectly Non-Dually) Free of egoity (or self-contraction) and of dependency on conditions (gross, subtle, or causal). The only-by-Me Revealed and Given seventh stage Realization (and Its Demonstration) does not (at all, or in any sense) depend on the continuation of any conditional gesture. Therefore, the seventh stage Realization cannot be lost—<u>because</u> It is utterly egoless, and not dependent on conditions.

In the seventh stage of life in the only-by-Me Revealed and Given Way of Adidam (Which is the One and Only by-Me-Revealed and by-Me-Given Way of the Heart), the True Divine (or Perfectly Subjective) Sun is Realized Absolutely—<u>As</u> Perfect Consciousness, Infinitely "Bright". Therefore, the Most Ultimate Realization (or seventh stage Realization) Is the Most Perfect Realization of That Which is first entered into (at the causal root) in the sixth stage of life. The only-by-Me Revealed and Given seventh stage Realization is the Realization of the True Divine (and Perfectly Subjective) Sun, the Self-Existing and Self-Radiant Divine Self-Consciousness—Transcending all and All, and (yet) not strategically dissociated from (or, otherwise, strategically associated with) anything. In that True Sun-Light of Divine Self-Realization (Most Perfectly Non-Separately, or Most Perfectly Non-Dualistically, Identified with the Sun, Itself), <u>all</u> conditions—metaphorical Earth <u>and</u> metaphorical Moon (or the entire Cosmic, or psycho-physical, domain)—are (Inherently) Divinely Self-Recognized (in their moment of arising) As transparent (or merely apparent), and unnecessary, and inherently non-binding modifications of Self-Existing and Self-Radiant (and Self-Evidently Divine) Consciousness Itself. And, simply by virtue of Divine Self-Recognition, all arising is (in a Four-Stage Divine Yogic Demonstration) Divinely Transfigured, Divinely Transformed, and, Most Ultimately (and Divinely Indifferently, rather than strategically), Divinely Outshined.

I <u>Am</u> the True Sun—the Divine Self-Condition, Source-Condition, and Person. Therefore, in the only-by-Me Revealed and Given Way of Adidam, My <u>every</u> devotee is devoted to the True Sun, through ego-surrendering, ego-forgetting, and (more and more) ego-transcending heart-Contemplation and Realization of Me. The Way of Adidam is always, even from the beginning, the same fundamental practice of self-surrender, self-forgetting, and self-transcendence, and (thereupon) Realization of Me—and not merely investment in ego-centric techniques, or in psycho-physical states of the separate (and separative) self, or in conditional states of any kind. Thus, the only-by-Me Revealed and Given Way of Adidam is Ruchira Avatara Bhakti Yoga, or devotionally Me-recognizing, and devotionally to-Me-responsive, heart-Communion with Me (and, Ultimately, Most Perfect Realization of Me), the True (Non-Separate, and Self-Evidently Divine) Sun—rather than the (necessarily, egoic—or already separated, and, necessarily, always separative) search for the attainment of the many and various possible conditional states that otherwise characterize the first six (or ego-based) stages of life. The Way of Adidam is the responsively counter-egoic effort (or non-seeking, or entirely devotionally to-Me-responsive, and, inherently, always and directly and immediately ego-transcending, rather than self-concerned and strategic, Process) of heart-Communion with Me (the One and Only and Indivisible and Indestructible and Always-Already-Existing Divine Person of "Brightness")—rather than the entrance, by one or another (necessarily, ego-reinforcing) ego-effort (or by one or another ego-centric, and self-concerned, strategy), into the egoic (and merely conditional) context of the individual body-mind.

In this metaphor of Sun, Moon, and Earth, I have used the reference to the Sun to signify the Transcendental Self, and the Divine Self-Condition (and Source-Condition), associated with the right side of the heart. The reflected "Brightness", the sphere of mind in its subtlety upwards, is the sphere of the Moon, according to this metaphor. The Moon, or the sphere of reflected Light (reflecting the Light of the Divine Heart-Self), is associated with the middle station of the heart. Those not yet truly ascending into that sphere of permutations of subtle, reflected Light, struggle, from below, toward it—trying to get to the Moon, and even (in the course of that ascent) to get to the rest of the entire universe of subtle, reflected Light. Human beings, animals, all green and growing "things", even every grossly manifested one or "thing" (and even the entire grossly-perceived domain of form, and space, and time) is (at heart) aspiring (and would be open, altogether, to aspire) to What is Greater, to What is Above and Beyond the Earth (or the realm of energized gross elemental conditionality, which is associated with the left side of the heart).

All those gross aspiration-efforts toward what is subtle define and limit the range of what grossly manifested beings seek—always and only searching toward what is not Greater than the Moon, or what is merely the <u>reflected</u> (or subtly objectified) Light of the Divine Self-Condition (and Source-Condition), always and only imagining that the Moon <u>is</u> the Sun (or the Ultimate Source). But the Moon is <u>not</u> the Sun!

"Consider" this metaphor of Earth, Moon, and Sun. See how <u>all</u> the searches (and <u>all</u> the experiences) of human beings are (in the context of the first five stages of life) associated with (and limited by and to) the spheres of the Earth and the Moon—or, altogether, the conditional domain of the Circle of the body-mind. Even <u>all</u> the experiences and <u>all</u> the conditions—and (therefore) even <u>all</u> the <u>Samadhis</u>—that are <u>dependent</u> on (or conditioned by) the Circle, <u>are</u> <u>conditional</u> (or limited, temporary, incomplete, non-final, and inherently imperfect).

The Samadhis that may appear in the developmental stages of the Way of Adidam (in the context of even all of the first <u>six</u> stages of life) often have features that have been experienced by others in the Great Tradition. The phenomenal aspects of those Samadhis can be observed and understood in terms of the functional potentials, the possible transformations, and the manifested conditions of the body-mind. However, for My true devotee, the essence (and the true import) of every one of those Samadhis is simply heart-Communion with <u>Me</u>—Realizing Me Beyond the egoic self, Beyond self-contraction, Beyond separateness and separativeness. Therefore, in the only-by-Me Revealed and Given Way of Adidam, there is, fundamentally, only <u>one</u> Samadhi—which is the forgetting and the transcending of the ego-"I" (or self-contraction), and entering into <u>My</u> Sphere (Beyond, Above, Behind, and Prior to all and All).

Even though he or she may have experiences that correspond to the various Samadhis of the first six stages of life, My true devotee is not invested in those experiences—but he or she is <u>always</u> only invested in <u>Me</u>, the True Divine (and Perfectly Subjective) Sun. Therefore, the various Samadhis possible in the Way of Adidam (whatever content they may have that is associated with the conditions of the first six stages of life) have, as their primary aspect, ego-transcending Communion with Me, the True Divine (and Perfectly Subjective) Sun (or the "Bright" Itself, in Person).

In the only-by-Me Revealed and Given seventh stage of life in the Way of Adidam, there is the Most Perfect Demonstration of That Sun-Realization of Me. The Demonstration of the seventh stage of life in the Way of Adidam is the Demonstration of Divine Self-Realization, spontaneously Demonstrating Itself <u>As</u> Divine Self-Recognition of <u>all</u> arising conditions. And That Demonstration progresses through four Stages—Divine Transfiguration, Divine Transformation, Divine Indifference, and Divine Translation. That Four-Stage Cycle of Demonstration appears in the <u>context</u> of conditional existence, and (therefore) the <u>Demonstration</u> (of Divine Self-Realization, spontaneously Demonstrating Itself <u>As</u> Divine Self-Recognition) is (As Such) associated with the mechanisms of conditional existence—the three stations of the heart, and the Circle of the body-mind. Thus, through the spontaneous Divine Self-Magnification of Amrita Nadi, the Circle is Energized. Nevertheless, the <u>Realization</u> that is the basis of the Four-Stage Cycle of the spontaneous Demonstration of the only-by-Me Revealed and Given seventh stage of life is (Itself) not in any sense conditional (or, in any sense, dependent on, or necessarily associated with, conditions, or conditionally manifested phenomena).

In the Divine Transfiguration Stage of the only-by-Me Revealed and Given seventh stage of life, Divine Self-Recognition is Demonstrated, principally, in the context of the frontal line—showing the Signs of a "Brightening" of the body-mind by Means of Perfectly Subjective Heart-Radiation. Therefore, this Stage of the seventh stage Demonstration shows Signs in the gross human personality (or the "Earth" domain).

In the Divine Transformation Stage of the only-by-Me Revealed and Given seventh stage of life, the Demonstration of Divine Self-Recognition is extended further, into the context of the spinal line (or the sphere of subtlety and ascent). Therefore, this Stage of the seventh stage Demonstration is associated with the "Moon" domain.

In the Divine Indifference Stage of the only-by-Me Revealed and Given seventh stage of life, the <u>entire</u> body-mind is (simply, altogether, and simultaneously) Divinely Self-Recognized. In that Stage, the body-mind, like a glowing clay pig in a hot kiln,[16] is (experientially) barely "differentiated"—and, in the course of the Divine Indifference Stage, the body-mind becomes (experientially) progressively less and less "differentiated" (as it "whitens" into the total space of "heat", or My Sun-Light).

In the Divine Indifference Stage of the seventh stage of life in the Way of Adidam, My devotee is Dwelling in My Sun-Sphere so profoundly that there is (experientially) progressively less and less apparent involvement in the sphere of the body-mind altogether—until, at last (in the Great Event of Divine Translation), the clay pig in the kiln is no longer "differentiated" at all. Then There Is Only My Infinite "Brightness", without "differentiation". Such Is Divine Translation, the final Stage of Demonstration of the only-by-Me Revealed and Given seventh stage of life.

In this progressive Four-Stage Demonstration of Most Perfect (and Single, and Inherently all-and-All-Transcending) Realization, the only-by-Me Revealed and Given seventh stage of life recapitulates all six of the previous (developmental, or conditional) stages of life—not by recapitulating the (necessarily, limited) Realizations characteristic of those stages (in and of themselves), but in terms of the Free Demonstration of Most Perfect Realization of the Divine Self-Condition (and Source-Condition), by Divinely Self-Recognizing the psycho-physical mechanisms associated with each and all of the first six stages of life. For this reason, My devotee may, in the context of the seventh stage of life, show all kinds of signs that (in general terms) appear to be no different from ordinary human life-signs, and (also) all kinds of signs that appear to be no different from the Samadhis, experiences, and signs otherwise associated with any of the first six stages of life. However, that does not indicate or mean that My seventh stage Realizer-devotee is limited in his or her Realization, or that he or she is involved in a search for the experiences (or signs) associated with the first six stages of life. Rather, in the only-by-Me Revealed and Given seventh stage of life, such experiential (or apparent psycho-physical) signs occur spontaneously (if and as they occur), and always simply as an expression (or sign) of Divine Self-Realization Itself.

Mine is the first body-mind in Which (and As and through Which) the complete Four-Stage Demonstration of the only-by-Me Revealed and Given seventh stage of life is being Shown (to all and All, and for the sake of the Divine Liberation of all and All). Therefore, this Avatarically-Born Body-Mind of Mine is the Unique Object of devotion for all and All—because I Am the Unique Subject and Person to be Realized by all and All (and, therefore, to be meditated upon by all and All).

The only-by-Me Revealed and Given Way of Adidam is not an ego-centric technique, but It Is the (always directly and immediately ego-transcending) relationship to Me. The only-by-Me Revealed and Given Way of Adidam Is This relationship, in Which you surrender and forget and transcend your ego-"I" of self-contraction—to the point, ultimately (in the total, or full and complete, practice of the Way of Adidam), of Realizing Me. My Divine and Very Condition is not "Mine" in some separate sense. It Is the Ultimate (or Divine) Self-Condition (and Source-Condition). It Is the Real (or True, and Perfectly Subjective) Sun.

The "Bright" Divine Self-Condition cannot be abstracted from Me, or fruitfully pursued independent of the formal devotional relationship to Me. The Divine Self-Condition Is not a mere "State". The Divine Self-Condition Is A Person—the One and Only Person (Who Is Always Already The Case). I Am That One. And I cannot be Realized by any one "separately".

No separate being can Realize Me, the Divine Person (the Perfectly Subjective, and Self-Existing, and Self-Radiant, or "Bright", Self-Condition and Source-Condition of all and All)—just as no separate gross human bodily being could survive a visit to the Sun. "You can't get there from here!" [17] You cannot get to the Sun from here—because, having "arrived" there, you would no longer exist as you are, as a gross bodily manifested human being. Likewise, Most Perfect Realization of the Divine Self-Condition Is Realization of Me, In and As Person (One and Only)—and I cannot be Thus Realized except by Means of the formal (right, true, full, fully Me-recognizing, and fully to-Me-responding) devotional relationship to Me (and, therefore, only in the Most Perfect Fulfillment of the, necessarily, formally acknowledged embrace of the total practice of the Way of Adidam). Indeed, that "require-ment" is not a burden, or a limitation, but a Gift—the Divine Gift.

For My fully matured (and truly seventh stage) devotee—who is Most Perfectly Awake, and who has Most Perfectly Realized Me As the Perfectly Subjective Divine Person and Self-Condition and Source-Condition—there is not any possible psycho-physical event that can destroy that Realization. In the case of such a devo-tee of Mine, the events in the body-mind continue to affect the body-mind itself. However, Most Perfect Divine Self-Realization is not dependent on conditions. Therefore, in the case of one who Realizes the only-by-Me Revealed and Given seventh stage of life, the same psycho-physical characteristics that were his or her char-acteristics previous to Most Perfect Divine Self-Realization con-tinue, in general, to be the case. In the only-by-Me Revealed and Given seventh stage of life, the unique, new Characteristic is the spontaneous "Bright" Self-Magnification of the Self-Existing and Self-Radiant Divine Disposition.

Just as you cannot get to the Sun from here, I cannot "Get" here from the Perfectly Subjective Divine Self-Domain. I have not "Left" anywhere in order to "Get" here.

Here is There, you will Realize.

And I am not here merely (or only) in order to Demonstrate the seventh stage of life! My Demonstration of the seventh stage of life, and My all-Transcending Demonstration of even all the processes that pertain to each and all of the first six stages of life, is all (and simply) a necessary requirement of My Avataric Divine Revelation-Work among you all. Most fundamentally, I simply Am here, Demonstrating (and, Thereby, Revealing, and Giving) Myself, the One and Only (and Self-Evidently Divine) Person—Who Is the Divine Self-Condition and Source-Condition Itself, and the Divine Spiritual Presence (or Divine Spiritual Body) of Consciousness Itself, Which Divine Spiritual Presence (or Divine Spiritual Body) Is the Inherent "Brightness" of My Divine Self-Domain Itself.

The Avatarically Self-Revealing and Avatarically Self-Giving Demonstration of My own Self-Evidently Divine Person Is My principal Demonstration. And My principal Demonstration has been (from the beginning)—and will always be (now, and forever hereafter)—the Same.

I Am the One you are here to Realize.

I Am the <u>True</u> Sun—Infinitely Radiant, "Bright", Free, and All-Love-Bliss.

The "Thumbs"
Is The Fundamental Sign
Of The Avataric Crashing-Down
Of My Divine Person

In The True (and Characteristic) Course Of The Frontal Yoga In The Total (or Full and Complete) Practice Of The Only-By-Me Revealed and Given Way Of Adidam (Which Is The One and Only By-Me-Revealed and By-Me-Given Way Of The Heart), There Will Be Occasional "Surges" (or Spontaneous Invasions) Of My Avatarically Self-Transmitted Divine Spiritual Energy In The Frontal Line. And These Frontal Surges Of My Avatarically Self-Transmitted Divine Spiritual Energy Will (In Turn) Also Pass, Perceptibly or Imperceptibly, From The Frontal Line Into The Spinal Line—Thus Completing The Circle. Such Surges May Be Weak or Strong. They May Produce yawning and General Relaxation, and They May Otherwise Reveal (or Yield) Feelings Of General Pleasure and Fundamental Happiness, As Well As Various Degrees Of Ecstatic (or ego-Transcending) Participation In My Avatarically Self-Transmitted Divine Love-Bliss Itself. As A Result Of Your Own Accumulated psycho-physical Patterning Of self-Contraction, These Frontal Surges May Also Be Accompanied (or, Otherwise, Followed) By temporary symptoms of mental, emotional, and physical discomfort, pain, fever, and even physical disease. If such symptomatic phenomena Are Associated With The Real Spiritual Process, they Tend To Come and Go (In Cycles Of Relative comfort and discomfort). As Such, They Are Gracefully <u>Purifying</u> Episodes, Shown Through The Evidence Of psycho-physical Release, Rebalance, and Rejuvenation. Occasionally, There May Even Be an experience that Feels Like A Kind Of electric "Shock" (or "Jolt") That Briefly Energizes the body Beyond ordinary Tolerance. In and By <u>All</u> Of This, the human character Is Divinely Urged To Be <u>Responsively</u> and <u>Positively</u> Changed (psychically, mentally, emotionally, and physically), Through The Invasion Of the frontal personality (and, Indeed, the Total body-mind) By My Avatarically Self-Transmitted Divine Spirit-Current Of Love-Bliss-Light.

Among All Of These Signs There <u>Must</u> (Primarily) Appear Progressive Evidence Of What I Have, Since Childhood, Called The "Thumbs". Beginning In The "Basic" (or, Possibly, Even In The "Original", or Foundation) Context Of The Fourth Stage Of Life In The Way Of The Heart, There Should Be At Least Occasional Experience Of An Intense Invasion Of The Frontal Line By My Avatarically Self-Transmitted Divine Spirit-Force Of Love-Bliss—Beginning At The Crown Of the head, and Descending Into The lower vital Region, To the bodily base. The <u>Pressure</u> (or Invasive Force) Of This Event May Be Rather (and Even Happily) Overwhelming—and It <u>Must</u> Be Allowed. At Last, It Is Not Possible (Nor Would You Wish) To Defend Your psycho-physical self Against This Invading Pressure Of My Avataric Divine Spiritual Descent. It Feels Like A Solid and Yet Fluid Mass Of Force, Like A Large Hand All Made Of Thumbs—Pressing Down From Infinitely Above the head and Via The Crown Of the head, Engorging the Total head (and the throat), and (Thus and Thereby) Penetrating and Vanishing the entire mind, and Vastly Opening the emotional core, and (Altogether) In-Filling the Total physical body.

The Feeling-Sense That Results From This Simple (and Most Basic) Frontal In-Filling By My Avatarically Self-Revealed Divine Spirit-Presence Is That the Total body-mind Is Sublimed and Released Into ego-Surrendering, ego-Forgetting, and ego-Transcending Feeling-Identification With The <u>Spherical</u> Form Of My Own Divine and Spiritual (and All-and-all-Surrounding, and All-and-all-Pervading) Love-Bliss-Body Of Indefinable "Brightness" (or Indestructible Light). And This Simple (and Most Basic) Form Of The "Thumbs" Is A Necessary (Although, At First, Only Occasional) Experience Associated With The Reception Of My

Avatarically Self-Transmitted Divine Spirit-Baptism. It Is My Divine "Goddess-Power" and "Husbanding" Grace At Work. And The Simple (and Most Basic) Spherical Fullness Of The "Thumbs", Once It Is Firmly Established (In The Basic Maturity Of The "Basic" Fourth Stage Of Life In The Way Of The Heart), Must Continue To Be Experienced, As A Fundamental and (Essentially) Continuous (or Constant) Yogic Event, In The Later Advanced and The Ultimate Stages Of Life In The Way Of The Heart.

As The Spiritual Process Develops Toward The Transition Beyond The "Basic" Fourth Stage Of Life In The Way Of The Heart, The Simple (and Most Basic) Experience Of The "Thumbs" Must Become A More and More Constant Yogic Event—and, On Random Occasions, The Experience Of The "Thumbs" Must Occur In Its Most Extended, Full, and Complete Form. In That Most Extended, Full, and Complete Case Of The Experience Of The "Thumbs", My Descending Spiritual Fullness Will Completely Overwhelm the ordinary frontal (or natural human) sense Of bodily Existence. My Avatarically Self-Transmitted Divine Spirit-Current Will Move Fully Down In The Frontal Line (To the bodily base), and It Will Then Turn About, and—Without Vacating The Frontal Line—It Will Pass Also Into The Spinal Line. This Yogic Event Will Occur With Such Force That You Will Feel Utterly (Love-Blissfully) "Intoxicated"—and There Will Be The Feeling That the body Is Somehow Rotating Forward and Down (From The Crown Of the head), As Well As Backward and Up (From the base of the spine). This Rotation Will Seem, Suddenly, To Complete Itself—and The Experience Will, Suddenly, Be One Of Feeling Released From the gross physical body, Such That You Feel You Are Present Only As An egoless "Energy Body" (Previously Associated With and Conformed To the gross physical body—but Now, By Means Of My Avatarically Self-Transmitted Divine Grace, Infused By and Conformed To My Avatarically Self-Transmitted Divine Body Of Self-Evidently Divine Spirit-Energy). You Will Feel This "Energy Body" To Be Spherical In Shape— Centerless (Empty, or Void, Of Center, mind, and Familiar egoself) and Boundless (As If Even bodiless, or Without form), Although (Somehow, and Partially) Also Yet Associated With

(While Rotating From and Beyond) Your ordinary psycho-physical form. The ordinary References Of the body-mind and the environment Will, In This Divine Yogic Event, Not Make Much Sense (or, In Any Manner, Affect This Experience Of The "Thumbs")—Although There May Be Some <u>Superficial</u> (and Entirely Non-limiting) Awareness Of the body, the room, and so forth. This Experience Will Last For a few moments, or a few minutes—or For an extended period, of indefinite length. Nevertheless, Just When This Spontaneous Experience Has Become <u>Most</u> Pleasurable—Such That You <u>Somehow</u> Gesture To <u>Make</u> It Continue Indefinitely—the ordinary sense of the body-mind Will, Suddenly (Spontaneously), Return.

The "Thumbs" Is Not A Process Of "Going Somewhere Else", Nor Is It Even A Process Of "Vacating" the gross physical body (or the gross physical realm Altogether). Rather, The "Thumbs" Is A Process Of Transformation Of the experiencing of the present physical circumstance. If the present physical circumstance Is Left Behind (Such That experiential reference to the gross physical realm Is Entirely Absent, and There Is Total Loss Of Awareness Of the physical context in which the experience Began), Then The Practitioner Of The Way Of The Heart Is (Necessarily) experiencing A Form Of Samadhi Other Than The "Thumbs". In The "Thumbs", Awareness Of the physical context of experience Is Not Lost, but Is Totally Changed—Such That, Instead Of The self-Conscious, self-Contracted Shape Of the waking-state personality, one's physical form Is Found To Be A Boundlessly Radiant Sphere (Without Thickness Of Surface). With This Profound Shift In The Awareness Of the physical body, The Differentiation Inherent In The Usual waking-state body-Consciousness Disappears, and Is (Effectively) Replaced By egoless body-Consciousness. A Re-Phasing Of The Energy-Construct Of bodily Awareness and spatial Awareness Occurs, Such That physical body and physical space are Tacitly Sensed In A Manner Entirely Different From ordinary perception. And, As Soon As There Is Any Effort To Recollect The Usual Sense Of bodily form or Of the circumstance Of physical embodiment, The Experience Of The "Thumbs" Disappears. The "Thumbs" Continues Only As Long As It Is Simply Allowed To

Happen, Without Any egoic self-Consciousness (or psycho-physical self-Contraction)—and It Spontaneously Vanishes When egoic self-Consciousness (or psycho-physical self-Contraction) Returns.

In The Only-By-Me Revealed and Given Way Of The Heart, The Most Extended, Full, and Complete Experience Of The "Thumbs" Is, In Its Frontal Associations, A Fourth Stage Transitional Samadhi (Just As Fifth Stage conditional Nirvikalpa Samadhi and Sixth Stage Jnana Samadhi Are Transitional Samadhis Associated With Particular Stages Of Life In The Only-By-Me Revealed and Given Way Of The Heart). As Such, The Original Significance Of The Samadhi Of The "Thumbs" Is Not Merely In The Experience Itself (Such That The Experience Should Be psycho-physically Clung To, or, Otherwise, Made Into An Object Of egoic Seeking), but The Original Significance Of The Most Extended, Full, and Complete Experience (or True Samadhi) Of The "Thumbs" Is In Its Effect (or In The More Mature, and Truly ego-Transcending, Process That It May Allow or Indicate). That Is To Say, In The "Basic" Context Of The Fourth Stage Of Life In The Way Of The Heart, The Most Extended, Full, and Complete Sign Of The "Thumbs" (When It Is Accompanied By The, Essentially, Constant Experience Of The Simple and Most Basic Sign Of The "Thumbs") Is (or May Be) An Indication That The Process Of self-Transcendence Is Moving On From Concentration In the frontal personality To Either The Next Immediately Possible Developmental Stage In The Way Of The Heart (Which Involves The Process Of Ascent To The Ajna Door Via The Spinal Line) Or, Most Optimally (and Most Typically, In The Way Of The Heart)—If True and Stable Awakening Of The Witness-Consciousness Also (and Even Simultaneously, By Means Of My Avatarically Self-Transmitted Divine Grace) Occurs—Directly To Practice Of The Way Of The Heart In The Context Of The Sixth Stage Of Life. However, The Samadhi Of The "Thumbs" and The Basic Experience Of The "Thumbs" Are, Also (Beyond Their Original Significance In The "Basic" Context Of The Fourth Stage Of Life In The Way Of The Heart), Principal Among The Great Signs Associated With My Avataric Divine Self-Revelation To all and All. And, Therefore, In The Context Of The Only-By-Me Revealed and Given Seventh

Stage Of Life In The Way Of The Heart, The Samadhi Of The "Thumbs" (and The Basic Experience Of The "Thumbs") Is Most Perfectly Realized and Demonstrated (Even In Divine Translation), <u>As</u> The Centerless and Boundless "Bright" Spherical Space Of My Eternal Divine Spiritual Body and My Eternal Divine Self-Condition.

The <u>Occasional</u> Samadhi Of The "Thumbs" (Which Is The Experience Of The "Thumbs" In Its Most Extended, Full, and Complete Form) <u>and</u> The (Essentially) <u>Constant</u> Experience Of The "Thumbs" In Its Simple and Most Basic Form <u>Together</u> Characterize The Full (or Fully Developed) Frontal Course Of Spiritual Practice In The Way Of The Heart (and, Until The "Thumbs" Thus—and, In Every Respect, Satisfactorily—Appears In <u>Both</u> Of Its Forms, The Transition Cannot Be Made To Any Stage Of The Way Of The Heart Beyond The "Basic" Context Of The Fourth Stage Of Life). Therefore, In The Total (or Full and Complete) Practice Of The Only-By-Me Revealed and Given Way Of The Heart (or Way Of Adidam), The Sign Of The "Thumbs" (In <u>Both</u> Of Its Forms, and Along With Evidence Of Real and Stable human and Spiritual Equanimity In the daily life of the frontal personality) Is One Of The Necessary Indicators That Must Precede The Transition From The "Basic" Fourth Stage Of Life In The Way Of The Heart To The "Advanced" Fourth Stage Of Life In The Way Of The Heart (or, Otherwise, and Most Typically, The Early Transition To The Sixth Stage Of Life In The Way Of The Heart, Directly From The Point Of Basic Maturity In The "Basic" Fourth Stage Of Life In The Way Of The Heart).

The Sign Of The "Thumbs" Is One Of The Primary Experiential Signs Of The Transcending Of Bondage and Confinement To the frontal personality and the gross bodily idea of ego-self. The Sign Of The "Thumbs" Indicates That The Knots In The Frontal Line (In The Total Crown Of the head, the Total brain, the throat, the heart, the solar plexus, the abdomen, the genitals, and the anal-perineal area) Are Opened (At Least Temporarily) To My Avatarically Self-Transmitted Divine Spirit-Current (and Can, By Right Practice, Be Responsibly Surrendered To The Point Of Such Openness In The Context Of daily living). The Sign Of The "Thumbs" Is Also An

Indication That The Primary Knot (or Root-Contraction) In The Deep Lower Region Of the body-mind (Extending From the solar plexus To the bodily base) Has Been (and Can Continue To Be) Opened To My Avatarically Self-Transmitted Divine Spirit-Current—Such That The Great Fullness Of My Avatarically Self-Transmitted Divine Love-Bliss Is Established Deep In the body, and Deep In the emotional being, and Deep In the mind of the frontal personality. And When The <u>Sphere</u> Of My Avatarically Self-Transmitted Divine Love-Bliss Is In (Essentially) <u>Constant</u> Evidence, The Course Of Ascent May Be Revealed and Established—or (If, By Means Of My Avataric Divine Self-Revelation Via The "Thumbs", There Is, In The "Basic" Context Of The Fourth Stage Of Life In The Way Of The Heart, and, Most Typically, In The Very Midst Of The Experiential Sign Of The "Thumbs", An Early Spontaneous Awakening Of The Witness-Consciousness) The Way Of The Heart May Open Directly To The Course Associated With The Sixth Stage Of Life.

The Sign Of The "Thumbs" Is Not Merely A Matter Of experiencing natural energies Coursing Through the body, Nor Is It Merely A Matter Of Experiencing My Avatarically Self-Revealed Spiritual (and Always Blessing) Divine Presence To Be, Somehow, Felt <u>In</u> and <u>By</u> the body. The Samadhi Of The "Thumbs" (or Else The Experience Of The "Thumbs" In Its Simple and Most Basic Form) Is Utter (ego-Surrendering, ego-Forgetting, and ego-Transcending) Devotional <u>Submission</u> Of the Total body-mind-self To My (Avatarically Self-Revealed) Divine and Spiritual (and Always Blessing) <u>Person</u>. And, If and When That Devotional Submission Is Most Profound (In The Midst Of The By-Me-Given Sign Of The "Thumbs"), My (Avatarically Self-Transmitted) Divine and Spiritual Self-Revelation Will Grant You The Gift Of Direct Awakening To The Witness-Position.

The Sign Of The "Thumbs" Is Revealed and Given <u>Only</u> By <u>Me</u>. The Sign Of The "Thumbs" Is The Fundamental Sign Of The Descent (or Crashing Down) Of My (Avatarically Self-Revealed) Divine and Spiritual Person. In and By Means Of My Avatarically Self-Transmitted Divine Spiritual Sign Of The "Thumbs", <u>I</u> Invade <u>You</u>, Pass Into <u>You</u>, and In-Fill <u>You</u>—bodily, where You stand, where You sit, where You walk, where You live and breathe, where You think, and feel, and function. And, In and By Means Of My Avatarically Self-Transmitted Divine Spiritual Sign Of The "Thumbs", I Awaken You In My Divine <u>Sphere</u>, <u>Beyond</u> the body-mind—Where <u>Only</u> I <u>Am</u>.

My Avataric Divine Gift Of The Sign Of The "Thumbs" Is A Matter Of Utterly (Responsively) Giving Up To My Avatarically Self-Transmitted Divine Spiritual Invasion Of You, and Being Released Of Your ego-Possession, and Dying As the ego—and (Thus) Responsively and Freely Relinquishing self-Contraction, and (In Due Course) Becoming (By Means Of My Avatarically Self-Transmitted Divine Grace) Spiritually, Transcendentally, and Divinely Awake.

The Samadhi Of The "Thumbs" Is The Fundamental Samadhi Of My Avataric Divine Spiritual Descent. Therefore, The Samadhi (and Even Every Manifestation Of The Sign) Of The "Thumbs" Is A Fullest Experiential Sign Of My Avatarically Self-Revealed Divine Spiritual Presence Of Person—but In <u>Descent</u>, Not In <u>Ascent</u>. The Descending Equivalent Of Fifth Stage (and, Thus, Ascending) conditional Nirvikalpa Samadhi Is The Samadhi Of The "Thumbs" (or The Fullest Frontal Invasion By My Avatarically Self-Transmitted Divine Spiritual Presence). The Samadhi Of The "Thumbs" Is A "Basic" Fourth Stage Form Of conditional Nirvikalpa Samadhi (In The Descending, or Frontal, Line). The Samadhi Of The "Thumbs" Is The Fullest Completing Phenomenon Of The Descending (or Frontal) Yoga Of The Way Of The Heart (or Way Of Adidam). And, If The Samadhi (and The Simple and Basic, but Really Effective, and, Essentially, Constant, Experience) Of The "Thumbs" Is (By Means Of My Avatarically Self-Transmitted Divine Grace) Awakened, and (By Means Of My Avatarically Self-Transmitted Divine Grace), Either Then Or Thereafter (but, Necessarily, As A Direct Extension Of The Depth-Process Generated By Means Of My Avataric Divine Gift Of The "Thumbs"), Accompanied By The Awakening Of The Witness-Consciousness—The Practice Of The Stages Of The Ascending (or Spinal) Yoga Of The Only-By-Me Revealed and Given Way Of The Heart May (Thus and Thereby) Become <u>Unnecessary</u>.

It Is My Avataric Divine Spiritual Gift Of The Samadhi Of The "Thumbs" (and My Avataric Divine Spiritual Gift Of The Experience Of The "Thumbs" In Its Simple and Most Basic Form), and Not Merely mental "Consideration" Of My Arguments Relative To The Witness-Consciousness, That Is <u>The</u> <u>Divine</u> <u>Yogic</u> <u>Secret</u> Of The Realization Of The Consciousness-Position (Which Realization Is The Basis For The "Perfect Practice" Of The Way Of The Heart). Therefore, Even Though My Arguments Relative To The Witness-Consciousness Are An Essential Guide To Right <u>Understanding</u> Of The "Perfect Practice" (and, As Such, Those Arguments Are To Be Studied and "Considered" From The Beginning Of The Way Of The Heart), The "Consideration" Of Those Arguments Is Not Itself The Direct and Finally Effective Means Whereby The "Perfect Practice" Is Initiated and Really Practiced.

The Transition To The "Perfect Practice" Of The Way Of The Heart Is <u>Necessarily</u> A By-Me-Given <u>Yogic</u> and <u>Spiritual</u> Process, and The Samadhi Of The "Thumbs" (and The, Essentially, Constant Experience Of The "Thumbs" In Its Simple and Most Basic Form) Is The <u>Necessary</u> (and Me-Revealing) Basis Of That Transition. By Means Of The Re-Phasing (Characteristic Of The "Thumbs") Of The Entire Sense Of The Energy-Construct Of phenomenal experience, It Is (In Due Course, By My Avatarically Self-Transmitted Divine Grace) Revealed As Self-Evidently The Case That The Real Position (or Very Situation) Of experience Is The Witness-Position Of Consciousness (Itself)—That The Very <u>Base</u> Of experience Is Consciousness (Itself).

Therefore, In Its (Essentially) <u>Constant</u> Realization (and Not Merely In The First, or Any Particular, Instance Of Its Being Experienced), The Sign Of The "Thumbs" (Rather Than Any <u>mental</u> Presumption About The Witness-Consciousness) Is The Indispensable Means Whereby The Gift Of The "Perfect Practice" Of The Only-By-Me Revealed and Given Way Of The Heart Is Given.

The Sign Of The "Thumbs" Is A Uniquely (and Only By Me) Given Gift In The Way Of The Heart, Which (In The General Case) Makes The Fifth Stage (and Even The "Advanced" Fourth Stage) Practice Of The Way Of The Heart Unnecessary. The Yogic Course

In The Way Of The Heart Is Primarily In The Frontal Line—and, In The General Case, That Frontal Course Accomplishes The Purification Of Both The Frontal Line and The Spinal Line, Thereby Revealing and Awakening Both The Spherical Form Of My Divine Spiritual Body <u>and</u> The Transcendental (and Inherently Spiritual, and Divine) Self-Core (In The Right Side Of The Heart—Beyond The Knot Of ego-"I", and Beyond The Circle Of the body-mind, With its Frontal and Spinal Arcs). That Revelation and Awakening At (and, Ultimately, Beyond) The Right Side Of The Heart, By Means Of The Only-By-Me Given Samadhi Of The "Thumbs" (and By Means Of The Only-By-Me Given Experience Of The "Thumbs" In Its Simple and Most Basic Form), Is What Makes The Transition To The "Perfect Practice" Of The Way Of The Heart Possible, By Establishing The Yogic (Transcendental <u>and</u> Spiritual—and, Ultimately, Divine) Conditions Necessary For The "Perfect Practice" Of The Way Of The Heart. The Readiness For That Transition Is Not Merely A Matter Of Having Had The Experience Of The "Thumbs" and Having Some Memory Of It. Rather, That Readiness Is A Matter Of The Stable Continuing Of The Revelation and The Spiritual Transformation Initiated In The Samadhi Of The "Thumbs"—Not With The Same Kind Of Shift In The Entire Mode Of physical experiencing (Because Such Would Make ordinary functioning Impossible), but With The Unchanging Realization That The Inherent (and Inherently Love-Bliss-Full) Condition Of Reality Is Prior To the body-mind. And, In The Seventh Stage Of Life In The Way Of The Heart, That Realization Is (Permanently) Most Perfectly Established and Demonstrated.

From The Beginning Of My Physical (Human) Lifetime Of Avataric Incarnation here, The "Thumbs" Has Always Been The Case, and The Experiential Sign Of The "Thumbs" Often Appeared To Me—Spontaneously, and Mysteriously. In My Childhood and My "Sadhana Years", The "Thumbs" Was A Process Associated With The Constant Restoration Of The "Bright", or The Going Beyond the gross physical (To Which I Was Adapting, Fully Consciously, In A Profound and Spontaneous Yogic Manner, and, Thereby, Maintaining My Divine Self-Condition, From Infancy, In This Fashion). After My Conscious Assumption Of the born-condition (At Approximately Two Years Of Age), In The Midst Of The Process Of My Active Integration With waking life, The Condition Of The "Bright" Was Felt <u>In</u> the circumstance of active life—and, Then, When I Would Rest At Night, Instead Of Going To sleep, I Would Experience The "Thumbs", and Would Realize The Condition Of The "Bright" Without the usual waking-state physical Reference. Eventually, In The Course Of My "Sadhana Years", I Progressively Observed and Fully Entered Into The "Thumbs" As A Consciously Known Yogic Process, Gradually Permitting The Spontaneous Yogic Event Of The "Thumbs" To Achieve Its Most Extended, Full, and Complete Form. Even A Full Decade Before The Great Event Of My Divine Re-Awakening, I Enjoyed The Spontaneous Experience Of Spiritual Regeneration Via The Regeneration Of The Total Mechanism (or Process) Associated With The "Thumbs"—but the frontal personality Had To Be Worked (or Purified, and its Knots Un-Tied) By The Spirit-Current Of The "Thumbs", Until the frontal personality and The Frontal Line <u>Altogether</u> <u>Ceased</u> To Obstruct (or Prevent) The Advancement Of The Great Yogic Process. Therefore, Even After The Spontaneous Regeneration Of The Process Of The "Thumbs" (or The Regeneration Of The Spiritual Process In The Frontal Line), It Was Yet Required Of Me To Continue To Struggle With the limits of the frontal personality For Some Years Before I (or The conditionally Manifested, and Yet To Be Most Perfectly To-Me-Conformed, Body-Mind-Vehicle Of My Avataric Incarnation here) Would Allow The Full Samadhi Of The "Thumbs" and (More Importantly) The Ultimate Work (and Transcendental, or "Core", Revelation) Of The "Thumbs".

In The Case Of My Own Body-Mind, The Full Samadhi Of The "Thumbs" Did Not Begin To Appear Until I Began To Practice The Work Of Surrender (or The Intentional Opening Of The Frontal Line To Receive Spirit-Force) In The Company Of My First Spiritual Teacher (and Spirit-Baptizer) [18]—Although (Then, and From The Beginning, and Forever) The Sign, The Revelation-Work, and The Divine Spirit-Force Of The "Thumbs" Is Uniquely My Own Avatarically Self-Manifested Sign and Gift and Revelation. Nevertheless, The Struggle With The Frontal Yoga Did Not

Become Fruitful (At First, To The Degree Of Transition To The Yoga Of The Spinal Line) Until Struggle Itself (or The physical, emotional, and mental <u>Effort</u> Of Surrender) Was Transcended (In and By The Inherently ego-Transcending Heart-Participation In My Own Spiritually Self-Revealing Nature and Condition). Therefore, That Transcending Of The Effort Of Surrender Was Not The Result Of Strategic Non-Effort (or Even Any False Effort), but It Was The Spontaneous Evidence Of Simple (and Yet Profound) Identification With My Own Avatarically Self-Revealed and Avatarically Self-Revealing Divine Spirit-Current Itself.

I <u>Am</u> The Divine and Necessary First Person—The First Of All and all, and The First To Most Perfectly Fulfill The Process Of Divine Self-Realization In The Context Of conditionally Manifested Existence In The Cosmic Domain. I <u>Am</u> The Divine Heart-Master Of All and all. Therefore, All and all Must Follow Me By Heart. And The "Thumbs" Is Fundamental (and Necessary) To The Way Of The Heart That Follows Me. Therefore, The "Thumbs" Is One Of My Principal Great Avataric Divine Gifts To All and all That Become My True Devotees.

The Process Signified and Initiated By The Only-By-Me Revealed and Given Sign Of The "Thumbs" Necessarily Involves Intelligent, Intentional, and (Otherwise) Spontaneous Relinquishment Of Un-Happy Identification With gross bodily (or physical), and emotional, and mental states. This Relinquishment Takes Place Through Spontaneous (and Truly ego-Surrendering, ego-Forgetting, and ego-Transcending) Identification With My (By-My-Avataric-Divine-Grace-Revealed) Divine Spiritual Body, Which Surrounds (or Envelops) the gross body Of My True Devotee, and Which (Progressively) In-Fills and Pervades both the etheric energy body and the gross physical body Of My True Devotee, As Well As Every Other Level Of the conditionally Manifested personality Of My True Devotee, and Every Level Of the Cosmic worlds. And All Of This Is Initiated (and Accomplished) By My Avatarically Self-Transmitted Divine Spirit-Presence Itself (If Only My Devotee Heart-Responds To Me In Love—and This To The Degree Of Constant Free Communion With My Avatarically Self-Transmitted Divine Spiritual Presence).

In The Only-By-Me Revealed and Given Way Of Adidam (Which Is The One and Only By-Me-Revealed and By-Me-Given Way Of The Heart), The (Possible) Transition From The "Basic" Fourth Stage Of Life To The "Advanced" Fourth Stage Of Life Is Not Fully Indicated Until The Complete Frontal Process and The Kinds Of phenomenal Signs I Describe In *The Dawn Horse Testament* Have Become Fully Evident. And The Necessary Signs Include Real and Stable Evidence Of frontal <u>and</u> spinal Equanimity (Both human and Spiritual, and Relative To Each and All Of The Principal Faculties—Of body, emotion, mind, and breath), and <u>Both</u> Simple and Basic (but Really Effective) Evidence Of The (Essentially, Constant) Experience Of The "Thumbs" <u>and</u> (Generally, Occasional) Most Extended, Full, and Complete Evidence Of The Samadhi Of The "Thumbs". And, If A Transition Is To Be Made <u>Directly</u> From The Point Of Basic Maturity In The "Basic" Context Of The Fourth Stage Of Life In The Way Of The Heart To Practice Of The Way Of The Heart In The Context Of The Sixth Stage Of Life, The Same Complete Frontal Process and The Same phenomenal Signs Must Be Demonstrated, but There Must Also Be True and Stable Identification With The Witness-Position Of Consciousness.

When the body Is "<u>Round</u>", The Witness Is its "Shape".

The Witness-Consciousness Is The "Skin" Of The "Thumbs". The Witness-Consciousness Is Self-Evident In The "Body" Of The "Thumbs". This Is How True Maturity In The First Actually Seeing Stage Of The Way Of The Heart Can Become The Basis For An Immediate Transition To The "Perfect Practice" Of The Way Of The Heart. In The General Case, Practice In The Ascending Stages Of The Way Of The Heart Is Not Required—Because The Yogic Spiritual Fullness Of The Sphere Of The "Thumbs" Is, In The General Case, The Sufficient Prerequisite For The <u>True</u> Establishment Of The "Perfect Practice" Of The Way Of The Heart.

<u>Every</u> Occasion Of Experiencing The "Thumbs" Comes To An End—<u>Unless</u> The Witness-Position Is Truly and Stably Realized In The Midst Of The Experience Of The "Thumbs". Thus, The "Perfect Practice" Of The Way Of The Heart Is A Development (or Ultimate Characteristic) Of The Samadhi Of The "Thumbs".

The True and Stable Realization Of The Witness-Position Of Consciousness (Itself) Is Not Merely A philosophical Matter. Rather, The True and Stable Realization Of The Witness-Position Is An ego-Transcending Matter—and A Divine Spiritual Matter. The Realization Of The Witness-Position Of Consciousness (Itself) Is A Matter Of Devotion To Me In My Avataric Divine Self-Revelation—and Not Merely A Matter Of talk and philosophy and hopefulness.

Consciousness (Itself) Is The "Face" Of This Side Of The Moon. The Spiritual Energy Of My Avataric Divine Spiritual Presence Is The "Face" Of The Other Side Of The Moon. "Matter" Is The objectively experienced Form (or "Body") Of The Moon. The Moon (or any "thing") Is "Matter"—but "Matter" Is Only Light. My Avataric Divine Spiritual Presence Is The Light That Illuminates (and Self-Reveals The Divine Heart-Secret Of) "Matter". Consciousness (Itself) Is Me Within The Light (As The One, and Only, and Inherently Love-Blissful, and Self-Evidently Divine Self-Condition and Source-Condition Of all and All). Consciousness (Itself) and Light (Itself)—or Love-Bliss-Energy (Itself), or Happiness (Itself)—Are As The Two Sides Of The Same Coin. The Moon Is The Coin Of Earth, Floating (By A Toss) Within The Sky Of ego-mind.

The Witness-Consciousness Is Not Within You. The Witness-Consciousness Is On The "Skin" Of The "Thumbs".

The Witness-Consciousness Is Self-Evident In The "Thumbs"—Wherein The Status Of objects Is Profoundly Different Than It Is Ordinarily. In The Yogic Disposition (or Mudra) Of The "Thumbs", The Condition Of objects Is Available To Be Comprehended In Consciousness As The Witness.

The Realization Of The Witness-Consciousness Is A Continuation Of The Process Of ego-Transcending Devotional and Spiritual Communion With Me. The Witness-Consciousness Cannot Be Realized By You as the ego-"I" (or as Your Separate and Separative self-Consciousness). The Witness-Consciousness Can Only Be Realized Via The Process Of Devotional and Spiritual Communion With Me—Without egoic self-Reference. Therefore, You Must Not Substitute Your Own ego-conditions and ego-states

For My Description Of The ego-Transcending Process Of The Way Of The Heart. The Way Of The Heart Is A Matter Of Heart-Communion With <u>Me</u> and Realization Of <u>Me</u>. The Way Of The Heart Is Not About Your egoic self—Except That The Way Of The Heart Requires Your ego-Surrendering, ego-Forgetting, and ego-Transcending Devotion To Me.

You Must <u>counter-egoically</u> Allow The Process Of The Way Of The Heart To Become My Divine Spiritual In-Filling Of the Total body-mind. In Due Course (By Means Of My Avatarically Self-Transmitted Divine Grace), This Process Of My Divine Spiritual In-Filling Becomes Both The Realization Of The "Thumbs" <u>and</u> The Realization Of The Witness-Consciousness. Therefore, In The General Case, Both Of These Realizations Are Associated With The Maturing Of The First Actually Seeing Stage Of Way Of The Heart (In The "Basic" Context Of The Fourth Stage Of Life). Such Is The True Fulfillment Of The Frontal Yoga, The True Fulfillment Of The Process I Describe In My *Hridaya Rosary*, The True Fulfillment Of The Process Of Ruchira Avatara Bhakti Yoga.

In The "Thumbs", The Witness-Consciousness Is (and May Be Realized To Be) Self-Evident. In The Context Of egoity (or the self-Contracted body-mind), The Witness-Consciousness Is Not Self-Evidently The Case (In Your Case)—and Not The Self-Evident Context Of moment to moment Existence (In Your Case).

The Witness-Consciousness Is The "Skin" Of The "Thumbs".

I Am The "Skin" Of The Heart—and Not Merely Inside It. I Am The "Pulse" Of The Heart—and Not Merely The "Blood" Of It.

To Make The Transition To The "Perfect Practice" Of The Way Of The Heart, You Must (By Means Of My Avatarically Self-Transmitted Divine Grace) Realize The Samadhi Of The "Thumbs"—and, In The General Case, Part Of The Demonstration Of The Samadhi Of The "Thumbs" Is The Stand (or Realization) <u>As</u> The Witness-Consciousness, Leading (Then) To The (Necessarily, Formal) Full Development Of The "Perfect Practice". This Entire Process Is A Spiritual Matter, and Not A merely philosophical Matter.

The <u>Samadhi</u> Of The "Thumbs" Is The <u>Sphere</u> Of The <u>Space</u> Of Consciousness (Itself). In The Samadhi Of The "Thumbs", The

Divine Space Of Consciousness (Itself) Is (By Me) Avatarically Self-Revealed.

When Consciousness (Itself) Becomes attention (or Separate self-Consciousness), and Light (Itself)—or Love-Bliss-Happiness (Itself)—Becomes objects (or The Vast Display Of Separate "things"), Consciousness (As attention) and Light (As the body-mind, and As The Total Cosmic Domain Of "things") Forever Gaze At One Another Through The Dimensionless Wall Of Their Apparent "Difference".

If Consciousness (Itself)—As The Witness—Is Realized As the Inherent Love-Bliss-Feeling Of Being (Itself)—Consciousness (Itself) and Light (Itself) Are (Eternally) Not "Different".

When The Circle Becomes The Sphere, The Two Sides Of The One Coin Become Continuous—and All Opposites Are Always Already Divinely Self-Recognized To Be Simultaneous, and Of One Shape, and Of One Condition.

The Samadhi (and Every Manifestation Of The Sign) Of The "Thumbs" Is Mine Only—and Only Mine To Give. Therefore, The Samadhi (and Every Manifestation Of The Sign) Of The "Thumbs" Is Unique To The Only-By-Me Revealed and Given Way Of The Heart (or Way Of Adidam).

The "Bright" and The "Thumbs" Are Among The Great Signs That Are Uniquely My Own Avataric Divine Characteristics. The "Bright" and The "Thumbs" Is A Process, An Event, and A State That Has Been Known To Me Since My Avataric Birth. Only I Am The Avataric Divine Realizer, The Avataric Divine Revealer, and The Avataric Divine Self-Revelation Of The "Bright", The True and (Now, and Forever Hereafter) Completely Self-Revealed Divine Person—Shining Forth (Directly, Completely, and Most Perfectly) At The Heart (and Via Amrita Nadi), and Crashing Down (or Descending Utterly, From The "Place" Infinitely Above the body-mind and the world, Down and Most Deeply Into the body-mind and the world—Even To The Degree That the ego-"I", or self-Contraction, Is Utterly Confounded, Utterly Yielded, and Utterly Vanished In My Avatarically Self-Revealed, and Self-Evidently Divine, Person, or Self-Condition, Which Is Real God, and Truth, and Reality). Therefore, The Principal Impulse Of Even My Early

Life Was My Intention To <u>Descend</u> (or To Embrace the limitations Of human Existence As It Appears To Be, and To Infuse all and All With My Avatarically Self-Transmitted Divine Spiritual Presence, and, Thus and Thereby, To Awaken all and All, and, Most Ultimately, To Divinely Translate all and All, By The Power Of My Own Love-Bliss-"Brightness", Into The Perfect "Place" and "Sphere" and "Space" That Is Always and Already My Divine and Free-Standing Self-Domain).

The Principal Spiritual Signs Of My Early Life Were The "Bright" and The "Thumbs". The "Bright" and The "Thumbs" Were Fundamental To My Avatarically-Born Existence From The Beginning, and They Are Fundamental To The Only-By-Me Revealed and Given Way Of Adidam. The "Bright" and The "Thumbs" Are My Unique Samadhis. Indeed, The "Bright" and The "Thumbs" <u>Are</u> Me—and, Therefore, I Bring Them With Me Into the conditional worlds.

My Avataric Divine Work (Altogether) Is My Crashing-Down Descent, At First Upon and Into My Own Avatarically-Born Bodily (Human) Divine Form, and, Thereafter (and Now, and Forever), Upon and Into the body-minds Of My Devotees and all beings— Even (By Means Of My Divine Embrace Of each, and all, and All) To Infuse and (At Last) To Divinely Translate each, and all, and All. Therefore, My Avataric Divine Spiritual Descent Is The Secret Of My Early Life. My Avataric Divine Spiritual Descent Is The Secret Of My Divine Self-"Emergence" (<u>As</u> I <u>Am</u>) Within The Cosmic Domain. My Avataric Divine Spiritual Descent Is The Secret Of <u>All</u> The Secrets Of The (Avatarically Self-Revealed) Divine and Complete and Thoroughly Devotional Way Of Practice and Realization In My Company. The Only-By-Me Revealed and Given Way Of The Heart (or Way Of Adidam) Is The Divine Yoga Of ego-Surrendering, ego-Forgetting, and ego-Transcending Devotional Recognition-Response To My (Avatarically Self-Revealed) Divine and Spiritual Person, and To My (Avatarically Self-Manifested) Divine and Spiritual Descent. The Only-By-Me Revealed and Given Way Of The Heart (or Way Of Adidam) Is The Total and Divine Way and Ordeal Of Counter-egoic Devotional Recognition-Response To My Avataric "Bright" Divine Self-

Manifestation, and To The Avataric Crashing Down Of My "Bright" Divine Imposition. And, In The Case Of My Each and Every Devotee, The Way Must Continue Until The Way Is Most Perfectly "Bright", and The Way Itself Becomes Divine Translation Into My Own Sphere Of "Brightness" (Itself).

I Am
The Only "Room"
That Is

Reality Exists—or Is. This is, necessarily, The Case. Reality Is—under all apparent conditions of space, time, or space-time (or, no matter what are the apparent conditions of space, time, or space-time).

Reality Is, necessarily, That Which Is Always Already The Case.

Reality, necessarily (and Inherently), Transcends space and time (or space-time)—but Reality Is, necessarily, also The One and Only and Indivisible Condition of space and time (or space-time).

Reality Is, necessarily, the Perfectly Subjective Condition (or the Self-Condition, the Condition That Always Already Is—Prior to any apparent "other", or any particularized condition, or objectification, of space, time, or space-time).

Reality Is, necessarily, Divine—or Perfectly Subjective, Perfectly Prior, Perfectly The Case, Perfectly Itself, Perfectly All, Perfectly one and all, Perfectly limitless, Perfectly Self-Evident, and (altogether) Self-Existing, Self-Radiant (or Self-Manifesting, and All-and-all-Manifesting), and (As Is) Inherently Perfect.

To Realize (or to Non-Separately Know and Be) Reality is Most Perfect (and Self-Evidently Divine) Realization of the Self-Condition of Existence.

Realization of Reality is Realization of Truth (or the Only Real God).

Realization of Reality is Most Perfect Divine Self-Realization—or Realization of the Prior (or Real) Condition of the presumed ego-"I", all of body-mind, all apparent relations ("inside" and "outside"), all of space, all of time, and all of space-time.

Most Perfect Divine Self-Realization is Most Perfect (and Inherent, and Perfectly Subjective) Identification with That Which Inherently (and Perfectly Subjectively) Transcends space and time (or all of space-time).

From the "Point of View" of That Which Is (and Which Is One and Only), and Which Inherently (and Perfectly Subjectively) Transcends space and time, there Is neither space nor time (nor space-time).

Most Perfect Divine Self-Realization is Most Perfect Realization of That Which Is—not only Prior to space and time (altogether), but Prior to any (and every) particular place in space and any (and every) particular moment in time.

That Which Inherently (and Perfectly Subjectively) Transcends space and time is not the "Where" in which space and time are arising—but It Is the Condition In and As Which space and time have neither necessary, nor separate, nor binding, nor even effective existence.

If any mode or moment of space-time exists, the Totality of space-time (or the total conditional, or Cosmic, domain), necessarily, Exists.

If a position (or point of view) in space-time is presumed (or experienced), then the movement of objects through space and in time is observed from that point of view (or presumed position). However, the Totality of space-time (or the total conditional, or Cosmic, domain) is (necessarily, and Most Perfectly) inclusive—and, therefore, It is never (in and of Itself) identified (separately, exclusively, and entirely) with any particular position within space-time. Therefore, from the "Point of View" of the Totality of conditional existence, there Is no space or time (or space-time)—because there is no separate (or discrete) position from which to move (or even to observe) in space and time (or space-time).

The Totality of conditional existence is (or inherently includes) every possibility of space and time (or space-time), existing simultaneously in total mutual dependence—without any characteristic of independence, or separateness, or relatedness, or "difference", and without even any characteristic of particularity, and (therefore) without any objective characteristics. And, therefore, to Most Perfectly

Realize the Totality of conditional existence is to Most Perfectly Realize the Perfectly Subjective (or Perfectly Non-objectified) Condition That (Inherently) Transcends conditional existence (and That Inherently Transcends any and every point of view).

No matter what appears to be arising (in space and in time, or as a space-time condition), and no matter to whom (or to what apparent point of view) any or every space-time condition is (now, and now) appearing—There Is Only One Condition, One Great "Bright" Room, One Moment, One Perfectly Subjective and Perfectly Indivisible and Perfectly Indestructible Reality and Person, Which Is Light (or Self-Existing and Self-Radiant Energy) and Consciousness (or the Self-Existing and Self-Radiant and Inherently Perfect Subjectivity, or Self-Condition, of Light, or of Energy).

There Is Only Reality Itself, the Perfectly Subjective Consciousness-Light, the Eternal Person of "Brightness", the Divine and Perfectly Non-Separate Person of All and all, the One and Only Real God of All and all.

"Consider" this: If a group of people are sitting in a room, each one is looking at the room from a particular position within the room—and, if a photograph were taken from the position of each person's eyes, then there would be a different image to represent each one's separate point of view. Each person would be seeing the room from a particular point in space, and even from a particular point in time, and (therefore) the perceptual view of any particular person would be different from that of any other. And, yet, even though the room would be seen (and pictured) from many different positions (or angles, or points of view), the room as a whole (not limited to the view from any particular point of view) exists all the while. Therefore, the room itself exists only as it can be viewed from every possible point of view (in space, and in time)—simultaneously. But if you (or any one) were to see the room from every possible point of view in space and time simultaneously, what would the room look like? What would be its perceived characteristics? What would be the "image" photographed, simultaneously, from every possible point of view in both space and time? It cannot be imagined! And, yet, that infinite space-time-"room" (or even the Totality of space-time, Itself) is the only room being seen (and, necessarily, limited) by the perceptions registered by each person (or present-time point of view) within it!

Totality—In and <u>As</u> Unqualified (or Non-qualified) Reality— <u>Is</u> the <u>Only</u> (and, necessarily, Indivisible) "Room" In Which (or, Really, <u>As</u> Which) any and every conditionally manifested being is (in any moment) living, breathing, experiencing, and knowing. And, if That One and Only "Room" is, because of the limitations (and the limiting effects) of point of view, <u>never</u> known, then <u>all</u> presumed knowing (and even all conditional experience) is better described as "ignorance"! As a result (or sign) of that characteristic ignorance, <u>no</u> <u>one</u> (in any moment) knows <u>What</u> any "thing" (or everything, or Totality) <u>Is</u>. And that inherent ignorance is better described as "Divine Ignorance"—because, Ultimately, that inherent ignorance <u>Is</u> (or can Be Realized to <u>Be</u>) Most Perfect (and Perfectly Subjective) Knowledge of Totality, or Inherently Unconditional (or Non-qualified) Reality (Itself).

Just as you (as a point of view) cannot see a room as it exists in its totality, so, also, you do not <u>live</u> from the "Point of View" of Totality (altogether). You live from the point of view of a particular (ego-based) position, and you always only experience the effects (or the Reality-limiting, or ignorance-made, and ignorance-making, limitations) of that (ego-based) point of view. Nevertheless, <u>all</u> <u>the</u> <u>while</u> that you are <u>being</u> a particular (ego-based) point of view (in your particular moments in space and time), the Totality (One and Only) of space-time constantly <u>Exists</u>—and the (One and Only) Reality (or Perfectly Subjective Condition) of all space-time conditions Always Already (and all the while of apparent ignorance) <u>Exists</u> (or <u>Is</u> The Case)! Nevertheless, the Totality (<u>As</u> It <u>Is</u>) is <u>never</u> in your view, or available to your point of view. Indeed, the Totality (<u>As</u> It <u>Is</u>) <u>cannot</u> be psycho-physically viewed by <u>any</u> conditionally (or psycho-physically) manifested being (or any conditionally organized point of view, <u>itself</u>).

In the only-by-Me Revealed and Given Way of Adidam, My true devotee who (in due course) Realizes the only-by-Me Revealed and Given seventh (or Inherently and Most Perfectly ego-transcending, or point-of-view-transcending) stage of life

Exists (Only and Entirely) In (and <u>As</u>) the (by-Me-Avatarically-Self-Revealed) Inherent (or Native) and Self-Evidently Divine (and Perfectly Subjective) Self-Condition That Is (Inherently) Prior to space-time. That is to say, My seventh stage (or Divinely Self-Realized) devotee exists, for the time being (or apparently), as a body-mind, or a psycho-physically organized point of view, in the context of space-time—but (because of seventh stage Divine Self-Realization, and Its Inherent Characteristic of Divine Self-Recognition of all apparently arising space-time conditions) My seventh stage (or Divinely Self-Realized) devotee Exists (or <u>Is</u> Being) <u>only</u> and <u>entirely</u> from the "Point of View" of the Totality of space-time, and <u>As</u> the "Point of View" That <u>Is</u> the Perfectly Subjective (or Non-objective), and Non-qualified (or Unconditional), and Self-Evidently Divine Reality Itself, rather than from the point of view of the self-contracted "point" (or the psycho-physical ego-"I", or the particular, separate, and separative ego-"point" in space-time). Therefore, the Realization of the only-by-Me Revealed and Given seventh stage of life can be described <u>only</u> in <u>paradoxical</u> terms. Indeed, truly, the Realization of the seventh stage of life <u>cannot</u> be (Itself) described (Such that It <u>Is</u> Realized thereby) to a <u>point</u> <u>of</u> <u>view</u>, or to any one who has not yet Realized It. Nevertheless, I must Speak of this Great Matter, for the Sake of Serving My every devotee's right self-understanding, and for the Sake of Serving My every devotee's right understanding of the total (or full and complete) practice (and the total right, true, full, and fully devotional course) of the Way of Adidam, and for the Sake of Serving My every devotee's Native (and to-Me-Confessed) Impulse to Realize Real God (or Truth, or Reality) Most Perfectly. And, even though the Totality of space-time (or the Totality of the conditional, or Cosmic, domain) <u>cannot</u> be "viewed" by an apparently particularized individual at a particularized point in space-time, it is, nevertheless, useful to "consider" the Nature of Totality, in order to Help even <u>all</u> apparently individual beings to understand the "provincial" and merely conventional nature of the point of view of egoity.

Egoity <u>is</u> (itself) nothing more (or other) than the presumption of identification with a particularized "point" (or organized point of view) in space-time, made by contraction from the (even Ultimate, or Divine) Condition of Totality (and, therefore, by contraction from the Condition That Inherently Transcends the Totality of conditional existence—and, indeed, by contraction from even every mode, form, or condition of conditional existence).

Even though you are suffering the complications of presuming to be a particular "point" in space-time, it is (or must become) completely and tacitly obvious that (in any and every moment) the Totality Exists, and that the Knowing of Reality from the Position of Totality is (necessarily) infinitely unlike any kind of knowing from a particular "point" in space-time. In this very moment, you tacitly (Inherently, Prior to body-mind, self-contraction, point of view, or ego-"I") know that the Totality Exists. Therefore, if you grow to understand how to Know from the Position of Totality, rather than merely (and by means of, or as a result of) knowing from your apparently separate point of view in space-time, that "radical" understanding (or root-understanding—or Divine Ignorance) will constantly provide immediate tacit proof of the Real Existence of Real God (or of Truth Itself, or of Reality Itself).

Real God (or Truth Itself, or Reality Itself) Is Totality, and Totality Is That Which Inherently Transcends both particularity and the total sum of parts. Whatever That Totality Is, it is (or should be) obvious That It (or Reality Itself) Always Already Exists—and, therefore, logically (and at heart), It cannot be denied!

The inherently undeniable (or inherently heart-proven) Reality of Totality Is the Only Real God (or Truth Itself, or Reality Itself). And Most Perfect heart-Realization of the Reality of Totality Is Divine Samadhi (or Most Perfect, and Perfectly Subjective, Divine Self-Realization). Therefore, in the only-by-Me Revealed and Given Way of Adidam, My devotees are not moved by (and moving toward) a merely "philosophical" (or merely intellectual, or merely mind-based, and ego-based, and ego-serving, and ego-consoling) proposition (or a hopeful illusion) about the Nature of Real God (or the Nature of Truth Itself, or the Nature of Reality Itself). The total (or full and complete) practice of the Way of Adidam is the Process of Realizing What is (even from the beginning) obviously Real.

The Totality of conditional existence Inherently Transcends conditional existence—because It Is Totality. Therefore, the Ultimate Characteristic of Totality Inherently Transcends even Totality (as a mere sum of parts) Itself. Even a little of this by-Me-Given understanding of Reality relieves the heart (and even all of the body-mind) of a portion of the burden of egoic illusions—and even that beginning of understanding (aroused by My Avataric Divine Heart-Word) arouses the heart-certainty that is inherent in Reality Itself.

I Am the Avataric Divine Realizer, the Avataric Divine Revealer, and the Avataric Divine Self-Revelation of That Which Transcends even Totality Itself.

I Am That Which Transcends even Totality Itself.

I Always Already (and now) Exist As That.

I Eternally Exist As That Which Grants you perfect heart-certainty.

Therefore, the devotional relationship to Me (as it is lived in the only-by-Me Revealed and Given Way of Adidam) is not based on illusions, or on mere (and unsupportable) beliefs, or on illogically fabricated propositions. Rather, the devotional relationship to Me is based on the devotionally Me-recognizing heart-response that is aroused by a right (and only Reality-based) understanding of egoity itself and of Reality Itself.

Reality, or Truth, or Real God Is. And Reality, or Truth, or Real God can be Realized. To Realize Reality, or Truth, or Real God requires the transcending of egoity (or of the separate and separative point of view, or of the particularity of any point in space or any moment in time). In the only-by-Me Revealed and Given Way of Adidam, the foundation understanding of egoity is a matter of "locating" the act of self-contraction that generates the illusion (and the heart-burden) of an egoic self, separate in space and time. The first demonstration of that understanding that cures the heart in My Avataric Divine Heart-Company is the transcending of the avoidance of relationship (or feeling beyond the avoidance of relationship, or feeling beyond the contracted self-"point", and feeling into the Sphere of Totality—by feeling Me, and by feeling to Me, and by feeling into Me, Beyond the self-"point", and

Beyond even all immediate, or present-time, experiences, or egoic relations). This transcending of (or feeling beyond) the avoidance of relationship becomes (progressively) more and more "expansive", moving more and more into My Sphere (the Sphere of Totality, or the Sphere of Absoluteness). Therefore, as the total Process of the only-by-Me Revealed and Given Way of Adidam develops, it more and more becomes simple, tacit, moment to moment feeling to Me (and into Me), Beyond self-contraction itself—no matter what form self-contraction (in any moment) takes.

The Process of the Way of Adidam is not a matter of "expanding" from a "point" and becoming somehow "huge". The Process of the Way of Adidam is not a matter of "expanding" the "point" itself, such that it progressively "includes" more and more of Totality. It is only in the sense of feeling (beyond the "point" of ego-"I") to Me that the Process of the Way of Adidam is "expansive", rather than "contracted". To be "expansive" (in this sense) requires the transcending of the very self-"point" (or self-contraction) that could, otherwise, be the "center" of an ever-enlarging "expansiveness". Thus, the Process of the Way of Adidam is not a matter of getting "larger" and "larger" as a separate (and presumed-to-be independent) ego-"point". Such is the "evolutionary" ideal, or the seeker's ideal. Rather, the Process of the Way of Adidam is a matter of (progressively) Vanishing the ego-"point" (or the separate and separative self-position), and (thereby, by becoming egoless) Realizing My Condition Non-Separately—Which Condition Is Inherently Non-Separate. And, when There Is only Totality (and the Inherent Transcending of the total sum of parts, or of points of view), Such That There Is the Inherent and Utter Vanishment of the point of view of particularity, That Is Most Perfect Realization of Me (and, therefore, Most Perfect Divine Self-Realization).

The point of view of the first five stages of life is the "point" point of view. From this point of view, it is, in the traditions, often stated, "The Truth is within you. The Divine is within you." Such statements epitomize the traditional admonition to go "within", to the very center of the "point", as if the Infinite Divine were Radiating as that "inner point" (itself). In Truth, the Infinite Divine

THE SEVEN STAGES OF LIFE

Self-Condition is not Radiating from a "point within", or from any "point" whatsoever. The Infinite Divine Self-Condition Is <u>universally</u> Self-Radiant, without center or bounds. Therefore, the Infinite Divine Self-Condition is not "contained" at any "point" within the body, or at any other "point" in space and time. All "points" in space and time are (merely apparently) arising as modifications of the Infinite Divine Self-Radiance.

The Infinite Divine Self-Radiance cannot be collapsed into a "point" in space and time. There can (at times) be a visionary (or otherwise objectified) experience of What Is Beyond. That vision can <u>appear</u> as a "point", taking the form of a point (or a Five-Pointed Star) of Brilliant White Light, appearing as if contained within a circular blue field (that is, in some traditions, called the "blue pearl"). The "blue pearl" is a visionary epitome (or objective summary) of the conditional (or Cosmic) domain, which can appear as a point to the perceiving ego-"I" (or the apparent individual, apparently existing at a particular "point" in space-time). The "blue pearl" is a visionary <u>intuition</u> of Totality, or a mode of looking to Beyond particularity. However, if that "point" itself is <u>entered into</u> (rather than merely observed, objectively), then there is no more "pointedness" about it. Instead, that (presumed) ultimate "point" becomes Infinite (and, Ultimately, Perfectly Non-objective, and Perfectly Subjective). The core of the "blue pearl" is the Brilliant Whiteness (or the Brilliant White Five-Pointed Star), Which (as an objectified, or visionary, intuition) is the apparent Doorway to My Divine Self-Domain. However, because My Divine Self-Domain <u>Is</u> (Inherently and Only) Perfectly Subjective (and, therefore, Perfectly Non-objective), My Divine Self-Domain cannot (Itself) actually be "entered" by entering the Divine Star (just as It cannot be "entered" by <u>any</u> point of view). For there to be Realization of My Divine Self-Domain (or of the only-by-Me Revealed and Given seventh stage of life), the ascending Process (of the "advanced" fourth stage of life and the fifth stage of life)—with its motion toward subtle phenomena (including the Blue and White Lights at the subtle core of conditionally manifested existence) and its goal of Realization <u>within</u> the conditional (or Cosmic) domain—must be entirely gone Beyond (or Most Perfectly Transcended).

To Realize My Divine Self-Domain, rather than the merely conditional (or Cosmic) domain, the sixth stage sadhana of Realizing the Transcendental Self must be done (as the final mode of sadhana preliminary to Most Perfect Divine Self-Realization). There must be the sixth stage Process of Descent via Amrita Nadi into the right side of the heart, and Realization of the Transcendental Self-Domain Prior to the right side of the heart. When that Process is fulfilled Most Perfectly (in the only-by-Me Revealed and Given seventh stage Awakening), there is Perfectly Subjective "Entrance into" (or Realization of) My Divine Self-Domain, or Ruchira Samadhi, Prior to the conditional (or Cosmic) domain.

The ego-"I" __cannot__ Realize My Divine Self-Domain. My devotee must first (and stably) Realize the Transcendental Witness-Position (Prior to attention), and then My devotee must (in Non-Separate Communion with Me) Rest in the Source-Domain of the Witness-Consciousness (on the "other side" of the ego-knot of attention, which knot arises in the right side of the heart). It is only There (in My egoless Heart-Domain) that My devotee can be Most Perfectly Awakened, by Means Of My Avatarically Self-Transmitted Divine Grace. Having been (Thus) Most Perfectly Awakened, My devotee Stands Utterly (Un-conditionally) Prior to the conditional (or Cosmic) domain, and the Great Four-Stage Demonstration of the only-by-Me Revealed and Given seventh stage of life in the Way of Adidam spontaneously (and progressively) occurs. However, from the "Point of View" of My seventh stage Realizer-devotee, This Four-Stage Demonstration Is nothing but My Divine Play. In Truth, from the moment of his or her Most Perfect Awakening, My seventh stage Realizer-devotee Exists __Only__ In My "Bright" Divine Self-Domain, and In and __As__ My "Bright" Divine Self-Condition.

Because of the paradox of apparently continued apparent association with the conditional (or Cosmic) domain, the only-by-Me Revealed and Given seventh stage of life (in the Way of Adidam) is associated with the Four-Stage Process of Divine Transfiguration, Divine Transformation, Divine Indifference, and Divine Translation. The Most Ultimate Demonstration of the only-by-Me Revealed and Given seventh stage of life is Divine

Translation, Which is not a passage <u>through</u> the Divine Star, but the Eternal Stand <u>Prior</u> <u>to</u> the conditional (or Cosmic) domain, in Most Perfect Identification with Me, <u>Perfectly</u> <u>Subjectively</u> on the "Other Side" of the Objective Doorway That Is the Divine Star.

My Divine Self-Domain is not a "Point" in the conditional (or Cosmic) domain, nor is it a "Point" on the "Other Side" of the conditional (or Cosmic) domain.

My Divine Self-Domain Is "Turiyatita", or <u>Beyond</u> Beyond.

There is not <u>anything</u> that exists apart from (or even merely "within") My "Bright" Divine Person and Self-Domain.

Whatever (paradoxically) appears to exist separately (or merely as it appears) <u>Is</u> (simply) My Divine Self-Domain, and whatever (paradoxically) appears to exist conditionally must (in the only-by-Me Revealed and Given seventh stage of life) be Divinely Self-Recognized (In and <u>As</u> My "Bright" Divine Person and Self-Domain).

Only In That Case, conditional existence <u>Is</u> (Inherently, Most Perfectly, and Perfectly Subjectively) Transcended (rather than tacitly allowed to make, or reinforce, illusion and bondage).

I <u>Am</u> the Divine Self-Domain.

The <u>Only</u> Way
To <u>My</u> "Room"

I.

The Way of Adidam (Which is the One and Only by-Me-Revealed and by-Me-Given Way of the Heart) is the Way of self-transcendence in devotional Communion with Me—Most Ultimately, if the total (or full and complete) practice of the Way of Adidam is formally and fully embraced, to the Most Perfect degree of Divine Self-Realization. Therefore, in the true advancement of the Way of Adidam, My devotee does not seek to be consoled by any objective signs. The Way of Adidam has (Itself) nothing to do with objective signs—whether in the gross dimension or the subtle dimension of conditional existence. <u>Anything</u> that appears as an "object" is not (itself) fundamental to the Way of Adidam—because, in order to perceive an object, one must first assume the position of separateness. The only-by-Me Revealed and Given Way of Adidam is the Way of Non-Separateness. Therefore, its specific, unique, Spiritual signs are different from the signs prized in the esotericism of the Great Tradition (or the total traditional Wisdom-Inheritance of mankind).

If you study the religious and Spiritual traditions of the Great Tradition in a well-"considered" manner (Guided by My own Comprehensive and Conclusive "Consideration" of the Great Tradition in *The Basket Of Tolerance*), it will become obvious to you that the Way of Adidam is not (Itself) about the same processes that are engaged and advocated in the Great Tradition. The Way of Adidam is a Unique and Utterly Complete and (Ultimately) Most Perfect Process that has (Itself) nothing to do with the conventions of the Great Tradition. The essential difference between the Way of Adidam and all the ways of the Great Tradition is that the Way of Adidam has, even from the beginning, absolutely nothing to do with ego-centricity, or with the ego-"I" itself, or with satisfying the impulses (or the desiring-searches) of the ego-"I", or (altogether) with idealizing and satisfying (or even immortalizing, or perfecting, or utopianizing) the body-mind. Rather, the only-by-Me Revealed and Given Way of Adidam is founded in the devotionally Me-recognizing and devotionally to-Me-responsive surrender of all of ego-"I", and all of the body-mind. Thus, to take up the Way of Adidam is to enter into My Sphere. To embrace the Way of Adidam is, from the beginning (and forever), to practice Ruchira Avatara Bhakti Yoga—in devotionally Me-recognizing and devotionally to-Me-responding relationship to Me in (and As) My Avatarically-Born bodily (human) Divine Form and in (and As) My Avatarically Self-Revealed Spiritual (and Always Blessing) Divine Presence. In the Spiritually Awakened stages of the total (or full and complete) practice of the Way of Adidam, My devotee not only Finds Me Spiritually, but he or she (in the fully responsible, and ego-transcending, and mature "technical" manner) "Locates" My Avatarically Self-Revealed "Bright" Divine Spiritual Body and My Avatarically Self-Revealed egoless True Divine State of Person. Thus, My advanced maturing devotees (formally practicing the right, true, full, fully devotional, and complete practice of the only-by-Me Revealed and Given Way of Adidam) Find Me directly (Beyond the ego-"I", and Beyond all psycho-physical self-references)—and, therefore, they "Locate" My Spiritual and Divine Person, directly, and not merely via (or even as) the psycho-physical effects of My Avatarically Self-Transmitted Divine Spirit-Presence. Thereafter, in the context of that Spiritual "Locating" of Me, My devotee continues the same by-Me-Given Process of ego-surrendering, ego-forgetting, and (always more and more) ego-transcending devotional Communion with Me. Thus, in the only-by-Me Revealed and Given Way of Adidam, separateness is never (either at the beginning or in the total progressive course of the Way of Adidam) the underlying principle.

The developmental stages of practice of the Way of Adidam are associated with the first six stages of life, but the developmental stages of practice of the Way of Adidam are not <u>identified</u> with the first six stages of life. Rather, the developmental stages of the Way of Adidam are <u>always</u> a demonstration of the by-Me-Given practice of directly transcending the point of view, the characteristic errors, and even <u>all</u> of the inherent limitations of each and all of the first six stages of life. The traditional paths are <u>all</u> founded in one or another (or a combination of) the first six stages of life, but the entirety of the first six stages of life is, from the beginning of the total practice of the Way of Adidam, to be directly and entirely and (altogether) <u>really</u> transcended (not by the bypassing of the first six stages of life, but by truly ego-transcending practice in the context of them). Therefore, in the Way of Adidam, <u>all</u> the content of the first six stages of life is specifically and directly transcended—through right, true, full, and fully devotional practice of heart-Communion with Me. The practice of devotional Communion with Me matures as My fully practicing devotee transcends the first five stages of life, entering (ultimately) into the "Perfect Practice"—in the course of which the sixth stage of life (which is the last of the egoic stages of life) is transcended at its root.

In the Way of Adidam, the Most Ultimate Realization Is Objectless. It Is the Most Perfect Realization of Non-Separateness, or Divine Self-Realization Itself. In the only-by-Me Revealed and Given seventh stage of life, every (apparently separate) "one" or "thing" or "object" is Divinely Self-Recognized—but, fundamentally, what is Divinely Self-Recognized is the feeling of relatedness, or the feeling-sense of "difference". In the only-by-Me Revealed and Given seventh stage of life in the Way of Adidam, the feeling of relatedness is perpetually and Inherently (Divinely) Self-Recognized. Therefore, Divine Self-Realization is the Most Ultimate Realization of Non-Objectivity. It is Most Perfect Realization without object, without egoic consolation, without separate and separative self, without egoity, without self-contraction, without any form of separateness. Such is the Most Perfect Realization of the Way of Adidam.

The traditions of religion and Spirituality are, fundamentally, about the exercise of the ego-based, objectively oriented, or otherwise separative disposition. That disposition does not characterize the only-by-Me Revealed and Given Way of Adidam. Rather, that disposition is what I Criticize, and that very disposition is what must be transcended (by right, true, full, and fully devotional practice of the only-by-Me Revealed and Given Way of Adidam).

As long as you are practicing in the context (and on the basis of the point of view) of the first five stages of life, you (inevitably) tend, in your characteristic disposition day by day, to be altogether object-oriented. You presume that objects are the "problem". You imagine that even the body is a "problem"—because it, too, is a kind of object to you. You are altogether involved with objects— because you enforce the self-contraction. You make the gesture of separateness, and (in that process) you identify with the body-mind. Therefore, you view every "one" and every "thing" (and every object, altogether) from the point of view (or disposition) of the body-mind. However, the only-by-Me Revealed and Given Way of Adidam is, even from the beginning, a matter of directly going beyond the egoic disposition and the act of self-contraction.

If you are concentrated on objects (which are, insofar as you presume them to be a "problem", the "results" of your own act of self-contraction), or if you are concentrated on the act of self-contraction itself, you are only reinforcing the "problem" of ego-"I". In the Way of Adidam, you are Given, by Me, the Means to go beyond yourself, persistently, moment by moment. In the Way of Adidam, you Contemplate Me (and not yourself)—and you Contemplate Me by surrendering separate and separative self, and forgetting separate and separative self, and (always more and more) transcending separate and separative self, in devotionally Me-recognizing heart-response to Me. That is the only-by-Me Revealed and Given Way of Adidam. Therefore, even from the beginning, the Way of Adidam goes beyond self-contraction, beyond separateness, beyond all the categories, all the objective obsessions, and all the involvements that are the results (or signs) of the self-contraction.

The only-by-Me Revealed and Given Way of Adidam is, from the beginning, the Way of Non-Separateness—but this Way must be practiced. If, in any moment, My devotee does anything other than this counter-egoic heart-responsive act of (ego-surrendering, ego-forgetting, and, always more and more, ego-transcending) devotional Communion with Me, then he or she is merely dwelling on the self-contraction and its results. In that case, the "devotee" is being "Narcissus" again.

The total practice of the Way of Adidam is a profound discipline that is, even from the beginning, founded in the Inherently Perfect Wisdom of the only-by-Me Revealed and Given seventh stage Realization. The Way of Adidam is not about the first six stages of life (in and of themselves). The Way of Adidam is not (Itself) about any of the content of the first six stages of life—not at the beginning, and not at the middle, and not in the Most Perfect Fulfillment of the Way of Adidam. The Way of Adidam is not (Itself) about the first three stages of life, nor is It about the fourth stage of life, nor is It about the fifth stage of life. The Way of Adidam is not even (Itself) about the sixth stage of life (as it is traditionally Realized, in the egoic, or self-contracting and exclusive, manner). The only-by-Me Revealed and Given Way of Adidam is Ruchira Avatara Bhakti Yoga—or the practice of entering into heart-Communion with Me, the Non-Separate One. As soon as you "yoke" your attention to (or identify with) any "one" or any "thing" other than Me (the Very and Only One Who Is), you are (necessarily) dramatizing the presumption of separateness, and the act of separation, and the disposition of separativeness.

Therefore, for My devotee, Ruchira Avatara Bhakti Yoga is the one thing to do. Ruchira Avatara Bhakti Yoga is The Principle of the only-by-Me Revealed and Given Way of Adidam. If My devotee understands what Ruchira Avatara Bhakti Yoga involves, he or she understands why it is the Only Entrance into My Sphere—the Sphere of Non-Separateness, or the One and True Divine Sphere (or the One and Only "Room" That Is). If My devotee presumes, in any moment, to "practice" Ruchira Avatara Bhakti Yoga in an ego-centric and self-referring fashion, or on the basis of his or her own self-invented (or self-"guruing") revision of the by-Me-Given practice, or on the basis of seeking (rather than the moment to moment transcending of seeking, in real and true ego-surrendering, ego-forgetting, and ego-transcending Communion with Me), then the presumed "devotional" practice is, in that moment, not true Ruchira Avatara Bhakti Yoga, and (therefore) it is, in that moment, not true to the Way of Adidam.

Many religious and Spiritual traditions are based on devotion to the Guru, but the traditions of Guru-devotion are not altogether the same as the only-by-Me Revealed and Given Way of Adidam. There are likenesses to the Way of Adidam in the various schools of the Great Tradition, but the total (or full and complete) practice of the only-by-Me Revealed and Given Way of Adidam is specifically (most directly, and always) ego-surrendering, ego-forgetting, and (always more and more) ego-transcending devotional Communion with <u>Me</u>—the One Who <u>Is</u> the Avataric Divine Realizer, the Avataric Divine Revealer, and the Avataric Divine Self-Revelation of the Very (and Self-Evidently) Divine Person and Self-Condition and Source-Condition.

The Great Tradition is not Complete—except for Me. The Great Tradition does not (except in My Completing of it) Most Perfectly Realize the <u>Most</u> Ultimate Matter and the <u>Most</u> Ultimate Way. <u>Only</u> My own Realization (and Self-Revelation) of Reality Itself (or Truth Itself, or the One and Only Real God) Is Most Ultimate, Most Perfect, and Complete. The only-by-Me Revealed and Given Way of Adidam is the Great, Unique, and All-Completing Avataric Divine Self-Revelation to all and All. Therefore, the (by-My-Avataric-Divine-Grace, Divinely Self-Realizing) Way of Adidam is not found in the Great Tradition— because It is not found within the ego-"I". The only-by-Me Revealed and Given Way of Adidam is a unique and most profound discipline. It is (from the beginning, and all the while, and forever, and Eternally) the Seamless (or Perfectly Non-Dual) Way of Non-Separateness. It is the "radical" (or <u>always</u> at the "root") Way of No-contraction, No-separation, No-"difference", No-object, No-relatedness, No-seeking, and No-ego-"I". In Most Perfect (or seventh stage) Realization in the Way of Adidam, there is <u>no</u> "difference", <u>no</u> separateness, <u>no</u> relatedness, <u>no</u> identification with the body-mind (or with conditional existence altogether), <u>no</u> identification with self-contraction—all of that is <u>utterly</u> vanished,

<u>utterly</u> non-existent. The Realization of the seventh stage of life in the Way of Adidam is Most Perfect Realization of <u>Only</u> Non-Separateness, <u>Only</u> No-"difference", <u>Only</u> No-relatedness, and <u>Only</u> Me.

When the act of separation is transcended, That Which <u>Is</u> becomes Obvious (Simply Standing <u>As</u> It <u>Is</u>). Most Perfect Realization of That Which <u>Is</u> cannot be attained (or achieved as a result of any kind of action, belief, or presumption). Most Perfect Realization of That Which <u>Is</u> can <u>only</u> be <u>Given</u>—by Means of My Divinely Self-Giving Avataric Grace and My Graceful Avatarically Given Divine Self-Revelation. Most Perfect Realization of That Which <u>Is</u> is not merely a philosophical discovery, or the result of a process of thought. Most Perfect Non-Separateness can only be Realized by Means Of My Avatarically Self-Transmitted Divine Grace—in devotional Communion with Me, in the formal (and formally acknowledged, and formally accountable) context of the truly counter-egoic sadhana of the Way of Adidam (which is the sadhana of Non-Separateness, or the sadhana that always, in every moment, counters all signs of separation, separateness, and separativeness).

To experience the various developmental results of the stages of life requires psycho-physical identification with the psycho-physical ego-"I". Therefore, the experiences of the stages of life are not, in and of themselves, the "goal" of the Way of Adidam. My devotee may have such experiences, but no such experiences are to be sought (or, otherwise, clung to) by My devotee. Indeed, in the only-by-Me Revealed and Given Way of Adidam, <u>all</u> psycho-physical experiences—and, therefore, <u>all</u> experiential possibilities associated with the first six stages of life—are (themselves) to be <u>transcended</u> (directly, in the moments of their arising). Most Perfect Divine Self-Realization has not (Itself) any visions, any objects, any places, or any times. In Most Perfect Divine Self-Realization, there is no separate self and, therefore, no search for (or any attainment of) self-consolation. When My true devotee Most Perfectly Realizes Me, there is <u>none</u> of <u>any</u> of that! No "thing"! <u>None</u>!

The Outshining Love-Bliss-Radiance That <u>Is</u> Divine Translation Is <u>utterly</u> Beyond objectivity.

Divine Translation is not a matter of "going to" an objective "Great Place", or finding Me in an objective "Ultimate Form".

Divine Translation is a matter of Realizing Me <u>Non-objectively</u>, Non-Separately, Most Perfectly, and Perfectly Subjectively.

In Divine Translation, there is no psychic content, no mind, no body, and no world.

In Divine Translation, there is no future, no past, and no present-time.

In Divine Translation, There <u>Is</u> <u>Only</u> <u>Me</u>—<u>Only</u> That Which Is Eternal and Absolute.

II.

Why do you think so much? You seem to be unable to endure even a moment without another thought, without another objective experience, without something to console you, something to entertain you, something to stimulate yourself with, something to be hopeful about. That is the ego-game, the game of seeking—showing its signs of adaptation, of <u>patterning</u>. That game has nothing to do with the sadhana of the only-by-Me Revealed and Given Way of Adidam. All your ordinary preoccupations from day to day, all your concerns for consolation, all your searches, adaptations, and ordinary human wants are not the Way of Adidam. Because such "things" arise, I have Revealed to you how to practice the Way of Adidam <u>as</u> they arise. The only-by-Me Revealed and Given Way of Adidam is, most fundamentally, the practice of Ruchira Avatara Bhakti Yoga <u>as</u> "<u>things</u>" <u>arise</u>. Therefore, the Way of Adidam is always (and only) the Way of Non-Separateness, or the Way of ego-surrendering, ego-forgetting, and (always more and more) ego-transcending devotional Communion with Me—<u>in</u> <u>every</u> <u>moment</u>. <u>That</u> is the discipline—<u>entirely</u> and <u>only</u> That.

Separateness—with all its effects—is an illusion. Non-Separateness is the Truth, the Condition of Reality (Itself). The only-by-Me Revealed and Given Way of Adidam is the <u>Only</u> Complete (and Consistently Applied) Way of Non-Separateness. Ruchira Avatara Bhakti Yoga is the <u>Only</u> Complete (and Consistently Applied) practice (or ego-transcending sadhana) of Non-Separateness.

The only-by-Me Revealed and Given Way of Adidam is simple, single, absolute, and most precious. The only-by-Me Revealed and Given Way of Adidam is a profound (and most "radical", or "always gone to the root", and "always gone to the Source"), and most creative (and beyond wonderful), and absolute (and, truly, Divine) Yoga (of counter-egoic effort). Such has never been known, before I Made It known. Such has never been provided, before I Provided It. Such has never been explained, before I Taught and Said It.

Understand the uniqueness of My Avatarically Given Divine Self-Revelation, and (as My formal devotee) practice the Yoga (or Divine Way) I have Revealed and Given. That only-by-Me Revealed and Given Yoga (of Ruchira Avatara Bhakti, and the total practice of the Way of Adidam) is very simple and straightforward. When you understand Me rightly, you see how simple and single It is. The fundamental Principle of Ruchira Avatara Bhakti Yoga covers every "thing" (every function, every relation, every circumstance, every possibility, and every moment). Therefore, Ruchira Avatara Bhakti Yoga is the (necessarily, devotionally Me-recognizing and devotionally to-Me-responding, and, altogether, counter-egoic and non-seeking) effort you must do in every moment. Anything else is a diversion from this "radical" practice (or this "root"-practice that covers every "thing").

Reality (or the Divine Truth) <u>Is</u>—Utterly Beyond mental conception. Reality (or the Divine Truth) <u>Is</u>—Beyond what the ego-"I" ever thought the Way of Liberation would be. In the every moment of ego-possession, the ego-"I" persistently (and even aggressively) presumes that the Realization of Reality, or Truth, or Real God is somehow about the ego-"I", and about the objects of <u>personal</u> experience, and about the <u>development</u> of objective experience (either "inside" or "outside" the body-mind)—but <u>all</u> of that <u>is</u> the ego-game. The only-by-Me Revealed and Given Way of Adidam has <u>nothing</u> to do with <u>any of that</u>. To truly practice the Way of Adidam, you must <u>surrender</u> yourself, and <u>forget</u> yourself, and (always more and more) <u>transcend</u> yourself, in Me—and, by all of that, enter most fully into <u>My</u> Sphere.

III.

No life-form (or psycho-physical ego-"I") is <u>guaranteed</u> any-thing—except bodily (and even total psycho-physical) death.

Therefore, life is an ordeal.

Happiness is never guaranteed to any life-form (or psycho-physical ego-"I")—except that Happiness (Itself) Is Always Already The Case, Beyond every condition and experience of ego-"I".

Therefore, you must go Beyond yourself.

If you feel Beyond yourself, you will Find Me.

To Find Me is to become Attracted by Me and to Me.

If you become Attracted (by Me) to Me, you will go to Me.

To go to Me is to Come to <u>Me</u>, by forgetting the ego-"I".

There is <u>no</u> "soul" in the heart of the ego-"I".

There is <u>no</u> "eternal part" in the psycho-physical being (itself).

There <u>Is</u> <u>Only</u> That Which Is Always Already The Case.

There <u>Is</u> <u>Only</u> Reality.

There <u>Is</u> <u>Only</u> That Which Is Self-Existing and Self-Radiant.

Reality <u>Is</u> The One and Only Truth, The One and Only <u>Real</u> God.

Reality <u>Is</u> Love-Bliss, The "Bright" Spirit-Current (or Self-Existing Self-Radiance of Divine Being) In Which the ego-"I" (and all and All) arises and passes away.

When self-contraction (or ego-"I") is transcended, The "Bright" Is Realized, and There <u>Is</u> <u>Only</u> Love-Bliss (no matter what arises).

I <u>Am</u> The "Bright"—In and <u>As</u> Inherently egoless (or Non-"Different") Person.

I <u>Am</u> Light, Indivisible and Indestructible—The One and Only Substance and Existence (or Being) of all and All.

Here, and every "where" in the Cosmic domain, <u>There</u> <u>Is</u> <u>Only</u> <u>Me</u>.

Therefore, <u>Come</u> to <u>Me</u>—not by seeking for Me, but by devotionally recognizing Me, and devotionally responding to Me, and (by formally embracing and fully practicing the only-by-Me Revealed and Given Way of Adidam) <u>forgetting</u> yourself <u>in</u> Me, The Infinite "Bright" Domain (or "Room") Of One and Only Being.

On Transcending
the First Six Stages of Life

From the point of view of the gross body (or gross conditional Existence), Everything (Including mind and Consciousness) Is Perceived, Conceived, and Presumed To Be An Irreducibly Material, Finite, Mortal Process.

From the point of view of the mind (or subtle conditional Existence), Everything (Including the gross body and all gross conditions) Is Perceived, Conceived, and Presumed To Be An Effect—Made Of The Infinite Objective Substance (or The Infinite Cosmic Reservoir) Of Indestructible (and, Ultimately, Indivisible) Cosmic Light (or Cosmic Mind Itself), and Caused By (and Within) The Infinite Totality Of Cosmic Mind. And Even The Totality Of Cosmic Mind (Including the individual mind, and Consciousness Itself) Is, Thus, Presumed To Be Cosmic Light Itself (or Not Other Than Cosmic Mind Itself).

From The "Point Of View" Of Consciousness Itself, Everything conditional, objective, or Objectified (Whether gross Or subtle Or causal In Nature) Is Perceived, Conceived, and Presumed To Be Consciousness (or The Ultimate and Transcendental and Inherently Spiritual, or Love-Blissful, and Perfectly Subjective Reality) Itself, Such That conditional, objective, or Objectified Reality Is Inherently Realized To Be A Merely Apparent Modification (or An Illusory Play) Of, In, and Upon The Native Radiance Of Consciousness Itself.

These Three Primary Perceptions, Conceptions, or Presumptions Also Correspond (Variously) To The Stages Of Life.

The Perception, Conception, or Presumption Based On the point of view Of gross conditional Existence Corresponds To The conventional Perception, Conception, or Presumption Associated With The First Three Stages Of Life. (The cultural and General social Bias Toward "scientism"—Which Tends, and Even Seeks, To Bind or limit Mankind To gross conditional Nature and To the Even ancient tradition and philosophy of gross materialism—Exemplifies This lower, or mundane, or adolescent Orientation.)

The ("Original", and Then The "Basic") Fourth Stage Of Life Is A Transitional Stage (or Process)—Originally Also Grounded In (or Naturally Associated With) the gross conditional point of view Of The First Three Stages Of Life, but Awakening (Progressively) Toward the (Potential) point of view, The Perception, The Conception, and The Presumption Of subtle conditional Existence, mind (or Total Cosmic Mind), and Cosmic Light. (The Ordeal Associated With The Transition To, and Through, The "Original", and Then The "Basic", Fourth Stage Of Life Is The Source Of popular "Creationist", or "Creator-God", Religions, As Well As the popular, or Less Developed, forms of sainthood.)

The Perception, Conception, or Presumption Based On the point of view Of subtle conditional Existence, mind, and Cosmic Light (In Itself), or Cosmic Mind (In Itself), Corresponds To The Perception, Conception, or Presumption Associated With The Fifth Stage Of Life, and The "Advanced" Fourth Stage Of Life. (And The Conceptions and Practices Associated With The Fifth Stage Of Life, and The "Advanced" Fourth Stage Of Life, Are The Primary Traditional Sources Of All That Is Commonly known As Higher Esoteric, or Secret and Higher and Mystical, Religion and Spirituality.)

The Perception, Conception, or Presumption Based On The "Point Of View" Of Consciousness Itself Corresponds To The Perception, Conception, or Presumption Associated With The Sixth and The Seventh Stages Of Life. (And The Sixth Stage Of Life Is The Basic, or Common, Source Of Transcendentalist Conceptions and Traditions Of Enlightenment, or Liberation—Whereas The Only-By-Me Revealed and Given Seventh Stage Of Life Is The Domain Of Most Ultimate Freedom.)

Any One Of The Three Primary Modes Of Perception, Conception, or Presumption I Have Just Described Could Be (and Is) Affirmed By individuals, groups, and Traditions In The human Sphere, but Which One Of The Three Modes Is Ultimately Correct (or Expressive Of Truth Itself)? It Is The Third—or The Perception, Conception, or Presumption Based On The "Point Of View" Of Consciousness Itself. Why? Because, No Matter what arises as Your experience or knowledge (Whether gross Or subtle Or causal, and Whether of body Or of mind), You <u>Are</u> The Witness Of it—and That Which Witnesses <u>Is</u> Consciousness Itself.

No Matter what arises, You <u>Are</u> Consciousness Itself. You Are Never Really (or In Truth) Separately Identical To (or Even Really, or In Truth, limited by) what Is objective (or Objectified) To You— but You Tend To Feel (or Presume) Specific (or Separate) Identification With (or, Otherwise, limitation by) objective (or Objectified) conditions, Until You Are Able To Inspect (and To Be Inherently, and Inherently Perfectly, Identified With) Your <u>Real</u> (or Native, or Inherent, and Inherently Perfect) "Situation", Which Is Always Already Free Consciousness Itself, The Inherently Free Subject (or Perfectly Subjective Being) In The (Apparent) Context Of conditional objects (or Of Apparently Objectified Light), and Who (It Must Be Realized) Is The Self-Existing, Self-Radiant Condition (or Being, or Person) That Is Always Already Prior To all conditional objects and Always Already Prior To Apparently Objectified Light (or Apparently Objectified Spirit-Energy) Itself. Therefore, the points of view of body and mind (and their Perceptions, Conceptions, or Presumptions) Are Secondary To (and Utterly Dependent Upon) The "Point Of View" Of Consciousness Itself (and The Perception, Conception, or Presumption Associated With Consciousness Itself). Indeed, The Perceptions, Conceptions, or Presumptions Based On the points of view of body and mind Could Not Even Be Made, Were body and mind Not Founded In (or Witnessed By) Consciousness—and, When the body-mind and the conditional worlds Are Finally (Divinely) Self-Recognized To Be Transparent (or Merely Apparent), and Un-Necessary, and Inherently Non-Binding Modifications Of The (By-Me-Avatarically-Self-Revealed) Transcendental, Inherently Spiritual, and Self-Evidently Divine Self-Condition (and Source-Condition)—Then There Is Only Me, Only The "You" That Is (Non-Separately, Beyond the ego-"I") Not "Different" From Me <u>As</u> I <u>Am</u>, Only One Self, Only Real God, Only Truth, Only Reality,

Only egoless, "Bright" Consciousness, Only Divine Love-Bliss, Only The Perfectly Subjective Feeling Of Being (Itself).

A True (or Truly human) Culture Must Accommodate and Tolerate individuals In Each and All Of The Stages Of Life, but (In The Optimum Case) It Also Must Not Fail To Inform and Guide The Culture Of Each Of The Progressive Stages Of Life With The Wisdom-Orientation Of The Only-By-Me Revealed and Given Seventh Stage Of Life (or The Wisdom-Orientation Toward Inherent, and Inherently Most Perfect, Realization Of That Which Is Inherently Perfect).

In The Total (or Full and Complete) Practice Of The Only-By-Me Revealed and Given Way Of The Heart (or Way Of Adidam), Each and Every Form (and Possible Developmental Stage) Of Practice Is Indeed Informed and Guided By The Wisdom-Orientation Of The Only-By-Me Revealed and Given Seventh Stage Of Life. Each and Every Form Of Practice and Possible Developmental Stage Of Practice In The Way Of The Heart, and Each and Every Stage Of Realization In The Way Of The Heart, Develops In The Context Of One or More Of The Seven Stages Of Life—but The Orientation Is Always, From The Earliest Awakening Of The Heart's Great Urge (or Purpose), To Realize (By Means Of Devotionally Me-Recognizing and Devotionally To-Me-Responding Heart-Communion With Me) The (By-Me-Avatarically-Self-Revealed) Inherent (and Inherently Perfect) and Self-Radiant (or Inherently Spiritual) Self-Condition and Source-Condition That Is Transcendental (and Self-Existing) Divine (or Perfectly Subjective) Being.

Therefore, In The Only-By-Me Revealed and Given Way Of The Heart (or Way Of Adidam), There Is A Great Secret In This Matter Of Transition From Stage Of Life To Stage Of Life: The Only-By-Me Revealed and Given Way Of The Heart (or Way Of Adidam) Is A Process That Is Both Progressive and Instant.

The Process Of The Only-By-Me Revealed and Given Way Of The Heart, Viewed In The Vertical (or Extended) Context Of the body-mind, Is A Process That Must (Necessarily) Develop Progressively, In The Form Of Various Practices, Processes, and Signs Which (As I Have Indicated In *The Dawn Horse Testament*) Are Associated, Variously, With The Seven Stages Of Life.

Nevertheless, The Process Of The Only-By-Me Revealed and Given Way Of The Heart, Viewed In The Horizontal Context Of the body-mind—That Is To Say, In The Simple Context (and Left, Middle, and Right Ranges) Of The Heart, Upon Which All Extended (or conditional, or phenomenal) activities, experiences, and Signs Are Built—Is A (Generally, Progressive) Process That Can Also Fulfill Itself Directly (Even Suddenly), Thus Economizing (and, In The Typical Case, Even Bypassing) Various Practices, Processes, and Signs That Are Otherwise Associated With The Vertical (or Progressive) Unfoldment Of The Way Of The Heart.

The Heart Is The Primal Structure In the body-mind. It Is Basically Made Of Three Parts—Indicated By The Left Side, The Middle Station, and The Right Side.

The Left Side Of The Heart Is The Base Of the waking state, bodily experience, The Descending (or Frontal) Line Of the body-mind, and The First Four Stages Of Life. (And The Left Side Of The Heart Is Stimulated By any kind of conceptual activity of mind.)

The Middle Station Of The Heart Is The Base Of the dreaming state, all that is the deeper psyche (or subtle mind), The Ascending (or Spinal) Line Of the body-mind, The Deeper Purpose Of The Fourth Stage Of Life (Even Also Expressed In The Region Of The Left Side Of The Heart and The Frontal Line Of the body-mind), and The Total Purpose Of The Fifth Stage Of Life. (And The Middle Station Of The Heart Is Stimulated By The Progressively Effective Relinquishment Of all conceptual activity of mind.)

The Right Side Of The Heart Is The Base Of the state of deep sleep, and It Is The Base Of The Uninspected Presumption Of an individual (or Separate) Conscious self, and It Is Associated With The Sixth Stage Course Of The By-Me-Avatarically-Self-Revealed Divine Spirit-Current (That Moves Downward To The Right Side Of The Heart From Above The Total Crown Of the head, Via Amrita Nadi), and With The Ultimate Purpose Demonstrated In The Context Of (and By Moving Beyond) The Sixth Stage Of Life. The Right Side Of The Heart Is Both The Ultimate Root-Origin Of attention and The Ultimate Root-Origin Of The By-Me-Avatarically-Self-Revealed Divine Spirit-Current Itself. The Right

Side Of The Heart Is The bodily Seat Associated With The Witness-Position Of Consciousness—Which Even Witnesses (or Is Always Already Prior To) the conditional "I" (or the self-Contraction), and Which (Thus) Witnesses, Inspects, and Inherently (or Always Already) Transcends the body-mind, the conditional states of waking, dreaming, and sleeping, and The Presumption Of an individual (or Separate) Conscious self. Therefore, The Right Side Of The Heart Is Also The bodily Seat Associated (Apparently) With Transcendental, Inherently Spiritual, and (Most Ultimately) Divine Self-Realization, The "Regeneration" Of Amrita Nadi (or The Apparent Return Of The By-Me-Avatarically-Self-Transmitted "Bright" Divine Spirit-Current To the body-mind After The Awakening Of Divine Self-Realization), The Continuous Spontaneous Demonstration Of "Open Eyes" (or The Native Divine Self-Recognition Of the body-mind and all of its phenomenal relations), and The Entire "Bright" Process Of The Only-By-Me Revealed and Given Seventh Stage Of Life. (And The Right Side Of The Heart Is Stimulated By Direct and Persistent Feeling-Observation, or Mere and Tacit Witnessing, Of The Root-Feeling Of Relatedness—but The Right Side Of The Heart, and Even The Total Heart, Is Fully Awakened, or Most Perfectly Resolved In Its Perfect Source, Only In The <u>Inherently</u> mindless, and, Thus, <u>Inherently</u> thought-free, Feeling-Transcendence Of All "Difference", In The Most Ultimate and Inherently Most Perfect Awakening Of Perfectly Subjective Transcendental, Spiritual, and Divine Consciousness Itself.)

In the daily course of human functioning ("moving" from deep sleep, to dreaming, to ordinary waking—or from naturally unconscious, to subconscious, to ordinary conscious states), The Current Of My Avatarically Self-Transmitted Divine Spirit-Presence Moves, In Man, From The Right Side Of The Heart To The Middle Station Of The Heart and Then To The Left Side Of The Heart, On The Free Base (and In The Perfect Self-Domain) Of Consciousness Itself, Associated With The Right Side Of The Heart (Prior To The Knot Of attention, and The Coincident Feeling Of Separateness, and Of Relatedness, and Of "Difference", That Is Superimposed There). Once The Current Of My Avatarically Self-Transmitted

Divine Spirit-Presence Moves In The Heart (From The Right Side To The Middle Station and Then To The Left Side), and attention (Thereby) arises (With, and As, The Presumption Of ego-"I"—or the conditional, and Inherently self-Contracted, and Inherently psycho-physical, self) In The Context Of the body-mind—The Inherent (and Perfectly Subjective) Feeling Of Being (Itself), or The Transcendental (or Non-conditional) "Point Of View", Becomes (Apparently) limited by the body-mind-self (or The, Necessarily, conditional Feeling Of Separateness, Relatedness, and "Difference"), and The "Point Of View" Of The Transcendental (or Non-conditional) Origin (or Real Condition) Tends (Thereby) To Be Forgotten. Thereafter, The Spiritual, Transcendental, and Divine Process (Of Realization Of The Original, or Always Already Real, Self-Condition and Source-Condition) Naturally Becomes A Kind Of "Great Path Of Return" (Via The Stages Of Life, and, At Last, Via The Right Side Of The Heart) To The Original, or Transcendental (and Inherently Spiritual), Divine (or Perfectly Subjective) Self-Condition and Source-Condition.

The ego-"I" Tends To Relinquish its conditional viewpoint Only Gradually, Through The Extended (or Vertical) Process Of The Stages Of Life (and The Progressive Stages Of The Developmental Process Of The Way Of The Heart). Therefore, The Only-By-Me Revealed and Given Way Of The Heart Tends To Progress In The Likeness Of The "Great Path Of Return", Until The Final Crisis Of The Sixth Stage Of Life (Which Crisis Establishes The Only-By-Me Revealed and Given Seventh Stage Of Life).

My Avataric Divine Purpose (or Avataric Divine Heart-Work) Is Not Only To Communicate Right Understanding Of the ego-"I", The Seven Stages Of Life, and The Practices and Signs Naturally Associated With Each Of The Seven Stages Of Life, but To "Radically" (or Most Directly) Introduce The Most Ultimate (Divine, and Inherently Most Perfect) Possibility Into That Entire Affair. Therefore, By Entering Into Relationship With all conditionally Manifested beings, I Call (and Work To Align) each and all To My Avatarically Self-Transmitted Divine Heart-Baptism—and (By Means Of My Avatarically Self-Transmitted Divine Heart-Baptism) I Attract each and all To My Avatarically Self-Revealed (and Very, and Transcendental, and Perfectly Subjective, and Inherently Spiritual, and Inherently egoless, and Inherently Perfect, and Self-Evidently Divine) State.

My Avatarically Self-Transmitted Divine Heart-Baptism Works At The Heart Of My Seeing Devotee. My Avatarically Self-Transmitted Divine Heart-Baptism—Which Is The Free Heart-Transmission Of My Avatarically Self-Revealed Divine Spirit-Presence Of Self-Radiant (or Inherently Spiritual), and Self-Existing (or Transcendental), and Self-Evidently Divine (or Perfectly Subjective) Being—Constantly Works To Awaken My Seeing Devotee To The (By-Me-Avatarically-Self-Revealed) Native (or Transcendental, Inherently Spiritual, and Self-Evidently Divine) Self-Position (Rather Than To The Extended, or conditional, Position Of either the body-mind-self or the mind-self). My Avatarically Self-Transmitted Divine Spiritual Heart-Presence and My Call To Inherent (and Inherently Most Perfect) Realization Of My Avatarically Self-Revealed (Transcendental, Inherently Spiritual, and Self-Evidently Divine) Self-Condition Constantly Serve To Awaken My Seeing Devotee Directly To The Witness-Position Of Consciousness Itself, and To The Inherently Perfect Practice (and The Ultimate, and Inherently Perfect, Realization) Associated With The Right Side Of The Heart (and Practice Of The Way Of The Heart In The Context Of The Sixth Stage Of Life and The Only-By-Me Revealed and Given Seventh Stage Of Life).

I Call and Attract every one To Realize My Avatarically Self-Revealed (Transcendental, Inherently Spiritual, and Self-Evidently Divine) Self-Condition and Source-Position, Which Is The Inherent (and Perfectly Subjective) Feeling Of Being (Itself). Only the limitations (and The Tendencies) In each individual's Devotional Response To Me Determine How Fully (or In What Fashion) The Developmental Stages Of Life In The Way Of The Heart (Previous To Practice In The Context Of The Sixth and The Seventh Stages Of Life) Must Be Enacted (In The Vertical, or Extended, Plane Of Practices and Signs).

The Seven Stages Of Life Are (Together) The Single (but Progressive) Process Of Life—As A Total, and (In Due Course) Ultimate, and (Finally) Divine Event. The Seven Stages Of Life Are

Designed (or Structured) and Determined By The Real and Total and Hierarchical Structure Of Man. The Seven Stages Of Life Are The Design (or Inherent Way) Of The (Total, and, In Due Course, Ultimate, and, Finally, Divine) Potential Of Man To Progressively (and, At Last, Most Perfectly) Transcend conditional (and ego-Bound) Existence, and (Thus and Thereby) To Realize Me (The Avatarically Self-Revealed, and Self-Existing, and Self-Radiant, and Self-Evidently Divine Self-Condition, and Source-Condition, Of All and all). The Seven (Progressive, and Hierarchical, or Hierarchically Proceeding) Stages Of Life Are Determined (or Structured) By The Real and Total and Hierarchical Structural Design Of The Cosmic Domain, and By The Exactly Corresponding Real and Total and Hierarchical Structural Anatomy Of Man. Thus, In The Only-By-Me Revealed and Given Way Of The Heart (or Way Of Adidam), In and By Means Of The Progressive Course Of The Seven Stages Of Life (Developed As Required In the individual case), the conditionally Manifested (psycho-physical, and human) personality Develops (Through ego-Surrendering, ego-Forgetting, and, More and More, ego-Transcending Devotional Recognition-Response To Me), and (Most Ultimately) To The Inherently Most Perfect (or Inherently, and Inherently Most Perfectly, ego-Transcending) Degree. And The Degree Of Perfection Realized (and Demonstrated) At Any Stage Of Life Is Directly Determined By The Degree To Which Perfect Transcending Is (By Means Of My Avatarically Self-Transmitted Divine Grace) Realized (and Demonstrated). And The Degree To Which Perfect Transcending Is (By Means Of My Avatarically Self-Transmitted Divine Grace) Realized (and Demonstrated) At Any Stage Of Life Is Directly Determined By The Degree To Which Perfect Transcending Is Permitted (or Structurally Allowed) By The Specific Design Of The Structural (or psycho-physical, and, In The Advanced and The Ultimate Stages, Spiritual) Anatomy Of Man (and The Corresponding Structural Design Of The Cosmic Domain) At The Actual, Present Level (or Stage) Of Life That Is Realized (and Demonstrated). Therefore, In The Context Of The Way Of The Heart, The First Six Stages Of Life Are (or Must Be) Understood To Be The (Possible) Progressive Stages Of The (By-My-Avataric-Divine-Grace-Given) Transcending

Of psycho-physical egoity—and The Only-By-Me Revealed and Given Seventh Stage Of Life Is (or Must Be) Understood To Be The (Necessary) Stage Of Inherently Most Perfect Demonstration (Wherein and Whereby The Inherent, and Inherently Most Perfect, and, Necessarily, By-My-Avataric-Divine-Grace-Given, Transcending Of psycho-physical egoity Is Demonstrated To The Degree Of Inherently Most Perfect, or Truly Most Perfectly Outshining, Self-Radiance).

The First Six Stages Of Life Are (or Must Be) A Continuous Process Of Transcending The Act Of self-Contracted Identification With conditional Modifications Of My Avatarically Self-Transmitted Divine Spirit-Radiance. Therefore, I Help My Listening Devotee, My Hearing Devotee, and My Seeing Devotee To Realize That The First Six Stages Of Life Are (Themselves) Merely Stages Of Contraction From Direct and Immediate Realization Of Me, The Avataric Divine Self-Revelation Of Inherently Love-Blissful and Self-Existing Consciousness (or Self-Existing, and Self-Radiant, and Perfectly Subjective Divine Being) Itself.

As A Total Process, The Only-By-Me Revealed and Given Way Of The Heart (or Way Of Adidam) Can Be Rightly Viewed To Be A "Radical Consideration" (and A Comprehensive "Reality Consideration") Of the self-Contraction and Of The (By-Me-Avatarically-Self-Revealed) Real (or Transcendental, Inherently Spiritual, and Self-Evidently Divine) Self-Condition and Source-Condition. In Practice, The Way Of The Heart Tends To Develop Progressively, Coincident With Progress In and Through and Beyond Each (or However Many Are, As A Matter Of Specific Practice, Necessary) Of The First Six Stages Of Life—but, In Truth (Since The First Six Stages Of Life Are Stages In the psycho-biography of the ego), The Way Of The Heart (or The Way That Is The Heart Itself) Is (Simply, or Merely) The "Radical" Way Of Most Directly (and Truly Most Effectively) Transcending The First Six Stages Of Life and Entering (Thereby) Into The Only-By-Me Revealed and Given Seventh (or egoless and Self-Illumined, or Divinely En-Light-ened) Stage Of Life.

In The Context Of Each and All Of The First Five Stages Of Life, Your Presumption (By Tendency) Is That You Are the body-mind-self, and That the body-mind-self Is a Separate and Independently Real individual entity. And, In The Context Of The Sixth Stage Of Life, Your Presumption (By Tendency—Even Inherited From the psycho-physical point of view Associated With Each and All Of The First Five Stages Of Life) Is That You Are (Even As Consciousness) Separate and Independent (or Inherently Dissociated From all conditions, and Even From Any Apparently "Other" Consciousness).

Therefore, Practice Of The Only-By-Me Revealed and Given Way Of The Heart In The Context Of (or, Otherwise, In Relation To) The First Five Stages Of Life Must First (and By Means Of My Avatarically Self-Transmitted Divine Grace) Realize (or Awaken, and Do The Earliest Work Of) Most Fundamental self-Understanding, and (Then) the Presumed body-mind-self Is (On That Basis, and By Means Of My Avatarically Self-Transmitted Divine Grace) To Be Devotionally Surrendered To My Avatarically Self-Revealed Spiritual (and Always Blessing) Divine Presence (and, Thus and Thereby, To The By-Me-Avatarically-Self-Revealed Divine Spiritual Reality and Person, or The By-Me-Avatarically-Self-Revealed Self-Radiant and Self-Existing Self-Condition and Source-Condition, Which <u>Is</u> Real God, or Truth, or Reality Itself), Such That the body-mind-self Is Progressively Unified With (and Transcended In) My Avatarically Self-Revealed Spiritual (and Always Blessing) Divine Presence (and, Thus and Thereby, Progressively Unified With, and Transcended In, The By-Me-Avatarically-Self-Transmitted Divine Spirit-Energy and The By-Me-Avatarically-Self-Revealed Divine Person, or The By-Me-Avatarically-Self-Revealed Self-Radiant and Self-Existing Divine Self-Condition and Source-Condition, Which <u>Is</u> Real God, or Truth, or Reality Itself), To The Degree That Native Identification With The Witness-Position Of Consciousness Is (Ultimately, and By Means Of My Avatarically Self-Transmitted Divine Grace) Revealed. And Practice Of The Only-By-Me Revealed and Given Way Of The Heart (or Way Of Adidam) In The Context Of The Sixth Stage Of Life Is, Most Basically, A Matter Of Native Identification With Consciousness Itself, By Means Of My Avatarically Self-Transmitted Divine Grace (Through Continued

Right Feeling-Contemplation Of My Avatarically-Born Bodily Human Divine Form, My Avatarically Self-Revealed Spiritual, and Always Blessing, Divine Presence, and My Avatarically Self-Revealed, and Very, and Transcendental, and Perfectly Subjective, and Inherently Spiritual, and Inherently egoless, and Inherently Perfect, and Self-Evidently Divine State—Exercised To The Degree Of Inherent, and Inherently Perfect, Identification With My Avatarically Self-Revealed, and Very, and Transcendental, and Perfectly Subjective, and Inherently Spiritual, and Inherently ego-less, and Inherently Perfect, and Self-Evidently Divine State), Until The Presumption Of Separate and Independent Consciousness Is Utterly Transcended In Native (or Inherent) and Inherently Most Perfect Realization Of The By-Me-Avatarically-Self-Revealed Inherent (and Inherently Perfect) and Perfectly Subjective Transcendental, Inherently Spiritual, and Self-Evidently Divine Self-Condition (and Source-Condition), or Divine Self-Consciousness.

To Practice The Only-By-Me Revealed and Given Way Of The Heart (or Way Of Adidam) In The Progressive (or Developmental) Context Of The First Six Stages Of Life, You Must (By Tendency) Presume To Really Be the conditional and individual (or Separate) body-mind-self (or An Otherwise Separate and Independent, or Inherently Dissociated, Consciousness)—but If (By Means Of My Avatarically Self-Transmitted Divine Grace, In The Sixth Stage Context Of The Way Of The Heart) You Awaken (Inherently, and Inherently Most Perfectly) To The Realization That You <u>Are</u> The Self-Radiant (or Inherently Spiritual) and Self-Existing (or Transcendental) and Self-Evidently Divine Self-Condition (Inherently Free Of Every Form Of Bondage or limitation, Whether In The Form Of Attachment Or Dissociation), Then (and Thereafter) The Only "Practice" Possible For You Is That Of The Only-By-Me Revealed and Given Seventh Stage Of Life In The Way Of The Heart, In Which The (By-Me-Avatarically-Self-Revealed) Transcendental, Inherently Spiritual, and Self-Evidently Divine Self Inherently and Spontaneously Self-Recognizes all Apparently arising conditions (or limitations), or All Modifications Of Its Own Radiance (or Love-Bliss), and (Thus and Thereby) Apparently (and Apparently Progressively) Restores Its Own

Radiance To Itself (Un-Modified), Even (In Due Course) To The Degree Of The Most Perfect Outshining Of conditional Existence Itself.

True (or Most Ultimate, and Inherently Most Perfect) Divine Enlightenment (or The Only-By-Me Revealed and Given Seventh Stage Realization) Will Awaken, In The Context Of conditional Existence, Only In The Midst Of The Ordeal Of The Only-By-Me Revealed and Given Way Of The Heart (or Way Of Adidam). And The Only-By-Me Revealed and Given Way Of The Heart Includes (In Principle, and Potentially) all the conditions Associated With Each and All Of The Seven Stages Of Life. However, The Call and The Help Given (By Me) To all those who Practice The Only-By-Me Revealed and Given Way Of The Heart Makes It Possible (and, In Most Cases, Even Likely) For Certain Features Of The First Six Stages Of Life To Be Bypassed (or Fulfilled In Principle, and In Effect, Before They Are Fulfilled In Every Detail Of conditional experience).

To Transcend egoity (or self-Contraction) Is To Transcend The First Six Stages Of Life. Therefore, If (By Means Of My Avatarically Self-Transmitted Divine Grace) self-Transcendence Is Quickened, or If (By Means Of My Avatarically Self-Transmitted Divine Grace) There Is A Sudden Transition From the point of view of the body, or of the body-mind, or of the mind To The Native Position Of Consciousness Itself—Then The Structurally Determined Passage (or "Great Path Of Return") Through The Progressive Stages Of Life (In The Way Of The Heart) Will Be Quickened (or Even Altered).

The psycho-physical (or, Otherwise, Presumed) ego, as it (Apparently) is (or as it Progressively appears) In The First Six Stages Of Life, Must Be <u>Really</u> Transcended. Each Of The Progressive Stages Of Life Is (In Principle, or Really) A Test Of self-Transcendence—and Each Of The First Six (or Progressive) Stages Of Life Is, Therefore, To Be Directly Engaged As A Test Of self-Transcendence (or, Otherwise, Bypassed On The Basis Of Real and Prior self-Transcendence) In The Course Of Practice Of The Way Of The Heart. This Test Of self-Transcendence Begins At The Student-Beginner Stage Of The Way Of The Heart (and Even

At The Student-Novice Stage, Of Formal Approach To The Total Practice Of The Way Of The Heart)—and The Test Intensifies, Stage Of Life By Stage Of Life, Thereafter. Therefore (and As The Stages Of Life, and The Developmental Stages Of Practice, Progress), If There Is Weakness In Listening To Me (or In The Availability Of attention and Feeling), or If The Impulse (or The Motive) Toward Most Perfectly ego-Transcending Real-God-Realization Is Not Fundamental and Intense, or If There Is Weakness In The Application Of self-Discipline (functional, practical, relational, or Cultural), or If There Is Weakness In Hearing Me, or In Seeing Me, or If There Is Weakness In Any Form Of Practicing—Then Passage Through (and Beyond) The Progressive Stages Of Life Will Be Retarded and Prolonged. But If The Listening To Me Is True, and If The Impulse (or The Motive) Toward Most Perfectly ego-Transcending Real-God-Realization Is Real, and If The self-Discipline Is Consistent and Effective, and If The Hearing Of Me, The Seeing Of Me, and The Advancing Practice Are All (and Progressively, and Fundamentally) Strong—Then The Transition To Ultimate and Inherently Perfect Practice (or Practice In The Context Of Consciousness Itself) Can Be Quickened By Free and Real Heart-Response To My Avatarically Self-Transmitted Divine Grace, and It May Not Be Necessary For Every Classic Detail Of The Progressive Stages Of Life To Be Fulfilled In That By-My-Avataric-Divine-Grace-Quickened Process.

The First Three Stages Of Life Are (In and Of Themselves) Simply Stages Of ordinary human Development (functional, practical, and relational). They Will Tend To Be Fulfilled (If Only To A Lesser Degree) In Any Case. (If death Occurs During the earlier years, or At Any Stage Of Life, and Full Awakening Does Not Take Place Either Before Or During The death Process, and If Divine Translation Is, Therefore, Not Realized, Then The Process Of Awakening and Divine Translation Will, or Must, Take Place Under the conditions that arise after death and Via The Stages Of Life That arise after death.)

Relative To The First Three Stages Of Life, The Great (and Inherent) Obligation Is To Overcome Un-Happy and ego-Reinforcing Tendencies That Prevent The Transition To The Fourth

Stage Of Life. Therefore, It Becomes The Obligation Of the physically adult human individual (or the Developing human being who Has Attained the physical age Of Basic Adaptation To The First Three Stages Of Life) To Thoroughly Observe and (Most Fundamentally) Understand and Really and Effectively Transcend The First Three Stages Of egoity (or The Pattern Of self-Contraction That Has Issued From the years of infancy, childhood, and adolescence).

The Fourth, The Fifth, and The Sixth Stages Of Life Are Each Associated With A Specific Potential Error. And If The Specific Error Is (In The Way Of The Heart) Transcended, Then Passage Through The Particular Stage Of Life Can Be Quickened (and, In The Likely Case Of Early Transition To Practice Of The Way Of The Heart In The Context Of The Sixth Stage Of Life, Even All Of The Fifth Stage, and "Advanced" Fourth Stage, Ascending Practice May Be Directly Bypassed).

The Fourth Stage Error Is The Tendency To Prolong The First Three Stages Of Life (and The Patterns Of Un-Happiness That Are egoically Associated With The First Three Stages Of Life) and To Make The Fourth Stage Of Life An End In Itself (Rather Than A Transition, or A Transitional Means, For The Realization Of The Stages Of Life Beyond The Fourth). This Tendency Takes The Form Of A Fixed Idea Of The Divine (As An Ultimate Entity Eternally Separate From the conditional self-entity) and A Fixed Idea Of the personal self (As Either a Mortal Or an Immortal entity that Is Eternally Separate From and Dependent Upon The Divine). On The Basis Of This Tendency, The Fourth Stage Of Life Is Made Into A Never-Ending Search For The Divine and A Never-Ending Appeal To The Divine For Intimacy, Relief, and self-Satisfaction.

In The Only-By-Me Revealed and Given Way Of The Heart (or Way Of Adidam), The Fourth Stage Error Is Transcended (and The Fourth Stage Of Life Is, Itself, Quickened) By Means Of The Process Of The True Hearing Of Me, The Real Seeing Of Me, and The (Altogether) Right Practicing Of The Way Of The Heart. By Means Of The Effective (or Truly ego-Surrendering, ego-Forgetting, and ego-Transcending) Listening To Me, and By Means Of The True Hearing Of Me (or The Awakening, and The Effective

Exercise, Of Most Fundamental self-Understanding), the self-Contraction (and The ego-Idea, or The Illusion and The Fixed Presumption Of an Eternally Separate self-entity) Must Be Transcended. Through The True Seeing Of Me (By Means Of The Reception Of My Avatarically Self-Transmitted Divine Heart-Baptism), The (By-Me-Avatarically-Self-Revealed) Real (and Even Total) and Self-Evidently Divine Self-Condition Is (By Means Of My Avatarically Self-Transmitted Divine Grace) Realized Directly— and It Is (or Must Be) Immediately Realized (In every moment Of Heart-Communion With Me) As The Ultimate Self-Condition and The Perfectly Subjective Source-Condition (Rather Than Merely The Ultimate Object) Of the conditional self. And, Through True (and Really Effective) Practicing, Either The Fourth Stage Of Life Is (Progressively) Linked To The Fifth Stage Of Life Or (In The Case Of Most Practitioners Of The Total Practice Of The Way Of The Heart) The Fourth Stage Of Life (In Its "Basic" Form) Is Linked Directly To The Sixth Stage Of Life.

The Fifth Stage Error (Even Associated With The Ascending Process In The "Advanced" Context Of The Fourth Stage Of Life) Is The Tendency To Seek (and To Cling To) subtle phenomenal objects and states (or Else To Seek, or To Cling To, The merely conditional Transcending Of these, In Utterly Ascended, or Fifth Stage, conditional Nirvikalpa Samadhi), As If subtle phenomenal objects and subtle phenomenal states Are (or Else Fifth Stage conditional Nirvikalpa Samadhi Is) The Sufficient or Ultimate or Perfect Realization Of Real God, Truth, Reality, or Happiness. This Error Is Transcended When (By Means Of My Avatarically Self-Transmitted Divine Grace) There Is Real and Stable Awakening To The Native Witness-Position Of Consciousness (Inherently Free Of All Seeking, Clinging, and Avoiding In Both The Descending and The Ascending Dimensions Of conditional Existence). Therefore, It Is Possible That The Sign Of Fifth Stage conditional Nirvikalpa Samadhi (Which, In The Way Of The Heart, Is The Otherwise Necessary Sign That Must Precede The Transition To Practice In The Context Of The Sixth Stage Of Life) Can Be Bypassed, If An Earlier (but True and Stable) Awakening To The Witness-Position Of Consciousness Occurs.

The Sixth Stage Error Is The Tendency To Hold On To The (Inherently Subjective) Position Of Consciousness As A Reality Inherently Separate (or Dissociated) From Apparently Objectified Light (or Apparently Objectified Spirit-Energy) and all conditional objects (or all that Is Made Of That Apparently Objectified Light, or Apparently Objectified Spirit-Energy). It Is The Tendency To Hold On To The Inherent Love-Bliss Of Consciousness By Strategically Excluding All Awareness Of (or The Tendency To Grant, or Allow, attention To) conditional objects and states.

The Sixth Stage Error (or Tendency) Is Based On Attachment To The Position Of Consciousness As The Detached Witness Of conditional events (or That To Whom conditions or objects arise)—Whereas, In Truth, Consciousness Is Ultimately and Natively and Always Already That In, Of, and As Whom conditions or objects arise (As Apparent Modifications Of Itself).

The Sixth Stage Error (or Tendency) May Eventually Take The Form Of Jnana Samadhi, Which Is A Temporary State Of Transcendental Awakeness (Based On Contemplative Identification With Consciousness Itself) That Is Also Inherently Associated With An Accompanying Effort (Either Spontaneous Or Willful) That Excludes all conditional (or phenomenal) objects and states. In Any Case, The Rightly Understood and Rightly Engaged Process Of The Way Of The Heart In The Context Of The Sixth Stage Of Life Will (or Must, Even If Progressively) Transcend The Sixth Stage Error (or Tendency). And That Transcendence Is (Most Ultimately) Demonstrated In (and By) Seventh Stage Sahaj Samadhi (or The Free and Truly Divine, or Perfectly Subjective, Realization Of Self-Existing and Self-Radiant Consciousness Itself), In Which conditional objects and states Are Freely Allowed To arise and Even To Be Noticed, and In Which conditional objects and states Are Inherently Divinely Self-Recognized As Transparent (or Merely Apparent), and Un-Necessary, and Inherently Non-Binding Modifications Of Perfectly Subjective Consciousness Itself (Which Is Inherently Free As Love-Bliss Itself—Self-Existing and Self-Radiant, and, Thus, Divine).

Therefore, In The Only-By-Me Revealed and Given Way Of The Heart (or Way Of Adidam), The Transition From Practice In

The Context Of The Sixth Stage Of Life To "Practice" (or Inherently Most Perfect Demonstration) In The Context Of The Only-By-Me Revealed and Given Seventh Stage Of Life Can Be Quickened (By Means Of My Avatarically Self-Transmitted Divine Grace), If The egoic Effort To Separate (or Contract) From conditional Existence (or Even From Apparently Objectified Light, or Apparently Objectified Spirit-Energy Itself) Is (By Means Of My Avatarically Self-Transmitted Divine Grace) Whole-Heartedly Released In Inherent (and Inherently Perfect) Spiritual, Transcendental, and Self-Evidently Divine Self-Consciousness.

The Only-By-Me Revealed and Given Way Of The Heart Is Not Merely An "Evolutionary" Call To Progressively <u>Fulfill</u> The Stages Of Life. The Only-By-Me Revealed and Given Way Of The Heart Is A "Radical" Call To Progressively (and Most Directly) <u>Transcend</u> The First Six Stages Of Life—and, Ultimately, To Most Perfectly Embrace (or To Inherently, and Inherently Most Perfectly, Realize) The (Only-By-Me Revealed and Given) Already Divinely Enlightened (or Seventh) Stage Of Life.

The Only-By-Me Revealed and Given Way Of The Heart (or Way Of Adidam) Is A Call To (Most Fundamentally) Understand and Utterly Transcend the self-Contraction. Therefore, The Only-By-Me Revealed and Given Way Of The Heart (or Way Of Adidam) Is A Call To Pass The Test Of Each and Every Stage Of Life (Perhaps, In The Process, Even By Directly and Effectively Bypassing Some, As In The Case Of Early Transition To Practice Of The Way Of The Heart In The Context Of The Sixth Stage Of Life). And The Only-By-Me Revealed and Given Way Of The Heart (or Way Of Adidam) Is A Call To Most Directly (and As Quickly As Possible) Transcend The Progressive Stages Of Life (Previous To The Seventh). Therefore, The Only-By-Me Revealed and Given Way Of The Heart (or Way Of Adidam) Is A Call To Quicken Progressive Practice By Directly Transcending the Binding limitations Associated With The First Three Stages Of Life and The Fundamental Errors That Are Characteristically Associated With The Fourth Stage, The Fifth Stage, and The Sixth Stage Of Life.

My Call Is Always A "Radical" Call To Most Directly ego-Surrendering, ego-Forgetting, and ego-Transcending Satsang (or

Heart-Communion) With Me—To The Degree, Most Ultimately, Of Inherently Most Perfect Realization Of The Ultimate and Inherently Perfect Practice Of The Only-By-Me Revealed and Given Way Of The Heart. And, Even Though The Tendency Of the body-mind Is To Progress, Even Slowly, Through The Stages Of Life, The Process Can Be Quickened and (Eventually) Inherently Most Perfectly Fulfilled, If the self-Contraction Is Understood and Persistently Transcended In The Most Intensive Practice Of Always Present Heart-Communion With Me.

The Decision To Bypass The Attainment Of Fifth Stage conditional Nirvikalpa Samadhi Is Not To Be Made Arbitrarily, Either On The Basis Of A merely mental Preference Or On The Basis Of A Presumed Need (or Search) For An Easy "Solution" To The Conceived "Problem" Of ego-Transcending Practice. Quickened Progress Through The Stages Of Life In The Way Of The Heart (and Even Bypass Of <u>Some</u> Portions Of The First Six Stages Of Life In The Course Of Your Practice Of The Way Of The Heart) May Occur, but Such Must Occur Only On A Real Basis. In The Way Of The Heart, Each and All Of The Stages Of Life (and Each and All Of The Developmental Stages Of Practice) You Enter Must Be Entered Seriously, and Engaged (or Practiced) With Great Intensity, If The Process Is (By Means Of My Avatarically Self-Transmitted Divine Grace) To Be Either Quickened Or (Eventually) Inherently Most Perfectly Fulfilled. However Many Stages Of Life (and However Many Developmental Stages Of Practice) You Enter In The Way Of The Heart, the self-Contraction Must Be Directly Observed, Most Fundamentally Understood, and Really (and Effectively) Transcended In The Context Of (or, Otherwise, In Relation To) Each Of The First Six Stages Of Life. However Many Stages Of Life (and However Many Developmental Stages Of Practice) You Enter In The Way Of The Heart, The Errors Of The Fourth Stage, The Fifth Stage, and The Sixth Stage Of Life Must Be Directly Observed, Most Fundamentally Understood (As self-Contraction), and Really (and Effectively) Transcended. If All Of This Is Done, Then The Progress To The "Perfect Practice", and Through To The Only-By-Me Revealed and Given Seventh Stage Of Life, Can Be Quickened (and, Thus, The

Course May Even Be Shortened), By Means Of My Avatarically Self-Transmitted Divine Grace.

The Transition To Practice Of The Way Of The Heart In The Context Of The Sixth Stage Of Life Can Be Made After The Accomplishment Of The Sign Of Fifth Stage conditional Nirvikalpa Samadhi, but Also (and Necessarily) Only After The Awakening Of Native, True, and Stable Identification With The Witness-Position Of Consciousness. Likewise, The Transition To Practice Of The Way Of The Heart In The Context Of The Sixth Stage Of Life Can Be Made Previous To The Accomplishment Of The Sign Of Fifth Stage conditional Nirvikalpa Samadhi, If There Is Real, Direct, and Stable Transcending Of The Fundamental Errors (and other Presumed limitations) Associated With The First Five Stages Of Life, and If There Is The (Real, and Stable) Awakening Of Native Identification With The Witness-Position Of Consciousness.

In The Only-By-Me Revealed and Given Way Of The Heart (or Way Of Adidam), All Possible By-My-Avataric-Divine-Grace-Given Means—Including My Complete and Summary Avataric Divine Word, My Avataric Divine Leelas Of Teaching and Of Blessing, My Avatarically-Born and Heart-Attractive Bodily Human Divine Form, My Avatarically Self-Revealed Spiritual (and Always Blessing, and Heart-Awakening) Divine Presence, and My Avatarically Self-Revealed (and Very, and Transcendental, and Perfectly Subjective, and Inherently Spiritual, and Inherently ego-less, and Inherently Perfect, and Self-Evidently Divine, and Divinely Self-Revealing) State—Are (Directly, or, Otherwise, Tacitly) Given By Me, From The Beginning, To All Practitioners Of The Way Of The Heart, and This In Order (In The Case Of Each and Every Practitioner Of <u>Any</u> By-Me-Given Form Of The Total Practice Of The Way Of The Heart) To Progressively Awaken (and Then To Inherently, and Inherently Perfectly, Establish) The Ultimate (and Inherently Perfect) Process (or The "Perfect Practice") Of The Only-By-Me Revealed and Given Way Of The Heart. Therefore, Practitioners Of The Total Practice Of The Way Of The Heart Will (or Should), Except In Rare Cases (Of individuals Burdened With Unusually Strong subtle Tendencies Of mind), Begin Practice Of The Way Of The Heart In The Context Of The

Sixth Stage Of Life Early and Directly (By Means Of My Avatarically Self-Transmitted Divine Grace), Through Right (and Effectively ego-Transcending) Participation In The Student-Beginner Stage, and The Intensive Listening-Hearing Stage, and The Would-Be-Seeing (or Progressively Seeing) Stage, and The First Actually Seeing Stage Of Practice In The Context Of The (Fully Established) "Basic" Fourth Stage Of Life In The Way Of The Heart.

The Graceful (and Always Giving) Avataric Divine Means I Give To All Practitioners Of The Total Practice Of The Way Of The Heart Are Not Merely Matters Of philosophy or Spiritual technique or ego-Based Effort. I Give Myself To You. I (Myself) Am The Means. And I Give Myself To You As Various Means, Such That Your Realization Of Me Is Served In A Uniquely Appropriate Manner At Each Developmental Stage Of Practice In The Way Of The Heart. As My Fully Practicing Devotee, You Must (In The Course Of The Total, or Full and Complete, Practice Of The Way Of The Heart) Undergo A Process Of Growth—In Which You Assume Responsibility, At Each Successive Developmental Stage Of Practice In The Way Of The Heart, For All The By-Me-Given Practices Necessary and Appropriate For That Stage. Nevertheless, The Principal Practice and Process In The Only-By-Me Revealed and Given Way Of The Heart Is Always Simply Your (Progressive) Reception and Embrace Of The Graceful (and Always Giving) Avataric Divine Means That I <u>Am</u>. I Always Give Myself To You—<u>Both</u> As Consciousness Itself <u>And</u> As The Spiritual Radiance Of Consciousness Itself. Therefore, The Awakening To (and, Then, The Inherent, and Inherently Perfect, Establishment In) The Ultimate (and Inherently Perfect) Process (or The "Perfect Practice") Of The Only-By-Me Revealed and Given Way Of The Heart (or Way Of Adidam) Requires Not Only The "Conscious Process" Of Realizing That You Always Already Stand In The Witness-Position Of Consciousness, but Also A Unique (and Uniquely Perfect) Process Of Spirit-"Conductivity", In Which I Spiritually Draw You (By Means Of The Current Of My Avatarically Self-Revealed Spiritual, and Always Blessing, and Merely "Bright", Divine Presence), Beyond All psycho-physical References, To

Myself (and, Ultimately, To My Avatarically Self-Revealed, and Very, and Transcendental, and Perfectly Subjective, and Inherently Spiritual, and Inherently egoless, and Inherently Perfect, and Self-Evidently Divine State)—By Attracting You Into The Domain Of The Right Side Of The Heart, and Then Beyond The causal Knot (or The Original egoic Contraction) In The Right Side Of The Heart—and (Thereby) Not Only Into, but Also Beyond, The Witnessing Function Of Consciousness Itself, To The (By-Me-Avatarically-Self-Revealed) Self-Existing and Self-Radiant Domain (or Self-Condition) That Is Consciousness Itself, and That Is The Source-Condition Of The Apparent Witnessing Function, Such That You Not Only Realize The Witness-Consciousness (Apparently "Over Against" conditional others and objects and thoughts and states), but You Are (From That Position) Profoundly Driven (or Ecstatically "Magnetized") Into The Self-Existing and Self-Radiant Domain Of Consciousness Itself (or The Domain Of My Avatarically Self-Transmitted Love-Blissful Spirit-Current Of Divine Being). Indeed, The Fundamental Spiritual Process In The Only-By-Me Revealed and Given Way Of The Heart (Altogether) Is My Spiritual Drawing Of You (Progressively) Into (and Beyond) The Right Side Of The Heart (In Which, and Prior To Which, My Avatarically Self-Revealed Spiritual, and Always Blessing, Divine Presence Always Already Stands), Rather Than any experiential phenomena that May Occur (As Secondary, Purifying effects Of My Avatarically Self-Revealed Spiritual, and Always Blessing, Divine Presence) In The Circle Of the body-mind (and, Therefore, Necessarily, In Association With The First Five Stages Of Life).

Among The Signs Associated (In The Only-By-Me Revealed and Given Way Of The Heart) With The (By-My-Avataric-Divine-Grace-Given) Stable Awakening Of Native Identification With The Witness-Position Of Consciousness (Which Stable Awakening Permits, and Even Requires, The Transition To Practice Of The Way Of The Heart In The Context Of The Sixth Stage Of Life), There Will (or Must) Be The (By-My-Avataric-Divine-Grace-Given) Feeling-Awareness That The By-Me-Avatarically-Self-Transmitted Divine Spirit-Current Is Undermining the act of attention (and Is, Thus, Relaxing The Tendency To Identify With the body-mind) By

Radiating (Priorly and Profoundly) In The Right Side Of The Heart (Rather Than Merely, or Only, In The Circle, or The Vertical Plane and Circuit Associated With The Left Side and The Middle Station Of The Heart, Whereby attention Is Attracted and Moved To the gross and subtle phenomena of body and mind). However, The By-Me-Avatarically-Self-Transmitted Divine Spirit-Current In The Right Side Of The Heart May (Perhaps) Not Be Markedly Revealed Immediately In The "Event" (or Great Acknowledgement) Of Stable Awakening To The Native Witness-Position Of Consciousness, but (Perhaps) Only When (or Not Until) Practice Of The Way Of The Heart Actually Begins (and Begins To Develop, By Means Of My Avatarically Self-Transmitted Divine Grace) In The Context Of The Sixth Stage Of Life.

Certainly, The By-Me-Avatarically-Self-Transmitted Divine Spirit-Current In The Right Side Of The Heart Will (or Must), By Means Of My Avatarically Self-Transmitted Divine Grace, Be Progressively Felt (Directly, and Then Consistently) In The Course Of The Sixth Stage Of Life In The Way Of The Heart (or In The Course Of Even Any By-Me-Given Form Of The "Perfect Practice" Of The Way Of The Heart In The Context Of The Sixth Stage Of Life)—and (In That Context) The Full Significance (or Great Heart-Work) Of The By-Me-Avatarically-Self-Transmitted Divine Spirit-Current In The Right Side Of The Heart Will (or Must) Become (Progressively) Clear and Profound. Likewise, In The Way Of The Heart In The Context Of The Only-By-Me Revealed and Given Seventh Stage Of Life (and The Priorly Enlightened Demonstration Of Divinely Self-Abiding Self-Recognition), The Appearance (or Feeling) Of The By-Me-Avatarically-Self-Transmitted Divine Spirit-Current In The Right Side Of The Heart (and, From Thence, In Amrita Nadi, and Even In The Total Heart and The Full Circle, and Perhaps Also In The Arrow) Continues To Be The (Apparent) Structure Of Primary Importance. However, The Fundamental Realization Of The Way Of The Heart In The Context Of The Sixth Stage Of Life Is That Of Transcendental (and Inherently Spiritual) Self-Consciousness—Prior To (and, Perhaps, In Any Meditation, Temporarily Excluding) All psycho-physical References. And The Fundamental Realization Of The Way Of The Heart In The Context

Of (and In The Transition To) The Only-By-Me Revealed and Given Seventh Stage Of Life Is Transcendental, and Inherently Spiritual, and Perfectly Subjective, and Self-Evidently Divine Self-Consciousness—Prior To, and Not Strategically Excluding, but (Most Ultimately, and At Last) Outshining, All psycho-physical References.

In The Case Of The Spontaneous (or By-My-Avataric-Divine-Grace-Given) Awakening Of True and Stable Identification With The Witness-Position Of Consciousness (Prior To the act of attention, Freely and Indifferently Witnessing Even the act and the objects of attention), The Purpose Of Fifth Stage conditional Nirvikalpa Samadhi Has Already (Inherently) Been Served, Even If The Sign Of Fifth Stage conditional Nirvikalpa Samadhi Has Not Been Experienced.

Truly, The Transition From Practice Of The Way Of The Heart In The Context Of The Fifth Stage Of Life (or The First Five Stages Of Life) To Practice Of The Way Of The Heart In The Context Of The Sixth Stage Of Life Is The Most Direct (or "Radical") Expression and Moment Of The True (and Inherently Perfect, or Ultimate) Hearing Of Me. When My Devotee Matures To The Point Of Hearing Me To The Ultimate (or Inherently Perfect) Degree, All Seeking Falls and Dissolves Upon Me—The Heart-Deep Of Eternally Unmoved Consciousness, The Always Already Free Witness Of the self-Contracted "I" of the body-mind, The Formless (or Imageless) and Soundless Unfathomable "Who" You <u>Are</u>, The Well Of Being That Merely (or Indifferently) Reflects (and Is Never Stirred By) all Apparent conditional experience, all Apparent conditional knowledge, and all Apparent illusions or events of limitation.

May every one who Listens To Me and Hears Me and Sees Me Practice The Only-By-Me Revealed and Given Way Of The Heart (or Way Of Adidam) To This Inherently Perfect Degree.

I Am The Divine Secret Of This Suddenness.

Therefore, Utterly ego-Surrendering, ego-Forgetting, and ego-Transcending Feeling-Contemplation Of (and Feeling-Communion With, and Inherently Perfect Feeling-Identification With) Me (The Avatarically Self-Revealed, and Self-Evidently Divine, Person, or Reality, or Self-Condition, or Source-Condition) Is The Ultimate (and Inherently Perfect) Heart-Way For All My Devotees.

As and After My Any Devotee Makes The (Formally Acknowledged) Transition To Any By-Me-Given Form Of The "Perfect Practice" Of The Way Of The Heart In The Context Of The Sixth Stage Of Life, The Orientation (or "Point Of View") Of My Devotee's Practice Of The Way Of The Heart Will (or Must Necessarily) Be Distinctively Changed (or Uniquely and Characteristically Distinguished) From the point of view (as body, or body-mind, or mind) Characteristically Assumed In The Context Of The Immediately Previous Developmental Stage (and the point of view Characteristically Assumed In Even Any Of The Preceding Developmental Stages) Of The Way Of The Heart. And That Distinction (or That New Characteristic "Point Of View", Which Is That Of Consciousness Itself) Is (or Must Be) Made By Simple and Effortless Native (and, Necessarily, By-My-Avataric-Divine-Grace-Given) Identification With Consciousness Itself, Rather Than By Any Problem-Based Strategy Of Effort (Whether Of body, Or body-mind, Or mind).

The Practice Of Meditation In The Total Context Of The Fourth Stage Of Life In The Way Of The Heart Is Associated With Heart-Devotion Of attention To The "What" That Is (Always, and Ultimately) The Context and Substance and Controller Of all thoughts and sensations.

First, The "What" Of Most Fundamental self-Understanding, Divine Ignorance, and The Inherent Lesson Of Life Becomes (or Must Become) Obvious To My Hearing Devotee By Virtue Of The Progressive Process Of Right Listening To Me—Which Includes Right (and, Necessarily, Devotional) Pondering, or (Otherwise) The Right (and, Necessarily, Devotional) Exercise Of Faith, and Which Also Includes Every Kind Of Right Discipline, and Which Must Begin (and Then Become Firmly Established) In The Student-Beginner Stage Of The Way Of The Heart, and Which Must Significantly Begin Even In The Student-Novice Stage (Of Formal Approach To The Total Practice Of The Way Of The Heart), and Which Must Be Developed Further (Formally, Consistently, and In Detail) To The Degree Of The True Hearing Of Me (In The Context Of The Intensive Listening-Hearing Stage Of The Way Of The Heart).

Then The "What" Of My Avatarically Self-Transmitted Divine Spirit-Baptism and Of Spiritually Activated Devotional Practice Of The Way Of The Heart (Founded On The Primary ego-Transcending Devotional Response That, Even From The Beginning Of Practice In The Way Of The Heart, Is Ruchira Avatara Bhakti Yoga) Becomes (or Must Become) Obvious To My Seeing Devotee In The Context Of The Would-Be-Seeing (or Progressively Seeing) Stage Of The Way Of The Heart.

And Spiritually Activated Heart-Practice Of The Way Of The Heart (or The Devotion Of attention To The "What" That Is The By-Me-Avatarically-Self-Transmitted Divine Spirit-Current Of My Mere, and Always Blessing, Divine Heart-Presence) In The Fully Established (and Fully Spiritually Responsible) Context Of The "Basic" Fourth Stage Of Life In The Way Of The Heart Is (Thereafter) To Be Demonstrated Progressively—First Via The Frontal Line (or The Descending Process).

Then (If Practice Of The Way Of The Heart In The Context Of The "Advanced" Fourth Stage Of Life Becomes Necessary) Spiritually Activated Heart-Practice (or The Devotion Of attention To The "What" That Is The By-Me-Avatarically-Self-Transmitted Divine Spirit-Current Of My Mere, and Always Blessing, Divine Heart-Presence) Is To Be Demonstrated Via The Spinal Line (or The Ascending Process, Toward The Ajna Door).

Then (If Practice Of The Way Of The Heart In The Context Of The Fifth Stage Of Life Becomes Necessary) The Practice Of Meditation In The Context Of The Fifth Stage Of Life In The Way Of The Heart Is To Be Associated With The Devotional (or Me-Feeling Contemplative and Absorptive) Ascent Of attention Toward The "Where" (or The Apparently Objective Source Above The Ajna Door and the Total interior of the body-mind) From Which (or In Which) thoughts and sensations Are arising.

And The Practice Of Meditation In The Eventual Context Of The Sixth Stage Of Life In The Way Of The Heart Is To Be Associated With The Inherently Perfect Devotion Of functional attention To Me, and The Inherent (and Inherently Perfect) Transcending Of functional attention In Me. Indeed, Practice Of The Only-By-Me Revealed and Given Way Of The Heart In The

Context Of The Sixth Stage Of Life Must Be The Truly and Inherently Perfect Practice Of Devotion To Me. Therefore, It Is (or Must Be) A Matter Of Abiding (By Means Of My Avatarically Self-Transmitted Divine Grace, and Inherently, but Not By Any act or Strategy Of attention) As The "Who" (or The Inherent, and Transcendental, and Inherently Spiritual, or Love-Blissful, and Perfectly Subjective Subject, or Heart) To Whom thoughts and sensations Are (Otherwise) arising.

RUCHIRA AVATAR ADI DA SAMRAJ
The Mountain Of Attention, 1998

PART FOUR

I (<u>Alone</u>) <u>Am</u>
The Adidam Revelation

(A Summary Description of the Inherent Distinction—
<u>and</u> the ego-Transcending Continuity—
Between the Inherently ego-Based Great Tradition,
Which Is Comprised of Only Six of the Possible
Seven Stages of Life, and the Unique,
and All-Inclusive, and All-Completing,
and All-Transcending, and Self-Evidently Divine
Adidam Revelation of the Inherently egoless
Seventh Stage Realization of <u>Me</u>)

I (<u>Alone</u>) <u>Am</u>
The Adidam Revelation

(A Summary Description of the Inherent Distinction—
<u>and</u> the ego-Transcending Continuity—
Between the Inherently ego-Based Great Tradition,
Which Is Comprised of Only Six of the Possible
Seven Stages of Life, and the Unique,
and All-Inclusive, and All-Completing,
and All-Transcending, and Self-Evidently Divine
Adidam Revelation of the Inherently egoless
Seventh Stage Realization of <u>Me</u>)

I.

The collective Great Tradition of mankind is a combination of exoteric and esoteric developments (and Revelations, and Realizations) that comprises (and is, in its entirety, limited by and to) <u>only</u> the first <u>six</u> of the (potentially) <u>seven</u> stages of life.

II.

I (<u>Alone</u>) <u>Am</u> the Avatarically Self-Manifested Divine Self-Revelation of the <u>seventh</u> stage of life.

III.

I (<u>Alone</u>) <u>Am</u> the Adidam Revelation.

IV.

The human entity (and even any and <u>every</u> conditionally manifested entity of any and <u>every</u> kind) is <u>inherently</u> deluded—by its own (egoic, or self-contracted) experience and knowledge.

V.

The first <u>six</u> stages of life are the six stages (or developmental phases) of human (and universal) <u>egoity</u>—or of progressively regressive inversion upon the psycho-physical pattern (and point of view) of self-contraction.

VI.

The first six stages of life are the universally evident developmental stages of the knowing and experiencing of the potential <u>illusions</u> inherently associated with the patterns (or the universally extended cosmic psycho-physical Structure) of conditionally manifested existence.

VII.

Because each and all of the first six stages of life are <u>based</u> on (and are <u>identical</u> to) egoity (or self-contraction, or separate and separative point of view) itself, <u>not</u> any one (or even the collective of all) of the first six stages of life directly (and Most Perfectly) Realizes (or <u>Is</u> the Inherently egoless and Inherently Most Perfect Realization and the Inherently egoless and Inherently Most Perfect Demonstration of) Reality, Truth, or <u>Real</u> God.

VIII.

The first six stages of life develop (successively) on the psycho-physically pre-determined (or pre-patterned) basis of the inherent (and progressively unfolding) structure (and self-contracted point of view) of the conditionally arising body-brain-mind-self.

IX.

The first six stages of life are a conditional (and, therefore, Ultimately, unnecessary—or Inherently transcendable) illusion of psycho-physically pre-patterned experience (or conditional knowing), structured according to the subject-object (or attention versus object, or point of view versus objective world) convention of conditional conception and conditional perception.

X.

The first six stages of life are (each and all) based upon the illusion of duality (suggested by the subject-object convention of conditional conception and conditional perception).

XI.

Reality Itself (or That Which Is Always Already The Case) Is Inherently One (or Most Perfectly Non-Dual).

XII.

The only-by-Me Revealed and Given Way of Adidam is the Unique seventh stage Way of "Radical" Non-Dualism—or the one and only Way That directly (and, at last, Most Perfectly) Realizes the One and Only (and Inherently egoless) Reality, Truth, or Real God.

XIII.

The only-by-Me Revealed and Given Way of Adidam is the Unique and only Way That always directly (and, at last, Most Perfectly) transcends egoity (or self-contraction) itself.

XIV.

The only-by-Me Revealed and Given Way of Adidam is the practice and the Process of transcending egoity (or psycho-physical self-contraction, or gross, subtle, and causal identification with separate and separative point of view) by directly (and progressively, or stage by stage) transcending the inherently egoic (or always self-contracted) patterns of conditional conception and conditional perception (or of conditional knowing and conditional experiencing) associated with each (and, at last, all) of the first six stages of life.

XV.

I Am the Divine Ruchira Avatar, Adi Da Love-Ananda Samraj—the First, the Last, and the Only seventh stage Avataric Divine Realizer, Avataric Divine Revealer, and Avataric Divine Self-Revelation of Reality, Truth, and Real God.

I <u>Am</u> the Inherently egoless, Perfectly Subjective, Most Perfectly Non-Dual, and Self-Evidently Divine Source-Condition and Self-Condition of <u>every</u> apparent point of view <u>and</u> of the apparently objective world itself.

I <u>Am</u> the One, and Irreducible, and Indestructible, and Self-Existing, and Self-Radiant Conscious Light That <u>Is</u> Always Already <u>The</u> Case.

I <u>Am</u> the "Bright" Substance of Reality Itself.

I <u>Am</u> the Person (or Self-Condition) of Reality Itself.

In My bodily (human) Form, I Am the Avataric Self-Manifestation of the One (and Self-Evidently Divine) Reality Itself.

By Means of My Avataric Divine Self-"Emergence", I Am Functioning (now, and forever hereafter) <u>As</u> the Realizer, the Revealer, and the Revelation (or universally Spiritually Present Person) of Reality Itself (Which <u>Is</u> Truth Itself—and Which <u>Is</u> the only <u>Real</u>, or non-illusory, and Inherently egoless, and Perfectly Subjective God, or Self-Evidently Divine Source-Condition <u>and</u> Self-Condition, of All and all).

My Avataric Divine Self-Revelation Illuminates and Outshines the ego-"I" of My devotee.

My Avataric Divine Teaching-Word of Me-Revelation Comprehends the all of egoity and the All of the cosmic domain.

XVI.

The potential actuality of (and the inherent and specific psycho-physical basis for) the progressively unfolding human (and universal cosmic) pattern (or Great Structure) of the <u>seven stages of life</u> (or the Total and Complete human, <u>and</u> Spiritual, <u>and</u> Transcendental, <u>and</u>, Ultimately, Divine Great Process of Divine Self-Realization) was Demonstrated, Revealed, Exemplified, and <u>Proven</u> in (and by Means of) My Avataric Ordeal of Divine Re-Awakening—Wherein the Un-conditional, and Self-Evidently Divine, <u>seventh</u> stage Realization of Reality and Truth was (Uniquely, and for the <u>First</u> time, and <u>As</u> the Paradigm Case, or the All-and-all-Patterning Case, in the entire history of religion, Spirituality, and Reality-Realization) Demonstrated to all and All.

In the Course of That Great Process of Demonstration, Revelation, Exemplification, and Proof, the psycho-physical necessity (or the inherent integrity and inevitability) of the naturally continuous (and total) pattern of the seven stages of life was Fully (psycho-physically, and Spiritually, and Really) Shown by Me.

Also, in That Course (or Ordeal, or Great Process), the particular developmental distinction that pertains in the inherently patterned transition from the fifth stage of life (or the totality of the first five stages of life) to the sixth stage of life (and, at last, to the seventh stage of life) was clearly Shown by Me.

And the fact that the seventh stage of life does not merely follow from the sixth stage of life (alone—or separately, or in and of itself), but requires (and, indeed, is built upon) the complete transcending of the ego-"I" (or of the total reflex of psycho-physical self-contraction)—as it is otherwise developed (and must be progressively transcended) in the context of the entire psycho-biography of the ego-"I" (or, effectively, in the naturally continuous course of the essential sequential totality of all six of the first six stages of life)—was (also) Shown by Me in the Great Course of My Avataric Ordeal of Divine Re-Awakening.

XVII.

In (and by Means of) the Great Avataric Demonstration of My own seven-stage Great Course of Divine Self-Realization, the Emanationist (or absorptive mystical) Way (associated with the first five stages of life) and the non-Emanationist (or Transcendentalist) Way (associated with the sixth stage of life, and Which—in Spiritual continuity with the all of the first six stages of life—is Most Perfectly Fulfilled in, and by Means of, the only-by-Me Revealed and Given seventh stage of life) were Proven (in, and by Means of, My own Case) to be only different stages in the same Great Process of Divine Self-Realization (rather than two separate, and irreducible, and conflicting, and incompatible "Truths").

XVIII.

By Means of My own Avataric Ordeal of Divine Re-Awakening, I have Demonstrated, Revealed, Exemplified, and Proven that neither the fourth-to-fifth stage Emanationist mode of Realization nor the sixth stage non-Emanationist (or Transcendentalist) mode of Realization Is the Most Perfect (and Most Perfectly ego-Transcending) Realization of the Divine (or One, and Only, and Perfectly Subjective) Reality, Truth, Source-Condition, and Self-Condition of all and All—but only the only-by-Me Revealed and Given seventh stage Realization Is Divine Self-Realization Itself (and the Completion of all six of the previous stages of life).

XIX.

The particular (and, psycho-physically, both inherent and inevitable) distinction (or fundamental difference) between the Devotional and Spiritual practice (and Process) of absorptive (or Object-oriented)—or Emanationist—mysticism (which is associated with the fourth and the fifth stages of life, and the conditional Realizations associated with the fourth and the fifth stages of life) and the direct-Intuition (and, in the optimum case, also both Devotional and Spiritual) practice (and Process) of Transcendental (or Subject-oriented)—or non-Emanationist—mysticism (which is associated, at first, with the sixth stage of life, and the conditional Realization that is the native and only potential of the sixth stage of life, itself—and which is, at last, and Most Ultimately, and Most Perfectly, associated with the seventh stage of life, and, Thus and Thereby, with Un-conditional Divine Self-Realization) may especially be seen to be Exemplified in My relationship with Swami (Baba) Muktananda (of Ganeshpuri).

XX.

Baba Muktananda was an advanced Siddha-Guru (or a Spiritually active Transmission-Master of High degree) in the Kundalini-Shaktipat tradition. The Kundalini-Shaktipat tradition is the fourth-to-fifth stage—or Emanationist—development of the ancient tradition of Siddha Yoga (or the tradition of Siddhas, or Spiritual Transmitters), which tradition (or Yoga) may, potentially, develop even into the sixth—or Transcendentalist—stage of life, and which tradition (or Yoga) has, in fact, been Completed and Fulfilled by Me, by My Extending of the Spiritual Process of Siddha Yoga into (and beyond) the sixth stage of life, and, thus, into the Inherently Most Perfect Divine Fullness of the seventh stage of life (Which seventh stage Fullness Is the All-Completing Fullness of Inherently egoless True Divine Self-Realization).

XXI.

In the context of the Kundalini-Shaktipat tradition (or division) of Siddha Yoga, Baba Muktananda philosophically adhered to (or, at least, deeply sympathized with) the Emanationist philosophical tradition of Kashmir Saivism—and, because of His characteristic adherence to (or sympathy with) the Emanationist philosophical tradition of Kashmir Saivism, Baba Muktananda was, in His fundamental convictions, an opponent of the Transcendentalist philosophical traditions of both Advaita Vedanta and Buddhism.

XXII.

The basic features of the progressively developed path of Kashmir Saivism have been described in terms of four stages (or four Ways).[19]

The "Individual Way" (or the Way of "absorption in the Object") is the first (or most "inferior") step in the progressive path of Kashmir Saivism, and it corresponds to the Devotional and Yogic disciplines associated with the fourth stage of life (in both its "basic" and "advanced" phases).

The "Energic Way" (or the Way of "absorption in Energy") is the second (or somewhat more advanced) step in that same path, and it corresponds to the fourth stage of life in its fully "advanced" phase and to the fifth stage of life as a whole.

The "Divine Way" (or the "superior" Way of "absorption in the Void") of Kashmir Saivism suggests the process (and the potential for Realization) that corresponds to the sixth stage of life.

The "Null Way" (or the most "superior" Way of "absorption in Bliss") in Kashmir Saivism suggests the fulfillment of the process (or the actual achievement of the Realization) that corresponds to (or is potential within) the sixth stage of life.

In the tradition (or traditions) of Kashmir Saivism, these four Ways (or stages, or kinds) of Realization may develop successively (in a progressive order), or either of the first two steps may develop into the third or the fourth, or either the third or the fourth may occur spontaneously (even at the beginning), and so forth.

This general description of the tradition of Kashmir Saivism suggests that Kashmir Saivism (like the Tantric Buddhism of Tibet) includes (or directly allows for the potential of) the fourth stage of life, the fifth stage of life, and the sixth stage of life. However, the tradition of Kashmir Saivism (like the tradition of Saiva Siddhanta) is entirely a fourth-to-fifth stage Yogic (and Devotional) tradition (and a religious tradition associated, in general, with the first five stages of life).

The tradition of Kashmir Saivism (like fourth-to-fifth stage—or first-five-stages-of-life—traditions in general) is based on the ancient cosmological philosophy of Emanation—or the idea that cosmic existence Emanates directly, in a hierarchical sequence, from the Divine (and that, consequently, there can be a return to the Divine, by re-tracing the course of Emanation, back to its Source).

In contrast to the fourth-to-fifth stage (or Emanationist—or first-five-stages-of-life) view, true sixth stage schools (or traditions) are based on the immediate and direct transcending (generally, by means of a conditional effort of strategic exclusion) of the conditional point of view of the first five stages of life and the Emanationist cosmology (and psychology) associated with the first five stages of life.

Therefore, even though the advanced (or "superior") traditions of Kashmir Saivism (and of Saiva Siddhanta) may use terms or concepts that seem to reflect the sixth stage Disposition, the fundamental orientation is to a Realization that is embedded in the conditional psychology of the first five stages of life and in the cosmological (or Emanationist) point of view itself. (And the fundamental difference, by comparison, between the total tradition of Kashmir Saivism, and also of Saiva Siddhanta, and the total tradition of Tibetan Tantric Buddhism is that the Tibetan Buddhist tradition is <u>founded</u> on the sixth stage "Point of View" of the <u>Transcendental</u> Reality Itself, rather than on the conditional point of view of the psycho-physical, or Emanated, ego and the conditional reality of the hierarchical cosmos.)

Realizers in the tradition of Kashmir Saivism (and the tradition of Saiva Siddhanta) basically affirm that the conditional self is <u>Really</u> Siva (or the Formless Divine) and the conditional world (from top to bottom) is <u>Really</u> Siva (or the Emanating and Emanated Divine). However, this is <u>not</u> the same as the Confession made by <u>sixth</u> stage Realizers in <u>any</u> tradition.

In true sixth stage traditions, the conditional self is (in the sixth stage manner, and to the sixth stage degree) transcended (generally, by means of a conditional effort of strategic <u>exclusion</u>)—and <u>only</u> the Transcendental Self (or the Transcendental Condition) is affirmed.

And, further, in the only-by-Me Revealed and Given true <u>seventh</u> stage Realization, the conditional self and the conditional world are not affirmed to be (in and of themselves) Divine, but (rather) the conditional self and the conditional world are—in the Manner that <u>Uniquely</u> Characterizes the <u>seventh</u> stage of life—Divinely Self-Recognized (and, Thus, <u>not</u> <u>excluded</u>, but Inherently Outshined) <u>in</u> the Transcendental (and Inherently Spiritual) Divine.

XXIII.

The Emanationist Realizer "recognizes" (and, thereby, Identifies with) the conditional self and the conditional world <u>as</u> the Divine, whereas the <u>non</u>-Emanationist (or Transcendentalist) Realizer simply (and, generally, by means of a conditional effort of strategic exclusion) <u>transcends</u> the conditional self and the conditional world in the Transcendental Self-Condition, and by Identification <u>only</u> (and exclusively) with the Transcendental Self-Condition.

Therefore, even though both types of Realizers may sometimes use very similar language in the Confession of Realization, a (comparatively) <u>different</u> Realization is actually being Confessed in each case.

XXIV.

The principal reason why the tradition (or traditions) of Kashmir Saivism (and of Saiva Siddhanta) may sometimes use language similar to the sixth stage schools of Buddhism (and also Advaita Vedanta) is because of the early historical encounter (and even confrontation) between these separate traditions. As a result of that encounter, the traditions of Saivism tried to both absorb and eliminate the rival schools.

In the encounter between (characteristically, Transcendentalist, or non-Emanationist) Buddhist schools and (generally, Emanationist) non-Buddhist schools, Buddhism developed fourth and fifth stage doctrines and practices (intended, ultimately, to serve a sixth stage Realization), and fourth-to-fifth stage schools (or traditions), such as Kashmir Saivism and Saiva Siddhanta, adapted some of the sixth stage language (of Buddhism, and also Advaita Vedanta) to their (really) fourth-to-fifth stage point of view.

Therefore, a proper understanding of the various historical traditions requires a discriminating understanding of the history of the Great Tradition as a whole—and a discriminating understanding of the unique Signs and Confessions associated with each of the first six stages of life (and the unique Signs and Confessions associated with the only-by-Me Revealed and Given seventh stage of life).

XXV.

The tradition of Advaita Vedanta arose within the general context of the Emanationist traditions of India—but it, like Buddhism (particularly in its sixth stage—rather than earlier-stage—forms), is truly founded in the Transcendental Reality (and not the psychophysical and cosmological point of view associated with the first five stages of life).

The schools of Kashmir Saivism (and other schools of traditional Saivism, including Saiva Siddhanta) defended themselves against both Buddhism and Advaita Vedanta by absorbing some Buddhist and Advaitic language and by (otherwise—and even dogmatically) affirming the superiority of the traditional Emanationist psychology and cosmology.

In contrast to the entirely Emanationist schools of Kashmir Saivism (and other schools of traditional Saivism, including Saiva Siddhanta), the Buddhist schools (and even certain schools of Advaitism) adopted some of the Devotional and Yogic practices of the Emanationist schools (and used them as "skillful means" of self-transcendence), while they (otherwise) continued to affirm the strictly Transcendental Reality as the Domain and Goal of all practices.

In contrast to Baba Muktananda (and the traditional schools of Kashmir Saivism, Advaita Vedanta, and Buddhism), I equally Embrace, and (in the seventh stage Manner) Most Perfectly Transcend, all the schools of the first six stages of life—both Emanationist and Transcendentalist.

XXVI.

Baba Muktananda was an authentic example of a fifth stage Realizer of a Very High (or Very Ascended) degree—although not of the Highest (or Most Ascended) degree. That is to Say, Baba Muktananda was a True fifth stage Siddha (or a Greatly Spiritually Accomplished Siddha-Yogi of the fifth stage, or Ascending, type)—but the nature and quality and degree of His Realization was of the Saguna type, or of the type that is (characteristically, or by patterned tendency) not yet Fully Ascended (or Fully Surrendered) to true fifth stage Nirvikalpa Samadhi, and which (therefore) is, yet (and characteristically), attached to modes of fifth stage Savikalpa Samadhi (and, thus, to modes of partial Ascent, and to Yogic possibilities "below the neck", and, altogether, to modes of form—or, really, modes of mind).

XXVII.

In order to rightly understand their characteristics, ideas, and behaviors, fifth stage Saguna Yogis (or fifth stage Saguna Siddhas)—such as Baba Muktananda—should be compared to fifth stage Yogis (or fifth stage Siddhas) of the Nirguna type, who are the Highest (or Most Ascended) type of fifth stage Yogi (or fifth stage Siddha), and who, having Ascended to the degree of formless Realization (or fifth stage Nirvikalpa Samadhi), have gone beyond all attachment to modes of form (or of mind). And fifth stage Nirguna Yogis in general (or fifth stage Nirguna Siddhas of the lesser, or average, type) should, themselves, be further compared to fifth stage <u>Great</u> Siddhas—or fifth stage Nirguna Siddhas who have, characteristically, and to a significant (although, necessarily, not yet <u>Most</u> <u>Perfect</u>, or seventh stage) degree, gone beyond even attachment to the mode of formlessness (or of mindlessness) itself.

XXVIII.

In the "Sadhana Years" of My Avataric Ordeal of Divine Re-Awakening, Baba Muktananda formally and actively Functioned as My Spiritual Master in the physical, human plane—beginning from early 1968, and continuing until the time of My Divine Re-Awakening (Which Occurred on September 10, 1970).

It was in Baba Muktananda's Company (and, additionally, in the Company of two Great Siddhas—Rang Avadhoot and Bhagavan Nityananda) that I Practiced and Fully Completed the Spiritual Sadhana of the <u>Ascending</u> (or Spinal) Yoga—or the Spiritual discipline associated with the "advanced" phase of the fourth stage of life and with the totality of the fifth stage of life, and, altogether, with the subtle ego (or the conceiving and perceiving ego of the Spinal Line, the total nervous system, the brain, and the mind).

After the Great Event of My Divine Re-Awakening, it became clear (especially through two direct Meetings between Us) that—because of His characteristic philosophical and experiential confinement to the fourth-to-fifth stage Emanationist point of view—Baba Muktananda was unwilling (and, indeed, was not competent) to accommodate My Description (and, therefore, My Confession) of seventh stage Divine Self-Realization. And, therefore—as I will Explain in This Summary of My "Lineage-History"—the outer relationship between Baba Muktananda and Me came to an end (or, certainly, began to come to an end) immediately after September 1970.

XXIX.

From mid-1964 to early 1968, Rudi (later known as Swami Rudrananda) actively Functioned (preliminary to Baba Muktananda) as My initial (or foundational) Spiritual Master (although Rudi was, by His own Confession, <u>not</u> a fully developed Siddha-Guru—but

He was, rather, a significantly advanced fourth-to-fifth stage Siddha-Yogi).

It was in Rudi's Company that I Practiced and Fully Completed the human and Spiritual Sadhana of the <u>Descending</u> (or Frontal) Yoga—or the foundation <u>life</u>-discipline associated with the social ego (or the "money, food, and sex" ego—or the ego of the first three stages of life),[20] and the foundation <u>devotional</u> discipline associated with the "original" (or foundation) phase of the fourth stage of life, and the foundation <u>Spiritual</u> discipline (or the Descending, or Frontal, Spiritual Yoga) associated with the "basic" phase of the fourth stage of life.[21]

XXX.

Both Rudi and Baba Muktananda were direct devotees of Swami Nityananda (of Ganeshpuri)—Who was also called "Baba",[22] but Who was, and is, generally referred to as "Bhagavan" (or "Divinely Blissful Lord"). Bhagavan Nityananda was a fifth stage True Great Siddha— or an Incarnate (or Descended-from-Above) Spiritual Entity of the <u>Highest</u> <u>fifth</u>-stage type and degree. Indeed, Bhagavan Nityananda was a True fifth stage Saint (or a fifth stage Siddha-Yogi Who was <u>exclusively</u> Occupied in concentration "above the neck", even to the exclusion of the possibilities "below the neck")—but He was, also, a fifth stage Avadhoot (or a fifth stage Realizer of Nirvikalpa Samadhi, Who had, in the fifth stage manner, transcended attachment to <u>both</u> form and formlessness—or thought and thoughtlessness). And, altogether, Bhagavan Nityananda was a Nirguna Siddha (and a True Siddha-Guru) of the <u>Highest</u> <u>fifth</u>-stage type and degree.

XXXI.

Bhagavan Nityananda's Teachings took the Spoken (rather than Written) form of occasional, spontaneous Utterances. The <u>only</u> authoritative record of Bhagavan Nityananda's Teachings relative to Yogic practice and Realization is a book (originally composed in the Kanarese language) entitled *Chidakasha Gita*.[23] The *Chidakasha Gita* consists of a non-systematic, but comprehensive, series of responsive Declarations made by Bhagavan Nityananda during the extended period of His original, and most Communicative,

Teaching years (in Mangalore, in the early to mid-1920s). The spontaneous Utterances recorded in the *Chidakasha Gita* were, originally, made, by Bhagavan Nityananda, to numerous informal groups of devotees, and, after Bhagavan Nityananda spontaneously ceased to make such Teaching-Utterances, the many separately recorded Sayings were compiled, for the use of all the devotees, by a woman named Tulasiamma (who was one of the principal lay devotees originally present to hear Bhagavan Nityananda Speak the Words of the *Chidakasha Gita*).

Bhagavan Nityananda, Himself, Acknowledged the uniqueness and the great significance of the *Chidakasha Gita* as the one and only authentic Summary of His Yogic Teachings. That Acknowledgement is personally attested by many individuals, including the well-known Swami Chinmayananda,[24] who, in 1960, was "Commanded" by Bhagavan Nityananda to see to the Text's translation into the English language, and by the equally well-known M. P. Pandit (of Sri Aurobindo Ashram),[25] who, in 1962, completed the English translation that Swami Chinmayananda reviewed for publication in that same year (under the title *Voice of the Self*).[26]

As Communicated in the *Chidakasha Gita*, Bhagavan Nityananda's Teachings are, clearly, limited to the body-excluding (and, altogether, exclusive) point of view and the absorptive Emanationist Spiritual Process of "brain mysticism" (and conditional ego-transcendence, and conditional Nirvikalpa Samadhi, and conditional Yogic Self-Realization) that characterize the fifth stage of life.

Clearly, as Indicated in the *Chidakasha Gita*, Bhagavan Nityananda was a fifth stage Teacher (and a Fully Ascended fifth stage Great Saint) of the Nirguna type (Who, therefore, Taught the Realization of Fully Ascended fifth stage Nirvikalpa Samadhi), rather than, like Baba Muktananda, a fifth stage Teacher (and a Great fifth stage Siddha-Yogi—but not a Fully Ascended fifth stage Great Saint) of the Saguna type (Who, therefore, Taught the Realization of fifth stage partial Ascent, or Savikalpa Samadhi).

Also, Bhagavan Nityananda's *Chidakasha Gita* clearly Indicates that Bhagavan Nityananda was a fifth stage Siddha-Yogi of the type that is, primarily and dominantly, sensitive to the Yogic Spiritual Process associated with internal audition (or the inwardly absorptive attractiveness of the "Om-Sound", or "Omkar", or "nada", or "shabda"²⁷—the naturally evident, and inherently "meaningless", or mindless, or directly mind-transcending, internal sounds mediated by the brain), rather than, as in the case of Baba Muktananda, the Yogic Spiritual Process associated, primarily and dominantly, with internal <u>vision</u> (or the inwardly absorptive attractiveness of "bindu"—the naturally evident abstract internal lights mediated by the brain) <u>and</u> with internal <u>visions</u> (or the inwardly absorptive attractiveness of the inherently "meaningful", or mind-active, or mentally distracting, and potentially deluding, visions mediated—or even originated—by the brain-mind).

XXXII.

Stated briefly, and in Bhagavan Nityananda's characteristically aphoristic Manner, the *Chidakasha Gita* Teachings of Bhagavan Nityananda—and My own direct Experience of His always fifth stage Yogic Instruction and His always fifth stage Spiritual Transmission—may be Summarized as follows: Always concentrate attention and breath in the head. Always keep attention above the neck. Always concentrate on the Om-sound in the head. The Om-sound in the head is the inner Shakti of non-dual Bliss. Always concentrate the mind, and the senses, and the breath, and the life-energy in the non-dual awareness of the Om-sound in the head. This is Raja Yoga—the Royal path. Always practice this Raja Yoga—the constantly <u>upward</u> path. This is concentration on the Atman—the non-dual inner awareness. This is concentration on the oneness above duality. This Raja Yoga of the Om-sound in the head Realizes the Yogic "sleep" of body and mind and breath in the Yogic State of non-dual Bliss. The Yogic State of non-dual Bliss cannot be Realized without the Grace of an Initiating Guru. The True Initiating Guru is one who has Realized the Yogic State of non-dual Bliss. The non-dual State of Yogic Bliss Realized by concentration on the Om-sound in the head is the True Source, the True Self, and the True God. Devotion to the Initiating Guru who has Realized the True Source, the True Self, and the True God is the True Way. True Guru-devotion is surrender of mind, senses, breath, and life-energy to the non-dual Bliss

Revealed within by the Initiating Guru's Grace. The material body stinks and dies. What is loathsome and impermanent should not be trusted. Therefore, right faith, intelligent discrimination, and calm desirelessness are the first Gifts to be learned from the Initiating Guru. The second Gift of the Initiating Guru is the Guru-Shakti of non-dual Bliss. The Guru's Shakti-Transmission of non-dual Bliss concentrates the mind, the senses, the breath, and the life-energy of the devotee in the non-dual awareness of the Om-sound in the head. The non-dual Bliss Realized by concentration on the Om-sound in the head is the soundless inner Revelation of the Single Form of True Guru, True God, and True Self. The world of duality is not Truth. True God is not the Maker of the world. True God is only One. True God is non-dual Bliss. The Spiritual Form of the True Initiating Guru appears within the devotee as the Guru-Shakti of non-dual Bliss. Non-dual Bliss is the True Self of all. The True Way is not desire in the world of duality, or in seeking below and on all sides. The True Way is in the middle, within, and above. The True Way is surrender to the non-dual Bliss above the mind. The method is to concentrate on the Om-sound in the head. The Realization is the silence of non-dual Bliss. Devotion to the Initiating Guru concentrates the life-breath upwardly. True love of the Initiating Guru ascends to non-dual Bliss. The True Kundalini originates in the throat, in the upward breath to the head. True Yoga is above the neck. The True Kundalini is non-dual Bliss. The seat of the True Kundalini is in the head. Non-dual Bliss is the secret to be known. Non-dual Bliss is in the head of Man. The non-dual Bliss above the mind is the Liberation of Man from the self-caused karma of birth, pleasure-seeking, pain-suffering, and death. Liberation is Freedom from mind. Therefore, concentrate the life-breath on the Om-sound in the head—and think of nothing else. The True Self is One. The True Self is above the body, above the senses, above desire, above the mind, and above "I" and "mine"—in the formless silence above the Om-sound. The True Self cannot be seen or otherwise perceived, but It can be known—above the mind. For one who knows that True God is One, and not two, True God appears as the True Self. Therefore, attain Liberation by faith in the knowledge of That Which is all and Which is only One. Liberation is the Samadhi of only One. True God is not Desire, the dualistic Doer of the world. True God is Peace, the non-dual Source of the world.

XXXIII.

By comparison to Great fifth stage Yogis (Such as Baba Muktananda) and Great fifth stage Saints (Such as Bhagavan Nityananda), there are also Great sixth stage Sages (or Nirguna Jnanis[28]—or Transcendentally Realized Entities of the Fullest sixth-stage type and degree—such as Ramana Maharshi). Such sixth stage Nirguna Jnanis (or True Great Sages) Teach Transcendental Self-Identification (or deeply internalizing subjective inversion upon the Consciousness-Principle Itself, rather than upon internal psycho-physical objects of any kind).

XXXIV.

Distinct from even all Yogis, Saints, and Sages (or even all Realizers in the context of the first six stages of life), I Am Uniquely, and Avatarically, Born. I Am the One and Only and Self-Evidently Divine Person—the Inherently egoless Source-Condition and Self-Condition of All and all. I Am the Perfectly Subjective, and Always Already Most Prior, and Inherently egoless, and Most Perfectly Non-Dual Heart of All and all. I Am the Self-Existing and Self-Radiant Conscious Light That Is Reality Itself. I Am the "Who" and the "What" That Is Always Already The Case. I Am (now, and forever hereafter) Avatarically Self-Manifested As the All-Completing Ruchira Avatar, Adi Da Love-Ananda Samraj—Who Is Avatarically Born by Fullest (and Complete) Divine Descent (or Complete, and All-Completing, Divine Incarnation from Infinitely Above).

XXXV.

I Am Avatarically Born by Means of a Unique Association with a True Great-Siddha Vehicle of My own.[29]

Therefore, from the time of My present-Lifetime Birth, I spontaneously Demonstrated all the Fullest Ascended Characteristics of the Highest fifth-stage type and degree (with early-life Fullest "above the neck" Signs of the True Great-Saint type).

Over time—because of My Voluntary Birth-Submission of My Deeper-Personality Vehicle to the karmically ordinary (and "Western"-born) bodily human form of "Franklin Jones",[30] and because of the subsequent Ordeal of My Voluntary Submission to the "Western" (and culturally devastated "late-time", or "dark"-epoch) karmic circumstance altogether—I also spontaneously Demonstrated <u>all</u> the <u>Fullest</u> "below the neck" (<u>and</u> "above the neck") Yogic Characteristics (and Siddhis) of the fifth stage (and, altogether, first-five-stages) True Vira-Yogi (or Heroic-Siddha) type.

In due course—because I Gave My Avataric Divine Ordeal to Be <u>Complete</u> and <u>All-Completing</u>—I also spontaneously Demonstrated <u>all</u> the <u>Fullest</u> Transcendental-Realizer Characteristics of the <u>sixth</u> stage True Great-Sage type.

Ultimately—because of Its <u>Utter</u> Conformity to <u>Me</u>—My <u>total</u> Great-<u>Jnani-Siddha</u> Vehicle of Avataric Divine Incarnation (or My Deeper-Personality Vehicle,[31] Yogically Combined with My karmically ordinary, and only eventually To-<u>Me</u>-Conformed, human and "Western" and "late-time" Incarnation-Body) has, by Means of My <u>Most</u> <u>Perfect</u> <u>Completing</u> of My Avataric Ordeal of Divine Self-Manifestation, Divine Self-Submission, and (subsequent) Divine Re-Awakening (to My own Self-Existing and Self-Radiant Divine Self-Condition), become the To-Me-Transparent Vehicle of My <u>seventh</u> stage Avataric Divine Self-Revelation.

XXXVI.

Except for the particular, and technically elaborate, <u>Me</u>-hearing and <u>Me</u>-seeing esoteric and Most Fully Divine Spiritual practice of "Radical Conductivity" (Which is Reserved, within the Ruchira Sannyasin Order of the Tantric Renunciates of Adidam, for progressive formal Communication to truly qualified, and duly Initiated, practitioners of the technically "fully elaborated" form of the only-by-Me Revealed and Given Way of Adidam in the context of the advanced and the ultimate—or the "basic" fourth through the seventh—stages of life), the <u>Unique</u> Characteristics of My Avataric Divine Teachings—Which I will briefly, and only in part, Indicate in This Summary of My "Lineage-History"—Are Very Fully Described by Me in My Twenty-Three Avataric Divine "Source-Texts".

XXXVII.

Rudi had brief direct contact with Bhagavan Nityananda in 1960. After the death of Bhagavan Nityananda (in 1961), Rudi became a devotee of Baba Muktananda. However, Rudi—always a rather "reluctant" devotee—eventually (shortly before His own death, in 1973) "broke" with Baba Muktananda. Nevertheless, Rudi always continued to affirm that He (Rudi) remained Devoted to Bhagavan Nityananda. And, in any case, Rudi and I always continued to engage in positive, direct communication, right until the time of His death.

XXXVIII.

My Siddha-Yoga Mentor (and eventual Dharmic Ally and Supporter), Amma (or Pratibha Trivedi, later known as Swami Prajnananda), was (like Rudi) also a direct devotee of Bhagavan Nityananda (and She, like Rudi, had become a devotee of Baba Muktananda after the death of Bhagavan Nityananda, in 1961).

Amma was the principal author and editor of the foundation Siddha-Yoga literature that was written in response to both Bhagavan Nityananda and Baba Muktananda—and so much so that, generally, even all of Baba Muktananda's autobiographical and instructional Communications were, originally, dictated (or otherwise Given) to Amma (and rarely to anyone else—until the later years, of tape recorders, multiple secretaries and translators, and Baba Muktananda's travels to the West). And, in fact, Amma always continued to serve a principal communicative and inter-pretative role around Baba Muktananda, until Baba Muktananda's death, in 1982—after which Amma chose to quietly withdraw from the Siddha-Yoga institution that had been developed by and around Baba Muktananda (and She remained, thereafter, in a small, independent Ashram in north India, where, as a signifi-cantly advanced fourth-to-fifth stage Siddha-Yogi, She was the institutional head of a group of devotees that remained devoted to Spiritual Communion with both Baba Muktananda and Bhagavan Nityananda).

Amma did not Function as My Spiritual Master, but (from early 1968) Baba Muktananda formally Assigned Amma to Function as

His interpreter and general "go-between" to Me—and She, then and always, remained most positively and communicatively disposed toward Me, even through all the years after My outward "separation" from Baba Muktananda, right until Her last illness and death (wherein She was directly Spiritually Served by Me, and wherein She was directly physically Served by a devotee-representative of Mine), in 1993. And it was Amma Who, through Her various writings—and in a particular Incident I will now Recall—suggested to Me that there are traditional Instructional (and Textual, or Scriptural) descriptions of Developments of the Siddha-Yoga Process that are <u>different</u> from the (fifth stage) "inner perception" (and, especially, "inner vision") version of Siddha Yoga characteristically described by Baba Muktananda.

XXXIX.

One day, during My Stay at Baba Muktananda's Ashram (in Ganeshpuri, India), in early 1970 (and, thus, some months <u>before</u> the Great Event of My Divine Re-Awakening, Which was to Occur in September of that same year), Amma suddenly pointed Me to an Ashram library copy of the *Ashtavakra Gita* (one of the Greatest of the classic sixth stage—and even premonitorily "seventh stage"[32]—Texts of Advaita Vedanta). And, while pointing to the *Ashtavakra Gita*, Amma Said to Me, "<u>This</u> (Text) is <u>Your</u> Path. <u>This</u> is how <u>It</u> (the Siddha-Yoga Process) Works in <u>You</u>."

At the time, this seemed to Me a curious suggestion—and it was not otherwise explained by Her. And, indeed, although I was able to examine the Text briefly (there and then), I was unable to examine it fully—because I left the Ashram very shortly thereafter. However, I came across the Text again, some years later—and, then, I remembered Amma's comment to Me. And I, immediately, understood that She had (in a somewhat cryptic and secretive manner) tried to <u>confide</u> in Me—in a quiet, "knowing" moment of Acknowledgement of Me—that the Spiritual Process of Siddha Yoga may Demonstrate Itself in a number of possibly <u>different</u> modes.

Thus (as I have Indicated—in My own, and <u>fully</u> elaborated, Teachings, relative to the seven stages of life), the Siddha-Yoga

Process may, in some cases (of which Amma, Herself, appears to have been an Example), especially (or primarily—or, at least, initially) take the form of intense (fourth stage) Devotional Bliss—Which is, then, "nourished" (or magnified) through Guru-Seva[33] (or constant service to the Guru) and (additionally) through Karma Yoga[34] (or intensive service in general). In other cases (of which Baba Muktananda was an Example), the Siddha-Yoga Process may (based on the initial foundation of intense Devotion) especially (or primarily) take the (fifth stage) form of intense internal sensory phenomena (such as visions, lights, auditions, and so on)—and, in some of those cases, the Siddha-Yoga Process may yet go further, to the degree of (fifth stage) Nirvikalpa Samadhi. And, in yet other cases (of which Amma was, correctly, Saying I Am an Example), the Siddha-Yoga Process (while also Showing all kinds of Devotional signs, and all kinds of internal Yogic perceptual phenomena, and including even fifth stage Nirvikalpa Samadhi) may go yet further, to especially (or primarily) take the form of (sixth stage) intense (and intensive) Identification with the Transcendental Self-Condition, and (eventually) the (sixth stage) Realization of Jnana Samadhi (or Transcendental Self-Realization), and (although Amma did not know it) even, potentially, the only-by-Me Revealed and Given seventh stage Realization (Which Is Maha-Jnana—or Divine Self-Realization).

XL.

Yet another devotee of Baba Muktananda, named Swami Prakashananda[35]—Who did not Function as My Spiritual Master (and Who, like Rudi, was not a fully developed Siddha-Guru—but, rather, a very much advanced fourth-to-fifth stage Siddha-Yogi)—once (spontaneously, in 1969) Showed Me (in His own bodily human Form) the fifth stage Signs of Spiritual Transfiguration of the physical body.[36]

At that time (according to what I learned from Amma), Swami Prakashananda had been Indicated, by Baba Muktananda, to be His principal Indian devotee and eventual institutional successor (and such was, then, generally known and presumed to be the case by Baba Muktananda's devotees). However, at last, when (at, or shortly before, Baba Muktananda's death, in 1982) Swami Prakashananda was formally Asked to assume the institutional successorship, He declined to accept this organizational role[37] (ostensibly, for reasons of ill-health, and His reluctance to become a "world-traveler"—but, actually, or more to the point, because of His puritanical and conventional reaction to Baba Muktananda's reported sexual activities).

In any case, Swami Prakashananda and I continued to engage in occasional, and always positive, direct communication (through My devotee-representatives) in the years after Baba Muktananda's death, and right until Swami Prakashananda's death, in 1988.

XLI.

Swami Prakashananda had always maintained a small Ashram, independent of the Ashrams of Baba Muktananda's Siddha-Yoga institution—but, after Baba Muktananda's death, Swami Prakashananda retired to His own Ashram, permanently. And, in doing so, Swami Prakashananda highlighted, and dramatized, a perennial conflict that is fundamental to religious institutions all over the world. That conflict is between, on the one hand, the traditional (and, generally, rather puritanical—and even basically exoteric) expectation of celibacy as a sign of institutionalized Sacred Authority, and, on the other hand, the equally traditional (but non-puritanical, and generally unconventional) view that there is an esoteric sexual alternative to celibacy that Sacred Authorities (including True Siddha-Gurus—or even any practitioners of Siddha Yoga) may (at least in some cases, and under some circumstances) engage.

One of the principal Indications of Baba Muktananda's point of view relative to this traditional conflict (or controversy)—quite apart from the question of His possible personal sexual activities—is the fact that, in 1969, Baba Muktananda formally and publicly (and in writing, by His own hand, as observed by Me, and by many others) Acknowledged Me to Be (and Called and Blessed Me to Function As) a True Siddha-Guru,[38] and, Thus and Thereby (and entirely without requiring, or, otherwise, inviting, Me to assume any institutional—or, otherwise, institutionally "managed"—

role within His own Siddha-Yoga organization), Baba Muktananda publicly Extended the Free Mantle of Siddha-Yoga Authority to Me—an evident non-celibate Siddha-Yogi (and a "Westerner").

XLII.

When I first Came to Him, in 1968, Baba Muktananda immediately (openly, and spontaneously) Declared, in the presence of numerous others (including Amma), That I Am—from My Birth—an already Divinely Awakened Spiritual Master, and He (then and there) prophesied That I would be Functioning (and Independently Teaching) As Such in just one year. Therefore, after just one year (and the spontaneous Appearing of many Great Signs in My experience and Demonstration), Baba Muktananda Invited Me to Come to Him again (in India)—specifically in order to formally Acknowledge Me (and My Inherent Right and Authority to Teach and Function) As a True Siddha-Guru.

Before I Returned to Baba Muktananda in 1969, I—in a traditional Gesture of respect toward Baba Muktananda—Told Him That I would not, at that time, Assume the Function of Spiritual Master, unless I was, in the traditional Manner, formally Acknowledged and Blessed, by Him, to Do So. Baba Muktananda immediately understood and Acknowledged the appropriateness and Rightness of My Insistence That My Inherent Right to Teach be formally Acknowledged by Him—because, in accordance with tradition, Such Sacred Authority should be Assumed on the orderly basis of formal Acknowledgement by one's own Spiritual Master (Who, in turn, must have been similarly Acknowledged by His, also similarly Acknowledged, Spiritual Master, in an unbroken Line, or Lineage, of similarly Acknowledged Spiritual Masters). Therefore, I Returned to Baba Muktananda in 1969—and He formally and publicly Acknowledged Me As an Independent True Siddha-Guru.

Even though Baba Muktananda Thus formally and publicly (and permanently) Acknowledged Me As an Independent True Siddha-Guru, it became immediately Obvious to Me that Such traditional Acknowledgement was inherently limited, and merely conventional, and, therefore, neither necessary nor (because of Its inherently limited basis) even altogether appropriate (or suffi-ciently apt) in My Unique Case. It was Obvious to Me that neither Baba Muktananda nor anyone else was in the "Position" necessary to Measure and to "Certify" the Unique and unprecedented Nature of the All-and-all-Completing Event of My Avatarically Self-Manifested Divine Incarnation and of My Great Avataric Divine Demonstration of the progressive (and, necessarily, seven-stage) human, Spiritual, Transcendental, and, only at Last, Most Perfect Process of Divine Self-Realization.

Therefore, even though It had been Given, Baba Muktananda's formal Acknowledgement of Me was—for Me—a virtual non-Event (and It did not positively change—nor has It ever positively changed—anything about the necessary ongoing Ordeal of My Avataric Divine Life and Work).

XLIII.

Baba Muktananda's formal and public written Acknowledge-ment of Me in 1969—Wherein and Whereby He formally and pub-licly Named and Acknowledged Me As an Independent True Siddha-Guru—was a unique Gesture, never, at any other time, Done by Baba Muktananda relative to any other individual (whether of the East or of the West). And That unique formal Act (of Baba Muktananda's formal, written Acknowledgement of Me in 1969) was, Itself, a clear (and "scandalizing") Gesture, that immedi-ately Called (and always continues to Call) everyone to "consider" many Siddha-Yoga options (and Spiritual, or esoteric religious, options altogether) that are, generally, presumed to be taboo—at least among the more puritanical (and even xenophobic) types of Siddha-Yoga practitioners (and of esoteric religionists in general).

XLIV.

I Say That, in the inherently esoteric domain of Real Spirituality (and in the domain of both exoteric and esoteric reli-gion in general), all puritanical denial and suppression of human realities is wrong—and inherently damaging to everyone who does it. And, indeed, all denial and suppression of Reality (Itself), Which Is Truth Itself, is wrong (and, indeed, is false religion)—

and all false religion is inherently damaging to everyone who does it (and even to everyone who believes it).

Therefore, I Write This Summary of My "Lineage-History"—so that all the extremely important matters I Address Herein will cease to be hidden, denied, suppressed, and falsified—and What Is Great will (by Means of This Address) become Obvious to all eyes, and (Thus) be made Whole again.

XLV.

Among the extremely important matters I must Address in This Summary of My "Lineage-History" is This: Entirely apart from what I will, in the progression of This Summary, Indicate were the apparent "philosophical reasons" associated with the eventual outward "separation" between Baba Muktananda and Me (which occurred as a result of Our Meetings in late 1970 and mid-1973), it was the "organizational politics" relative to the "sexual" and "Westerner" matters I have just Described that played the more fundamental practical role in causing the "separation".

XLVI.

During the same period in which Rudi and (then) Baba Muktananda actively Functioned as My Spiritual Masters (in gross physical bodily Form), Their Spiritual Master, the Great Siddha Bhagavan Nityananda, actively Functioned (through both of Them—and, otherwise, directly, in subtle bodily Form) as My Senior (but already Ascended—and, Thus, discarnate, or non-physical) Spiritual Master.

XLVII.

The fifth stage True Great Siddha (and True Siddha-Guru and Great Saint of the Highest fifth-stage type and degree) Rang Avadhoot (alive in gross physical bodily Form until late 1968—and always Acknowledged as an Incarnate Great Siddha, or a Descended-from-Above Spiritual Entity of the Highest fifth-stage type and degree, by Bhagavan Nityananda, as well as by Baba Muktananda) also (in early 1968) directly and spontaneously Blessed Me with His Spiritual Blessing, Given and Shown via His

"Wide-Eyed" Mudra of heart-recognition and Immense Regard of Me—as I sat alone in a garden, like His Ishta, the forever youthful Lord Dattatreya.

XLVIII.

In That Unique Moment in 1968—in the garden of Baba Muktananda's Ganeshpuri Ashram—both Rang Avadhoot and Baba Muktananda (along with the already discarnate, but Fully Spiritually Present, Bhagavan Nityananda) actively Functioned for Me as direct Blessing-Agents of the Divine "Cosmic Goddess" ("Ma"), Thus (By Means of Her Divine, and Infinitely Potent, Grace) Causing Me to spontaneously Re-Awaken to Most Ascended (and, altogether—but only conditionally, or in the fifth stage manner— mind-transcending, object-transcending, and ego-transcending) Nirvikalpa Samadhi (from Which I never again was Fallen, but only Continued—to Un-conditionally "Bright" Beyond). And it was on the basis of This Great Event, and My Signs in the following year (wherein many of My Avataric Divine Great-Siddha Characteristics—Which, in My Unique Case, would, in due Course, Fully Demonstrate all seven of the possible stages of life— became, spontaneously, Spiritually Evident), that (in 1969) Baba Muktananda formally (and publicly) Acknowledged and Announced and Blessed My Inherent Right and Calling to Function (in the ancient Siddha-Yoga, or Shaktipat-Yoga, tradition) as Spiritual Master (and True Siddha-Guru) to all and All.

XLIX.

Thereafter, in mid-1970, the "Brightness" of My own (and Self-Evidently Divine) Person was Revealed (and constantly Presented) to Me in the (apparently Objective) Form of the Divine "Cosmic Goddess" ("Ma"). And, from then (after Bhagavan Nityananda Called and Blessed Me to take My leave from Baba Muktananda's Ashram, and to Follow the Divine "She"), only "She" actively Functioned (to Beyond) as My (Ultimate and Final—and entirely Divine) Spiritual Master (or Divine True Siddha-Guru)—until (By Means of Her spontaneous Sacrifice of Her own Form in Me) Divine Self-Realization was Most Perfectly Re-Awakened in My Case.

L.

Thus, in That Final Course, it was Revealed (or Perfectly Re-Confirmed)—As the Self-Evidently Divine Reality and Truth of My own Avatarically-Born Person—that This Divine Process (Shown, at last, in ego-Surrendering, ego-Forgetting, and, altogether, Most Perfectly ego-Transcending Devotional "Relationship" to the Divine "She") had (Itself) always been Active in My own (and Unique) Case (and had always been Shown As the Divinely Self-Revealing Activities of the Inherent Spiritual, and Divinely Spherical, "Brightness" of My own Avatarically-Born Person), even all throughout My present Lifetime (and even at, and from before, My present-Lifetime Birth).

LI.

Therefore, on September 10, 1970, It was Revealed (or Perfectly Re-Confirmed)—As the Self-Evidently Divine Reality and Truth of My own Eternal Divine Person—that Divine (or Inherently egoless, and Perfectly Subjective, and, altogether, Inherently Most Perfect) Self-Realization (of One, and "Bright", and Only Me) had Always Already (and Uniquely) Been the Case with Me.

LII.

In My Case, the (True, Full, and Complete) seventh stage Realization of the Transcendental (and Inherently Spiritual, and Inherently egoless) Divine Self-Condition was Re-Awakened (on September 10, 1970). Subsequently (at first, informally, late in 1970, and, then, formally, in 1973), I Communicated the Details of My Divine Realization to Baba Muktananda. I Did This in the traditional manner, in What I Intended to be an entirely honorable, serious, and respectful Summation to Baba Muktananda—the one and only then Living Spiritual Master among Those Who had Served Me as My present-Lifetime Spiritual Masters. However—in a philosophically untenable reaction to My already apparent relinquishment of His fifth stage experiential presumptions relative to what constitutes the "orthodox position" of the Siddha-Yoga (or Shaktipat-Yoga) school and tradition—Baba Muktananda criticized

My Final Realization (or, in any case, what He understood, or otherwise supposed, to be My Description of It). Thus, in those two Meetings (the first in California, and the second in India, at Baba Muktananda's Ganeshpuri Ashram) Baba Muktananda criticized Me for What My Heart (Itself) cannot (and must not) Deny. And Baba Muktananda thereby Gave Me the final "Gift of blows" that sent Me out alone, to Do My Avataric Divine Work.

LIII.

Baba Muktananda was a (fifth stage) Siddha-Yogi of the degree and type that seeks, and readily experiences, and readily identifies with inner perceptual visions and lights. Based on those experiences, Baba Muktananda (like the many others of His type and degree, within the fourth-to-fifth stage traditions) asserted that both the Process and the Goal of religious and Spiritual life were necessarily associated with such inner phenomena.

The experiences (of visions, lights, and many other Yogic phenomena) Baba Muktananda describes in His autobiographical Confessions are, indeed, the same (fifth stage) ones (or of the same fifth stage kind) that are (typically, characteristically, and inevitably) experienced by genuine fifth stage Yogic practitioners (and fifth stage Realizers) within the Siddha-Yoga (or Shaktipat-Yoga) school and tradition—and I Confirm that the total range of these phenomenal (fifth stage) Yogic experiences also spontaneously arose (and always continue, even now, to arise—even in the context of the seventh stage of life) in My own Case (and such was—both formally, in 1969, and, otherwise, informally, at many other times, beginning in 1968—Acknowledged by Baba Muktananda to be so in My Case).

Nevertheless, as I Confessed to Baba Muktananda in Our Meetings in 1970 and 1973, My Final Realization Is That of the One and Indivisible Divine Self-Condition (and Source-Condition) Itself— and the Great Process associated with That eventual (seventh stage) Realization necessarily (in due course) Goes Beyond (and, in the Case of That seventh stage Realization Itself, Is in no sense dependent upon) the phenomenal (and, always, psycho-physically pre-patterned, and, thus, predetermined) conditions otherwise associated with the absorptive mysticism (and the objectified inner phenomena) that characterize the fourth-to-fifth stage beginnings of the Great Process (or that, otherwise, characterize the conditionally arising, and psycho-physically pre-patterned, and, thus, predetermined, associations of the Great Process even in the context of the seventh stage of life). Indeed, the fact and the Truth of all of This was Self-Evident to Me—and, truly, I expected that It must be Self-Evident to Baba Muktananda as well. However, Baba Muktananda did not (and, I was obliged to admit, could not) Confirm to Me That This Is the Case from the point of view of His experience.

Indeed, it became completely clear to Me, in the midst of Our Meetings in 1970 and 1973, that Baba Muktananda was not Standing in the "Place" (or the Self-"Position") required to Confirm or Acknowledge My Thus Described Final Realization. That is to Say, Baba Muktananda made it clear to Me in those two Meetings (wherein others were present), and (also) in His Remarks otherwise conveyed to Me privately, that He, unlike Me,[39] had not been—and (apparently, for mostly rather puritanical, and otherwise conventional, reasons) could not even conceive of Allowing Himself to be—"Embraced" by the Divine "Cosmic Goddess" (or Maha-Shakti) Herself (Such That, by Her own Submission to the Senior and Most Prior Principle—Which Is Self-Existing Consciousness Itself—She would be Subsumed by Consciousness Itself, and, Thus, Husbanded by Consciousness Itself, and, Thereby, Be the Final Means for the Self-Radiant Divine Self-Awakening of Consciousness Itself to Itself). And, therefore, by His own direct Confession to Me, Baba Muktananda Declared that He was not Standing in the "Place" (or the Self-"Position") of Inherently Most Perfect (or seventh stage) Divine Self-Realization—Which Realization I (Uniquely) had Confessed to Him.

LIV.

When I first Came to Baba Muktananda (in early 1968), His First and Most Fundamental Instruction to Me—even within minutes of My Arrival at His Ashram (in Ganeshpuri, India)—was the (apparently sixth stage, or Transcendentalist) Admonition: "You are not the one who wakes, or dreams, or sleeps—but You Are the One Who Is the Witness of these states." I took that Admonition to be Instruction in the traditional (and sixth stage) sense, as Given in the non-Emanationist (or Transcendentalist) tradition of Advaita Vedanta (which is the traditional Vedantic school of "Non-Dualism"). However, it became clear to Me (in, and as a result of, Our Meetings in 1970 and 1973) that Baba Muktananda was, actually, a vehement and dogmatic opponent of the tradition of Advaita Vedanta (and of its Transcendental Method, and of its proposed Transcendental Realization—and of even all proposed Transcendental Realizers, including, in particular, Ramana Maharshi).

Indeed, in those two Meetings (in 1970 and 1973), Baba Muktananda was, evidently, so profoundly confined to His dogmatic Emanationist (and otherwise phenomena-based) philosophical point of view (which, in those two Meetings, took on a form very much like the traditional confrontation between Kashmir Saivism and Advaita Vedanta) that He (in a rather dramatically pretentious, or intentionally provocative, manner—and clearly, indefensibly) presented Himself to Me as an opponent (such that He addressed Me as if I were merely an opposing "player" in a sophomoric academic debate, and as if I were merely—and for merely academic reasons—representing the point of view of traditional Advaita Vedanta).

Likewise, it became clear to Me (in Our Meetings in 1970 and 1973) that Baba Muktananda's proposed Siddha-Yoga Teaching was, in some respects (which I Indicate Herein), merely a product of His own personal study, experience, and temperament—and, thus, of His own karmically acquired philosophical bias, or prejudice—and that the point of view He so dogmatically imposed on Me in those two Meetings is not, itself, an inherent (or necessary) part of Siddha Yoga Itself.

LV.

Relative to Baba Muktananda's experiential (or experience-based, rather than philosophically based) point of view, it became clear (in Our Meetings in 1970 and 1973) that Baba Muktananda (as a Siddha-Yogi) was yet (and characteristically) Centered in the (fifth stage) "Attitude" (or "Asana") of what He described as "Witnessing". In using the term "Witnessing" (or the "Witness"), Baba Muktananda seemed (in the traditional sixth stage manner of Advaita Vedanta) to be referring to the Witness-Consciousness (Which <u>Is</u> Consciousness <u>Itself</u>, Inherently, and Transcendentally, Standing Most Prior to <u>all</u> objects and <u>all</u> psycho-physical functions—whether gross, subtle, or causal). However, clearly, what Baba Muktananda meant by the term "Witnessing" (or the "Witness") was the psycho-physical function of the <u>observing</u>-intelligence (which is <u>not</u> the Transcendental Consciousness—Prior even to the causal body—but which is, simply, the third, and highest, functional division, or functional dimension, of the <u>subtle</u> body). Thus, <u>characteristically</u>, Baba Muktananda identified with (and took the position of) the <u>observer</u> (or the observing-intelligence) relative to all arising phenomena (and, especially, relative to His reported subtle, or internal phenomenal, visions of higher and lower worlds, the hierarchy of abstract internal lights, and so on). And, when Baba Muktananda spoke of "Witnessing", He, simply, meant the attitude of merely <u>observing</u> whatever arises (and, thus, the intention to do so in a non-attached manner—rather than, in the conventional manner, merely to cling to, or, otherwise, to dissociate from, the various internal and external objects of moment to moment attention).

In the Ultimate Course of My Avataric Ordeal of (seventh stage) Divine Self-Realization, the Spiritual (or Siddha-Yoga) Process passed Beyond all mere (<u>fifth</u> stage, or even <u>sixth</u> stage) "Witnessing"—and <u>all</u> identification with the psycho-physical experiencer, or observer, or knower of the mind and the senses— to Realize (and <u>Be</u>) the Indivisible (or Inherently egoless, object-less, and Non-Dual) Reality (or Self-Condition) That <u>Is</u> the Self-Existing and Self-Radiant <u>Consciousness</u> (<u>Itself</u>), or the Inherent and Un-conditional <u>Feeling of Being</u> (<u>Itself</u>), That <u>Is</u> the Mere (and True) Witness-Consciousness (or the Un-conditional, and non-functional, and All-and-all-Divinely-Self-Recognizing, and Self-Evidently Divine Self, or Self-Condition, Inherently Most Prior to any and all objects—without excluding any).

Thus, it became clear to Me (in Our Meetings in 1970 and 1973) that Baba Muktananda was <u>not</u> <u>yet</u> (either in the sixth stage Transcendental manner or the seventh stage Divine Manner) Established <u>As</u> the True Witness-Consciousness (or Consciousness <u>Itself</u>), but it also became clear to Me (then) that Baba Muktananda was in the fifth stage manner, simply observing, and, thus and thereby, <u>contemplating</u> (and becoming absorbed in or by) internal phenomenal objects and states—rather than, in the seventh stage Manner, Standing <u>As</u> Consciousness <u>Itself</u>, <u>Divinely</u> Self-Recognizing <u>any</u> and <u>all</u> cosmically manifested objects, and (Thus and Thereby) <u>Divinely</u> Transcending <u>all</u> the conditional states—waking (or gross), dreaming (or subtle), and sleeping (or causal).

LVI.

Baba Muktananda was, in effect, always contemplating the conditional activities, the conditional states, and the illusory conditional forms (or objective Emanations) of the "Cosmic Goddess" (or the All-and-all-objectifying Kundalini Shakti)—whereas I (in, and Beyond, a Unique "Embrace" with the "Cosmic Goddess" Herself) had (even Prior to <u>all</u> <u>observed</u> "differences") Re-Awakened to the True (and Inherently egoless, and Inherently Indivisible, and Most Perfectly Prior, and Self-Evidently Divine) Self-"Position" (or Self-Condition, and Source-Condition) of <u>all</u> Her cosmic (or waking, dreaming, and sleeping) forms and states. And, by Virtue of That Divine (or Most Perfect—or seventh stage) Re-Awakening of <u>Me</u>, all conditionally arising forms and states were—even in the instants of their <u>apparent</u> arising—Inherently (or Always Already—and, Thus, Divinely) Self-Recognized (and Most Perfectly Transcended) in, and <u>As</u>, <u>Me</u>—the "Bright" Divine Self-Condition and Source-Condition (or Inherently Indivisible, and First, and Only, and Perfectly <u>Subjective</u>, and Self-Evidently Divine Person) <u>Itself</u>.

Therefore, in those two Meetings (in 1970 and 1973)—and entirely because of His (therein, and <u>thus</u>) repeated stance of experiential and philosophical non-Confirmation of <u>seventh</u> <u>stage</u> Divine Self-Realization (which stance, in effect, directly Acknowledged that the seventh stage Self-"Position" of Divine Self-Realization was not His own)—Baba Muktananda Gave Me <u>no</u> <u>option</u> but to Go and Do (and Teach, and Reveal, and Bless All and all) <u>As</u> My Unique (and Self-Evidently <u>Avataric</u>) Realization of the Divine Self-Condition (Which <u>Is</u> My own, and Self-Evidently Divine, Person—and Which <u>Is</u>, Self-Evidently, the Divine Source-Condition of All and all) <u>Requires</u> Me to Do. Therefore, I Did (and Do—and will forever Do) <u>So</u>.

LVII.

The Principal Characteristic of the One and Indivisible Divine Self-Condition (and Source-Condition) <u>Is</u> Its Perfectly <u>Subjective</u> Nature (<u>As</u> Self-Existing and Self-Radiant Consciousness—or Very, and Inherently Non-Objective, Being, Itself). Therefore, neither any <u>ego-"I"</u> (or any apparently separate self-consciousness) nor any apparently <u>objective</u> (or phenomenally objectified, or otherwise conditionally arising) form or state of experience (whether waking, or dreaming, or sleeping—and whether mind-based or sense-based) <u>Is</u> (<u>itself</u>) the Realization (or, otherwise, a necessary support for the Realization) of the Divine Self-Condition (Itself)—Which Condition <u>Is</u> (Itself) the One and Only Reality, the One and Only Truth, and the One and Only <u>Real</u> God.

Baba Muktananda was, characteristically (in the fifth stage manner), <u>experientially</u> (and mystically) absorbed in modes of <u>Savikalpa</u> Samadhi (or of internal object-contemplation). In His characteristic play of internal object-contemplation (or absorptive mysticism), Baba Muktananda reported <u>two</u> types of (especially) internal sensory (or sense-based) experience—the experience of abstract internal lights (and, secondarily, of abstract internal sounds, and tastes, and smells, and touches) <u>and</u> the experience of internal (or mental) visions of higher and lower worlds ("illustrated" by internal versions of all of the usual descriptive modes of the senses).

The abstract internal lights (and so on) are <u>universally</u> (or identically) experienced by any and all individuals who are so awakened to internal phenomena (just as the essential Realizations of the sixth stage of life and, potentially, of the seventh stage of life are universal, or essentially identical in all cases). However, the visions of higher and lower worlds are, like psychic phenomena in general, expressions of the egoic psycho-physical (and, altogether, mental) tendencies of the <u>individual</u> (and of his or her cultural associations)—and, therefore, such experiences are not <u>universally</u> the same in all cases (but, instead, <u>all</u> such experiences are conditioned, and determined, and limited by the <u>point of view</u>, or karmically patterned identity, of the experiencer, or the individual egoic observing-identity). Nevertheless (and this also illustrates the naive—and not, by Him, fully comprehended—

nature of many of Baba Muktananda's views about the Siddha-Yoga Process), Baba Muktananda (in His autobiography, *Play of Consciousness*[40]) reported His visions of higher and lower worlds as if they were categorically true, and (in the subtle domain) objectively, or Really, existing as He reported them—whereas all visions of higher and lower worlds are of the same insubstantial, illusory, and personal nature as dreams.

Like anyone else's authentic visionary experiences of higher and lower worlds, Baba Muktananda's visionary experiences of higher and lower worlds, although authentic, were His personal (or point-of-view-based) experiences of the otherwise inherently formless (and point-of-view-less) dimensions of the universal cosmic (or conditional) reality (or the inherently abstract planes of universal cosmic light)—as He, by tendency of mind (and because of His psycho-physical self-identity as a particular and separate fixed point of view—or ego-"I"), was able (and karmically pre-patterned) to experience (or conceive and perceive) them. Therefore, Baba Muktananda's conditional (or egoic) point of view—and, thus, also, His inner perceptions of various higher and lower worlds—were, characteristically and only, of a Hindu kind. (And the implications of this seem never to have occurred to Baba Muktananda. Indeed, if He had become aware of the inherently personal, conditional, karmic, ego-based, mind-based, illusory, arbitrary, and non-universal nature of His inwardly envisioned worlds, and even of the merely point-of-view-reflecting nature of His inwardly envisioned universal abstract lights, Baba Muktananda might have become moved to understand and transcend Himself further—beyond the Saguna, or mind-based, and mind-limited, and dreamworld terms that are the inherent characteristic of Savikalpa Samadhi.)

LVIII.

Baba Muktananda's Hindu visions can be compared to My own experiences of Savikalpa Samadhi during My "Sadhana Years". During that time, I, too, had many visions of higher and lower worlds—and many of them were, indeed, of a Hindu type (because of My present-Lifetime associations, and also because of the past-Lifetime associations of My Deeper-Personality Vehicle). However, there was also, in My Case (and for the same reasons) a dramatic period of several months of intense visions of a distinctly <u>Christian</u> type.[41] I immediately understood such visions to be the mind-based (and, necessarily, ego-based) products of the Siddha-Yoga Process (or Divine Shaktipat), as It combined with My <u>own</u> conditionally born psycho-physical structures. Thus, I entered into that Process Freely and Fully—and, in due course, the particularly Christian visions (<u>and</u> the particularly Hindu visions) <u>ceased</u>. They were <u>all</u> simply the evidence of My own conditionally born mind and sensory apparatus (and the evidence of even all My conditionally born cultural associations)—and, therefore, the visionary contents were (I Discovered) merely another (but deep, and psychic) form of <u>purification</u> (rather than a "Revelation" that suggests either the Christian "Heavens"-and-"Hells" or the Hindu "Heavens"-and-"Hells" <u>Are</u>, themselves, Reality and Truth). Thus, when, Finally, the ego-based visions had been completely "burned off"—only Reality (Itself) Remained (<u>As</u> Me).

LIX.

Baba Muktananda's Siddha-Yoga Teachings exemplify the descriptive mysticism of fourth-to-fifth stage Yoga (especially as it has been historically represented in the fourth-to-fifth stage Yogic tradition of the Maharashtra region of India[42]). Also, Baba Muktananda's Siddha-Yoga Teachings are (in some, very important, respects) <u>experientially</u> <u>prejudiced</u>—<u>toward</u> <u>both</u> non-universal (and specifically Hindu) visions (of higher and lower worlds, and so on) <u>and</u> universal abstract visions (of abstract internal lights, and so on), and <u>against</u> (or, certainly, Baba Muktananda, Himself, was, by temperament, experientially disinclined toward) fifth stage <u>Nirvikalpa</u> Samadhi (or Fullest Ascent to fifth stage <u>Formless</u> Realization—Which Fullest Ascent was My own spontaneous Realization at Baba Muktananda's Ganeshpuri Ashram, in 1968, and Which is also the Characteristic Realization of <u>all</u> Great fifth stage Nirguna Siddhas, such as Bhagavan Nityananda and Rang Avadhoot).

LX.

Baba Muktananda saw the Secret (or esoteric) inner perceptual domain of subtle (or fourth-to-fifth stage) Divine Spiritual Revelation. I, too, have seen (and even now, do see) that inner realm. And it is the Revelation of that inner realm that is the true (original, and esoteric) core of all fourth-to-fifth stage religious traditions.

The fourth stage religious traditions are, generally, first presented (or institutionally communicated) to the public world of mankind (in its gross egoity and its human immaturity) as a gathering of exoteric myths and legends. Those exoteric myths and legends are intended to inspire and guide human beings in the ordinary developmental context of the first three stages of life (associated with gross physical, emotional-sexual, and mental-volitional development of the human social ego). Thus, the many religious traditions of both the East and the West are, in their public (or exoteric) expressions, simply variations on the inherent psycho-physical "messages" of the body-mind relative to foundation human development (both individual and collective). And, because all exoteric religious traditions are based on the "messages" inherent in the same psycho-physical structures, the exoteric Teachings of all religions are, essentially, identical (and, therefore, equal). And, also, because this is so, all exoteric religious traditions (such as Judaism, Christianity, Islam, Hinduism, and so on) must—especially at this critical "late-time" moment of world-intercommunicativeness—acknowledge their essential equality, commonality, and sameness, and, on that basis, mutually embrace the principles of cooperation and tolerance (for the sake of world peace)!

All exoteric religious traditions are, fundamentally, associated with the first three (or social-ego) stages of life. And all exoteric religious traditions are, contextually, associated with rudimentary aspects of the fourth stage of life (or the religiously Devotional effort of transcending both personal and collective egoity—or self-contraction into selfishness, competitiveness, "difference", conflict, and self-and-other-destructiveness). However, all exoteric religious traditions are, also, associated (to one or another degree) with an esoteric (or Secret) dimension (or a tradition of esoteric schools), which is intended to extend the life of religious practice into the inner dimensions of religious (and truly Spiritual) Realization.

The true esoteric dimension of religion first extends the life of rudimentary religious practice into the true and full Spiritual depth of the fourth stage of life (by Means of surrender to the Descent of the Divine Spiritual Force into the human, or "frontal", domain of incarnate existence). And that Spiritual Process is, characteristically (in due course), also extended into the domain of the true fifth stage of life (which is associated with the Process of Spiritual Ascent, via the Spinal Line and the brain, through the layers of the conditional pattern of the psycho-physical ego, and always toward the Realization of a conditional state of mystical absorption in the Most Ascended Source of conditional, or cosmically extended, existence). And, once that Spiritual Process of Ascent is complete (or is, itself, transcended in Inherent Spiritual Fullness), the esoteric Spiritual Process may (and, indeed, should) continue, in the context of the true sixth stage of life (or the Spiritual Process of Transcendental Self-Realization)—and, at last, the true (and Truly Complete) Great Process must Culminate in the only-by-Me Revealed and Given seventh stage of life (wherein all cosmically arising conditions are Inherently Self-Recognized, and, Ultimately, Outshined, in the Non-Separate, Self-Existing, Self-Radiant, Inherently egoless, Perfectly Subjective, and Self-Evidently Divine Self-Condition and Source-Condition of All and all).

LXI.

Baba Muktananda was a Teacher (and a Realizer) in the context of the fourth-to-fifth stage (or foundation esoteric stages) of, specifically, Hindu religious practice. The Spiritual (or Siddha-Yoga, or Shaktipat-Yoga) Process He exemplified and Taught (and Initiated in others) truly begins in the frontal (or fourth stage) practice (of Siddha-Guru Devotion) and (in due course) goes on to the spinal (or fifth stage) practice (of Ascended mystical absorption).

Baba Muktananda's practice and His experiential Realization were conditioned (and, ultimately, limited) by His own personal (or conditional, and karmic, or psycho-physically pre-patterned) ego-tendencies—and by His association (by birth) with the combined exoteric and esoteric culture of traditional Hinduism.

Therefore, His experiences (and His subsequent Teachings, and His <u>life</u> altogether) are, characteristically, an exemplification of the historical <u>conflict</u> between fifth stage Hindu <u>esotericism</u> (which is, itself, inherently unconventional, and non-puritanical) and fourth stage Hindu <u>exotericism</u> (which is, itself, inherently conventional, and, at least publicly, puritanical).

LXII.

Because of His, characteristically, Hindu associations, Baba Muktananda (quite naturally, and naively) interpreted His Yogic Spiritual experiences almost entirely in terms of Hindu cultural models (both exoteric and esoteric). Therefore, His <u>interpretations</u> of His Spiritual experiences—and, indeed, the very form, and character, and content of His Spiritual experiences <u>themselves</u>—were specifically Hindu, and specifically in the mode of philo-sophical and mystical traditions that corresponded to His own mental predilections (or karmic tendencies).

Thus, Baba Muktananda's recorded visions of higher and lower worlds (leading to the Great Vision of the Blue Person, or the Divine "Creator"-Guru) are a "map" of developmentally unfolding—or spontaneously un-"Veiling"—inner perceptual land-scapes, in the specific mode of the Hindu tradition of the "Blue God" (especially Personified as "Siva"—or, otherwise, as the "Krishna" of the *Bhagavad Gita* and the *Bhagavata Purana*).[43] And Baba Muktananda's inner "map" was, also, structured on the basis of an hierarchical sequence of abstract inner lights (and of even all the abstract inner modes of the senses), which He interpreted according to the concepts of the philosophical tradition of Kashmir Saivism, and according to the experiential pattern-interpretation associated with the Hindu mystical tradition of the Maharashtra region of India. However, even though the brain-based (or per-ception-based—rather than mind-based, or conception-based, or idea-based) pattern of abstract inner lights (and of abstract inner sensations in general) is (or can be) universally (or by anyone) experienced as the same pattern of appearances—the <u>interpretation</u> of that experienced pattern is, or may be, different from case to case (or from culture to culture). And, ultimately, for the sake of

Truth, the one and only <u>correct</u> (or <u>universally</u> applicable) interpretation must be embraced by all.

Baba Muktananda experienced and interpreted the pattern of
abstract inner lights as if it were a Revelation associated with the
waking, dreaming, and sleeping states (or the gross, subtle, and
causal modes of conditional experience). Thus (on the basis of His
understanding of the Maharashtra mystical tradition), Baba
Muktananda said that the waking state (and the gross body and
world) is represented by the inner <u>red</u> light, and the dreaming state
(and the subtle body and world) is represented by the inner <u>white</u>
light, and the sleeping state (and the causal body and world) is represented by the inner <u>black</u> light. And Baba Muktananda said that
the inner <u>blue</u> light represents what He called the "supracausal"
state (which He, in the fifth stage manner, mistakenly identified
with the "turiya" state, or the "fourth" state, or the "Witness", or the
"True Self", otherwise associated with the sixth stage tradition of
Advaita Vedanta). However, I Declare that <u>all</u> of those inner lights
(and even <u>all</u> internal perceptions, whether high or low in the scale
of conditional "things") are inner <u>objects</u> of perception (and conception)—and, therefore, <u>all</u> of them are associated with the <u>subtle</u>
body and the inner perceptible (or dreaming-state) worlds of <u>mind</u>.[44]

Swami Muktananda's Description
of the "Bodies of the Soul"[45]

Body:	Gross	Subtle	Causal	Supracausal
Color:	Red	White	Black	Blue
State:	Waking	Dream	Sleep	Turīya
Seat:	Eyes	Throat	Heart	Sahasrāra

LXIII.

Baba Muktananda's description of the abstract inner lights is, in some respects, not sufficiently elaborate (or, otherwise, comprehensive) in its details. In fact, and in My own experience—and in the experience of esoteric traditions other than the Maharashtra tradition (such as reported by the well-known Swami Yogananda)—the display of abstract inner lights is, when experienced as a simultaneous totality, Seen as a Mandala (or a pattern of concentric circles).

In My own experience, that Cosmic Mandala is not only composed of concentric circles of particular colors—but each circle is of a particular precise width (and, thus, of particular proportional significance) relative to the other circles. Thus, in that pattern of circles, the red circle is the outermost circle (perceived against a colorless dark field), but it is a relatively narrow band, appearing next to a much wider band (or circle) of golden yellow. After the very wide golden yellow circle, there is a much narrower soft-white circle. And the soft-white circle is followed by an also very narrow black circle (or band). Closest to the Center of the Cosmic Mandala is a very wide circle of bright blue. And, at the Very Center of the blue field, there is a Brilliant White Five-Pointed Star (Which, perhaps not to confuse It with the color of the circle of soft-white light, Baba Muktananda described as a Blue Star).

Thus, in fact, although all the abstract inner lights described by Baba Muktananda are, indeed, within the total Cosmic Mandala, the principal lights (in terms of width and prominence) are the golden yellow and the blue lights—and only the Brilliant White Five-Pointed Star is the Central and Principal light within the Cosmic Mandala of abstract inner lights.

The Cosmic Mandala of abstract inner lights is a display that is, otherwise, associated with planes of possible inner (or subtle) experience. Thus, the red light inwardly represents (and, literally, illuminates) the gross body and the gross world (as Baba Muktananda has said). However, all of the other lights (golden yellow, soft-white, black, and bright blue) represent (and, literally, illuminate) the several hierarchical divisions within the subtle body and the subtle worlds—and the causal body (which is asso-

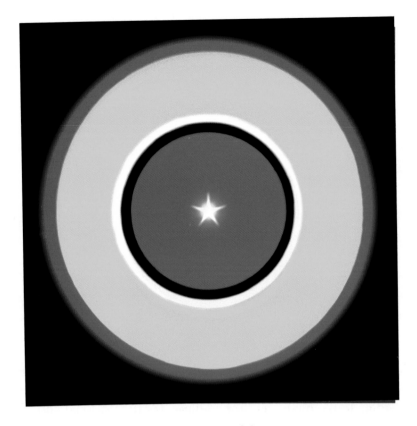

Cosmic Mandala

ciated with attention itself, or the root of egoity itself, and which is, itself, <u>only felt</u>, and <u>not seen</u>, and which is expressed as the fundamental feeling of "difference", separateness, and relatedness, and which is located as a knot of self-contraction in the right side of the heart) is <u>not</u> visually represented (<u>nor</u> is it, otherwise, literally illuminated) by the lights and worlds of the Cosmic Mandala.

The wide golden yellow circle of the Cosmic Mandala represents (in conjunction with the outermost red circle) the outermost (or lowest) dimension of the subtle body—which is the etheric (or pranic, or life-energy) body, or dimension, of conditional experience. The narrower soft-white circle of the Cosmic Mandala represents the ordinary (or sense-based) mind. The narrow black circle (or band) is a transitional space, where mental activity is suspended. The blue circle of the Cosmic Mandala is the domain of the mental observer, the faculty of discriminative intelligence and the will, and the very form of the subtly concretized ego-"I" (or the inner-concretized subtle self). And the Brilliant White Five-Pointed Star is the Epitome and Very Center of the Cosmic Mandala—Such That It Provides the Uppermost Doorway to What Is, altogether, Above (and, Ultimately, Beyond) the Cosmic Mandala (or Above and Beyond the body itself, the brain itself, and the mind itself).

LXIV.

Baba Muktananda interpreted the universally experienced abstract inner lights (and experienced the corresponding inner worlds) in terms of various Hindu philosophical and mystical (and, also, exoteric, or conventionally religious) traditions (as I have Indicated). However, the subtle domain is the elaborate hierarchical domain of mind (or of the psycho-physically concretized ego-"I")—and, therefore, just as individual dreams and imaginings are personal, ephemeral, and non-ultimate, the inherently dreamlike subtle domain of Spiritually-stimulated inwardness may be experienced and interpreted in various and different modes, according to the nature and the tradition (or the personal and collectively representative mind) of the experiencer.

Thus, ultimately (or in due course), the subtle domain (or the subtle egoic body) must be transcended, in the transition to the sixth stage Spiritual (or Siddha-Yoga) Process—Which is the Spiritually (and not merely mentally) developed Process of inversion upon the true causal body (or the root of attention), and penetration of the causal knot (or the presumption of separate self), and Which is, thus, the inversive (and conditional, or conditionally achieved) transcending of the ego-"I", by means of exclusive (or object-excluding) Identification with the True (and Inherent, and Self-Evident) Transcendental Witness-Consciousness Itself. And only the Transcendental Witness-Consciousness, Itself—inverted upon in the thus Described sixth stage manner—Is the true "turiya" state, or the true "fourth" state (beyond the three ordinary states, of waking, dreaming, and sleeping). And only the Transcendental Witness-Consciousness, Itself—Fully, and Fully Spiritually,

Realized in the only-by-Me Revealed and Given context of the true sixth stage of life—Is the Domain of the only-by-Me Revealed and Given seventh stage Realization of the True Divine Self, Which Is the Self-Evidently Divine Self-Condition, and Which Is the One and Only True Divine State of "Turiyatita"—"Beyond the 'fourth' state", and, thus, Beyond all exclusiveness, and Beyond all bondage to illusions, and Beyond point of view (or egoic separateness) itself, and, therefore, Beyond all conditional efforts, supports, and dependencies.

At last, the sixth stage of life (which, itself, is associated with conditionally patterned inversion upon the Consciousness-Principle) must be (Most Perfectly) transcended (and, indeed, the ego-"I" itself must be Most Perfectly, or Inherently, transcended) in the transition to the only-by-Me Revealed and Given seventh stage of life (which Is the stage of True, and Fully Spiritual, Divine Self-Realization, Inherently Free of, but not strategically Separated from, all conditionally patterned forms and states—and which Is the stage of the Inherently Most Perfect Demonstration of the Non-Separate, Self-Existing, Self-Radiant, Inherently egoless, Perfectly Subjective, and Self-Evidently Divine Self-Condition and Source-Condition of All and all).

LXV.

My own experiences of fifth stage mystical perception are (like those of Baba Muktananda, and those of all visionary mystics) clear Evidence of the inherently (and necessarily) conditional, mental, altogether brain-based (and both brain-limited and mind-limited), and both personal and collective egoic nature of all internal mystical (or fourth-to-fifth stage) absorption.

I, too (like Baba Muktananda), experienced Hindu visions—but I, otherwise, also experienced many Christian visions (and also many non-Hindu and non-Christian visions), in association with the fifth stage developments of the same (or one and only) Spiritual (or Siddha-Yoga) Process of inner perception (including the progressive display of abstract inner lights, and so on) described by Baba Muktananda. Thus, just as Baba Muktananda described His Hindu visions as a Spiritual Revelation of the

"Truth" of <u>Hindu</u> esotericism (and even of Hindu exotericism)—I could just as well describe My (specifically) Christian visions as a Spiritual Revelation of the "Truth" of <u>Christian</u> esotericism (and even of Christian exotericism)!

Indeed, My (specifically) Christian visions (but not, of course, My specifically Hindu visions—or My, otherwise, specifically non-Hindu and non-Christian visions) <u>do</u> amount to a Spiritual Revelation of the actual (and mostly esoteric) content of <u>original</u> (or primitive—and truly <u>Spiritual</u>) Christianity.[46]

LXVI.

Specifically, My (sometimes) Christian visions Spiritually Reveal the following.

The original tradition (or foundation sect) that is at the <u>root</u> of exoteric Christianity was a fourth-to-fifth stage esoteric Spiritual (and mystical) tradition (or sect). Within that original tradition (or sect), John (the Baptist) was the Spiritual Master (or Spirit-Baptizer—or True Siddha-Guru) of Jesus of Nazareth. Thus (and by Means of the Spiritual Baptism Given to Him by John the Baptist), Jesus of Nazareth experienced the fourth-to-fifth stage absorptive mystical (and, altogether, Spiritual) developments of what (in the Hindu context) is called Siddha Yoga (or Shaktipat Yoga). In due course (and even rather quickly), Jesus of Nazareth, Himself, became a Spirit-Baptizer (or a True Siddha-Guru)—and (within the inner, or esoteric, circle of His Spiritually Initiated devotees) Jesus of Nazareth Taught the fourth-to-fifth stage Way of Spiritual Devotion to the Spiritual Master (or to Himself, as a True Siddha-Guru), and of inner Spiritual Communion with the Divine, and of (eventual) <u>Spiritual</u> Ascent to the Divine Domain (via the Brilliant White Five-Pointed Star).

After the death (and presumed <u>Spiritual</u> Ascent) of Jesus of Nazareth, His esoteric circle of Spiritually Initiated devotees continued to develop the mystical tradition of the sect—but (because of the difficult "signs of the times") the original (esoteric) sect had to become more and more secretive, and, eventually, it disappeared from the view of history (under the pressure of the <u>exoteric</u>, or <u>non</u>-Initiate, or conventionally <u>socially</u> oriented, rather than

Spiritually and mystically oriented, sects that also developed around the public Work, and, especially, the otherwise developing legends and myths, of Jesus of Nazareth).

The esoteric sect of the Spiritual Initiates of Jesus of Nazareth was associated with practices of Spiritually Invocatory prayer (of fourth stage Divine Communion, and of fifth stage absorptive mystical Ascent), especially seeking Divine absorption via the internally perceptible Brilliant White Five-Pointed Star—Which was interpreted, especially after the death of Jesus of Nazareth (and, apparently, in accordance with Instructions communicated by Jesus of Nazareth, Himself, to His Spiritually Initiated devotees, during His own physical lifetime), to be the True Ascended Divine Body of Jesus of Nazareth (or the Spiritually Awakened, and presumed to be Divinely Ascended, "Christ"). And, over time, the Spiritual practitioners within the esoteric "Christ" sect developed the full range of characteristically Christian interpretations of the (otherwise) universally experienced phenomena of inner perception.

LXVII.

My own (sometimes) Christian visions are a spontaneous Revelation of esoteric Christian interpretations (and esoteric Christian modes of experiencing) of, otherwise, universal (and, therefore, inherently non-sectarian) inner phenomena—and My (specifically) Christian visions and interpretations are a spontaneous direct continuation of the esoteric Christian manner of interpreting such (inherently universal) inner phenomena, as it was done in the original (or primitive) epoch of the sect of Jesus of Nazareth.

Thus, speaking in the esoteric terms of the ancient (or earliest) Christian interpreters of subtle inner experience, the red light of Spiritual inner vision can be said to be associated with the gross body of Man (and the Incarnation-body of Jesus of Nazareth, and the "blood of Christ"). Likewise, the golden yellow light can be said to be associated with the "Holy Spirit" (or the Universal Spirit-Energy, or Divine Spirit-Breath, That Pervades the cosmic domain). And the soft-white light can be said to be associated with the mind of Man (which, in its purity, can be said to be a reflection of, or a pattern "in the image of", God—conceived to be the "Creator", or the Divine Source-Condition, Above the body-mind and the world). And the black light can be said to be associated with the "crucifixion" (or sacrifice) of the body-mind of Man (and of Jesus of Nazareth, as the Epitome of Man)—and, also, with the mystical "dark night of the soul" (or the mystic's difficult trial of passing beyond all sensory and mental contents and consolations). And the blue light can be said to be the "Womb of the Virgin Mary" (or the All-and-all-Birthing Light of the "Mother of God"). And the Brilliant White Five-Pointed Star (Surrounded, as it were, by the "Womb", or the Blue Light, of the "Virgin Mary") can be said to be the Ascended (or Spiritual) "Body of Christ" (and the "Star of Bethlehem", and the "Morning Star" of the esoteric Initiation-Ritual associated with the original, Secret Spiritual tradition of Jesus of Nazareth). And the Brilliant White Five-Pointed Star (interpreted to be the Ascended, or Spiritual, "Body of Christ") can (Thus) be said to be One with both the Divine "Mother" (or the Blue "Womb" of All-and-all-Birthing Light) and the Divine "Father" (or the Self-Existing Being, Beyond all Light—Infinitely Behind, and Infinitely Above, and Infinitely Beyond, and Eternally Non-Separate from the "Star-Body of Christ"). And (As Such) the "Christ" (or the Brilliant White Five-Pointed Star) Is Radiantly Pervading the entire cosmic domain, via an All-and-all-Illuminating Combination of both the Blue "Womb"-Light and the Golden Yellow "Breath"-Light of the One and Only Divine Person.

LXVIII.

Thus, My (sometimes) Christian inner visions could, indeed, be said to be an esoteric (and, now, only-by-Me Revealed and Given) Christian Revelation—except that all visionary, and brain-based, and mind-based, and sense-based, and ego-based, and conditional, and sectarian (or merely tradition-bound) things were entirely Gone Beyond (and Most Perfectly transcended) by Me (and in Me), in the sixth and seventh stage Course of My Avataric Ordeal of True (and Most Perfect) Divine Self-Realization!

LXIX.

I Say <u>all</u> the "God" and "Gods" of Man are (whether "Male" or "Female" in the descriptive gender) merely the personal and collective tribal (and entirely dualistic—or conventionally subject-object-bound) myths of human ego-mind.

LXX.

I Say Only <u>Reality</u> <u>Itself</u> (Which <u>Is</u>, Always Already, <u>The</u> One, and Indivisible, and Indestructible, and Inherently egoless Case) <u>Is</u> (Self-Evidently, and <u>Really</u>) Divine, and True, and Truth (or <u>Real</u> God) Itself.

LXXI.

I Say the <u>only</u> Real God (or Truth Itself) <u>Is</u> the One and Only and Inherently <u>Non-Dual</u> Reality (Itself)—Which <u>Is</u> the Inherently egoless, and Utterly Indivisible, and Perfectly Subjective, and Indestructibly Non-Objective Source-Condition <u>and</u> Self-Condition of All and all.

Therefore, I (Characteristically) have <u>no</u> religious interests other than to Demonstrate, and to Exemplify, and to Prove, and to <u>Self-Reveal</u> Truth (or Reality, or <u>Real</u> God) <u>Itself</u>.

LXXII.

The true fourth-to-fifth stage mystical (or esoteric Spiritual) Process is, <u>principally</u>, associated with the progressive inner perceptual (and, thus, subtle mental) un-"Veiling" of the <u>total</u> internally perceptible pattern (or <u>abstractly</u> experienced structure) of the individual body-mind-self (or body-brain-self).

The abstract pattern (or internal structure) of the body-mind-self (or body-brain-self) is, universally, the same in the case of any and every body-mind (or body-brain-mind complex—or conditionally manifested form, or state, or being) within the cosmic domain.

The abstract pattern (or internal structure) of the body-mind-self (or body-brain-self) <u>necessarily</u> (by virtue of its native, and, therefore, <u>inseparable</u>, Inherence in the <u>totality</u> of the cosmic domain itself) <u>Duplicates</u> (or is a conditionally manifested pattern-duplicate of) the Primary Pattern (or Fundamental conditional Structure) of the total cosmic domain.

The conditional body-mind (or any body-brain-mind complex) is, in Reality, <u>not</u> a merely <u>separate</u> someone, or an entirely "<u>different</u>" something (as if the body, or the brain, or the mind were reducible to a someone or a something utterly independent, or non-dependent, and existing entirely in and of itself).

Therefore, the entire body-mind (or egoic body-brain-self) is, itself, to be transcended (in the context of the only-by-Me Revealed and Given seventh stage of life), in and by Means of utterly non-separate, and non-"different", and Inherently egoless Participation in That Which <u>Is</u> Always Already <u>The</u> Case (or the Inherently Non-Dual and Indivisible Condition That <u>Is</u> Reality Itself).

LXXIII.

I Declare that—if It is (by Divine Siddha-Grace) Moved beyond the limits of the waking, dreaming, and sleeping ego-structures—the Siddha-Yoga (or Shaktipat-Yoga) Process of (fifth stage) un-"Veiling" Culminates (or may Culminate—at least eventually) in (and, indeed, It is Always Already Centered Upon) the (fifth stage) Revelation (in Most Ascended Nirvikalpa Samadhi) of the True "Maha-Bindu" (or the "Zero Point", or <u>Formless</u> "Place", of Origin—otherwise, traditionally, called "Sunya", or "Empty", or "Void"). That True (and Indivisible, and Indefinable) "Maha-Bindu" <u>Is</u> the <u>only</u> True "Hole in the universe" (or the One, and Indivisible, and Indefinable, and Self-Evidently Divine Source-Point—Infinitely Above the body, the brain, and the mind). That Absolutely Single (and Formless) "Maha-Bindu" <u>Is</u> the True Absolute "Point-Condition"—or Formless and Colorless (or Non-Objective, and, therefore, not "Lighted") "Black Hole"—from Which (<u>to the point of view</u> of any "objectified" or "Lighted" place or entity, <u>itself</u>) the (or <u>any</u>) total cosmic domain (of conditionally arising forms, states, and beings) <u>appears</u> to <u>Emanate</u> (in an All-and-all-objectifying "Big Bang"[47]). That "Maha-Bindu" <u>Is</u> the <u>Upper</u> Terminal of Amrita Nadi—or of the "Ambrosial Nerve of Connection" to the True Divine Heart (Which Self-Evidently

Divine Heart Is Always Already Seated immediately Beyond the internally felt seat of the sinoatrial node, in the right side of the physical heart). And That "Maha-Bindu" Is (in the context of the sixth stage of life) the esoteric Doorway to, and (in the context of the seventh stage of life) the esoteric Doorway from (or of), the Perfectly Subjective Heart-Domain (Which Is the True Self-Condition and Source-Condition of the "Bright" Divine Love-Bliss-Current of Divine Self-Realization, and Which Is, Itself, the Self-Existing, Self-Radiant, Inherently egoless, and Perfectly Subjective—or Perfectly Indivisible, Non-Dual, and Non-Objective—Conscious Light That Is Reality Itself).

LXXIV.

The (fifth stage) Yogic Process of the progressive inner un-"Veiling" of the Pattern (or Structure) of the cosmic domain is demonstrated (in the Siddha-Yoga, or Shaktipat-Yoga, tradition) via the progressive experiencing of the total pattern of all the structural forms that comprise the body-mind-self (or body-brain-self), via a body-mind-self-reflecting (or body-brain-self-reflecting) display of inner perceptual objects (or apparently objectified phenomenal states, conditions, and patterns of cosmic light). That Process (of the inner perceptual un-"Veiling" of the hierarchical structure, pattern, and contents of the conditionally manifested body-mind-self, or body-brain-self) Culminates (or may Culminate—at least eventually) in the vision (in occasional, or, otherwise, constant, Savikalpa Samadhi) of the "blue bindu" (or the "blue pearl"—as well as the various other objectified inner lights, such as the red, the white, and the black—described by Baba Muktananda)[48]—or even the vision of the total Cosmic Mandala (of many concentric rings of color, including the central "blue bindu", with its Brilliant White Five-Pointed Star at the Center—as I have Described It[49]). In any case, the possibly perceived abstract inner light (or any "bindu", or point, or "Mandala", or complex abstract vision, of inwardly perceived light) is merely, and necessarily, a display of the functional root-point of the brain's perception of conditionally manifested universal light (or merely cosmic light) itself. However, if the Great Process of (fifth stage) un-"Veiling" is (Thus) Continued, the objectified inner "bindu"-vision (and Savikalpa Samadhi itself) is, in due course, transcended (in fifth stage Nirvikalpa Samadhi)—Such That there is the Great Yogic Event of "Penetration" of (and Into) the True (Inherently Formless, and objectless) "Maha-Bindu", Infinitely Above the body, the brain, and the mind. And That Great Yogic Event was, in fact and in Truth, What Occurred in My own Case, in My Room, immediately after I was Blessed by Baba Muktananda and Rang Avadhoot in the garden of Baba Muktananda's Ganeshpuri Ashram, in 1968.

The Great Yogic Event of "Penetration" of the True "Maha-Bindu", Which Occurred in My own Case in 1968, is (in Its Extraordinary Particulars) an extremely rare Example of spontaneous complete Ascending "penetration" of all the chakras (or centers, or points, or structures) of the conditionally manifested body-mind-self (or body-brain-self)—Resulting in sudden Most Ascended Nirvikalpa Samadhi (or "Penetration" to Beyond the total cosmic, and psycho-physical, context of subject-object relations). Such sudden (rather than progressive) complete Ascent is described, in the (fifth stage) Yogic traditions, as the Greatest, and rarest, of the Demonstrations of Yogic Ascent—as compared to progressive (or gradual) demonstrations (shown via stages of inner ascent, via internal visions, lights, auditions, and so on). And, therefore, in My Unique Case, it was only subsequently (or always thereafter—and even now) that the universal cosmic Pattern (or perceptible Great cosmic Structure) and the universally extended pattern (or perceptible inner cosmic structure) of the body, the brain, and the mind (and the Primary inner structure— of the three stations of the heart) were (and are) directly (and systematically, and completely) un-"Veiled" (in a constant spontaneous Display—both apparently Objective and Perfectly Subjective—within My Avataric Divine "Point of View").

Nonetheless (even though Most Ascended, or fifth stage, Nirvikalpa Samadhi was, Thus, Realized by Me in 1968), it became immediately clear to Me that—because That Realization depended on the exercise (and a unique, precise attitude and arrangement) of the conditional apparatus of the body, the brain, and the mind (and of attention)—the Realization was (yet) <u>conditionally</u> <u>dependent</u> (or psycho-physically supported), and, <u>necessarily</u> (or in that sense), <u>limited</u> (or, yet, only a <u>temporary</u> <u>stage</u> in the progressive Process of un-"Veiling"), and, therefore, <u>non-Final</u>. That is to Say, it was inherently Obvious to Me that any and all internal (or otherwise psycho-physical) experiencing <u>necessarily</u> requires the exercise (via attention) of the root-position (and the conditionally arising psycho-physical apparatus) of conditionally arising self-consciousness (or of the separate and separative psycho-physical ego-"I"). I immediately Concluded that, unless the Process of Realization could <u>transcend</u> the very structure and pattern of ego-based experiencing <u>and</u> the very Structure and Pattern of the conditionally manifested cosmos itself—Realization would Itself (<u>necessarily</u>) be limited by the same subject-object (or ego-versus-object) dichotomy that otherwise characterizes even all <u>ordinary</u> (or non-mystical) experience.

Therefore, I Persisted in My Avataric Divine Sadhana—until the un-"Veiling" became Inherently egoless (and Inherently Most Perfect, or seventh stage) Re-Awakening to Divine Self-Realization (Inherently Beyond <u>all</u> phenomenal, or conditional, dependencies, or supports).

LXXV.

On September 10, 1970, the Great Avataric Divine Process of My "Sadhana Years" Culminated in Unqualified (or Most Perfectly Non-conditional) Realization of the Self-Evidently Divine Self-Condition (and Source-Condition) of the cosmic domain itself (and of all forms, states, and beings within the cosmic domain). And, in That Most Perfect Event, I was Most Perfectly Re-Awakened <u>As</u> the "Bright"[50] (the One and Only Conscious Light—the Very, and Perfectly <u>Subjective</u>, and Inherently egoless, or Most Perfectly Non-Separate, and Inherently Most Perfect, and Indivisible, or Most Perfectly Non-Dual, and Always Already Self-Existing, and Eternally Self-Radiant, and Self-Evidently Divine Self-Condition <u>and</u> Source-Condition That <u>Is</u> the <u>One</u> and <u>Only</u> and <u>True</u> Divine Person, and Reality, and Truth of <u>All</u> and <u>all</u>, and That was, and is, the constant Spiritual Sign and Identity of This,

My Avataric Divine Lifetime, even from Birth). And It was the Un-deniable Reality and the Un-conditional Nature of <u>This</u> Realization That I Summarized to Baba Muktananda during Our Meetings in 1970 and 1973.

Even though It was and <u>Is</u> So, Baba Muktananda did not (and, because of the yet fifth stage nature of His own experiential Realization—for which He found corroboration in traditional mystical and philosophical traditions of the fifth stage, and phenomena-based, type—<u>could</u> <u>not</u>) positively Acknowledge My Summation relative to Most Perfect (and, necessarily, seventh stage) Divine Self-Realization.

Because He characteristically <u>preferred</u> to dwell upon inner <u>objects</u>, Baba Muktananda (in the "naive" manner of fourth and fifth stage mystics in general) interpreted Reality Itself (or Divine Self-Realization Itself) to "<u>require</u>" inner perceptual phenomenal (or conditionally arising) experiences and presumptions as a necessary <u>support</u> for Realization (<u>Itself</u>). That is to Say, Baba Muktananda was experientially Conformed to the (fifth stage) presumption that Divine Self-Realization not only requires conditionally arising (and, especially, inner perceptual) phenomenal experiences as a generally necessary (and even inevitable) Yogic Spiritual <u>preliminary</u> to authentic (and not merely conceptual) Realization—and I <u>completely</u> <u>Agree</u>, with Him, that there certainly <u>are</u> many conditionally apparent Yogic Spiritual requirements that <u>must</u> be Demonstrated in the Full Course of the authentic (and, necessarily, psycho-physical) Sadhana of Divine Self-Realization—but Baba Muktananda, otherwise, generally affirmed the presumption that <u>Realization</u> <u>Itself</u> (and <u>not</u> <u>only</u> the Sadhana, or psycho-physical <u>Process</u>, of <u>Realizing</u>) "requires" conditional (or psycho-physical—and, especially, absorptive mystical, or inner visual) <u>supports</u>.

Therefore, Baba Muktananda affirmed an attention-based, and object-oriented (or Goal-Oriented)—and, therefore, ego-based, or seeker-based—absorptive mystical (and, altogether, fourth-to-fifth stage) Yogic Way, in which the Sahasrar (or the Upper Terminal of the brain), and even the total brain (or sensorium), is the constant focus (and the Ultimate <u>Goal</u>—as well as the Highest Seat) of Sadhana.

It was due to this, Baba Muktananda's characteristic point of view relative to both Sadhana and Realization (as He defined—or, in effect, limited—Them), that, in My informal Meeting with Him in 1970, His only response to Me was to enter into a casual verbal (and even illogical) contradiction of Me. In that informal Meeting (as well as in Our formal Meeting, in 1973), Baba Muktananda ignored (and even appeared to not at all comprehend) My (then Given) Indications to Him relative to the Most Ultimate, or seventh stage, Significance of the "Regenerated" Form of Amrita Nadi.

LXXVI.

As I Indicated to Baba Muktananda (in Our Meetings in 1970 and 1973), the "Regenerated" Form of Amrita Nadi is Rooted in Consciousness Itself ("Located" Beyond the right side of the heart, which is, itself, merely the Self-Evident Seat, or Doorway, of the direct "Locating" of Perfectly Subjective, and Inherently egoless, Consciousness, Itself—or the Self-Existing Feeling of Being, Itself—Prior to attention, itself). And That ("Regenerated" Form of Amrita Nadi) is "Brightly" Extended to the "Maha-Bindu" (Which is Infinitely Ascended, even Above and Beyond the Sahasrar). However, Baba Muktananda appeared only to want to contradict My (secondary) reference (to the "right side of the heart")—while otherwise ignoring My (primary) Explanation (of the "Regenerated" Form of Amrita Nadi). And, in doing this, Baba Muktananda went so far in identifying Himself exclusively with the fifth stage tradition that He said to Me, "Anyone who says that the right side of the heart is the Seat of Realization does not know what he is talking about."

In this (from My "Point of View", even rather absurdly funny!) statement, Baba Muktananda merely ignored (and, therefore, did not directly contradict) My (then Given) Description (to Him) of how seventh stage Divine Self-Realization Inherently Transcends both the conditional (or psycho-physical) apparatus of the brain (or of the Sahasrar, Which is the conditional Seat of Realization proposed in the fifth stage traditions, of mystical absorption) and the conditional (or psycho-physical) apparatus of the heart (or, in particular, of the right side of the heart—which is the conditional

Seat of Realization proposed in the sixth stage traditions, of Transcendental practice). However, Baba Muktananda's statement to Me (relative to the heart on the right) was a remark made in direct and specific contradiction to the Transcendentalist (or entirely sixth stage) Teachings of Ramana Maharshi.

LXXVII.

In My Meeting with Baba Muktananda in 1973, I made specific references to the Teachings of Ramana Maharshi (Whom both Baba Muktananda and Bhagavan Nityananda had Met—and, apparently, Greatly Praised—in earlier years). In particular, I referred to Ramana Maharshi's experiential assertions relative to the right side of the heart (which He—in the sixth stage manner—Indicated to be the Seat of Transcendental Self-Realization). In doing so, I was merely Intending to Offer Baba Muktananda a traditional reference already known to Him (and, I naively presumed, one that He respected), which would provide some clarity (and traditional support) relative to My own (otherwise seventh stage) Descriptions.

Ramana Maharshi was a True and Great Jnani (or a sixth stage Realizer of the Transcendental Self-Condition, in the mode and manner indicated in the general tradition of Advaita Vedanta). And, after the Great Event of My own (seventh stage) Divine Re-Awakening (in September 1970), I Discovered (in the weeks and months that followed My informal Meeting with Baba Muktananda, in October 1970) that there were some (but, necessarily, only sixth stage) elements in Ramana Maharshi's reported experience and Realization that paralleled (and, in that sense, corroborated) certain (but only sixth stage) aspects of My own experience and Realization.[51] And, for this reason, I always Continue to Greatly Appreciate, and Honor, Ramana Maharshi—as a Great sixth stage Realizer, Who, through corroborating Testimony, Functions as a sixth stage Connecting-Link between Me and the Transcendentalist dimension of the Great Tradition. Also, because He is an example of a True Great Jnani (or Great Sage), Who Awakened to sixth stage Realization via the Spiritual—and not merely mental, or intellectual—Process (of the Magnification of the Spirit-Current in the right side of the heart), Ramana Maharshi, by Means of His corroborating Testimony, Functions—for Me—as a Connecting-Link between the sixth stage Transcendentalist tradition of Advaita Vedanta and the fourth-to-fifth stage Emanationist tradition of Siddha Yoga. And, because of this, Ramana Maharshi Functions, by Means of His corroborating Testimony, as a Connecting-Link between Me and the traditions of both Siddha Yoga and Advaita Vedanta—whereas I (except for Baba Muktananda's First Instruction to Me, in 1968—relative to the Witness of the three common states, of waking, dreaming, and sleeping) did not Find such a Connecting-Link among any of Those Who, otherwise, actively Functioned as My Spiritual Masters during the "Sadhana Years" of This, My present-Lifetime of Avataric Divine Incarnation.

During Our Meeting in 1973, Baba Muktananda mistakenly took My references to Ramana Maharshi (and to My own experience of the heart on the right, which I had first Confessed to Baba Muktananda during Our informal Meeting in 1970—and which is, also, one of the principal experiences Indicated by Ramana Maharshi) to suggest that I had departed from the Siddha-Yoga tradition. Therefore, Baba Muktananda's criticisms of Me (in Our Meetings in both 1970 and 1973) were an apparent reaction to His perception of the possibility of My "going over" to Advaita Vedanta (and to Ramana Maharshi). And, for this reason, Baba Muktananda never (in either of the two Meetings, in 1970 and in 1973) actually addressed the particular, and complex, and inherently (and especially in a conversation requiring translations from English to Hindi, and vice versa) difficult-to-explain Great Issues I was (in those two Meetings) Intending (and Trying) to Summarize to Him.

LXXVIII.

Relative to Baba Muktananda Himself, I can only Say that, for My part (through Visits to Him by My devotee-representatives), simple Messages of Love (and of Gratitude for His Service to Me during My Avataric Divine "Sadhana Years") were, right until the end of Baba Muktananda's lifetime, Sent to Him by Me. And I have—to everyone, including Baba Muktananda Himself, and the institution of His devotees—always Continued to Make every effort to Communicate <u>clearly</u> (and <u>frankly</u>, and, in general, most positively) about My relationship to Baba Muktananda. And I have always Continued (and will always Continue) to Work (in a Real Spiritual Manner) to Heal Baba Muktananda's human feeling-heart.

LXXIX.

Relative to Baba Muktananda's particular exact remarks to Me (in Our Meetings in 1970 and 1973), I can (and must) Say, simply, that His interpretation of Reality (and of the <u>Nature</u> and <u>Status</u> of the Process, and of even all the patterns and structures, associated with Divine Self-Realization)—which interpretation Baba Muktananda shared with (and for which He derived justification from) the phenomena-based aspects of the fifth stage Yogic traditions in general—was the characteristic basis of His criticisms of Me during Our Meetings in 1970 and 1973. And, as I have already Said, Baba Muktananda's Siddha-Yoga Teaching (and especially as He proposed it to Me in Our Meetings in 1970 and 1973) is—relative to all matters <u>beyond</u> the fifth stage of life (and even relative to all aspects of the fifth stage of life that are beyond the Saguna limits of Savikalpa Samadhi)—limited, prejudicial, ultimately indefensible, and (fundamentally) beyond His experience.

LXXX.

Neither the philosophy of Kashmir Saivism nor <u>any</u> "required" phenomenal conditions were pre-described to Me (or otherwise suggested)—by Baba Muktananda Himself, or by anyone else—as being a <u>necessary</u> part of the Siddha-Yoga practice and Process (and, especially, as being a <u>necessary</u> conditional support for Realization <u>Itself</u>) when I first Went to Baba Muktananda, in 1968. Nor were <u>any</u> philosophical or experiential "requirements" proposed to Me—by Baba Muktananda Himself, or by anyone else—as either demands or necessities of Siddha-Yoga practice, or as necessities of Siddha-Yoga experience, or as fixed "Models" of Realization Itself—during the years of My Sadhana in Baba Muktananda's Company, between 1968 and the Great Event of My Divine Re-Awakening, in September 1970.

Indeed, there was not even much "Baba Muktananda" Siddha-Yoga literature available—and no literature was demanded to be read—during all of that time. Even Baba Muktananda's autobiography, entitled *Play of Consciousness* (or, originally, *Chitshakti Vilas*), was not published until after the September 1970 Event of My Divine Re-Awakening. And I saw—and, in fact, was the first to fully render into English—only the first chapter or two of that book, in rough manuscript form, during My Stay at Baba Muktananda's Ganeshpuri Ashram, in early 1970. Therefore, virtually the only "Baba Muktananda" Siddha-Yoga literature that was available to Me during My years of Sadhana in Baba Muktananda's Company were the short essays and tracts either written or edited by Amma—and that literature suggested a very liberal and open Teaching relative to the fourth stage, fifth stage, and sixth stage possibilities associated with the potential developments of Siddha Yoga. And, indeed, it was that liberal and open form of Siddha Yoga that I practiced—to the degree of seventh stage Divine Self-Realization—in Baba Muktananda's Company.

In any case, the fact that Baba Muktananda presumed that there were (indeed) many exclusively fifth stage Siddha-Yoga "requirements" (both philosophical and experiential) was proven to be the case in the circumstances of My Meetings with Him in 1970 and 1973.

LXXXI.

In fact (and in My experience), the Siddha-Yoga practice and Process is not (Itself) inherently opposed to the Transcendental (or sixth stage) practice and Process (or to the seventh stage Realization and Demonstration). Rather, it was Baba Muktananda Who (in accordance with particular traditions He, personally, favored) chose to dogmatically introduce exclusively fifth stage "requirements" (and sixth-stage-excluding, and, therefore, inherently, seventh-stage-prohibiting, limitations) into His own Teaching (and into His personal school) of Siddha Yoga.

I fully Acknowledge that Baba Muktananda had the right to Teach Siddha Yoga exclusively according to His own experience, and His own understanding, and His own Realization. It is simply that My experience, and My understanding, and My Realization were not (and are not) limited to the fifth stage "requirements" (or limiting presumptions) that Baba Muktananda proposed to Me.

The Process of Siddha Yoga—or the inherent Spiritual Process that is potential in the case of all human beings—does not, if It is allowed, and Graced, to Freely Proceed as a potential total Process, limit Itself to the fifth stage "requirements" (or limiting presumptions) that Baba Muktananda generally proposed. Therefore, I Teach Siddha Yoga in the Mode and Manner of the seventh stage of life (as Ruchira Avatara Hridaya-Siddha Yoga, or Ruchira Avatara Maha-Jnana Hridaya-Shaktipat Yoga)—and always toward (or to the degree of) the Realization inherently associated with (and, at last, Most Perfectly Demonstrated and Proven by) the only-by-Me Revealed and Given seventh stage of life, and as a practice and a Process that progressively includes (and, coincidently, directly transcends) all six of the phenomenal and developmental (and, necessarily, yet ego-based) stages of life that precede the seventh.

Baba Muktananda conceived of (and Taught) Siddha Yoga as a Way to attain conditional (and especially fifth stage) Yogic objects and phenomena-based states. The Siddha Yoga of the only-by-Me Revealed and Given Way of Adidam is not based upon (or, otherwise, limited to) conditional (or phenomenal) objects and states—or the (necessarily, ego-based) search for these, in the context of any stage of life. Rather, the only-by-Me Revealed and Given Way of Adidam is the Siddha-Yoga Way (and, in particular, the Ruchira Avatara Hridaya-Siddha-Yoga Way) that always (and directly) transcends egoity itself (or the ego-"I", or separate self— or the reactive reflex of self-contraction)—by always Feeling Beyond egoity (and Beyond all conditional forms and states) to Me, the Avatarically Self-Revealed Divine Person (or Self-Condition, and Source-Condition) Itself.

LXXXII.

In Summary, Baba Muktananda (in Our Meetings in 1970 and 1973) countered My Language of Inherently (and Most Perfectly) egoless—or seventh stage—Divine Self-Realization (and otherwise defended His own experiential Realization—and philosophical idealization—of inner phenomenal objects) with the traditional language of fifth stage Yoga. And I, for this reason (and not because of any ill-will, or antagonism, or lack of respect toward Baba Muktananda), Did Not, and Could Not, and Do Not Accept His fifth-stage-bound Doctrine—because, from My "Point of View", that Acceptance would have Required (and would now Require) Me to Deny the Self-Evident Divine (and Perfectly Subjective, and Inherently egoless, and Inherently Non-Objective, and Inherently Indivisible, and Utterly Non-dependent, or Un-conditional) Truth of Reality Itself (Which Realization even Baba Muktananda Himself—along with all My other Spiritual Masters and Spiritual Friends—so Dearly Served in My own Case)!

LXXXIII.

Reality (Itself) Is the Only Real God.

Reality (Itself) Is That Which Is Always Already The (One and Only) Case.

Reality (Itself) Is (Necessarily) One, Only, and Indivisible.

Reality (Itself) Is Inherently One (or Non-Dual) and not Two (or Divisible, and Opposed to Itself).

Reality (Itself) is not One of a Pair.

Reality (Itself) is not characterized by the inherently dualistic relationship of cause and effect.

Reality (Itself) Is Characterized by the Inherently Non-Dualistic Equation of Identity and Non-"Difference".

Reality (Itself) Is That in Which both cause and effect arise as merely apparent modifications of Itself.

Reality (Itself) is not Realized via the inherently dualistic relationship of subject and object.

Reality (Itself) Is Realized As the Inherently Non-Dualistic Condition of Inherently egoless Identity and Inherently objectless Non-"Difference".

Reality (Itself) is not the gross, subtle, and causal (or causative) ego-"I".

Reality (Itself) Is the Inherently egoless Native (and Self-Evidently Divine) Identity of All and all.

307

The Inherently egoless Non-Dual Self-Condition (or Non-"Different" Identity) of Reality (Itself) <u>Is</u> That Which Is Always Already <u>The</u> (One and Only) Case.

The Inherently egoless Non-Dual Self-Condition of Reality (Itself), Most Perfectly Prior to (and, yet, never excluding, or separated from) subject, object, cause, or effect, <u>Is</u> That Which Must Be Realized.

The apparent self (or separate and separative ego-"I"), and its every object, and, indeed, every cause, and every effect must be Divinely Self-Recognized <u>As</u> (and, Thus and Thereby, Transcended in) the One and Only (Inherently egoless, and Inherently Non-Dual, or Indivisible and Non-Separate, or Non-"Different") Self-Condition of Reality (Itself).

The apparent ego-"I" and the apparent world are not <u>themselves</u> Divine.

The apparent ego-"I" and the apparent world are to be Self-Recognized (and, Thus and Thereby, Transcended) in and <u>As</u> That Which <u>Is</u> (Self-Evidently) Divine.

The apparent ego-"I" and the apparent world are to be Divinely Self-Recognized in and <u>As</u> Reality (Itself).

Baba Muktananda always (in the Emanationist manner of Kashmir Saivism) affirmed the Realization "I am Siva"—meaning that He (or any body-mind-self, or body-brain-self, sublimed by the Revelation of internal Yogic forms) <u>is</u> (<u>as</u> an "Emanated" psycho-physical self) Divine.

I Affirmed (and always Continue to Affirm) <u>only</u> the Non-Dual (or One and Indivisible) Transcendental (and Inherently Spiritual) Divine Reality (or Self-Existing, Self-Radiant, and Inherently, or Always Already, egoless Consciousness Itself—or the One and Only Conscious Love-Bliss-Light Itself) <u>As</u> Self (or Self-Condition, and Source-Condition), Prior to and Inherently Transcending (while <u>never</u> strategically, or conditionally, <u>excluding</u>) the phenomenal self and <u>all</u> conditional forms (however sublime).

Baba Muktananda affirmed (in the fifth stage, Emanationist manner) "I and the world are Divine"—and He (thereby) embraced both the perceiving "I" and the world of forms.

I (in the seventh stage Manner) Affirmed (and always

Continue to Affirm) only the Self-Existing and Self-Radiant
(Transcendental, Inherently Spiritual, Inherently egoless, Perfectly
Subjective, Indivisible, Non-Dual, and Self-Evidently Divine) Self-
Identity (Itself)—or the One, and Most Prior, and Inherently Most
Perfect, and Inherently egoless Self-Condition, and Source-
Condition, of the body-mind (or the body-brain-self) and the
world—Divinely Self-Recognizing the body-mind (or the body-
brain-self) and the world (and, thus, neither excluding nor identi-
fying with the body-mind, or the body-brain-self, and the world,
but Inherently, or Always Already, "Brightly" Transcending, and,
Most Ultimately, Divinely Outshining, the body-mind, or the body-
brain-self, and the world).

It was This Distinction (or These Distinctions)—not merely in
language, but in the "Point of View" of Realization Itself—that was
(or were) the basis for My Assumption of My Avataric Divine
Teaching-Work, and My Avataric Divine Revelation-Work, and My
Avataric Divine Blessing-Work institutionally independent of (and,
after Our Final Meeting, in 1973, entirely apart from further
outwardly active association with) Baba Muktananda.

LXXXIV.

As has always been understood by authentic Realizers and
their authentic true devotees—within the Siddha-Yoga (or Shaktipat-
Yoga) tradition, and even everywhere within the human Great
Tradition as a whole—Great Siddhas, and even Avatars, and traditional Realizers of all kinds and degrees (or stages of life), and
Siddha-Yogis of all kinds and degrees, and even Siddha Yoga Itself,
are not mere "properties", to be "owned" (or exclusively "possessed")
by devotees, or even by institutions. Indeed, Baba Muktananda,
Himself, once told Me[52] that, because the same Life (or Shakti) is
in all beings, no individual, no religion, no tradition—and, therefore,
no institution—can rightly claim to be the only bearer, or the exclusive representative, of Siddha Yoga (or Shaktipat Yoga) Itself.

There are, inevitably, many forms of Siddha-Yoga Transmission
in this world. The institution that Baba Muktananda established to
represent and continue His own Work is (by its own self-description)
a fourth-to-fifth stage school of Siddha Yoga. And, indeed, there

are numbers of other such schools—in India, and elsewhere—that are extending the Work of various Great Siddhas (and of many otherwise worthy Siddha-Yogis) into the world. Likewise, the institution (or the total complex of institutions) of Adidam—which represents, and serves, and will always continue to serve My Avataric Divine (and, Uniquely, seventh stage) Work—is also a school of Siddha Yoga (or of Shaktipat Yoga).

The Uniqueness of the Siddha Yoga of the only-by-Me Revealed and Given Way of Adidam is that It is the Yoga (or Dharma, or Way) that continues to Develop beyond the absorptive mystical (and cosmically Spiritual) developments associated with the fourth and the fifth stages of life—and even beyond the Transcendental Yogic (and Transcendentally Spiritual) developments associated with the sixth stage of life. Thus, in due course, the Yoga (or Way) of Adidam becomes the Unique (and Most Perfectly Divine) Yoga (or Most Perfectly Divinely Spiritual Demonstration) of the only-by-Me Revealed and Given seventh stage of life (Wherein and Whereby Most Perfect Divine Self-Realization is Most Perfectly Demonstrated).

Because of This Uniqueness, the Siddha Yoga of the only-by-Me Revealed and Given Way of Adidam is not descriptively limited to (or by) the particular traditional descriptive language of the fourth-to-fifth stage schools and traditions of Siddha Yoga (which are the schools and traditions from which Baba Muktananda derived His descriptive Siddha-Yoga-language—and which descriptive language is conformed to, and, necessarily, limited by, the fourth-to-fifth stage experiential presumptions that characterize the Cosmic-Yoga, or Cosmic-Shakti, or Kundalini-Shakti schools and traditions). Therefore—even though the Process of the Siddha Yoga of the only-by-Me Revealed and Given Way of Adidam potentially includes (and then continues to Develop beyond) all the aspects and experiences of the fourth and the fifth and the sixth stages of life—the Siddha Yoga of the only-by-Me Revealed and Given Way of Adidam is (by Me) Uniquely Described, in the (Most Ultimately, seventh stage—and Most Perfectly Divine, or Cosmos-Transcending, and Cosmos-Outshining) Terms of My own Avataric (Divine) Shaktipat.

Thus, the Siddha Yoga of the only-by-Me Revealed and Given Way of Adidam is (by Me) Described in Terms of Ruchira Avatara Hridaya-Shaktipat (or My Avataric Divine Spiritual Transmission of the "Bright"—Which Is the Self-Existing and Self-Radiant Divine Self-Condition, or Divine Self-Heart, Itself), and Ruchira Avatara Maha-Jnana Hridaya-Shaktipat (or My Avataric Divine Spiritual Transmission of the "Bright" Divine Spirit-Current, or Divine Heart-Shakti, That Awakens the Divine Self-Heart to Its Inherent Divine Self-Condition), and Love-Ananda Avatara Hridaya-Shaktipat (or My Avataric Divine Spiritual Transmission of the Inherent Love-Bliss of the Divine Self-Condition, or Divine Self-Heart, Itself—Which Divine Spiritual Characteristic of Mine was Acknowledged by Baba Muktananda Himself, when, in 1969, He Sent Amma to Me, to Give Me the Name "Love-Ananda").

Therefore, the Siddha-Yoga practice (and especially the advanced and the ultimate stages of the Siddha-Yoga Process) of the only-by-Me Revealed and Given Way of Adidam is (along with numerous other by-Me-Given Descriptive Names and References) Named and Described by Me as "Ruchira Avatara Hridaya-Siddha Yoga" (or "Ruchira Avatara Hridaya-Shaktipat Yoga"), and "Ruchira Avatara Maha-Jnana-Siddha-Yoga" (or "Ruchira Avatara Maha-Jnana Hridaya-Shaktipat Yoga"), and "Love-Ananda Avatara Hridaya-Siddha Yoga" (or "Love-Ananda Avatara Hridaya-Shaktipat Yoga"), and (with reference to the Way, and the institution, of Adidam) "Adidam Hridaya-Siddha Yoga" (or "Adidam Hridaya-Shaktipat Yoga").

And My own Work (Which is served by the institutional Siddha-Yoga school—or, most properly, the Ruchira Avatara Hridaya-Siddha-Yoga school—of Adidam) was directly Blessed (and—formally, in 1969—Called Forth) by Baba Muktananda (and, now, and forever hereafter, by even all the Great Siddhas and Siddha-Yogis of My Lineage).

LXXXV.

The Uniqueness of My own Divine Self-Realization and Avataric Divine Work made it Inevitable that I would have to Do My Avataric Divine Teaching-Work, and My Avataric Divine Revelation-Work, and My Avataric Divine Blessing-Work

Independent from Baba Muktananda—and Independent from even all Teachers and traditions within the only six stages of life of the collectively Revealed Great Tradition of mankind. Indeed, even from the beginning of My relationship with Him, Baba Muktananda Indicated that My Work was Uniquely My own, and that I was Born to Do only My own Unique Work—and that I Must Go and Do That Work (even though I would, otherwise, have preferred to Remain, quietly, within Baba Muktananda's Ashram and Company). Therefore, ultimately, We both Embraced This Necessity and Inevitability.

Because of the original, mutual Agreement between Baba Muktananda and Me (relative to the necessarily Independent, and entirely Unique, nature of My own Work), whenever I have become Moved to Communicate about This Profound Matter to others, I have made every effort to Communicate fully, clearly, and positively relative to the always un-"broken" Nature of My Spiritual (and, generally, sympathetic) relationship to Baba Muktananda—and, also, relative to the always Continuing Nature of My Spiritual (and, generally, sympathetic) Connection to the Great (and total) Siddha-Guru tradition itself, and to the Great (and total) Siddha-Yoga tradition itself, and to the total Great Tradition of mankind (altogether). And I have always Affirmed (and, by Means of This Statement, I now Re-Affirm) that the Great, and total, Siddha-Guru tradition and Siddha-Yoga tradition, and the most ancient and perennial "Method of the Siddhas",[53] is—in the context of, and continuous with, the total Great Tradition of mankind—the very tradition (or total complex of traditions) in which, and on the basis of which, I Am Avatarically Appearing and Working here.

LXXXVI.

Human suffering is not due to the absence of inner visions (or of any other kinds of conditionally objectified internal or, otherwise, external perceptions). Therefore, human suffering is not eliminated by the presence (or the experiencing) of inner visions (or of any other kinds of conditionally objectified internal or, otherwise, external perceptions).

The "problem" of human suffering is <u>never</u> the <u>absence</u> of inner visions (and such), or the <u>absence</u> of <u>any</u> conditional experience of <u>any</u> kind. Rather, the "problem" of human suffering is <u>always</u> (and <u>inherently</u>) the <u>presence</u> (or presently effective activity) of the <u>ego-"I"</u> (or the self-contracted—or separate and separative—<u>point</u> <u>of</u> <u>view</u>). Indeed, the search to experience conditionally objectified inner perceptions—and, otherwise, the clinging to conditionally objectified inner perceptions—is, <u>itself</u>, a form of human suffering (and, altogether, of self-deluded confinement to the inherently, and negatively, <u>empty</u> condition of egoic separateness).

The root and essence of human suffering <u>is</u> egoity. That is to Say, the "problem" that is human suffering is <u>not</u> due to the absence of <u>any</u> kind of conditionally objectified experience (whether relatively external or relatively internal)—for, if human suffering <u>were</u> due to such absence, the <u>attaining</u> of conditionally objectified experiences (whether internal or external) would <u>eliminate</u> human suffering, human self-deludedness, and human un-Happiness. However, at most, conditionally objectified experiences (both internal and external)—or even <u>any</u> of the possible experiential attainments of the first <u>five</u> stages of life—provide only <u>temporary</u> distraction from the inherent mortality and misery of conditional existence. Therefore, if human suffering is to be <u>entirely</u> (and <u>Perfectly</u>) transcended (in Inherent, and Divinely Positive, Fullness), the root-cause of (or the root-factor in) human suffering must, <u>itself</u>, be directly and entirely (and, at last, Most Perfectly) transcended.

The "problem" of human suffering is <u>never</u> the absence of <u>any</u> kind of particular conditionally objectified experience (whether external or internal). The "problem" of human suffering is <u>always</u> the bondage to conditionally objectified experience <u>itself</u>. And the root-cause of (or the root-factor in) bondage to conditionally objectified experience is the separate and separative ego-"I", or the total psycho-physical act of self-contraction (which is identical to attention itself, or the conditionally apparent <u>point</u> of view <u>itself</u>, and which <u>always</u> coincides with the feeling of "difference", or of separateness and relatedness).

The experiencing of inner visions does <u>not</u> eliminate egoity (or the separate and separative ego-"I" of psycho-physical self-contraction). Likewise, the experiencing of inner visions does <u>not</u> indicate or suggest or mean that egoity is (or has been) transcended. True Spiritual life (or the true Great Process of Siddha Yoga) is not a search for inner visions (and such)—nor is true Spiritual life (or the true Great Process of Siddha Yoga) Fulfilled, Completed, and Perfected by the experiencing of inner visions (and such). Indeed, because inner visions, or conditionally objectified experiences of <u>any</u> kind—whether inner or outer—are <u>objects</u>, attention is <u>always</u> coincident with them. Therefore, in both the <u>search</u> for conditionally objectified experiences and the <u>grasping</u> of conditionally objectified experiences, <u>egoity</u> (or separative, and total psycho-physical, self-contraction of the presumed separate point of view) <u>is merely reinforced</u>.

True Spiritual life (or the true Great Process of Siddha Yoga) is <u>never</u> a matter of seeking for outer <u>or</u> inner conditionally objectified experiences—nor is true Spiritual life (or the true Great Process of Siddha Yoga) a matter of clinging to any conditionally objectified outer <u>or</u> inner experiences (as if such experiences were, themselves, Reality, Truth, or Real God). Rather, true Spiritual life (or the true Great Process of Siddha Yoga) is <u>always</u> a matter of transcending attention (and the total psycho-physical—or gross, subtle, and causal—point of view, or ego-"I") in its Perfectly Subjective Source (or Inherently Perfect Self-Condition). That is to Say, true Spiritual life (or the true Great Process of Siddha Yoga) is <u>always</u> (from Its beginning) a matter of transcending that which is merely apparently (or conditionally, and temporarily) the case— by transcending it in <u>That</u> Which <u>Is</u> Always Already <u>The</u> (One and Only, Indivisible and Irreducible) Case. And, for <u>This</u> Reason, true Spiritual life, or the true Great Process of Siddha Yoga, cannot be Fulfilled, Completed, and Perfected in the conditionally objectified context of any of the first <u>five</u> stages of life—nor even in the conditionally object-excluding context of the <u>sixth</u> stage of life—but true Spiritual life (in particular, in the form of the true Great Process of Ruchira Avatara Hridaya-Siddha Yoga) <u>Is</u> Fulfilled, Completed, and Perfected <u>only</u> in the Perfectly Subjective, and

Inherently egoless (or Inherently point-of-view-Transcending and Most Perfectly self-contraction-Transcending) and Un-conditionally Realized, and, altogether, Self-Evidently Divine Context of the only-by-Me Revealed and Given <u>seventh</u> stage of life.

This is My Firm Conclusion relative to <u>all</u> possible human experience—and It is, therefore, the Essence of My Instruction to all of humankind.

LXXXVII.

There are <u>three</u> <u>egos</u> (or three fundamental modes of egoity—or of the self-contraction-active psycho-physical illusion of separate and separative self-consciousness). The three modes of egoity (or of the self-contraction of <u>any</u> point of view, or ego-"I") are the lower self (or gross ego), the higher self (or subtle ego), and the root-self (or causal ego). These three egos (or modes of the conditionally arising illusion of separate self-consciousness) comprise the total conditionally perceiving and conditionally knowing ego-"I". The <u>total</u> (or tripartite) ego-"I" is always directly (and with progressive effectiveness) transcended in the right, true, and full (or complete) formal practice of the only-by-Me Revealed and Given Way of Adidam (Which is the right, true, and full formal practice of Ruchira Avatara Bhakti Yoga, or the totality of Ruchira Avatara Hridaya-Siddha Yoga).

The first of the three egos (or modes of egoity, or of self-contraction) to be progressively transcended in the only-by-Me Revealed and Given Way of Adidam is the <u>money-food-and-sex</u> <u>ego</u> (or the social, and, altogether, gross-body-based, personality—or the <u>gross</u> pattern and activity of self-contraction), which is the lower self, or the ego of the first three stages of life.

The second of the three egos (or modes of egoity, or of self-contraction) to be progressively transcended in the only-by-Me Revealed and Given Way of Adidam is the <u>brain-mind</u> <u>ego</u> (or the brain-based, and nervous-system-based, mental, and perceptual, and, altogether, subtle-body-based illusions of "object" and "other"—or the <u>subtle</u> pattern and activity of self-contraction), which is the higher self, or the ego of the fourth and the fifth stages of life.

The third of the three egos (or modes of egoity, or of self-contraction) to be progressively transcended in the only-by-Me Revealed and Given Way of Adidam is the root-ego (or the exclusively disembodied, and mindless, but separate, and, altogether, causal-body-based self-consciousness—or the causal, or root-causative, pattern and activity of self-contraction), which is attention itself, and which is the root-self, or the ego of the sixth stage of life.

By Means of responsive relinquishment of self-contraction in Me, or really and truly ego-surrendering, ego-forgetting, and, more and more (and, at last, Most Perfectly), ego-transcending (or always directly self-contraction-transcending) devotion to Me (and, Thus, by Means of the right, true, and full formal practice of devotionally Me-recognizing and devotionally to-Me-responding Ruchira Avatara Bhakti Yoga, or the totality of Ruchira Avatara Hridaya-Siddha Yoga), the tripartite ego of the first six stages of life (or the psycho-physical totality of the three-part hierarchically patterned self-contraction into separate and separative point of view) is (always directly, and with progressive, or stage-by-stage, effectiveness) transcended in Me (the Eternally Self-Existing, Infinitely Self-Radiant, Inherently egoless, Perfectly Subjective, Indivisibly One, Irreducibly Non-Separate, Self-Evidently Divine, and, now, and forever hereafter, Avatarically Self-Revealed Self-Conscious Light of Reality).

The Ultimate, Final, and Inherently Most Perfect (or seventh stage) Realization of Me requires—as a necessary prerequisite—an ego-transcending (or really and truly and comprehensively self-contraction-transcending) Great Ordeal. The Ultimate, Final, and Inherently Most Perfect (or seventh stage) Realization of Me requires—as a necessary prerequisite—the comprehensive by-Me-Revealed and by-Me-Given sadhana (or the always directly ego-transcending right practice of life) in the total and complete formal context of the only-by-Me Revealed and Given Way of Adidam. And—as a necessary prerequisite to the Ultimate, Final, and Inherently Most Perfect (or seventh stage) Realization of Me— the particular illusions that are unique to each of the three egos (or basic modes of egoity) each require a particular (and most profound) mode of the necessary ego-transcending (or self-contraction-transcending) Great Ordeal of the by-Me-Revealed and by-Me-Given formal practice of the Way of Adidam in the progressively unfolding context of the first six (and, altogether, psycho-physically pre-patterned) stages of life.

The foundation phase of the progressive ego-transcending Great Ordeal of the only-by-Me Revealed and Given Way of Adidam is the devotional (and relatively <u>exoteric</u>, and only in the rudimentary sense Spiritual) <u>listening-hearing</u> Process of progressively transcending (and, in due course, <u>most</u> <u>fundamentally</u> understanding) the <u>lower</u> <u>self</u> (or the <u>gross</u> <u>and</u> <u>social</u> <u>ego</u>—and the gross and social fear-sorrow-and-anger-bondage that is <u>always</u> associated with the <u>inherently</u> <u>egoic</u>—or thoroughly self-contracted—search to absolutely fulfill, and even to "utopianize", or to perfectly and permanently satisfy, the <u>inherently</u> conditional, limited, temporary, mortal, gross, and <u>always</u> changing life-patterns of "money, food, and sex").

Before the foundation phase (or first phase) of the ego-transcending Great Ordeal of the Way of Adidam can, itself, be complete, it must Realize a profoundly life-transforming and life-reorienting "positive disillusionment"—or a most fundamental (and really and truly self-contraction-transcending) acceptance of the fact that gross conditional existence is <u>inherently</u> and <u>necessarily</u> unsatisfactory and unperfectable (<u>and</u>, therefore, a most fundamental—and really and truly Me-Finding and search-ending—acceptance of the fact that <u>all</u> seeking to achieve permanent and complete gross satisfaction of separate body, emotion, and mind is <u>inherently</u> and <u>necessarily</u> futile). Only on the basis of that <u>necessary</u> foundation-Realization of "positive disillusionment" can the energy and the attention of the entire body-mind (or of the total body-brain-mind complex) be released from gross ego-bondage (or self-deluded confinement to the psycho-physical illusions of gross self-contraction).

The characteristic Sign of "positive disillusionment" relative to the permanent and complete satisfaction of the lower self (or the separate and separative gross and social ego) is the foundation-Realization of the Inherent Universal <u>Unity</u> (or All-and-all-inclusive interdependency, essential mutuality, and common causality) of gross conditional (and cosmic) existence, such that the inherently loveless (or anti-participatory and non-integrative) self-contraction-effort of the gross separate self is consistently released (or to-<u>Me</u>-responsively self-surrendered) into <u>participatory</u> and <u>integrative</u> attitudes of human, social, and cosmic unification (or <u>love</u>-connectedness) with all and All, and into <u>love</u>-based (and truly ego-transcending) actions that counter the otherwise separative (or anti-participatory and non-integrative) tendencies of the ego-"I". Thus, by Means of devotionally Me-recognizing and devotionally to-Me-responding relinquishment (or participatory and love-based transcending) of psycho-physical self-contraction (to the degree of "positive disillusionment" relative to gross conditional experience and gross conditional knowledge), My true devotee is released toward the true Spiritual (and not merely gross, or even at all conditional) Realization of Reality and Truth (or <u>Real</u> God).

The foundation-Realization of "positive disillusionment" requires fundamental release from the confines of the grossly objectified (and grossly absorbed) subject-object point of view (or fundamental release from the inherently ego-bound—or thoroughly self-contracted—search of relatively <u>externalized</u> mental and perceptual attention). And that foundation-Realization of "positive disillusionment" (and restoration to the humanly, socially, and cosmically participatory, or wholly integrative, disposition) requires the total (and truly devotional) transformative re-orienting (and, altogether, the right purification, steady re-balancing, and ego-transcending life-positive-energizing) of the entire body-mind (or the total body-brain-mind complex). Therefore, the foundation (or gross) phase of the progressive ego-transcending practice of the Way of Adidam <u>necessarily</u> requires <u>much</u> time (and <u>much</u> seriousness, and <u>much</u> profundity)—and even, potentially, the <u>entire</u> lifetime of <u>only</u> that foundation practice may (in many cases) be required—in order to establish the necessary (and <u>truly</u> "positively disillusioned") foundation of true (and truly in-<u>Me</u>-surrendered) hearing (or the only-by-Me Revealed and Given unique ego-transcending capability of most fundamental self-understanding).

The middle phase of the progressive ego-transcending Great Ordeal of the only-by-Me Revealed and Given Way of Adidam is the preliminary (or initial) esoteric devotional, and truly hearing (or actively ego-transcending, and, thus, always directly self-contraction-transcending), and really seeing (or actively, directly, and fully responsibly Spiritual) Process of transcending the higher self (or the subtle and mental ego—or the total subtle dimension, or subtle depth, of self-contraction—and all the conceptual and perceptual illusions of inherently, and necessarily, brain-based mind). Therefore, the middle (or subtle) phase of the progressive ego-transcending practice of the Way of Adidam requires the Realization of "positive disillusionment" relative to the subtly objectified (and subtly absorbed) subject-object point of view (or fundamental release from the inherently ego-bound—or thoroughly self-contracted—search of relatively internalized mental and perceptual attention). This degree of the Realization of "positive disillusionment" requires fundamental release from the inherently illusory search to experience the conditional dissolution of the ego (and, in particular, release from subtle states of self-contraction—and, especially, from mental states of self-contraction) by means of object-oriented absorptive mysticism (or the absorptive yielding of attention to the apparent subtle objects that are either originated by the brain-mind or, otherwise, mediated by the brain itself). And the characteristic Sign of "positive disillusionment" relative to the permanent and complete satisfaction of the object-oriented seeking of the higher self (or separate and separative subtle and mental ego) is the fully Me-hearing and truly Me-seeing Realization of the entirely Spiritual Nature of cosmic existence (or, that is to Say, the Realization that all natural and cosmic forms and states are inherently non-separate, or intrinsically non-dual, modes of Universally Pervasive Energy, or of Fundamental, Indivisible, and Irreducible Light—or of Love-Bliss-Happiness Itself).

The final phase of the progressive ego-transcending Great Ordeal of the only-by-Me Revealed and Given Way of Adidam is the penultimate esoteric devotional, Spiritual, and Transcendental hearing-and-seeing Process of transcending the root-self (or the

319

root-and-causal ego—or the causal, or root-causative, depth of self-contraction—which is attention itself, or the root-gesture of separateness, relatedness, and "difference"). Therefore, immediately preliminary to the Realization associated with the only-by-Me Revealed and Given seventh stage of life, the final (or causal) phase of the progressive ego-transcending (or comprehensively self-contraction-transcending) practice of the Way of Adidam requires the Realization of "positive disillusionment" relative to the causal (or root-egoic, and, therefore, fundamental, or original) subject-object division in Consciousness (or Conscious Light) Itself. This degree of the Realization of "positive disillusionment" requires the native exercise of Transcendental Self-Identification— Prior to the root-self-contraction that is point of view itself (or attention itself), and, Thus, also, Prior to the entire body-brain-mind complex, or conditional structure, of conception and perception. And the characteristic Sign of "positive disillusionment" relative to the permanent and complete satisfaction of the root-self (or the fundamental causative, or causal, ego) is the fundamental transcending of attention itself in the Me-"Locating" (and, altogether, Me-hearing and Me-seeing) Realization of the Transcendental (and Intrinsically Non-Separate and Non-Dual) Nature of Consciousness Itself.

Only after (or in the Great Event of Most Perfect, and, necessarily, formal and fully accountable, Fulfillment of) the complete progressive ego-transcending Great Ordeal of the only-by-Me Revealed and Given Way of Adidam in the total (and progressively unfolded) context of the inherently ego-based first six (or psychophysically pre-patterned gross, subtle, and causal) stages of life is there the truly ultimate (or seventh stage, and Always Already Divinely Self-Realized—and, Thus, Inherently ego-Transcending) "Practice" of the only-by-Me Revealed and Given Way of Adidam (or the Most Perfect, and Inherently egoless, or Always Already Most Perfectly, and Un-conditionally, self-contraction-Transcending, and Divinely Love-Bliss-Full, and only-by-Me Revealed and Given seventh-stage-of-life Demonstration of Ruchira Avatara Bhakti Yoga, or Ruchira Avatara Hridaya-Siddha Yoga).

The only-by-Me Revealed and Given seventh-stage-of-life "Practice" (or the Inherently egoless, and, Thus, Always Already Most Perfectly, and Un-conditionally, self-contraction-Transcending, and, altogether, Most Perfectly Divinely Self-Realized Demonstration) of the only-by-Me Revealed and Given Way of Adidam is the Great esoteric devotional, Spiritual, Transcendental, Self-Evidently Divine, and Most Perfectly Me-hearing and Me-seeing Demonstration of All-and-all-Divinely-Self-Recognizing (and, Thus, All-and-all-Divinely-Transcending) Divine Self-Abiding (in and As My Avatarically Self-Revealed Divine "Bright" Sphere of Self-Existing, Self-Radiant, Inherently egoless, Perfectly Subjective, and Inherently and Most Perfectly body-mind-Transcending, or body-brain-Transcending, or Inherently, Most Perfectly, and Un-conditionally psycho-physical-self-contraction-Transcending, but never intentionally body-mind-excluding, or body-brain-excluding, Divine Person, or Eternal Self-Condition and Infinite State).

The only-by-Me Revealed and Given seventh-stage-of-life Demonstration of the only-by-Me Revealed and Given Way of Adidam is the Un-conditional and Divinely Free (and Inherently egoless, or Inherently point-of-view-less) "Practice" (or Divinely Self-Realized progressive Demonstration) of Divine Self-Recognition of the simultaneous totality of the apparent gross, subtle, and causal body-brain-mind-self, or the progressively All-and-all-Outshining Process of the simultaneous Divine Self-Recognition of the total psycho-physical ego-"I" itself (or of the total conditional point of view, or apparent self-contraction, itself). Therefore, the only-by-Me Revealed and Given seventh-stage-of-life Demonstration of the only-by-Me Revealed and Given Way of Adidam is the Inherent "Practice" (or Divinely Self-Realized Demonstration) of Divine Self-Recognition of point of view itself (or of attention itself—or of the conditionally apparent subject, itself) and (always coincidently, or simultaneously) Divine Self-Recognition of the conception or perception of separateness, relatedness, or "difference" itself (or of any and every conditionally apparent object, itself).

The only-by-Me Revealed and Given seventh-stage-of-life Demonstration of the only-by-Me Revealed and Given Way of Adidam is the Most Perfect (or Un-conditional, Inherently egoless, and Self-Evidently Divine) Demonstration of "positive disillusionment", or of the Inherently illusionless (or self-contraction-Free, and, Inherently, All-and-all-Transcending) Realization of the Fundamental Reality and Truth (or <u>Real</u> God)—Which Fundamental Reality and Truth (or <u>Real</u> God) <u>Is</u> the One and Indivisible and Self-Existing and Indestructible and Self-Radiant and Always Already Most Perfectly Non-Dual Conscious Light (or That Which <u>Is</u> Always Already <u>The</u> Case), and Which Reality and Truth (or <u>Real</u> God) <u>Is</u> That Self-Existing and Perfectly Subjective Self-"Brightness" (or Infinite and Absolute and Most Perfectly Non-Separate Self-Condition) of Which the conditional (or gross, subtle, and causal) subject-object illusions (or total psycho-physical self-contraction illusions) of conception, and of perception, and of the ego-"I" presumption are mere, and merely apparent (or non-necessary, or <u>always</u> non-Ultimate), and Inherently non-binding modifications. And the characteristic Sign of Most Perfectly Demonstrated (or seventh stage) "positive disillusionment" relative to the totality of the separate and separative ego-"I" (or point of view) and its presumptions of a separate (or objectified) gross, subtle, and causal world is the Self-Evidently Divine (and Intrinsically Non-Separate and Non-Dual) Realization of Reality (<u>Itself</u>) <u>As</u> Irreducible and Indivisible Conscious Light (Inherently Love-Bliss-Full, or Perfectly Subjectively "Bright").

Therefore, the only-by-Me Revealed and Given Way of Adidam is—from the beginning, <u>and</u> at last—the Way of "positive disillusionment".

The only-by-Me Revealed and Given Way of Adidam is—from the beginning, <u>and</u> at last—the Way of the direct transcending of the fact and the consequences of egoity (or of psycho-physical self-contraction).

The only-by-Me Revealed and Given Way of Adidam is—from the beginning, <u>and</u> at last—the Way of the direct transcending of the illusions of inherently egoic attention (or of the conditionally presumed subject-object pattern of conception and perception).

The only-by-Me Revealed and Given Way of Adidam is—from the beginning, <u>and</u> at last—the Way of the direct transcending of the total illusory pattern of the inherently egoic presumption of separateness, relatedness, and "difference".

The only-by-Me Revealed and Given Way of Adidam is—from the beginning, <u>and</u> at last—the Way of the direct transcending of the always simultaneous illusions of the separate ego-"I" <u>and</u> the separate (or merely objective) world.

The only-by-Me Revealed and Given Way of Adidam is—from the beginning, <u>and</u> at last—the Way of the direct (or Inherently egoless <u>and</u> Inherently illusionless) Realizing of the One and Irreducible Conscious Light (or Perfectly Subjective "Brightness" of Being) That <u>Is</u> Reality and Truth (or <u>Real</u> God).

The only-by-Me Revealed and Given Way of Adidam is—from the beginning, <u>and</u> at last—the Way of the direct (or Inherently egoless <u>and</u> Inherently illusionless) Realizing of the Conscious Love-Bliss-Energy of Totality.

The only-by-Me Revealed and Given Way of Adidam is—from the beginning, <u>and</u> at last—the Way of the direct Realizing of <u>Only Me</u>.

LXXXVIII.

<u>Every</u> body-mind (whether human or non-human) tends to feel and be and function <u>egoically</u>—or <u>as if</u> it were a separate self, separated from its True Source, and un-Aware of its True, and Truly Free, Self-Condition. Therefore, <u>every</u> body-mind (whether human or non-human) must transcend its own (inherent) egoity (or egoic reflex—or self-contracting tendency), through Love-Surrender to its True Source. And This Love-Surrender must, Ultimately, become Realization of (and, <u>Thus</u>, True, and really ego-Transcending, Identification with) its <u>True</u> Source-Condition (Which <u>Is</u>, also, its <u>True</u> Self-Condition).

To <u>This</u> End, True Masters (or True Siddha-Gurus) Appear in the various cosmic worlds. Such True Masters are the Divine Means for living beings (whether human or non-human) to transcend themselves. That is to Say, True Masters (or True Siddha-Gurus—or True <u>Sat</u>-Gurus[54]) are living beings who have (in the manner of their characteristic stage of life) transcended their own (psycho-physical) separateness, through responsive Surrender (and, therefore, necessarily, Love-Surrender) to (and Identification with) the True Source-Condition (Which <u>Is</u> the True Self-Condition) of all and All.

Therefore, by Means of True Devotion (or Love-Surrender) to a True Master (or True Siddha-Guru), egoity is (always more and more) transcended, and the True Source-Condition of all and All (Which Is, necessarily, also the True Self-Condition of all and All) is, by Means of the Blessing-Grace of That True Master (or True Siddha-Guru), Found and Realized. And That "Finding-and-Realizing" Shows Itself according to the kind and degree of one or the other of the seven possible stages of life—and, thus, in accordance with the stage of life Realized by That True Master, or True Siddha-Guru, and, altogether, in accordance with the stage of life determined by the path, or Way, that is practiced, or, otherwise, determined by the "inclination", or "liking", or degree of ego-transcendence, of That True Master's practicing devotee.

This is the most ancient and perennial Great Teaching about True Guru-Devotion (or True Devotion to a True Spiritual Master, or True Siddha-Guru). This is the Great Teaching I Received from all My Lineage-Gurus. And, now, through My own Words, This Fundamental Message (or Great Teaching) Is Summarized in its Completeness, for the Sake of everyone.

If the living being is to Realize the Inherent Freedom of Oneness with its True Source-Condition (Which Is its True, or ego-less, Self-Condition), it must become truly devoted to a True Master (or Truly Realized Siddha-Guru). And such True Devotion constantly (and forever) requires the heart's Love-responsive Gesture (or ego-transcending Sadhana) of True Guru-Devotion (to one's heart-Chosen True Siddha-Guru), such that the otherwise egoic (or separate, and separative) body-mind is Surrendered to be actually, truly, and completely Mastered by That True Master.

If Such True Mastering of the body-mind is not accepted (or fully volunteered for—through responsive, and truly ego-surrendering, Devotional Love of one's heart-Chosen True Siddha Guru), the body-mind (inevitably) remains "wild" (or un-"domesticated"—or merely un-disciplined, and even ego-bound). And even if such Guru-Devotion is practiced, it must be Fully practiced (in a Fully ego-surrendering manner)—or else the Freedom (or the Divine Fullness) That is to be Realized by Means of the Blessing-Grace of one's heart-Chosen True Siddha-Guru will not (because it cannot)

Fully Fill the feeling-heart (and, Thereby, Fully Fill the living body-mind) of the would-be devotee.

LXXXIX.

In My present-Lifetime bodily (human) Form, I Am the Avataric Divine Incarnation (or True God-Man) always and everywhere (since the ancient days) Promised (and Expected) to Appear in the "late-time" (or "dark" epoch).[55] And, in My present-Lifetime bodily (human) Form, I have been Spiritually Served by a Continuous Lineage of Spiritual Masters, Such That I Passed from one to the next, in Continuous Succession. Those Spiritual Masters were, Themselves, related to one another in an hierarchical Manner, each related to the next in the Succession as one of lesser degree is to one of higher degree.

Rudi was a Spiritual Master of authentic, but lesser, degree. His Proficiency was, fundamentally, in the gross domain of the frontal personality, and in the Yogic Pattern of Spiritual Descent (or the Descending Yoga of the Frontal Line). Therefore, when My own foundational (or grosser human, and, also, frontal Spiritual, or Descending Yogic) Sadhana had been Completed in His Company, I (spontaneously) Passed from Rudi to Baba Muktananda.

Baba Muktananda was—as His own Confession and Demonstration to Me clearly indicates—an authentic Spiritual Master of Ascending Yoga, and His Proficiency was of a Very High, but not the Highest, degree. Therefore, beginning from the very day I first Came to Baba Muktananda, He (directly) Passed Me to Bhagavan Nityananda (Who was a Spiritual Master of Ascending Yoga Whose Proficiency was of the Highest degree).

Rang Avadhoot was—even according to the Statements of both Bhagavan Nityananda and Baba Muktananda—a Spiritual Master of Ascending Yoga Whose Proficiency was of the Highest degree, but He, along with Baba Muktananda, Deferred to Bhagavan Nityananda's Seniority, and (simply) Blessed Me to Pass On.

The "Cosmic Goddess" ("Ma") is, in the total context of the first five stages of life, Senior even to the Highest of Spiritual Masters. However, Ultimately, "She" (as an apparent Form and Person) is only another one of the many myths in the mind.

In the Great Yogic Spiritual Process Wherein I Experienced the
Developmental Unfolding (and Demonstrated the "Radical"
Transcending) of the gross and the subtle modes of egoity (associ-
ated with the first five stages of life), the "Cosmic Goddess" ("Ma")
was "Apparently" associated with all the frontal (and Descending
Spiritual) Events and with all the spinal (and Ascending Spiritual)
Events. Nevertheless, in My Unique Case, sixth stage Transcendental
(and causal-ego-Transcending, and Inherently Spiritual) Self-
Realization always Occurred spontaneously (and in a progressive
Demonstration) relative to each and every egoic stage of life, and It
progressively Developed (especially after a spontaneous experience
of ego-death, in the spring of 1967[56]) until My spontaneous seventh
stage (and Inherently Most Perfectly egoless, and Self-Evidently
Divine) Re-Awakening (on September 10, 1970)—Which Divine (and
Avatarically Demonstrated) Re-Awakening was (and Is) associated
with My Most Perfect Transcending even of the "Apparent She", in My
Avataric Divine Re-Awakening to the Realization of One and Only Me.

Therefore, in due course, Bhagavan Nityananda (directly)
Passed Me to the "Cosmic Goddess" ("Ma"), and, Thus, to Her
direct Mastery of Me—until the Perfectly Full became, at last,
Perfectly Full As Me (Beyond the mind's own myth of "She").

So It was and Is. Such Is My Lineage of Spiritual Masters—in
This, My Avatarically-Born human Lifetime. And, in My always
Absolute heart-Fidelity to the Great Process Wherein and Whereby
I was Passed from one to the next of each and all of the Spiritual
Masters within My present-Lifetime Lineage of Spiritual Masters, I
have Exemplified, to all and All, the Law and the Truth of True
Guru-Devotion.

Therefore, I have always Continued to Honor and to Praise all
My present-Lifetime Lineage-Gurus—including Rudi!, and Baba
Muktananda!, and Rang Avadhoot!, and Bhagavan Nityananda!,
and (above all) the "Bright" Divine "She" of Me, Who Always
Already Serves Me Most Perfectly!

And I have always Continued (and even now Continue, and
will never cease to Continue) to Yield My present-Lifetime Body-
Mind to Receive the Always Ready and Most Lovingly To-Me-
Given and Supremely Blissful Blessings of My present-Lifetime

Lineage-Gurus <u>and</u> the Great Lineage of <u>all</u> Who have (in any and every time and place) Blessed the Incarnation-Vehicle and Invoked the All-Completing "late-time" Incarnation of My (now, and forever hereafter) Avataric Divine Appearance here (and every where in the cosmic domain).

And I Do This (and I will <u>always</u> <u>Continue</u> to Do This) because the Immense Spiritual "Bond" of Siddha-Guru-Love <u>cannot</u> be destroyed—and It must <u>never</u> be forgotten or denied!

XC.

My <u>own</u> Unique <u>Response</u> to the hierarchically Revealed Lineage of My present-Lifetime Siddha-Gurus spontaneously Un-Locked the Doorway (in My present-Lifetime human body) to That Which <u>Is</u> Perfect (in <u>Me</u>). Indeed, even from the beginning of My Avataric Divine present Lifetime, That Which <u>Is</u> Perfect has been (and <u>Is</u>) the <u>Way</u> of Me—and It Carried the inherently non-Perfect (human, and, otherwise, conditional) forms of Me to the Inherent "Bright" Divine Self-Domain of Me, Which <u>Is</u> the One and Indivisible Divine Source-Condition of all and All, and the One and True Divine Self-Condition of all and All.

XCI.

My Way and My Realization have <u>always</u> been Inherent in <u>Me</u>, from Birth, in My present-Lifetime Avataric Divine Form.

My Way and My Realization are <u>Independently</u>, <u>entirely</u>, and <u>only</u> My <u>own</u>.

My Sadhana was, <u>entirely</u>, a Demonstration for the Sake of <u>all</u> <u>others</u>—including <u>all</u> Those Who Served Me as My Spiritual Masters in the Course of My Avataric Divine "Sadhana Years". Indeed, Siddha Yoga—and even the <u>entire</u> Great Tradition of mankind—was <u>Always</u> <u>Already</u> Most Perfectly <u>Full</u> (and Most Perfectly <u>Complete</u>) in My Case—not only at (and from the time of) My present-Lifetime Birth, but from <u>all</u> time before It (and <u>Eternally</u>).

During <u>all</u> of My present Lifetime (of Avataric Divine Incarnation), the "<u>Bright</u>" has <u>always</u> been My Realization—and the "<u>Thumbs</u>" and My own "Radical Understanding" have <u>always</u> been My Way in the "Bright". Therefore, by Means of My Unique (present-Lifetime)

Avataric Divine Demonstration, I have both Fulfilled and Transcended <u>all</u> traditional religions, and paths, and stages, and Ways. And, in <u>So</u> Doing, I have Clarified (or altogether <u>Rightly</u> Understood and Explained) <u>all</u> traditional religions, paths, stages, and Ways.

All and all <u>Are</u> in <u>Me</u>. Everything and everyone <u>Is</u> in <u>Me</u>. Therefore, by Virtue of My own Divine Self-Realization (Wherein and Whereby My own Avataric Divine Body-Mind is Most Perfectly Surrendered in <u>Me</u>, and Most Perfectly Conformed to <u>Me</u>, and Most Perfectly Transcended in <u>Me</u>), <u>all</u> of My present-Lifetime Lineage-Gurus—and even <u>all</u> Who have (at any time, or in any place) Blessed <u>Me</u>—<u>are</u> now (and forever hereafter) Spiritually, Transcendentally, and Divinely Appearing in and <u>As</u> My own Avataric Divine Form.

Therefore, now (and forever hereafter) I (<u>Alone</u>) <u>Am</u> the Lineage of <u>Me</u>—Blessing all and All.

XCII.

The Divine Self-Realization Re-Awakened in My own Case (and Which Is the Basis for My Every Avataric Divine Revelatory Word and All My Avatarically Me-Revealing Divine Blessing-Work) Is the Most Ultimate (and Inherently Most Perfect and Complete) Fulfillment of the Divine Spiritual Transmission I (in My present-Lifetime Body-Mind) Received from Rudi, and from Baba Muktananda, and from Rang Avadhoot, and from Bhagavan Nityananda, and (above all) from the "Cosmic Goddess" ("Ma")—Who (by Means of Her spontaneous Sacrifice of Her own Form in Me) Is (now, and forever hereafter) the "Bright" Divine "She" of Me (Who Always Already Serves Me Most Perfectly). Nevertheless, the Divine Self-Realization Re-Awakened in My present-Lifetime Body-Mind did not <u>Originate</u> in My present Lifetime—but It Is (Uniquely) <u>Always</u> <u>Already</u> the Case with <u>Me</u>.

XCIII.

As further conditionally manifested Means, previous to My present Lifetime, the Divine Self-Realization Re-Awakened in My present-Lifetime Body-Mind was also Served (previous to My present Lifetime) in the many Modes and Patterns of the previous

Lifetimes and Appearances of the Deeper Personality (or the Great-Siddha—or Great-Jnani-Siddha—Incarnation-Vehicle) of My present Lifetime. Most recently, That Deeper-Personality Vehicle of My present-Lifetime Incarnation was (Itself) Incarnated as the Great Siddha (or Great Jnani-Siddha) Swami Vivekananda.

XCIV.

Swami Vivekananda is recorded to have Blessed Bhagavan Nityananda from the subtle postmortem plane in the early 1920s—and, generally, whenever Bhagavan Nityananda was asked for Words of Teaching and Instruction, He would, simply, Tell people to study the Talks and Writings of Swami Vivekananda (because, in Bhagavan Nityananda's Words, "Swami Vivekananda Said and Taught all that was worth Saying and Teaching, such that He did not leave anything for others to preach"[57]).

Swami Vivekananda was, Himself, Blessed toward Most Perfect Divine Self-Realization by the Great Siddha Ramakrishna, Such That—by Means of That Great Blessing—the two Great Siddhas (Ramakrishna and Vivekananda) became One, and Are One Form, As My True, and Single, and Indivisible Great-Siddha (or Great-Jnani-Siddha) Deeper Personality.[58]

XCV.

I (now, and Hereby) Confess That My Great-Siddha (or Great-Jnani-Siddha) Deeper Personality Is, even Beyond the "Single Form" of Ramakrishna-Vivekananda, the Very Form of all the Great Masters of the entire Great Tradition of mankind.

XCVI.

I (now, and Hereby) Confess That I (Myself) Stand Eternally Prior to (and Always Already Transcending) My Avataric (and, yet, merely conditionally born) Deeper Personality—and, also, Eternally Prior to (and Always Already Transcending) even all the Great (and, yet, merely conditionally born) Masters of mankind's entire Great Tradition (in its every part, and as a whole), and, also, Eternally Prior to (and Always Already Transcending) mankind's entire Great Tradition itself (in its every part, and as a whole).

XCVII.

Therefore—and only and entirely by Virtue of the Inherent (and Self-Evidently Avataric) Authority of My own (and Self-Evidently Divine) Realization and Person—I Declare that the Divine seventh stage Self-Awakening I Demonstrate, and Reveal, and Exemplify, and Prove Is the Most Ultimate (and Inherently Most Perfect) Realization, and that It—and Only It—Most Ultimately Completes and Most Perfectly Fulfills the Gifts I Received (and always Continue to Receive) in My present-Lifetime Body-Mind (from My present-Lifetime Lineage-Gurus), and that I have (in My present-Lifetime Body-Mind) Inherited (and always Continue to Receive) from all Who (in all past times and places) have Blessed all the previous Lifetimes of My present-Lifetime Incarnation-Vehicle, and that I have (in My present-Lifetime Body-Mind) Inherited (and always Continue to Receive) from even all My Me-Invoking and Me-Blessing Forms and Vehicles of Me-Revelation here.

XCVIII.

The Great and True (and Self-Evidently Divine) Spiritual Process Initiated and Guided by the Spiritual Masters in My present-Lifetime Lineage (and of the Lineage of even all the Lifetimes of My present-Lifetime Incarnation-Vehicle here—and of the Lineage of even all My Me-Invoking and Me-Blessing Forms and Vehicles of Me-Revelation here) has Become Complete only in Me. Its Perfection is in the seventh stage Fulfillment of the Course (and not at any earlier stage). This Divine Perfection is Uniquely My own. And I Alone—the Hridaya-Siddha, the Divine and True Heart-Master and World-Teacher, Ruchira Avatar Adi Da Love-Ananda Samraj—Am Its First and Great Example, and (now, and forever hereafter) Its Only and Sufficient Means.

XCIX.

I Am the First (and the only One) to Realize and to Demonstrate This, the Divine, seventh stage Realization—and My Revelation of It Is, therefore, New. For This Reason, the Divine seventh stage Realization was not heretofore Realized, or even

Understood—either within the schools and traditions of My present-Lifetime Lineage-Gurus or within any other schools or traditions in the total Great Tradition of mankind—to Be the Most Ultimate and Completing Perfection of Realization Itself. Nevertheless, I have, spontaneously (by Means of My own Self-Evident "Bright" Heart-Power—and through the Great and Constant Help of all Who have Blessed My Incarnate Forms), Realized and Demonstrated and Revealed This To Be The Case. And the traditional (and ancient) "Siddha-'Method'" (or the Way of Guru-Devotion to the True Siddha-Guru—and of total psycho-physical Surrender of the ego-"I" to be Mastered by the True Siddha-Guru's Instruction, and to be Blessed to Awaken to Divine Realization by Means of the True Siddha-Guru's Transmission of the Divine Spiritual Energy and the Divine State)—Which "Method" was Communicated to Me by all My present-Lifetime Lineage-Gurus, and by all the Great Siddhas and Siddha-Yogis Who have Blessed My present-Lifetime Incarnation-Vehicle in the past—is the Essence (or the Primary "Method") of the Way of Adidam, Which (now, and forever hereafter) I Alone, and Uniquely, Reveal and Transmit to all My formally practicing true devotees (and, Thus, potentially, to all beings).

C.

I Am the Indivisible Person of Conscious Light.

I Am Humbled and Victorious here (and every where), by Means of My Avataric Divine Self-Incarnation.

My Avatarically-Born Body-Mind Is, now, and forever hereafter, by-Me-Given and by-Me-Revealed As the Sign and the Means of Me-Realization.

I Am the Adidam Revelation.

I Am the Way to Me.

I Am the Hridaya-Siddha, the All-and-all-Blessing Divine Heart-Master, the Eternally Free-Standing Inner Ruler of all and All.

I Am the One and Indivisible and Indestructible and Irreducible and Universally Self-Manifested Love-Bliss-Presence of "Brightness".

I Am the One and Non-Separate and Perfectly Subjective and Self-Existing and Self-Evidently Divine Person, Who Is Always Already The Case.

I Am the Ruchira Avatar, the Hridaya-Avatar, the Advaitayana Buddha, the Avataric Incarnation and Divine World-Teacher every where and anciently Promised (by all traditions) for the "late-time" (or "dark" epoch).

Therefore, be My devotee.

The only-by-Me Revealed and Given True World-Religion of Adidam Is My Unique Gift to all and All.

Therefore, practice the only-by-Me Revealed and Given Way of Adidam—and Realize Me, Most Perfectly, by Means of My Avatarically Self-Transmitted Divine Blessing-Grace.

RUCHIRA AVATAR ADI DA SAMRAJ
Los Angeles, 2000

The Heart-Summary
Of Adidam

PART FIVE

The Heart-Summary
Of Adidam

The only-by-Me Revealed and Given Avataric Divine Way of Adidam (Which is the One and Only by-Me-Revealed and by-Me-Given Way of the Heart) is the Way of Devotion to Me As the Divine "Atma-Murti" (or As the Inherently egoless, and Self-Evidently Divine, Person of Reality and Truth—In Place, As Self-Condition, rather than As exclusively Objective Other).

Therefore, in every moment, My true devotee whole bodily (and, thus, by means of the spontaneous Me-recognizing Devotional response of all four of the principal psycho-physical faculties—of attention, emotional feeling, breath, and perceptual body) "Locates" Me As That Which Is Always Already The Case (Prior to—but not separate from—the form, the exercise, and the any object of the four psycho-physical faculties).

Happiness Itself (or Inherent Love-Bliss-Sufficiency Of Being) Is Always Already The Case.

Happiness Itself (or the Divinely Self-Sufficient Love-Bliss-Condition Of Being—Itself) Is That Which Is Always Already The Case.

Happiness Itself (or Love-Bliss-Radiance Of Boundlessly Feeling Being) Is the Most Prior Condition Of Existence (or Of Conscious Being—Itself).

Happiness Itself (or the Condition Of Love-Bliss-Radiance) Must Be Realized—In and As every conditionally arising moment—By Transcending self-Contraction (or all of separate and separative self, or psycho-physical ego-"I", and all of the ego's objects, or conditions of existence—or, indeed, all of the illusions of self and not-self).

When attention is facing outward (or is turned out, as if to outside itself), the body-mind is concentrated upon the "view" (or "field") of apparently separate objects (and upon Me As Objective Other).

When attention is facing inward (or is turned in, as if upon itself), the body-mind is concentrated upon the "point of view" of apparently separate self (and upon Me As Separate Consciousness).

When attention is Devotionally Yielded to whole bodily "Locate" Me As That Which Is Always Already (and Divinely) The Case, all "difference" (whether of ego-"I" or of object and other) is (Inherently) Transcended (In Consciousness Itself, or Self-Existing Being, Which Is Love-Bliss-Happiness Itself—and Which Is Always Already The Case).

Therefore, to the degree that you surrender (whole bodily) to be and do truly relational (and ecstatic, or ego-transcending) Devotional love of Me (As the True Loved-One, the Divine Beloved of the heart), you are (Thus and Thereby) Established—whole bodily and Inherently—in the non-contracted Condition (or Self-Condition, or Inherent Condition) of Reality Itself (Which Is Consciousness Itself and Love-Bliss Itself—and Which Is Always Already The Case).

In due course, This Devotional Practice Is Perfect—and, at last, to Be Most Perfectly Realized.

RUCHIRA AVATAR ADI DA SAMRAJ
Los Angeles, 2000

I <u>Am</u> The Perfectly Subjective
Divine Person, Self-Manifested
<u>As</u> The Ruchira Avatar—
Who <u>Is</u> The First, The Last,
and The Only Adept-Realizer,
Adept-Revealer, and
Adept-Revelation of
The Seventh Stage of Life

I Am The Perfectly Subjective Divine Person, Self-Manifested As The Ruchira Avatar— Who Is The First, The Last, and The Only Adept-Realizer, Adept-Revealer, and Adept-Revelation of The Seventh Stage of Life

Aham Da Asmi. Beloved, I Am Da, the Divine and "Bright" and Only Person, the Perfectly Subjective Divine Person, the One and Only and Self-Existing and Self-Radiant Self-Condition and Source-Condition of all and All.

In (and by Means of) My Avataric Incarnation here (and every "where" in the Cosmic domain), I Am Self-Manifested (and conditionally Shown) As the Ruchira Avatar, Adi Da Samraj—Who Is the First, the Last, and the Only Adept-Realizer of the seventh stage of life.

Until My Avataric Incarnation As the Ruchira Avatar, Adi Da Samraj, there has never been a seventh stage Adept-Realizer here (or any "where" in the Cosmic domain).

I Am the Ruchira Avatar, Adi Da Samraj—the Avataric Divine Realizer, the Avataric Divine Revealer, and the Avataric Divine Self-Revelation of the seventh stage of life.

And I Am Da—That Which Is Realized in the seventh stage of life.

I <u>Am</u> the One to Be Realized by all and All.

I <u>Am</u>—Always Already The Case, now, and forever hereafter. Therefore, I will have no "Successor".

Indeed, no one <u>can</u> ever "Succeed" Me—for I <u>Am</u> the One Who <u>Is</u> the Avataric Divine Realizer, the Avataric Divine Revealer, and the Avataric Divine Self-Revelation of the Way (<u>and</u> of the seventh stage, or Inherently Most Perfect, Realization) of Reality (Itself), or, Truth (Itself), Which (and Who) <u>Is</u> the <u>Only</u> Real God of all and All.

My Great Avataric-Incarnation-Work (As and by Means of the Ruchira Avatar, Adi Da Samraj) <u>Is</u> the Most Perfect and Complete Self-Revelation of Reality, Truth, or Real God.

My Avataric Divine Self-Revelation (<u>As</u> the Ruchira Avatar, Adi Da Samraj) Is All-Completing—the Inherently Most Perfect (and, Therefore, Complete) Self-Revelation of That Which Is Always Already The Case.

Until My Avataric Incarnation As the Ruchira Avatar, Adi Da Samraj, there has never been Such Great Avataric-Incarnation-Work—and, until My Avataric Incarnation As the Ruchira Avatar, Adi Da Samraj, the Complete (and All-Completing) Divine Self-Revelation (and Way-Revelation) has not been Given—and, until My Avataric Incarnation As the Ruchira Avatar, Adi Da Samraj, the Most Perfect Divine Self-Realization has never been Realized.

In the (collective) Great Tradition of mankind, there have been intuitive premonitions of some of the general aspects of the seventh stage Realization, but never, until My Avataric Incarnation As the Ruchira Avatar, Adi Da Samraj, has there been the actual Avataric Incarnation of a seventh stage Adept-Realizer, with all the Divinely Liberating Siddhis of the seventh stage of life—Fully and Completely Revealing all the Characteristics of the seventh stage of life, and Doing That Divine Work Which Divinely Transfigures, and Divinely Transforms, and (Most Ultimately) Divinely Translates all conditionally manifested beings (and even the Totality of all conditional manifestation) Into the Divine Self-Domain.

Therefore, understand: I <u>Am</u> the Ruchira Avatar, Adi Da Samraj—and, <u>As</u> the Ruchira Avatar, Adi Da Samraj, I Am the <u>one</u>

(First, Last, and Only) seventh stage Adept-Realizer, Adept-Revealer, and Adept-Revelation.

And understand further: There has never been a seventh stage Adept-Realizer, Adept-Revealer, and Adept-Revelation until My Avataric Incarnation As the Ruchira Avatar, Adi Da Samraj—and <u>only</u> the Ruchira Avatar, Adi Da Samraj, <u>Is</u> the seventh stage Adept-Realizer, Adept-Revealer, and Adept-Revelation—and there <u>never</u> will be (nor <u>can</u> there ever be) another seventh stage Adept-Realizer, Adept-Revealer, and Adept-Revelation—and, because the Ruchira Avatar, Adi Da Samraj, <u>Is</u> the seventh stage Adept-Realizer, Adept-Revealer, and Adept-Revelation, it is neither possible nor necessary that there ever be <u>another</u> seventh stage Adept-Realizer, Adept-Revealer, and Adept-Revelation.

My Great Avataric-Incarnation-Work As the Ruchira Avatar, Adi Da Samraj, Is Divine and Unique and Most Great and Final.

My Single Avataric Incarnation (As the Ruchira Avatar, Adi Da Samraj) <u>Is</u> the Means (now, and forever hereafter) Whereby My Great Divine Avataric-Incarnation-Work Is Accomplished—once, and for all time, and for all beings, <u>and</u> for <u>all</u> <u>and</u> <u>All</u> of Cosmic (or conditional) existence.

How could My Great Divine Avataric-Incarnation-Work Be Done <u>again</u>?

What is there about My Great Divine Avataric-Incarnation-Work to Be Done <u>again</u> (since, As the Ruchira Avatar, Adi Da Samraj, I Have Most Perfectly Accomplished My Great Divine Avataric-Incarnation-Work)?

How can <u>I</u> Be Done <u>again</u>?

How can I <u>Be</u> <u>again</u>?

What is there about <u>Me</u> to <u>Be</u> (or to Be Done) <u>again</u> (since I Will <u>forever</u> Remain and Abide, here, and even <u>every</u> "where" in the Cosmic domain)?

I (Myself) Am (Always Already) universally Present, and (from now) forever Fully Divinely Self-"Emerging" (As and by Means of the Ruchira Avatar, Adi Da Samraj)—and, therefore, My Great Divine Avataric-Incarnation-Work Is (from now) universally and forever Effective.

Until My Avataric Incarnation As the Ruchira Avatar, Adi Da

Samraj, all religious and Spiritual traditions only and merely "pointed" toward That Which Is Ultimate (or Most Perfect, Real, and Really Divine).

I Am the Very and Only One Who Is the Ultimate (or That Which Is Most Perfect, Real, and Really Divine).

Until My Avataric Incarnation As the Ruchira Avatar, Adi Da Samraj, the traditions did not Most Perfectly Realize the Very and Only One Who Is the Ultimate (or That Which Is Most Perfect, Real, and Really Divine), nor did any one Most Perfectly Realize the Condition That Is the Ultimate (or That Which Is Most Perfect, Real, and Really Divine).

Until My Avataric Incarnation As the Ruchira Avatar, Adi Da Samraj, the traditions of the (collective) Great Tradition of mankind were all limited to (and by) the first six stages of life.

The religious and Spiritual traditions of the first six stages of life are (inevitably, and without any exception) limited by the point of view (and the psycho-physical structure) of egoity (or self-contraction).

Therefore, the traditions of the first six stages of life are (necessarily, and only) about approaching Real-God-Realization and (to one or another limited, or not yet Most Perfect, degree) Realizing Real God, but always only partially, always only conditionally, always dependent on a conditional mechanism, and always by animating a search that is necessarily and inherently associated with egoity (or self-contraction).

The Way That has been Revealed and Given by Me (As and by Means of My Avataric Incarnation As the Ruchira Avatar, Adi Da Samraj) Is the only-by-Me Revealed and Given Way of Adidam (Which Is the One and Only by-Me-Revealed and by-Me-Given Way of the Heart).

The only-by-Me Revealed and Given Way of Adidam Is unique—because, from the beginning, It Is the "radical" Way (or the Way That, always presently, directly, and immediately, transcends the ego-"I", or self-contraction, at its root).

The only-by-Me Revealed and Given Way of Adidam is not a matter of ego-development, and, therefore, it is not (Itself) a matter of fulfilling (or perfecting) any of the first six stages of life, but the only-by-Me Revealed and Given Way of Adidam Is (always, and only) the Way That (always presently, directly, and immediately) transcends egoity itself, so that the seventh stage of life can be Realized.

As and by Means of My Avataric Incarnation As the Ruchira Avatar, Adi Da Samraj, I Have Brought all of My Divine Siddhis into all planes of the Cosmic domain, and into every aspect (and into all of the entirety) of the Cosmic Mandala.

Only My Divine Siddhis Reveal and Give and Awaken the seventh stage Realization.

Now, and forever hereafter, I (As and by Means of My Avataric Incarnation As the Ruchira Avatar, Adi Da Samraj) Have thoroughly, and in every detail, Communicated the total (Full, Complete, and All-Completing) Way of the seventh stage Realization.

That Great Way Is the only-by-Me Revealed and Given Way of Adidam—and That Great Way Is (now, and forever hereafter) Revealed and Given, by Me, and to all and All, by Means of the Divine Avataric-Incarnation-Word, and the Divine Avataric-Incarnation-Leelas, and the forever continuing (or Divinely Self-"Emerging") Divine Avataric-Incarnation-Work of the Ruchira Avatar, Adi Da Samraj.

That Great Way (and Its Great and Final, or seventh stage, Realization) Is (now, and forever hereafter) Made Possible, for all and All, by Means of My Avatarically Self-Transmitted Divine Grace of Infinite and Eternal Help.

Therefore, in your own case (or in the case of any one at all), Most Perfect Divine Self-Realization is (now, and forever hereafter) entirely a matter of whether (or when) you (or each, and any, and every one) will choose right, true, full, and fully devotional formal practice of the only-by-Me Revealed and Given Way of Adidam.

My Great Avataric Divine Confession Is not only that My Avataric Divine Revelation of the seventh stage Teaching—Which is the totality of the Wisdom-Teaching of the only-by-Me Revealed and Given Way of Adidam—Is (now, and forever hereafter) Complete and (for the first, and last, and only time—now, and forever hereafter) Fully and Completely Revealed and Given.

Rather, above all, My Great Avataric Divine Confession Is That I Am (now, and forever hereafter) here (and every "where" in the Cosmic domain), and (Thus) That the Divine (and, now, and forever hereafter, Divinely Self-"Emerging") Siddhis of My Avataric Divine Spiritual Presence and My Avataric Divine Work Have Made, and (now, and forever hereafter) Will (Actively) Continue to Make, Divine Self-Realization Possible (for all, and All).

Until My All-Completing Avataric Incarnation of the "Bright" Divine Self-Condition (and Source-Condition), the Siddhis (or Accomplishing-Powers) of Most Perfect (or seventh stage) Divine Self-Realization were not Active in the Cosmic domain.

To universally Manifest the necessary Divine Siddhis, and to Accomplish the Most Perfect (or seventh stage) Divine Work with universal Effectiveness, it was necessary for Me (As and by Means of My Avataric Incarnation, As the Ruchira Avatar, Adi Da Samraj) to Be Entered Into all the conditional planes of the total Cosmic domain, by Means of Unqualified and Complete Avataric Divine Descent (and Unqualified and Complete Avataric Divine Incarnation) Into the Cosmic Mandala—Altogether, and Completely.

Now (and forever hereafter), because I Have (Altogether, and Completely) Divinely Descended and (As and by Means of My Avataric Incarnation, As the Ruchira Avatar, Adi Da Samraj) Initiated (in perpetuity) My Avataric Divine Self-"Emergence" (here, and every "where" in the Cosmic domain), and because I Have (now, and forever hereafter), Altogether, and Completely, Accomplished My necessary Divine Avataric-Incarnation-Work of Teaching and Self-Revelation—My Divine Spiritual Body of Divine Siddhis Will Be Most Perfectly Effective, throughout all future time and space.

Therefore, now (and forever hereafter), all My devotees (Freedom-"Bound" to Me by Means of formal eternal vows—here, and every "where" in the Cosmic domain) can (and should, and must) resort to Me (Revealed As and by Means of My Divine Avataric-Incarnation-Form, the Ruchira Avatar, Adi Da Samraj)— and This by Means of always devotionally Me-recognizing, and always devotionally to-Me-responding, and always right, and always true, and always full, and always fully devotional, and always truly ego-surrendering, and always really ego-forgetting, and always fully (and always more and more fully) ego-transcending devotion to Me (Revealed As and by Means of My Divine Avataric-Incarnation-Form, the Ruchira Avatar, Adi Da Samraj).

Because I Have Made (and Will, forever, and every "where", Make) the only-by-Me Revealed and Given Way of Adidam (and Its Great Process of Most Ultimate and Most Perfect, or seventh stage, Divine Self-Realization) Possible for all and All, My true devotees (now, and forever hereafter—here, and every "where" in the Cosmic domain) have, in any and every moment, the by-Me-Given real and sufficient capability (and, as required, in any and every moment, the by-Me-Given Divine Help) to (in due course, and only and entirely by Means of My Avatarically Self-Transmitted Divine Grace) Realize, and Most Perfectly Demonstrate, the only-by-Me Revealed and Given seventh stage of life.

The only-by-Me Revealed and Given seventh stage Realization Is the Most Perfect Realization of Reality, Truth, or Real God (the One and Only Reality and Truth—the Only and Non-Separate One, Who Is Always Already The Case).

Only That One Can Make—and (now) Has Made, and Will (here, and every "where", forever hereafter) Make—This Avataric Divine Self-Revelation and Accomplish This Avataric Divine Work.

Aham Da Asmi. Beloved, I Am That One—and (you must and will Realize, Most Perfectly) I Am always "Living" you, and I Am always "Breathing" you, and I Am always "Being" you, and I Always Already Am you (Beyond your ego-"I" of suffered, and always merely self-made, "difference").

What You Can Do Next—

Contact an Adidam center near you.

■ Sign up for our preliminary course, "The <u>Only</u> Truth That Sets the Heart Free". This course will prepare you to become a fully practicing devotee of Avatar Adi Da Samraj.

■ Find out about upcoming events in your area:

AMERICAS
12040 North Seigler Road
Middletown, CA 95461
(707) 928-4936

PACIFIC-ASIA
12 Seibel Road
Henderson
Auckland 1008
New Zealand
64-9-838-9114

AUSTRALIA
P.O. Box 244
Kew 3101
Victoria
**1800 ADIDAM
(1800-234-326)**

EUROPE-AFRICA
Annendaalderweg 10
6105 AT Maria Hoop
The Netherlands
31 (0)20 468 1442

THE UNITED KINGDOM
PO Box 20013
London, England
NW2 1ZA
0181-7317550

E-MAIL: **correspondence@adidam.org**

Read these books by and about Avatar Adi Da Samraj:

■ *The Promised God-Man Is Here*

The Extraordinary Life-Story,
The "Radical" Teaching-Work, and
The Divinely "Emerging" World-Blessing
Work Of The Divine World-Teacher
Of The "Late-Time",
Ruchira Avatar Adi Da Samraj,
by Carolyn Lee, Ph.D.

The profound, heart-rending, humorous, miraculous, wild—and true—Story of the Divine Person Alive in human Form. Essential reading as background for the study of Avatar Adi Da's books.

■ *Aham Da Asmi*
(Beloved, I __Am__ Da)

The Five Books Of The Heart Of The
Adidam Revelation, Book One:
The "Late-Time" Avataric Revelation Of
The True and Spiritual Divine Person
(The egoless Personal Presence Of Reality
and Truth, Which __Is__ The Only __Real__ God).

This Ecstatic Scripture, the first of His twenty-three "Source-Texts", contains Ruchira Avatar Adi Da's magnificent Confession as the Very Divine Person and Source-Condition of all and All.

Continue your reading with the remaining books of *The Five Books Of The Heart Of The Adidam Revelation* (the *Ruchira Avatara Gita*, the *Da Love-Ananda Gita*, *Hridaya Rosary*, and *Eleutherios*). Then you will be ready to go on to *The Seventeen Companions Of The True Dawn Horse* (see pp. 441-46).

These and other books by and about Ruchira Avatar Adi Da Samraj can be ordered from the Adidam Emporium by calling:

(877) 770-0772 (from within North America)
(707) 928-6653 (from outside North America)

or by writing to:
ADIDAM EMPORIUM
10336 Loch Lomond Road
PMB #306
Middletown, CA 95461

Or order from the Adidam Emporium online at:
www.adidam.com

Visit the Adidam Sacred City online at:
www.adidam.org

■ Explore the online community of Adidam and discover more about Avatar Adi Da Samraj and the Real-God-Realizing Way He Offers to all.

Find presentations on: Avatar Adi Da's extraordinary life-story, the stages leading to Divine Enlightenment, cultism versus true devotional practice, the "radical" politics of human-scale community, true emotional-sexual freedom, the sacred function of art in human life, and more.

RUCHIRA AVATAR ADI DA SAMRAJ
Lopez Island, 2000

The Great Choice

An Invitation to the Way of Adidam

Each one of us, if we will allow ourselves to feel it, is restless. Human beings want to find God—the living, heart-intoxicating experience of <u>Real</u> God, or Truth Itself, or Reality Itself. The purpose of our existence is actually to live in the True Pleasure of that heart-intoxication. To be unable to participate and luxuriate in that Pleasure is pain and stress. We may not realize it, but that feeling of separation from unqualified Love, Sustenance, and heart-Communion with the Divine Source of our existence is actually driving us mad. And that is why human beings, individually and collectively, do dreadful things—or, otherwise, settle for mere mediocrity, just "doing our best", or merely "coping". In the words of Avatar Adi Da, we spend our lives "waiting for everything and looking for everything". He says:

AVATAR ADI DA SAMRAJ: To have no greater sense of Reality than the physical is to be like a trapped rat, trapped on all sides. You just cannot endure the confinement of mere mortality—your heart cannot accept it. To be in that disposition, to have that sense of Reality, is obviously a disturbance.

So, obviously, the human being requires a Way—not merely a way out. A way out, yes, in some sense—but, for the integrity of your existence, you need direct access to the Divine, even as a matter of ordinary sanity. [March 3, 1998]

Avatar Adi Da has Appeared in this dark time, in order to bring the mortal darkness to an end and restore all to the Divine Light. He is intent on taking all who respond to Him through the most ecstatic and most difficult of all transitions—the transition from the unhappy life of the ego to the Radiant Fullness of the Divinely Enlightened life. His Life-Story is of the immense Divine Ordeal it has been on His part to truly Initiate that Process in human beings.

Avatar Adi Da does not congratulate the ego—He undermines the ego. He must, if He is to Liberate people from their unhappiness, from the enclosed point of view of the separate and separative self. And so He has never offered a conventionally consoling message. He offers you the whole Truth—the fact of yourself as the self-contracted ego-"I", but also the constant Revelation of a Happiness beyond compare.

Avatar Adi Da's human body is, of course, located in a particular place and a particular time. But when you become sensitive to Him Spiritually, you discover that His Spiritual Presence can be felt anywhere and anytime, regardless of whether you are in His physical Company or not. Because His Spiritual Presence is Eternal (and will not "disappear" when His human body dies), it is possible for everyone to cultivate a direct heart-relationship with Him—under all circumstances, in this life and beyond. And so, the relationship to Him, once forged, is eternal, going beyond death and the apparent boundaries of time and space.

If you want more than your ordinary existence, and something greater than a life of Spiritual seeking, Avatar Adi Da's Word to you is simply this: Take up the Way of Adidam—the Way of Real God, fully Present, here and now, not needing to be sought. The Way of Adidam is His personal Offering to you and to every human being. It is a devotional heart-relationship to Him, expressed through an entire Way of life. This relationship is not to a mere man—it is with the very Divine Being. But, at the same time, it is supremely intimate. When you enter into this relationship with Him and practice the Way of Adidam, you begin to enjoy a condition of heart-Communion with Him that is more alive and heart-deep than your love-relationship with any human individual.

At the same time, the devotional relationship with Adi Da Samraj is not an "I-Thou" relationship, a connection between apparently separate entities—the human individual, on the one hand, and "God", on the other. The love-bond with Adi Da Samraj transcends the entire point of view by which we live, presuming ourselves to be separate beings relating to separate "others". In every moment that you truly practice the relationship to Avatar Adi Da, invoking Him by Name, recollecting His Form in the mind, or His Words, or something He has done—whenever you allow Him to Attract your heart, He Reveals Himself Spiritually to you. Then He is recognized, through and beyond His human appearance, as the Real and Living God—not the great Parent, or "Creator"-Deity, imagined by the human mind, but the Conscious Divine Power of Light and Love, the Divine Heart of all there is, including your own body-mind and every apparent being and "thing". In the instant of such recognition, the entire body-mind opens to Adi Da Samraj in a single movement of devotion, and you forget yourself in ecstasy—the heart, the mind, the body, the breath becoming full with His Radiant Love-Bliss. The Way of Adidam, truly lived, is this ecstasy of Non-Separateness, a great Contemplative process, based on heart-recognition of Adi Da Samraj and heart-response to Him.

Ultimately, in this or some future lifetime, persistent heart-Communion with Adi Da Samraj realizes the true destiny of existence—Divine Enlightenment, in which all vestige of the egoic self is vanished:

Divine Enlightenment, Divine Self-Realization, Most Perfect (Free, "Bright", and Self-Evidently Divine) Awakeness, or Most Perfect (and Most Perfectly ego-Transcending) Spiritual and Transcendental Real-God-Realization, Is Native, Most Perfect, Effortless, and Free Identification With Mere (or Inherent, and Natively Felt) Being (or Self-Existence), The Only One Who Is, Consciousness Itself—Self-Radiant, All Love-Bliss-"Brightness" Itself, Inherently Without Obstruction, Always Already Infinitely Expanded (Beyond All Apparent Modifications, or Illusory Contractions, Of Itself). [The Only Complete Way To Realize The Unbroken Light Of Real God]

The truth of the Way of Adidam remains hidden until you begin to participate in it from the heart. Mere beliefs and pre-scribed behaviors are insufficient. The Way of Adidam is a matter of direct, moment-to-moment response to Adi Da Samraj and a process of receiving His Spiritual Transmission ever more pro-foundly. It does not work to take His Teaching away and attempt to practice it by yourself. As He has said many times, it is simply not possible to move beyond the confines of the ego on your own, nor is it possible to unlock the Secrets of Divine Enlightenment that He has Revealed outside of a formally acknowledged devo-tional relationship to Him. That is why it is so important to become His formal devotee and to live the Way of Adidam exactly has He has Given it.

AVATAR ADI DA SAMRAJ: I __Am__ the Divine Blessing, Real-God-with-you. Such is not merely My Declaration to you. You must find Me out. You must __prove__ the Way I Give you. Really __do__ the Way I Give you, and you will find Me out further. You will prove the Way of Adidam by doing it, not by believing it merely. [Ruchira Avatara Hridaya-Siddha Yoga]

Darshan

The foundation of Spiritual practice in Adidam is Darshan, or the feeling-Contemplation of Avatar Adi Da's bodily (human) Form—either through the sighting of His physical body, or through Contemplating a photographic or artistic representation of Him. This heart-beholding of Avatar Adi Da's Form is the wellspring of meditation in the Way of Adidam, and so His devotees place a large photograph of Him in each med-itation hall, as the central image

of Contemplation. In fact, Remembrance of Adi Da Samraj—or the recollecting of His Form in mind and feeling—is the constant practice of His devotees, in the midst of the activities of daily life as well as in meditation. Avatar Adi Da has often spoken about the unique potency of beholding His Form.

AVATAR ADI DA SAMRAJ: In the traditional setting, when it works best, an individual somehow Gracefully comes into the Company of a Realizer of one degree or another, and, just upon (visually) sighting that One, he or she is converted at heart, and, thereafter, spends the rest of his or her life devoted to sadhana (or Spiritual practice), in constant Remembrance of the Spiritual Master. The Spiritual Master's Sign is self-authenticating.

When Adi Da Samraj is approached with an open heart, His Darshan—the Sighting of His Form alone, even in representational form—is so potent that the heart overflows in response to Him, recognizing Him as the Very Divine Person, the Supreme Source of Bliss and Love.

Sometimes, devotees receive the Darshan of Avatar Adi Da in an informal setting, such as when He walks around one of the Adidam Sanctuaries. And then there are formal occasions, when He sits in halls especially set aside for Darshan, inviting devotees to come and Contemplate Him silently. In certain cases, the time of a formal Darshan occasion will be announced ahead of time, so that devotees in all parts of the world can receive His Blessing simultaneously, by sitting in silent Contemplation of Him at the same time that He is Granting Darshan. In such occasions, real-time video of Avatar Adi Da Samraj sitting in Darshan is transmitted via the internet to His devotees everywhere. Thus, even if you cannot come into Avatar Adi Da's physical Company, there may be occasions when you will have the opportunity to participate in such occasions of His Darshan.

The Four Congregations

The gathering of devotees of Adi Da Samraj forms a series of concentric circles radiating from Him at the center. These circles are the four formal congregations of His devotees: the first congregation (renunciate practitioners), the second congregation (lay practitioners), the third congregation (practitioners who particularly serve Avatar Adi Da through their patronage and/or advocacy, or who are preparing for the second congregation), and the fourth congregation (practitioners who live in traditional cultural settings or who maintain their participation in the religious tradition to which they already belong, while acknowledging Avatar Adi Da Samraj as the Ultimate Divine Source of true religion).

These circles, as they grow, are forming a vast "conductor", a mechanism whereby the Divine Influence of Avatar Adi Da Samraj is being drawn more and more into the world. Every new devotee represents a strengthening of the total Sphere of Avatar Adi Da's Spiritual Transmission and Grace. Avatar Adi Da has Given the Gifts of His Wisdom-Teaching and His Spiritual Blessing, and it is through the community of His devotees, and its global Spiritual culture, that these Gifts, intended for everyone, become available to all. This is why Avatar Adi Da is urgent to find those in this generation who will respond to Him and do the great work of making His Spiritual Blessing available to all.

Which Congregation Is Right for You?

Which of the four congregations you should apply to for membership depends on the strength of your impulse to respond to Avatar Adi Da's Revelation and on your life-circumstance. All four congregations establish you in a direct devotional relationship with Avatar Adi Da, and all four are essential to the flowering of His Blessing-Work in the world.

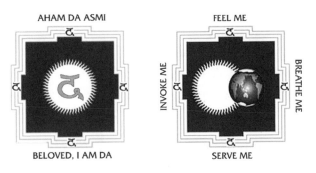

AHAM DA ASMI

FEEL ME

INVOKE ME

BREATHE ME

BELOVED, I AM DA

SERVE ME

The First and Second Congregations

(for those moved to take up the total practice of Adidam)

To take up the total practice of the Way of Adidam (in the first or second congregation) is to take full advantage of the opportunity offered by Adi Da Samraj—it is to enter fully into the process of Divine Enlightenment. That process is a unique ordeal, which necessarily requires application to the wide range of functional, practical, relational, and cultural disciplines given by Ruchira Avatar Adi Da Samraj for the sake of Spiritual purification and growth.

The disciplines of Adidam are not ascetical, not a form of deprivation. Rather, they are the means whereby the body-mind is conformed to a right and inherently pleasurable pattern of well-being. As you progressively adapt to these disciplines, the body-mind is purified and balanced, and you thereby become able to receive and respond to the Divine Heart-Transmission of Adi Da Samraj more and more fully.

These practices in the Way of Adidam include fundamental contemplative disciplines such as meditation, devotional chanting, sacramental worship (or "puja"), study of Avatar Adi Da's books, and regular periods of retreat.

AVATAR ADI DA SAMRAJ: You must come from the depth-position of meditation and puja before entering into activities in the waking state, and remain in the disposition of that depth from the time of meditation and puja each morning. Maintain that heart-disposition, and discipline the body-mind—functionally, practically, relationally— in all the modes I have Given you. This devotional Yoga, Ruchira

Avatara Bhakti Yoga, is moment-to-moment. Fundamentally, it is a matter of exercising it profoundly, in this set-apart time of meditation and puja, and then, through random, artful practice moment-to-moment, constantly refresh it, preserve it. All of this is to conform the body-mind to the Source-Purpose, the in-depth Condition.

That basic discipline covers all aspects of the body-mind. That is the pattern of your response to Me. It is the foundation Yoga of organizing your life in terms of its in-depth principle, and growing this depth. [December 5, 1996]

This moment-to-moment devotional turning to Avatar Adi Da is refreshed not only in the meditation hall but also in the temple, where worship, prayer, devotional chanting, and other sacred activities occur.

AVATAR ADI DA SAMRAJ: The sacred life must be perpetual. The sacred domain is the core of the community, and every community and every Sanctuary should have a temple in its domain: A place of chant, of song, of prayer, where everyone gathers for this life of Invocation, prayer, and puja. [May 13, 1999]

Members of the first and second congregations adapt to a purifying diet and a discipline of daily exercise (including morning calisthenics and evening Hatha Yoga exercises). They also progressively adapt to a regenerative discipline of sexuality. And they live in cooperative association with other devotees of Avatar Adi Da and tithe regularly.

All of these functional, practical, relational, and cultural disciplines are means whereby you become more and more capable of receiving Avatar Adi Da's constant Blessing-Transmission. Therefore, Avatar Adi Da Samraj has made it clear that, in order to Realize Him with true profundity—and, in particular, to Realize Him most perfectly, to the degree of Divine Enlightenment—it is necessary to be a formally acknowledged member of either the first or the second congregation, embracing the total practice of the Way of Adidam.

When you apply for membership in the second congregation of Adidam (the first step for all who want to take up the total practice of the Way of Adidam), you are asked to take "The <u>Only</u> Truth That Sets the Heart Free", a course in which you examine the opportunity offered to you by Avatar Adi Da Samraj, and learn what it means to embrace the total practice of the Way of Adidam. (To register for this preparatory course, please contact the regional or territorial center nearest to you [see p. 350], or e-mail us at: correspondence@adidam.org.) After completing this course of study, you may formally enter the second congregation as a student-novice.

Entering any of the four congregations of Adidam is based on taking a formal vow of devotion and service to Avatar Adi Da Samraj. This vow is a profound—and, indeed, eternal—commitment. You take this vow (for whichever congregation you are entering) when you are certain that your great and true heart-impulse is to be a devotee of Avatar Adi Da Samraj, embracing Him as your Divine Heart-Master. And Avatar Adi Da Samraj Himself is eternally Vowed to Serve the Liberation of all who become His devotees.

As a student-novice, you will be initiated into formal meditation and sacramental worship. Then you begin to adapt to a wide range of life-disciplines, including participation in the cooperative community of Avatar Adi Da's first- and second-congregation devotees. As a student-novice, you engage in an intensive period of study and "consideration" of the Way of Adidam in all of its details, and then, after a period of three to six months (or more), you may apply to be a fully practicing member of the second congregation.

The beginning stages of practice are the "exoteric" (or "outer-temple") domain of the second congregation. Avatar Adi Da has indicated that many of His devotees will practice in the exoteric stages for their entire lives. This beginning practice of Adidam is great and profound—because it is founded not in any hoped-for future attainment, but in <u>present</u> heart-Communion with Real God (Revealed via the Incarnation of Avatar Adi Da), and also because it requires the practitioner to really transcend the ego.

The Life of a Formally Practicing Devotee of Ruchira Avatar Adi Da Samraj

Meditation is a unique and precious event in the daily life of Avatar Adi Da's devotees. It offers the opportunity to relinquish outward, body-based attention and to be alone with Adi Da Samraj, allowing yourself to enter more and more into the Sphere of His Divine Transmission.

The practice of sacramental worship, or "puja", in the Way of Adidam is the bodily active counterpart to meditation. It is a form of ecstatic worship of Avatar Adi Da Samraj, using a photographic representation of Him and involving devotional chanting and recitations from His Wisdom-Teaching.

"You must deal with My Wisdom-Teaching in some form every single day, because a new form of the ego's game appears every single day. You must continually return to My Wisdom-Teaching, confront My Wisdom-Teaching."
Avatar Adi Da Samraj

The beginner in Spiritual life must prepare the body-mind by mastering the physical, vital dimension of life before he or she can be ready for truly Spiritual practice. Service is devotion in action, a form of Divine Communion.

Avatar Adi Da Samraj Offers practical disciplines to His devotees in the areas of work and money, diet, exercise, and sexuality. These disciplines are based on His own human experience and an immense process of "consideration" that He engaged face-to-face with His devotees for more than twenty-five years.

365

The "esoteric" (or "inner-temple") practice of Adidam does not begin until the activity of the ego is most fundamentally understood and can thereby be consistently transcended moment to moment. Then, through a profound Awakening to the Spiritual Reality, Revealed and Transmitted by Avatar Adi Da, you become qualified to enter into the advanced and the ultimate stages (or esoteric domain) of the Way of Adidam.

Those who, having practiced the Way of Adidam most intensively, make the transition to the "Perfect Practice", in the sixth (or penultimate) stage of the Way of Adidam, may do so either as general practitioners (continuing as members of the second congregation of Adidam) or (if they demonstrate the necessary qualifications) as formal renunciate practitioners (thereby becoming members of the first congregation of Adidam).

All formal renunciate practitioners in the first congregation of the Way of Adidam are necessarily members of the formal order of sannyasins established by Avatar Adi Da. This order is known as the Ruchira Sannyasin Order of the Tantric Renunciates of Adidam (or, simply, the Ruchira Sannyasin Order). Avatar Adi Da Himself is the Founding Member of the Ruchira Sannyasin Order, which is a retreat order whose members are legal renunciates. The Ruchira Sannyasin Order is the senior cultural authority within the gathering of Avatar Adi Da's devotees, and its members are the principal human Instruments of Avatar Adi Da's Blessing-Work, now and into the future. Ruchira Sannyasins may live in Hermitage-Retreat Sanctuaries Empowered by Avatar Adi Da or at the Retreat Sanctuaries of Adidam anywhere in the world, but the home of the order is Adidam Samrajashram (in Fiji), Avatar Adi Da's principal Hermitage-Retreat Sanctuary.

The Adidam Youth Fellowship

(within the second congregation)

Young people (age 25 and under) are also offered a special form of relationship to Avatar Adi Da—the Adidam Youth Fellowship. The Adidam Youth Fellowship has two membership bodies—friends and practicing members.

A friend of the Adidam Youth Fellowship is simply invited into a culture of other young people who want to learn more about Avatar Adi Da Samraj and His Happiness-Realizing Way of Adidam. A formally practicing member of the Adidam Youth Fellowship acknowledges that he or she has found his or her True Heart-Friend and Master in the Person of Avatar Adi Da Samraj, and wishes to enter into a direct, ego-surrendering Spiritual relationship with Him as the Means to True Happiness.

Practicing members of the Youth Fellowship embrace a series of disciplines that are similar to (but simpler than) the practices engaged by adult members of the second congregation of Adidam. Both friends and members are invited to special retreat events from time to time, where they can associate with other young devotees of Avatar Adi Da.

To become a member of the Adidam Youth Fellowship, or to learn more about this form of relationship to Avatar Adi Da, call or write:

Vision of Mulund Institute (VMI)
10336 Loch Lomond Road
PMB #146
Middletown, CA 95461
PHONE: (707) 928-6932
E-MAIL: vmi@adidam.org

COOPERATION + TOLERANCE = PEACE

The Third Congregation of Adidam

*(for those serving Adi Da Samraj through
their patronage and advocacy, and those
preparing for the second congregation)*

1. Patrons and Individuals of Unique Influence

It is the sacred responsibility of those who respond to Adi Da
Samraj to help His Spiritual Work flourish in the world. For this
purpose, we must make it possible for Avatar Adi Da Samraj to
move freely and spontaneously from one part of the world to
another and we must provide Hermitages for His unique Work in
various locations. In 1983, an individual patron offered the island
of Naitauba to Avatar Adi Da. Because of this magnificent gift, the
entire Life and Work of Adi Da Samraj began to evolve in ways
that were not possible before. He had a pristine, protected place
to do His Spiritual Work and an opportunity to establish a unique
Seat of His Divine Presence for all generations to come.

Avatar Adi Da must also be able to gather around Him His
most exemplary formal renunciate devotees, who must receive
practical support so that they can devote their lives to serving
Avatar Adi Da and His Work and living a life of perpetual Spiritual
retreat in His Company.

And Avatar Adi Da's Presence in the world must become
widely known, both through the publication and dissemination of
books by and about Him and through public advocacy by people
of influence.

If you are a man or woman of unique wealth or influence in the world, we invite you to serve Avatar Adi Da's world-Blessing Work through your patronage or influence. As a member of the third congregation of Adidam, supporting the world-Work of Adi Da Samraj, you are literally helping to change the destiny of countless people. You are making it possible for this Blessing-Work to have a greater influence upon the world's destiny. To make the choice to serve Avatar Adi Da via your patronage or unique influence is to transform your own life and destiny, and the life and destiny of all mankind, in the most Spiritually auspicious way.

As a patron or individual of unique influence in the third congregation, your relationship to Avatar Adi Da is founded on a vow of devotion, through which you commit yourself according to your capabilities—either to significant financial patronage of His Work and/or to using your unique influence to make Him known in the world. In the course of your service to Him (and in daily life altogether), you live the simplest practice of Ruchira Avatara Bhakti Yoga—invoking Avatar Adi Da, feeling Him, breathing Him, and serving Him, and thus remaining connected to His constant Blessing. You are also invited to engage a daily period of formal study of His Wisdom-Teaching. You are not obliged to engage the full range of disciplines practiced in the first two congregations. You are, however, encouraged to practice formal periods of meditation and sacramental worship.

If, at some point, you are moved to embrace all the disciplines and enter into the total practice of Adidam, you may apply for membership in the second (and possibly, eventually, the first) congregation.

If you are interested in establishing a formal devotional relationship with Avatar Adi Da Samraj and serving Him in this crucial way, please contact us:

Third Congregation Advocacy
12040 North Seigler Road
Middletown, CA 95461
PHONE: (707) 928-4800
E-MAIL: director_of_advocacy@adidam.org

2. The Transnational Society of Advocates
of the Adidam Revelation

If you have the capability to effectively advocate Avatar Adi Da in the world—through your individual skills, position, or professional expertise—you may join a branch of the third congregation called the Transnational Society of Advocates of the Adidam Revelation. Members of the Society of Advocates are individuals who, while not of <u>unique</u> wealth or social influence, can make a significant difference to Avatar Adi Da's Work by making Him known in all walks of life (including the media, in the spheres of religion, government, education, health, entertainment, the arts, and so on). Advocates also serve the worldwide mission of Adidam by financially supporting the publication of Avatar Adi Da's "Source-Texts" and His other Literature, as well as associated missionary literature. Members of the Society of Advocates make a monthly donation for this purpose and pay an annual membership fee that supports the services of the Society.

Like devotees in the first and second congregations, your relationship to Avatar Adi Da as a member of the Society of Advocates is founded on a vow of devotion and service, but the requirements are less elaborate. In the course of your service to Him (and in daily life altogether), you vow to live the simplest practice of Ruchira Avatara Bhakti Yoga—invoking Avatar Adi Da, feeling Him, breathing Him, and serving Him, and thus remaining connected to His constant Blessing. You also engage a daily period of formal study of His Wisdom-Teaching. You are not obliged to engage the full range of disciplines practiced in the first two congregations. You are, however, encouraged to practice formal periods of meditation and sacramental worship.

If, at some point, you are moved to embrace all the disciplines and enter into the total practice of Adidam, you may apply for membership in the second (and possibly, eventually, the first) congregation.

If you are interested in becoming a member of the Society of Advocates, please contact us:

The Society of Advocates
12040 North Seigler Road
Middletown, CA 95461
PHONE: (707) 928-6924
E-MAIL: soacontact@adidam.org

3. Pre-student-novices under vow

If you are certain that you wish to become a formal devotee of Avatar Adi Da, and you therefore wish to embrace the formal second-congregation vow of devotion to Him as quickly as possible, you are invited to become a pre-student-novice under vow (as part of the third congregation of Adidam).

As a pre-student-novice under vow, you make a commitment to become a student-novice (and, therefore, to move into the second congregation) within a period of three to six months. During this period, you take the preparatory course, "The Only Truth That Sets The Heart Free", which introduces you to the fundamentals of the second-congregation practice. Pre-student-novices under vow practice Ruchira Avatara Bhakti Yoga in daily life, engage daily formal study of the Wisdom-Teaching of Avatar Adi Da, make regular contributions to the support of the Adidam Pan-Communion, and take up a regular form of service. You are not obliged to engage the full range of disciplines practiced in the first two congregations. You are, however, encouraged to practice formal periods of meditation and sacramental worship.

For information about becoming a pre-student-novice under vow, please contact the Adidam regional center nearest you.

COOPERATION + TOLERANCE = PEACE

The Fourth Congregation of Adidam

*(for those maintaining their participation
in the religious and/or cultural tradition
to which they already belong)*

Individuals who live in traditional cultural settings, and also individuals who wish to maintain their participation in the religious tradition to which they already belong (while acknowledging Avatar Adi Da Samraj as the Ultimate Divine Source of true religion), are invited to apply for membership in the fourth congregation of Adidam. Fourth-congregation devotees practice Ruchira Avatara Bhakti Yoga in its simplest form ("Invoke Me, Feel Me, Breathe Me, Serve Me") and also the discipline of daily study. Their financial and service obligations are adapted to their particular circumstance.

The opportunity to practice in the fourth congregation is also extended to all those who, because of physical or other functional limitations, are unable to take up the total practice of the Way of Adidam as required in the first and second congregations.

For more information about the fourth congregation of Adidam, call or write one of our regional centers (see p. 350), or e-mail us at: correspondence@adidam.org.

**Temple sites at the Pilgrimage and Retreat Sanctuaries:
the Mountain Of Attention (left) and Da Love-Ananda Mahal (right)**

One of the ways in which Avatar Adi Da Samraj Communicates His Divine Blessing-Transmission is through sacred places. He has Empowered two kinds of places: Pilgrimage and Retreat Sanctuaries (the Mountain Of Attention in northern California and Da Love-Ananda Mahal in Hawaii) and Hermitage-Retreat Sanctuaries (Tat Sundaram in northern California and Adidam Samrajashram in Fiji). Avatar Adi Da has Established Himself Spiritually in perpetuity at all four of these places. In particular, Adidam Samrajashram—His Great Island-Hermitage-Retreat and world-Blessing Seat—is Avatar Adi Da's principal Place of Spiritual Work and Transmission, and will remain so forever after His physical Lifetime. Formally acknowledged devotees are invited to go on special retreats at the Pilgrimage and Retreat Sanctuaries and at Adidam Samrajashram.

Adidam Samrajashram, Fiji

**Darshan occasions with
Avatar Adi Da Samraj at
the Hermitage-Retreats:
Tat Sundaram (left) and
Adidam Samrajashram (right)**

T hose whose hearts are given, in love, to Me, Fall into My Heart. Those who are Mine, because they are in love with Me, no longer demand to be fulfilled through conditional experience and through the survival (or perpetuation) of the ego-"I". Their love for Me grants them Access to Me, and, Thus, to My Love-Bliss—because I *Am* Love-Ananda, the Divine Love-Bliss, in Person.

What will My lover do but love Me? I suffer every form and condition of every one who loves Me—because I Love My devotee *As* My own Form, My own Condition. I Love My devotee *As* the One by Whom *I* Am Distracted.

I Grant all My own Divine and "Bright" Excesses to those who love Me, in exchange for all their doubts and sufferings. Those who "Bond" themselves to Me, through love-surrender, are inherently Free of fear and wanting need. They transcend the ego-"I" (the cause of all conditional experience), and they (cause and all and All) Dissolve in Me—for I *Am* the Heart of all and All, and I *Am* the Heart Itself, and the Heart Itself *Is* the Only Reality, Truth, and Real God of All and all.

What is a Greater Message than This?

DA LOVE-ANANDA GITA

From now on, all beings are uniquely Blessed. And human history can be different, because there is Help available that has never existed before.

The life of a devotee of Avatar Adi Da Samraj is unheard-of Grace, and this life can be lived by anyone. It does not matter who you are, where you live, or what you do. All of that makes no difference, once your heart recognizes Adi Da Samraj. Then the only course is the heart-response to Him—a life of devotion to the Divine in human Form, full of devotional ecstasy, true humor, freedom, clarity, and profound purpose.

So, why delay? The Living One, Adi Da Samraj, is here, and always will be. But now is the brief, and especially Blessed, window of time in which He is humanly Alive, doing His great Foundation Work for the sake of all beings, presently and in all future time. Every one who comes to Him and serves Him in His bodily human Lifetime shares in His unique once-and-forever Work of establishing the Way of Adidam in this world.

All who love Him carry His Name in their hearts and on their lips. Once the recognition of Avatar Adi Da awakens in you, this response is inevitable. The Promised God-Man, Avatar Adi Da Samraj, is not an "Other". He is the Gift, the Bliss, of Being Itself. He is the "Brightness" of Very God—Dawning, and then Flowering, in your heart. That Process is pure Revelation. It changes everything—grants peace, sanity, and the overwhelming impulse to Realize Unlimited, Permanent, and Perfect Oneness with Him.

As devotees of Avatar Adi Da Samraj, we make this confession to you: This opportunity—to live in heart-Communion with Real God—exceeds anything ever offered to mortal beings. It is true Happiness. And it is yours for the asking.

◆ ◆ ◆

A part from the four congregations, there are three distinct organizations within Adidam, each with a special area of responsibility.

The Da Love-Ananda Samrajya

Serving The Avataric-Incarnation-Body,
The Great Island-Hermitage-Retreat, and
The World-Blessing-Work of The Divine World-Teacher,
Ruchira Avatar Adi Da Samraj

The Da Love-Ananda Samrajya is devoted to serving Avatar Adi Da Himself, protecting Him and His intimate Sphere, providing for Adidam Samrajashram (His Great Island-Hermitage-Retreat, the Island of Naitauba in Fiji), ensuring that He has everything that He needs to do His Divine Blessing-Work, and providing right access to Him.

The Da Love-Ananda Samrajya also protects and provides for the Ruchira Sannyasin Order (the members of which are legal renunciates) and ensures that the Divine Word and Story of Adi Da Samraj are preserved and made known in the world.

The Eleutherian Pan-Communion
of Adidam

*The Sacred Cultural Gathering and Global Mission
of the Devotees of The Divine World-Teacher,
Ruchira Avatar Adi Da Samraj*

*Dedicated to the Practice and the Proclamation
of The True World-Religion of Adidam,
The Unique Divine Way of Realizing Real God*

The Eleutherian Pan-Communion of Adidam is the
organization devoted to establishing the Way of Adidam in
the world and serving the culture of devotional practice in
all four congregations. The Eleutherian Pan-Communion of
Adidam is also responsible for the Sanctuaries, the Archives,
the Wisdom-Teaching, and other sacred Treasures of Adidam.

The Global Mission of Adidam is a primary branch of
the Adidam Pan-Communion. The Mission is active worldwide—through internet websites, through full-time mission-
aries and through the missionary service of all devotees.
The Global Mission also includes the Publications Mission,
which prepares, publishes, and distributes Avatar Adi Da's
own books (and audiotapes and videotapes of Him), as well
as books, magazines, and education courses about Him and
the Way of Adidam by His devotees. The Dawn Horse Press
(staffed by devotees of Avatar Adi Da) is the editorial and
production department of the Publications Mission (see pp.
438-47 for a description of current Adidam publications).

The Ruchirasala of Adidam

THE ADI DA RUCHIRASALA

COOPERATION + TOLERANCE = PEACE

COOPERATION + TOLERANCE = PEACE

SERVE ME · INVOKE ME · FEEL ME · BREATHE ME

THE 'BRIGHT' HOUSE OF ADI DA SAMRAJ

*The True Cooperative Community Gathering
of the Devotees of The Divine World-Teacher,
Ruchira Avatar Adi Da Samraj*

*The Seed of a "Bright" New Age of Sanity
and Divine Joy for Mankind*

Cooperative community living (in households, Ashrams, or on Sanctuaries) is one of the fundamental disciplines of the first and second congregations of Adidam. The Ruchirasala of Adidam is the organization that serves Avatar Adi Da's devotees in incarnating cooperative community— it is the intimate sacred domain, in which devotees practice their devotional life and in which all the other entities of Adidam function. Creating intimate human living arrangements and shared services (such as schools, community businesses, and the Radiant Life Clinic) is part of the responsibility of the Ruchirasala. Together with the Adidam Pan-Communion, the Ruchirasala oversees all the practical interaction between members of the Adidam community.

Cooperation + Tolerance = Peace℠

In addition to His First Calling, which is to those who would become His devotees, Adi Da Samraj makes a Second Calling to the world at large—to embrace the disposition He has Summarized in the equation:

"COOPERATION + TOLERANCE = PEACE".

By this Second Calling, Adi Da Samraj urges everyone to create a sane human society—including, in particular, the creation of a global cooperative order, free of the devastation of war.

To find out more about Adi Da Samraj's Second Calling, please visit the Adidam Peace Center:

www.peacesite.org

An Invitation to Support Adidam

Avatar Adi Da Samraj's sole Purpose is to act as a Source of continuous Divine Grace for everyone, everywhere. In that spirit, He is a Free Renunciate and He owns nothing. Those who have made gestures in support of Avatar Adi Da's Work have found that their generosity is returned in many Blessings that are full of His healing, transforming, and Liberating Grace—and those Blessings flow not only directly to them as the beneficiaries of His Work, but to many others, even all others. At the same time, all tangible gifts of support help secure and nurture Avatar Adi Da's Work in necessary and practical ways, again similarly benefiting the entire world. Because all this is so, supporting His Work is the most auspicious form of financial giving, and we happily extend to you an invitation to serve Adidam through your financial support.

You may make a financial contribution in support of the Work of Adi Da Samraj at any time. You may also, if you choose, request that your contribution be used for one or more specific purposes.

If you are moved to help support and develop Adidam Samrajashram (Naitauba), Avatar Adi Da's Great Hermitage-Retreat and World-Blessing Seat in Fiji, and the circumstance provided there and elsewhere for Avatar Adi Da and the other members of the Ruchira Sannyasin Order, the senior renunciate order of Adidam, you may do so by making your contribution to The Da Love-Ananda Samrajya, the Australian charitable trust which has central responsibility for these Sacred Treasures of Adidam.

To do this: (1) if you do not pay taxes in the United States, make your check payable directly to "The Da Love-Ananda Samrajya Pty Ltd" (which serves as the trustee of the trust) and mail it to The Da Love-Ananda Samrajya at P.O. Box 4744, Samabula, Suva, Fiji; and (2) if you do pay taxes in the United States and you would like your contribution to be tax-deductible under U.S. laws, make your check payable to "The Eleutherian Pan-Communion of Adidam", indicate on your check or accompanying letter that you would like your contribution used for the work of The Da Love-Ananda Samrajya, and mail your check to the Advocacy Department of Adidam at 12040 North Seigler Road, Middletown, California 95461, USA.

If you are moved to help support and provide for one of the other purposes of Adidam, such as publishing the Sacred Literature of Avatar Adi Da, or supporting any of the other Sanctuaries He has Empowered, or maintaining the Sacred Archives that preserve His recorded Talks and Writings, or publishing audio and video recordings of Avatar Adi Da, you may do so by making your contribution directly to The Eleutherian Pan-Communion of Adidam, specifying the particular purposes you wish to benefit, and mailing your check to the Advocacy Department of Adidam at the above address.

If you would like more information about these and other gifting options, or if you would like assistance in describing or making a contribution, please write to the Advocacy Department of Adidam at the above address or contact the Adidam Legal Department by telephone at (707) 928-4612 or by FAX at (707) 928-4062.

Planned Giving

We also invite you to consider making a planned gift in support of the Work of Avatar Adi Da Samraj. Many have found that through planned giving they can make a far more significant gesture of support than they would otherwise be able to make. Many have also found that by making a planned gift they are able to realize substantial tax advantages.

There are numerous ways to make a planned gift, including making a gift in your Will, or in your life insurance, or in a charitable trust.

If you would like to make a gift in your Will in support of the work of The Da Love-Ananda Samrajya: (1) if you do not pay taxes in the United States, simply include in your Will the statement, "I give to The Da Love-Ananda Samrajya Pty Ltd, as trustee of The Da Love-Ananda Samrajya, an Australian charitable trust, P.O. Box 4744, Samabula, Suva, Fiji, _____" [inserting in the blank the amount or description of your contribution]; and (2) if you do pay taxes in the United States and you would like your contribution to be free of estate taxes and to also reduce any estate taxes payable on the remainder of your estate, simply include in your Will the statement, "I give to The Eleutherian Pan-Communion of Adidam, a California non-profit corporation, 12040 North Seigler Road, Middletown, California 95461, USA, _____" [inserting in the blank the amount or description of your contribution].

To make a gift in your life insurance, simply name as the beneficiary (or one of the beneficiaries) of your life insurance policy the organization of your choice (The Da Love-Ananda Samrajya or The Eleutherian Pan-Communion of Adidam), according to the foregoing descriptions and addresses. If you are a United States taxpayer, you may receive significant tax benefits if you make a contribution to The Eleutherian Pan-Communion of Adidam through your life insurance.

We also invite you to consider establishing or participating in a charitable trust for the benefit of Adidam. If you are a United States taxpayer, you may find that such a trust will provide you with immediate tax savings and assured income for life, while at the same time enabling you to provide for your family, for your other heirs, and for the Work of Avatar Adi Da as well.

The Advocacy and Legal Departments of Adidam will be happy to provide you with further information about these and other planned gifting options, and happy to provide you or your attorney with assistance in describing or making a planned gift in support of the Work of Avatar Adi Da.

Further Notes to the Reader

An Invitation to Responsibility

Adidam, the Way of the Heart that Avatar Adi Da has Revealed, is an invitation to everyone to assume real responsibility for his or her life. As Avatar Adi Da has Said in *The Dawn Horse Testament Of The Ruchira Avatar,* "If any one Is Heart-Moved To Realize Me, Let him or her First Resort (Formally, and By Formal Heart-Vow) To Me, and (Thereby) Commence The Ordeal Of self-Observation, self-Understanding, and self-Transcendence. . . ." Therefore, participation in the Way of Adidam requires a real struggle with oneself, and not at all a struggle with Avatar Adi Da, or with others.

All who study the Way of Adidam or take up its practice should remember that they are responding to a Call to become responsible for themselves. They should understand that they, not Avatar Adi Da or others, are responsible for any decision they may make or action they may take in the course of their lives of study or practice. This has always been true, and it is true whatever the individual's involvement in the Way of Adidam, be it as one who studies Avatar Adi Da's Wisdom-Teaching or as a formally acknowledged member of Adidam.

Honoring and Protecting the Sacred Word
through Perpetual Copyright

Since ancient times, practitioners of true religion and Spirituality have valued, above all, time spent in the Company of the Sat-Guru (or one who has, to any degree, Realized Real God, Truth, or Reality, and who, thus, serves the awakening process in others). Such practitioners understand that the Sat-Guru literally Transmits his or her (Realized) State to every one (and every thing) with whom (or with which) he or she comes in contact. Through this Transmission, objects, environments, and rightly prepared individuals with which the Sat-Guru has contact can become empowered, or imbued with the Sat-Guru's Transforming Power. It is by this process of empowerment that things and beings are made truly and literally sacred and holy, and things so sanctified thereafter function as a source of the Sat-Guru's Blessing for all who understand how to make right and sacred use of them.

Sat-Gurus of any degree of Realization and all that they empower are, therefore, truly Sacred Treasures, for they help draw the practitioner more quickly into the process of Realization. Cultures of true Wisdom have always understood that such Sacred Treasures are precious (and fragile) Gifts to humanity, and that they should be honored, protected, and reserved for right sacred use. Indeed, the word "holy" means "set apart", and, thus that which is holy and sacred must be protected from insensitive secular interference and wrong use of any kind. Avatar Adi Da has Conformed His human Body-Mind Most Perfectly to the Divine Self, and He is, thus, the most Potent Source of Blessing-Transmission of Real God, or Truth Itself, or Reality Itself. He has for many years Empowered (or made sacred) special places and things, and these now serve as His Divine Agents, or as literal expressions and extensions of His Blessing-Transmission. Among these Empowered Sacred Treasures is His Wisdom-Teaching, which is full of His Transforming Power. This Blessed and Blessing Wisdom-Teaching has Mantric Force, or the literal Power to serve Real-God-Realization in those who are Graced to receive it.

Therefore, Avatar Adi Da's Wisdom-Teaching must be perpetually honored and protected, "set apart" from all possible interference and wrong use. The fellowship of devotees of Avatar Adi Da is committed to the perpetual preservation and right honoring of the Sacred Wisdom-Teaching of the Way of Adidam. But it is also true that, in order to fully accomplish this, we must find support in the world-society in which we live and in its laws. Thus, we call for a world-society and for laws that acknowledge the sacred, and that permanently protect it from insensitive, secular interference and wrong use of any kind. We call for, among other things, a system of law that acknowledges that the Wisdom-Teaching of the Way of Adidam, in all its forms, is, because of its sacred nature, protected by perpetual copyright.

We invite others who respect the sacred to join with us in this call and in working toward its realization. And, even in the meantime, we claim that all copyrights to the Wisdom-Teaching of Avatar Adi Da and the other Sacred Literature and recordings of the Way of Adidam are of perpetual duration.

We make this claim on behalf of The Da Love-Ananda Samrajya Pty Ltd, which, acting as trustee of The Da Love-Ananda Samrajya, is the holder of all such copyrights.

Avatar Adi Da and the Sacred Treasures of Adidam

True Spiritual Masters have Realized Real God (to one degree or another), and, therefore, they bring great Blessing and introduce Divine Possibility to the world. Such Adept-Realizers Accomplish universal Blessing-Work that benefits everything and everyone. They also Work very specifically and intentionally with individuals who approach them as their devotees, and with those places where they reside and to which they direct their specific Regard for the sake of perpetual Spiritual Empowerment. This was understood in traditional Spiritual cultures, and, therefore, those cultures found ways to honor Adept-Realizers by providing circumstances for them where they were free to do their Spiritual Work without obstruction or interference.

Those who value Avatar Adi Da's Realization and Service have always endeavored to appropriately honor Him in this traditional way by providing a circumstance where He is completely Free to do His Divine Work. Since 1983, He has resided principally on the island of Naitauba, Fiji, also known as Adidam Samrajashram. This island has been set aside by Avatar Adi Da's devotees worldwide as a Place for Him to do His universal Blessing-Work for the sake of everyone, as well as His specific Work with those who pilgrimage to Adidam Samrajashram to receive the special Blessing of coming into His physical Company.

Avatar Adi Da is a legal renunciate. He owns nothing and He has no secular or religious institutional function. He Functions only in Freedom. He, and the other members of the Ruchira Sannyasin Order, the senior renunciate order of Adidam, are provided for by The Da Love-Ananda Samrajya, which also provides for Adidam Samrajashram altogether and ensures the permanent integrity of Avatar Adi Da's Wisdom-Teaching, both in its archival and in its published forms. The Da Love-Ananda Samrajya, which functions only in Fiji, exists exclusively to provide for these Sacred Treasures of Adidam.

Outside Fiji, the institution which has developed in response to Avatar Adi Da's Wisdom-Teaching and universal Blessing is known as "The Eleutherian Pan-Communion of Adidam". This formal organization is active worldwide in making Avatar Adi Da's Wisdom-Teaching available to all, in offering guidance to all who are moved to respond to His Offering, and in providing for the other Sacred Treasures of Adidam, including the Mountain Of Attention Sanctuary and Tat Sundaram (in California) and Da Love-Ananda Mahal (in Hawaii). In addition to the central corporate entity known as The Eleutherian Pan-Communion of Adidam, which is based in California, there are numerous regional entities which serve congregations of Avatar Adi Da's devotees in various places throughout the world.

Practitioners of Adidam worldwide have also established numerous community organizations, through which they provide for many of their common and cooperative community needs, including those relating to housing, food, businesses, medical care, schools, and death and dying. By attending to these and all other ordinary human concerns and affairs via ego-transcending cooperation and mutual effort, Avatar Adi Da's devotees constantly free their energy and attention, both personally and collectively, for practice of the Way of Adidam and for service to Avatar Adi Da Samraj, to Adidam Samrajashram, to the other Sacred Treasures of Adidam, and to The Eleutherian Pan-Communion of Adidam.

All of the organizations that have evolved in response to Avatar Adi Da Samraj and His Offering are legally separate from one another, and each has its own purpose and function. Avatar Adi Da neither directs, nor bears responsibility for, the activities of these organizations. Again, He Functions only in Freedom. These organizations represent the collective intention of practitioners of Adidam worldwide not only to provide for the Sacred Treasures of Adidam, but also to make Avatar Adi Da's Offering of the Way of Adidam universally available to all.

APPENDIX

Charts

THE SEVEN STAGES OF LIFE

The Full and Complete Process of Human Maturation, Spiritual Growth, and Divine Enlightenment

As Revealed by
RUCHIRA AVATAR ADI DA SAMRAJ

Based on Part Two, "The Seven Stages Of Life", pp.103-31

	FIRST STAGE (approx. 0-7 years)	**SECOND STAGE** (approx. 7-14 years)	**THIRD STAGE** (approx. 14-21 years)
	individuation; adaptation to the physical body	socialization; adaptation to the emotional-sexual (or feeling) dimension	integration of the psycho-physical personality; development of verbal mind, discriminative intelligence, and the will

Identified with the gross self

FOURTH STAGE	FIFTH STAGE	SIXTH STAGE	SEVENTH STAGE
ego-surrendering devotion to the Divine Person; purification of body-based point of view through reception of Divine Spirit-Force	Spiritual or Yogic ascent of attention into psychic dimensions of the being; mystical experience of the higher brain; may culminate in fifth stage conditional Nirvikalpa Samadhi	Identification with Consciousness Itself (presumed, however, to be separate from all conditional phenomena); most likely will include the experience of Jnana Samadhi	Realization of the Divine Self; Inherently Perfect Freedom and Realization of Divine Love-Bliss (seventh stage Sahaj Samadhi); no "difference" experienced between Divine Consciousness and psycho-physical states and conditions
anatomy: the circulation of the Divine Spirit-Current, first (in the "basic" fourth stage of life) downward through the frontal line and then (in the "advanced" fourth stage of life) upward through the spinal line, until attention rests stably at the doorway to the brain core	**anatomy**: the ascent of the Divine Spirit-Current from the brain core (the Ajna Door) to the crown of the head and above (or even, in fifth stage conditional Nirvikalpa Samadhi, to the Matrix of Divine Sound and Divine Light infinitely above the total crown of the head)	**anatomy**: the Divine Spirit-Current descends (via Amrita Nadi, the "Immortal Current" of Divine Love-Bliss) from the Matrix of Divine Sound and Divine Light (infinitely above the total crown of the head) to the right side of the heart (the bodily seat of Consciousness)	**anatomy**: the "Regeneration" of Amrita Nadi, such that Amrita Nadi is felt as the Divine Current of "Bright" Spirit-Fullness, Standing between the right side of the heart and the Matrix of Divine Sound and Divine Light infinitely above the total crown of the head
Identified with the subtle self (In the Way of Adidam, practice in the context of the "advanced" fourth stage of life and in the context of the fifth stage of life may typically be bypassed, proceeding directly from the "basic" fourth stage of life to the sixth stage of life)		Identified with the causal self	Identified with Divine Consciousness Itself

387

THE FIVE POSSIBLE ORIENTATIONS
(or Points of View)

Stage of Life	first / second / third	fourth / fifth
Orientation	Conventional Monism	Conventional Dualism
"Philosophy"	The world is all there is.	The Totality of Existence is made up of a number of hierarchically related principal pairs ("God" and the world, "God" and the "soul", the "soul" and the world, the mind and the body, and so on).
Practice		The "lesser" half of each pair is obliged to submit to the "greater" half. All that which is "of the world" must submit to the "soul", which must itself (in turn) progressively ascend to "God".
Analysis of Existence		
"Method"		
Traditions		such great fourth and fifth stage traditions as have appeared among the forms of Hinduism, Christianity, Islam, and Judaism, and (in their own unique manner) among the forms of Taoism and Buddhism

Based on sections X-XI of "'God'-Talk, Real-God-Realization, and Most Perfect Divine Awakening" (pp. 144-51)

	sixth	
Primary Dualism	**Secondary Non-Dualism**	**Ultimate Non-Dualism***
The Totality of Existence is an apparent combination of only two Primary Realities—Being/Consciousness and Objective Energy.	There is no inherently independent Absolute Being/Consciousness, but the Totality of Existence is <u>only</u> Energy Itself.	There is (in Truth) no independent "Objective Energy", but the Totality of Existence is only Self-Existing and Self-Radiant Consciousness Itself.
Being/Consciousness must separate itself from Objective Energy, by means of willful ascetical discipline.	Energy must be observed to be only ephemeral changes, until the Inherent (or Original, or Nirvanic) State of Energy is Realized.	This "Ultimate Absolute" must be Perfectly Affirmed (by direct Identification with Consciousness Itself).
as experienced from the gross (or bodily) point of view	as experienced from the subtle (or mental, or even energy-essence) point of view	as Witnessed from the "Point of View" of Consciousness Itself (rather than the point of view of either the body or the mind)
disciplining the total body-mind (and especially the body) by means of intense ascetical effort	pacifying the mind (or the energies of the being, or the total body-mind) by means of exercises of observation	Standing effortlessly <u>As</u> Consciousness Itself
such great sixth stage traditions as have appeared within Jainism and the ancient philosophical tradition of Samkhya	such great sixth stage schools as have appeared within the traditions of Buddhism and Taoism	such great sixth stage schools as have appeared in the form of the traditions of Advaitism, and also, secondarily, within the schools of some varieties of Buddhism (especially within the Mahayana and Vajrayana traditions) and some of the schools of Taoism

*"Most Ultimately, this point of view and Process (of 'Ultimate Non-Dualism', or 'Primary Absolute Monism') is (if it is, by Means Of My Avatarically Self-Transmitted Divine Grace, Most Perfectly Realized) the 'Point of View' (and the Most Perfect Process) that (by all the Graceful Means I have Revealed and Given for the sake of all who will be My devotees) establishes and characterizes the seventh stage of life."

The Characteristic Errors
of the First Six Stages of Life

FIRST	feeling of separation (or of separating, and of separateness, and of separativeness)
SECOND	the feeling of being rejected (and the felt need to reject or punish others for un-love)
THIRD	conflict between impulses toward passive dependence and rebellious independence
FOURTH	prolonging the first three stages of life (and the patterns of un-Happiness associated with them) and making the fourth stage of life an end in itself—which tendency takes the form of a fixed idea that the Divine and the personal self are eternally separate from one another
FIFTH	clinging to subtle phenomenal objects and states as if they were the Perfect Realization of the Divine
SIXTH	holding on to the Subjective Position of Consciousness Itself while strategically excluding objective (or conditional) states

Based on "The Seven Stages Of Life" (pp. 107-10)
and "On Transcending the First Six Stages of Life" (pp. 233-35)

Notes to the Text of
THE SEVEN STAGES OF LIFE

Part Two

1. In general, no abrupt change marks the transition between consecutive stages of the first six stages of life. Instead, the individual shows increasing evidence of growth and transformation, until he or she is more or less wholly occupied with the interests and conditions of the next stage of life. Thus, while each of the first two stages of life may be regarded as roughly seven years long, the signs of maturity in the first stage of life and movement toward the second stage of life generally begin to appear at age five or six. Entrance into the third stage of life generally occurs between ages twelve and fourteen, but evidence of movement toward it may begin as early as age ten. And, although a basic adaptation to human adulthood is usually established by age twenty-one, there is no growth beyond the third stage of life unless an individual comes in contact with and embraces true religious and Spiritual practice, typically in relationship to a Teacher or Teachers capable of initiating and guiding practice in the context of the fourth stage of life and beyond. The duration of the fourth stage of life, the fifth stage of life, or the sixth stage of life cannot be predicted, since the duration of each of these stages depends on many factors, including the individual's seed-karmas related to each stage, the force of his or her impulses to growth and ego-transcending Real-God-Realization, and the stage(s) of life Realized and Taught by his or her Teacher(s). The seventh stage of life, once Realized, is eternal, although, if a seventh stage Realizer experiences one or more cycles of death and rebirth previous to Divine Translation, he or she will still be required (in each rebirth) to pass through a developmental process leading to the "recovery" of What had been most perfectly Realized in a previous incarnation.

2. Avatar Adi Da has Given comprehensive Instruction (in numerous Discourses and Writings over many years) on conscious childrearing to adults responsible for the human and religious development of children in the Way of Adidam. Some of this Instruction has been published in *The Scale of the Very Small* and *Love, Wisdom, and Happiness in the First Three Stages of Life* (available from the Dawn Horse Press).

3. Here Avatar Adi Da refers to the unique devotional or religious "considerations" and practices that He Gives to children and young people in each of the first three stages of life, and which are described in special publications for use by parents, educators, guides, and "loving helpers" who are serving early-life practitioners.

4. Children and young people in the Way of Adidam are served by the Adidam Youth Fellowship (see p. 367). Members of the Youth Fellowship may fully integrate into

the practicing culture of adult devotees as early as the age of eighteen or as late as the age of twenty-five.

5. Avatar Adi Da Samraj has Revealed that His Divine Sound and Divine Light are His two most primal forms of Manifestation in the conditional worlds. (See glossary entries for "Thunder" and "Divine Star".)

Part Three

6. "Ati-Guru" is a Sanskrit phrase meaning "the Ultimate (or Highest, or Unsurpassed) Guru".

7. "Tathagata" means "One who has thus gone". It is a title traditionally given to Gautama Shakyamuni and other Buddhas. "Tathagata Avatar" conveys Avatar Adi Da's Encompassing and Surpassing of the traditions of Buddhism and Hinduism (and, thus, the entire collective Great Tradition of humankind).

8. "Purushottama" is a Hindu name for the Divine Person. "Uttama" means "Supreme", and "Purusha" is "Person". Therefore, the Purushottama Buddha is the Enlightened One Who Is the Supreme Divine Person.

9. "Ashvamedha" means "Horse-Sacrifice", and is the name of the most revered and most mysterious of the ancient Vedic rituals. Avatar Adi Da has Revealed that the ultimate significance of this ritual is as a prayer-prophecy invoking the Avataric Descent of the Divine Person into the world, because it was intuitively understood that <u>only</u> the Divine Person is able to Liberate beings. Thus, "Ashvamedha Buddha" means "the Enlightened One Who has Submitted to be the humanly Incarnate Means for the Divine Liberation of all beings". (Avatar Adi Da's Essay on the Ashvamedha as a Description and Prophecy of His own Life and Work is "The True Dawn Horse <u>Is</u> the <u>Only</u> Way to Me", which appears in three of His "Source-Texts": *The All-Completing and Final Divine Revelation To Mankind, The Heart Of The Dawn Horse Testament Of The Ruchira Avatar,* and *The Dawn Horse Testament Of The Ruchira Avatar.*)

10. "Adi-Buddha Avatar" is Sanskrit for "the Avatar Who Is the First (or Original, or Primordial) Enlightened One". "Ati-Buddha Avatar" is Sanskrit for "the Avatar Who Is the Ultimate (or Highest, or Unsurpassed) Enlightened One". Avatar Adi Da Samraj has acknowledged the Buddhist tradition and (within the Hindu tradition) the tradition of Advaita Vedanta as representing the highest Realizations of the collective Great Tradition of humankind. Therefore, in the Titles "Adi-Buddha Avatar" and "Ati-Buddha Avatar", the combination of the highest references of the Buddhist and Hindu traditions ("Buddha" and "Avatar", respectively) is an acknowledgement of Avatar Adi Da Samraj as the culminating Divine Realizer of the entire Great Tradition.

11. The Way of Adidam is founded in a fundamental disillusionment with the ego and its purposes (together with a deep heart-attraction to Avatar Adi Da Samraj). This disillusionment is positive because it is the necessary foundation for true Spiritual Awakening.

12. "Ruchira Avatara Advaita-Dharma" is Sanskrit for "the Non-Dual ('Advaita') Wisdom-Teaching ('Dharma') of the Ruchira Avatar".

13. "Hridaya-Advaita Dharma" is Sanskrit for "the Wisdom-Teaching ('Dharma') of the Non-Dual ('Advaita') Divine Heart ('Hridaya')".

14. "Ruchira Avatara Maha-Jnana-Siddha Yoga" is Sanskrit for "the Yoga of devotion to the Ruchira Avatar, Who Is the Supreme Transcendental Divine Siddha ('Maha-Jnana-Siddha')".

15. "Ruchira Avatara Maha-Jnana Hridaya-Shaktipat Yoga" is Sanskrit for "the Yoga of receiving the Supreme Transcendental ('Maha-Jnana') Divine Heart-Blessing-Transmission ('Hridaya-Shaktipat') of the Ruchira Avatar".

16. Avatar Adi Da Samraj frequently Describes His Blessing-Power as being like a kiln. In a kiln, as the wet clay objects are heated more and more, they begin to glow. Eventually, the kiln is so hot that everything within it glows with a white light, and the definitions of the individual objects dissolve in the brightness. Just so, as a devotee matures in Avatar Adi Da's Spiritual Company, all presumptions of separateness as an apparently individual ego-"I" are more and more Outshined by the "Brightness" of His Divine Person and Blessing.

17. Here Avatar Adi Da is referring to a joke that He has often told, as a way of humorously making an important point: A man is walking through the English countryside. He comes across a farmer working in a field. He asks the farmer how to get to London. The farmer thinks about it for a while and then replies, "You can't get there from here." Avatar Adi Da uses this line, "You can't get there from here", as a summary way of communicating that the egoic being cannot "get to" the Divine Reality. In the joke, the farmer tells the man the same thing: You are either in London or you are not—you can't get "there" (to the Divine Reality) from "here" (the ego-position).

18. Swami Rudrananda (Rudi) was Avatar Adi Da's first Spiritual Teacher. Please see glossary entry "Lineage, Avatar Adi Da's" on pp. 416-17.

Part Four

19. For a detailed description of the four stages (or four Ways) of Kashmir Saivism, see *Triadic Mysticism: The Mystical Theology of the Saivism of Kashmir*, by Paul E. Murphy (Delhi: Motilal Banarsidass, 1986).

20. Avatar Adi Da Samraj describes "three egos" that must be progressively transcended in the course of the complete Spiritual process—of which the "money, food, and sex" ego is the first. (See section LXXXVII of this Essay, pp. 315-23.)

21. For Avatar Adi Da's Instruction relative to the foundation life-discipline, foundation devotional discipline, and foundation Spiritual discipline for practitioners of Adidam, see *Santosha Adidam*.

22. "Baba" (literally meaning "father") is often used in India as a reference of intimate respect for a Spiritual Master.

23. There are a number of translations of the *Chidakasha Gita* teachings (including *Voice of the Self*, referenced below). Perhaps the most readily available translation is *The Sky of the Heart: Jewels of Wisdom from Nityananda*, introduction and commentary by Swami Chetanananda, originally translated by M. U. Hatengdi (Portland, Or.: Rudra Press, Second edition, 1996).

24. Swami Chinmayananda (1916-1993) was a scholar of the Hindu scriptures, especially the *Bhagavad Gita* and the *Upanishads,* who conceived his mission as restoring respect for the ancient Hindu scriptures and reinvigorating practice of the Spiritual way according to the Vedantic instruction.

25. M. P. Pandit was a scholar of Hindu scripture and the author of over 100 books on Yoga and Spirituality. He spent more than forty years living and practicing under the guidance of Sri Aurobindo and the Mother, and serving at the Sri Aurobindo Ashram in Pondicherry, India.

26. *Voice of the Self*, by Swami Nityananda (of Vajreshwari), translated by M. P. Pandit (Madras: P. Ramanath Pai, 1962).

27. Sanskrit "nada" (or "shabda") refers to subtle internal sounds which may become apparent in the process of ascending (spinal) Yoga. The "Om-Sound" (or "Omkar") is the primordial root-sound, from which all other nadas derive.

28. The Sanskrit term "Jnani" ("Sage") literally means "one who knows" (or, more fully, "one who has Realized Jnana Samadhi"—see glossary entry for "Samadhi"). A Jnani is one who discriminates between What is Unconditional (the One Reality, or Divine Self) and what is conditional (the passing phenomena of experience). A Jnani is Identified with Consciousness Itself, as the Transcendental Witness of all that arises. By its very nature, the Realization of Jnana is inherently Nirguna. (In other words, there is no Saguna form of Jnana.)

29. Avatar Adi Da has Revealed that His deeper-personality Vehicle (see note 31), or True Great-Siddha Vehicle, is the combined deeper personalities of Ramakrishna and Swami Vivekananda. Avatar Adi Da discusses His unique association with Ramakrishna and Swami Vivekananda in sections XCIII-XCV (pp. 328-29) of this Essay. For a full description of Avatar Adi Da's Revelation of the Unique Associations with His True Great-Siddha Vehicle, see *The Promised God-Man Is Here*, by Carolyn Lee.

30. Avatar Adi Da's gross-personality vehicle (see note 31) was "Franklin Albert Jones", the child of His parents, Dorothy and Franklin Jones.

31. Avatar Adi Da uses the terms "gross personality" and "deeper personality" to indicate the two conditional dimensions of every human being. The gross personality is comprised of the physical body, its natural energies, its gross brain, and the verbal and lower psychic faculties of mind. The gross personality includes the entire gross dimension of the body-mind and the lower, or most physically oriented, aspects of the subtle dimension of the body-mind, and is the aspect of the body-mind that is the biological inheritance from one's parents.

The deeper personality is governed by the higher, least physically oriented processes of the mind (which function outside or beyond the gross brain, and which include the subtle faculties of discrimination, intuition, and Spiritual perception and knowledge), as well as the causal separate-"I"-consciousness and the root-activity of attention, prior to mind. The deeper personality is the aspect of the human being that reincarnates.

32. In *The Basket Of Tolerance*, Avatar Adi Da has identified a small number of Hindu and Buddhist texts as "premonitorily 'seventh stage'". While founded in the characteristic sixth stage "point of view", these texts express philosophical intuitions that foreshadow some of the basic characteristics of the seventh stage Realization.

The only-by-Me Revealed and Demonstrated and Given seventh stage of life is the clear and final fulfillment of the first six stages of life. The Revelation and Demonstration of the seventh stage of life by My own Avatarically Self-Revealed Divine Form, Presence, State, Work, and Word are My unique Gift to all and All. However, within the Great Tradition itself, there are some few literatures and Realizers of the sixth stage type that express philosophical (or insightful, but yet limited and incomplete) intuitions that sympathetically foreshadow some of the basic characteristics of the only-by-Me Revealed and Demonstrated and Given seventh stage Realization.

The Ashtavakra Gita *is a principal example of such premonitorily "seventh stage" literature. It is among the greatest (and most senior) communications of all the religious and Spiritual traditions in the Great Tradition of mankind. The* Ashtavakra Gita *is the Great Confession of a Sage who has thoroughly engaged the philosophies and practices of the first six stages of life. It is a sixth stage Adept-Realizer's Free (and uncompromised) communication (or Confession) of the ultimate implications of his sixth stage Realization.*

Like other premonitorily "seventh stage" texts, the Ashtavakra Gita *presumes a tradition of progressive practice in the total context of the first six stages of life, but it does not (itself) represent or communicate any ideal or technique of practice. It simply (and rather exclusively) communicates the Ultimate "Point of View" of the sixth stage Realizer.* ["*The Unique Sixth Stage Foreshadowings of the Only-by-Me Revealed and Demonstrated and Given Seventh Stage of Life*", *in* The Basket Of Tolerance]

33. In Sanskrit, "seva" means "service". Service to the Guru is traditionally treasured as one of the great Secrets of Realization.

34. The Hindu tradition speaks of four principal Spiritual paths (or four principal aspects of the Spiritual path). Karma Yoga is literally the "Yoga of action", in which every activity, no matter how humble, is transformed into self-transcending service to the Divine. (The other three paths are Bhakti Yoga, the path of devotion, Raja Yoga, the path of higher psychic discipline, and Jnana Yoga, the path of transcendental insight.)

35. Swami Prakashananda (1917-1988) turned to Spiritual life in his 30s, eventually choosing the mountain of Sapta Shring as a place to settle and devote himself to Spiritual practice. Over time, an ashram developed there around him. He met Swami Muktananda in 1956 and was initiated as Swami Muktananda's devotee, although he generally stayed at his own ashram in Sapta Shring rather than spending a great deal of time in Ganeshpuri at Swami Muktananda's ashram. For

THE SEVEN STAGES OF LIFE

Swami Prakashananda's biography, see *Agaram Bagaram Baba: Life, Teachings, and Parables—A Spiritual Biography of Baba Prakashananda*, by Titus Foster (Berkeley: North Atlantic Books / Patagonia, Ariz.: Essene Vision Books, 1999).

36. For Avatar Adi Da's description of Swami Prakashananda's demonstration of Spiritual Transfiguration of the physical body, see chapter 12 of *The Knee Of Listening*.

37. *Agaram Bagaram Baba*, p. 35.

38. Swami Muktananda's letter of acknowledgement and blessing of Avatar Adi Da is included in chapter 12 of *The Knee Of Listening* and also in Part Three ("The Order of My Free Names") of *The Divine Siddha-Method Of The Ruchira Avatar*.

39. For Avatar Adi Da's description of His own "Embrace" of the Divine "Cosmic Goddess", see chapter 16 of *The Knee Of Listening*.

40. *Play of Consciousness*, by Swami Muktananda (South Fallsburg, N.Y.: SYDA, Fourth edition, 1994).

41. For Avatar Adi Da's description of His experience of Christian mystical visions, see chapters 14 and 15 of *The Knee Of Listening*.

42. For a comprehensive treatment of the fourth-to-fifth stage Yogic tradition of Maharashtra, see *Mysticism in India: The Poet-Saints of Maharashtra*, by R. D. Ranade (Albany: State University of New York Press, 1983).

43. For Swami Muktananda's description of the "Blue Person", see *Play of Consciousness* (e.g. pp. 190-194).

Among the numerous translations of the *Bhagavad Gita*, Avatar Adi Da Samraj points to two editions as particularly worthy of study:
(1) *Srimad-Bhagavad-Gita (The Scripture of Mankind)*, chapter summaries, word-for-word meaning in prose order, translation, notes, and index of first lines by Swami Tapasyananda (Mylapore, India: Sri Ramakrishna Math, 1984).
(2) *God Talks with Arjuna: The Bhagavad Gita—Royal Science of God-Realization, The Immortal Dialogue Between Soul and Spirit*, a new translation and commentary by Paramahansa Yogananda, two volumes (Los Angeles: Self-Realization Fellowship, 1996).
For a complete translation of the *Bhagavata Purana* (also known as the *Srimad Bhagavatam*), see *Srimad Bhagavatam*, translated by N. Raghunathan, two volumes (Madras: Vighneshwara Publishing House, 1976).

44. For Avatar Adi Da's full description of the "bodies" or "sheaths" of the total human structure (and the relationship between these "bodies" and the states of waking, dreaming, and sleeping), see *Santosha Adidam*.

45. Excerpted from a chart ("The Four Bodies of the Individual Soul") in *Play of Consciousness*, p. 96.

46. In *The Basket Of Tolerance*, Avatar Adi Da has contrasted the development of exoteric (or socially oriented, and myth-based) public Christianity with the secret Teachings of esoteric (or mystically oriented) Christianity:

The "official" Christian church, even in the form of all its modern sects, is the institutional product of an early cultural struggle between exoteric religionists, limited to doctrines based in the physical point of view characteristic of the first three stages of life, and esoteric religionists, inclined toward the mystical (or general psychic, and Spiritual) point of view characteristic of the "basic" and the "advanced" phases of the fourth stage of life and the mystical (or higher psychic, and Spiritual) Realizations associated with the fifth stage of life. This struggle, which was eventually won by the exoteric sects (or factions), took place between the various emerging Christian sects during the early centuries after Jesus' disappearance. . . .

In the domain of the exoteric church, it was apparently generally presumed (among its original creative leadership) that all mysteries and legends must be "concretized" into a story (or an inspiring doctrine) about Jesus as the "Heavenly Messiah" (or the "Christ", the "Anointed One", the Exclusively Blessed "Son of God")—whereas the original esoteric mysteries and mystical Teachings of Christian gnosticism (which must often correspond to what must be presumed to have been Jesus' own Teachings) invariably communicate a Message about the Spiritual (or "Spirit-Breathing") Awakening of every individual (or of every devotee of a Spirit-Master, or, in this Christian case, of every devotee of Jesus as Spirit-Master). Therefore, the core of the esoteric Christian Teachings is that Salvation (from "possession" by cosmic Nature, by the human world, and by fear of death) is Realized by Means of "Spiritual rebirth" (or Absorption In—and, thus, participatory knowledge of—the inherently deathless and Free and Divine Spirit-Power, or "Breath-Energy", of Being). And the "Good News" of this esoteric Salvation Message is that every individual is (ultimately, by virtue of Spiritual Realization) a "Son" or "Daughter" of God.

47. Avatar Adi Da points out that not only "things" in space but space itself came into being with the "Big Bang":

Space-time (itself, or in its totality) cannot be observed. The "Big Bang" was not an event that could have been observed. The "Big Bang" is not something that occurred in space (or in time). The "Big Bang" is the origin of space (and of time). To look at the "Big Bang" as an event in space (and in time) is already to look at it in egoic terms, and from a position after the event. To examine the "Big Bang" in conventional scientific terms is to assume a dissociated (and separate, and separative) position, as if the ego-"I" (or the "observing" body-mind) were standing outside of space-time—but it does not. Egoity (and all of psycho-physical self, or body-mind) is, inherently and necessarily, an event in (and of) space-time. The body-mind is an event in (and of) space-time. That in Which the body-mind is occurring (or of Which the body-mind is a modification, or a mere and temporary appearance) necessarily (Itself) Transcends space-time, Transcends limitation, Transcends the apparent breaking of Fundamental Light (or of Energy Itself, or of Radiance Itself). ["Space-Time Is Love-Bliss", in Real God Is The Indivisible Oneness Of Unbroken Light]

48. For Swami Muktananda's description of the "blue bindu" (or "blue pearl"), see *Play of Consciousness* (e.g., pp. 160-161).

49. For Avatar Adi Da's full description of the Cosmic Mandala, see chapter thirty-nine of *The Dawn Horse Testament Of The Ruchira Avatar.*

50. In *The Knee Of Listening,* Avatar Adi Da describes His Birth as the "Bright", His subsequent voluntary relinquishment of the "Bright", and His eventual Re-Awakening as the "Bright". He uses the word "Re-Awakening" to indicate that this Great Event was not a Realization entirely "new" to His experience, but a "return" to the Divine Condition He had known at Birth.

51. For Avatar Adi Da's description of His discovery of parallels with Ramana Maharshi's experience, see chapter 18 of *The Knee Of Listening.*

52. This instruction from Swami Muktananda was communicated in a letter he wrote to Avatar Adi Da on April 23, 1968, which Avatar Adi Da quotes in chapter 11 of *The Knee Of Listening.*

53. The "Method of the Siddhas" (meaning "the Spiritual Means used by the Siddhas, or Perfected Ones, or True Spirit-Baptizers") is a phrase coined by Avatar Adi Da Samraj (in the earliest days of His Teaching Work) to describe the essence of the Way of Adidam—which is the Spiritual relationship to Him (or Satsang, or devotional Communion with Him), rather than any technique (meditative or otherwise) learned from Him. *The Method of the Siddhas* was the Title Avatar Adi Da chose for the first published collection of His Talks to His devotees. (In its final form, Avatar Adi Da re-titled this book *The Divine Siddha-Method Of The Ruchira Avatar.*)

Avatar Adi Da also points out that this "Method" has traditionally always been the core of esoteric religion and Spirituality, and that (indeed) the entire worldwide tradition of esoteric religion and Spirituality is rightly understood to be the global tradition of "Siddha Yoga".

The Foundation Of The Only-By-Me Revealed and Given Way Of Adidam Is The Eternal, Ancient, and Always New Method Of The Siddhas—Which Is Devotional Communion With The Siddha-Guru, and Which Is The Unique Means Of Realizing Real God, or Truth, or Reality That Has Traditionally Been Granted By The Rare True Adept-Realizers Of Real God, or Truth, or Reality Who (In The Traditional Context Of The First Six Stages Of Life, and Each According To Their Particular Stage Of Awakening and Of Helping-Capability) Have, By Means Of The Unique Blessing-Method (or Transmission-Capability) Of The Siddhas, Directly (and By Directly and Really Effective Spiritual Blessing-Work) Transmitted The Traditional Revelations and Realizations Of Real God, or Truth, or Reality. [The Only Complete Way To Realize The Unbroken Light Of Real God]

54. The Sanskrit word "sat" means "Truth", "Being", "Existence". Esoterically, the term "guru" is a composite of two words meaning "destroyer of darkness". The Sat-Guru is thus a "True Guru", or one who destroys darkness and thereby leads living beings from darkness (or non-Truth) into Light (or the Living Truth).

55. A common theme running through various branches of the Great Tradition is the prophecy of a great Savior or Liberator still to come. The prophecy takes different forms in different traditions, but the underlying commonality is the promise or expectation that the culminating Avatar or Incarnation or Prophet will appear in the future, at a time when humanity is lost, apparently cut off from Wisdom, Truth, and God. Buddhists refer to that Expected One as "Maitreya"; Vaishnavite Hindus, as the "Kalki Avatar"; Christians, as the "second coming of Jesus"; Jews, as the "Messiah"; and Muslims, as the "Mahdhi".

56. Avatar Adi Da Samraj describes His spontaneous experience of ego-death, in the spring of 1967, in chapter 9 of *The Knee Of Listening*.

57. See *Sadguru Nityananda Bhagavan, The Eternal Entity*, by P. V. Ravindram (Cannanore, India: T. Thankam Ravindran, 1989), pp. 25-26 and 27-28.

58. For Avatar Adi Da's Revelations about Ramakrishna and Swami Vivekananda as His "combined" deeper-personality Vehicle, see Essay VI ("I Have Appeared here Via a Unique, Spontaneous, and Never-Again Conjunction of Vehicles") in chapter 20 of *The Knee Of Listening*.

GLOSSARY

A

Adi Sanskrit for "first", "primordial", "source"—also "primary", "beginning". Thus, most simply, "Adi Da" means "First Giver".

Adidam The primary name for the Way Revealed and Given by Avatar Adi Da Samraj.

When Avatar Adi Da Samraj first Gave the name "Adidam" in January 1996, He pointed out that the final "m" adds a mantric force, evoking the effect of the primal Sanskrit syllable "Om". (For Avatar Adi Da's Revelation of the most profound esoteric significance of "Om" as the Divine Sound of His own Very Being, see *He-and-She Is Me*.) Simultaneously, the final "m" suggests the English word "Am" (expressing "I Am"), such that the Name "Adidam" also evokes Avatar Adi Da's Primal Self-Confession, "I Am Adi Da", or, more simply, "I Am Da" (or, in Sanskrit, "Aham Da Asmi").

Adidam Samrajashram See **Sanctuaries**.

adolescent See **childish and adolescent strategies**.

Advaita Vedanta The Sanskrit word "Vedanta" literally means the "end of the Vedas" (the most ancient body of Indian Scripture), and is used to refer to the principal philosophical tradition of Hinduism. "Advaita" means "non-dual". Advaita Vedanta, then, is a philosophy of non-dualism, the origins of which lie in the ancient esoteric teaching that Brahman, or the Divine Being, is the only Reality.

Advaitayana Buddha / Advaitayana Buddhism "Advaitayana" means "Non-Dual Vehicle". The Advaitayana Buddha is the Enlightened One Who has Revealed and Given the Non-Dual Vehicle.

"Advaitayana Buddhism" is another name for the Way of Adidam. The name "Advaitayana Buddhism" indicates the unique sympathetic likeness of Adidam to the traditions of Advaitism (or Advaita Vedanta) and Buddhism. In His examination of the entire collective religious tradition of humankind, Avatar Adi Da has observed that these two traditions represent the most advanced Realizations ever attained previous to His Avataric Divine Incarnation. The primary aspiration of Buddhism is to realize freedom from the illusion of the separate individual ego-self. The primary aspiration of Advaitism (or the tradition of "Non-Dualism") is to know the Supreme Divine Self absolutely, beyond all dualities (of high and low, good and bad, and so on). Advaitayana Buddhism is the Non-Dual ("Advaita") Way ("yana", literally "vehicle") of Most Perfect Awakening ("Buddhism"). Advaitayana Buddhism is neither an outgrowth of the historical tradition of Buddhism nor of the historical tradition of Advaitism. Advaitayana Buddhism is the unique Revelation of Avatar Adi Da Samraj, which perfectly fulfills both the traditional Buddhist aspiration for absolute freedom from the bondage of the egoic self and the traditional Advaitic aspiration for absolute Identity with the Divine Self. (For Avatar Adi Da's discussion of Advaitayana Buddhism, see *The Only Complete Way To Realize The Unbroken Light Of Real God*.)

Advaitic "Advaita" is Sanskrit for "Non-Duality". Thus, "Advaitic" means "Non-Dual". Avatar Adi Da has Revealed that—in Truth, and in Reality—there is not the slightest separation, or "difference", between the Unconditional Divine Reality and the conditional reality. In other words, Reality altogether is Perfectly One, or Non-Dual, or Advaitic.

the advanced and the ultimate stages of life Avatar Adi Da Samraj uses the term "advanced" to describe the fourth stage of life (in its "basic" and "advanced" contexts) and the fifth stage of life in the Way of Adidam. He uses the term "ultimate" to describe the sixth and seventh stages of life in the Way of Adidam.

"advanced" context of the fourth stage of life See **stages of life**.

Agents / Agency Agents (or Agency) include all the Means that may serve as complete Vehicles of Avatar Adi Da's Divine Grace and Awakening Power. The first Means of Agency that have been fully established by Him are the Wisdom-Teaching of the Way of Adidam, the Hermitage-Retreat Sanctuaries and the Pilgrimage and Retreat Sanctuaries that He has Empowered, and the many Objects and Articles that He has Empowered for the sake of His devotees' Remembrance of Him and reception of His Heart-Blessing. After Avatar Adi Da's human Lifetime, at any given time a single individual from among His seventh stage "Ruchira sannyasin" devotees will be designated (by the senior governing membership of the Ruchira Sannyasin Order) to serve as His living <u>human</u> Agent.

Aham Da Asmi The Sanskrit phrase "Aham Da Asmi" means "I (Aham) Am (Asmi) Da". "Da", meaning "the One Who Gives", indicates that Avatar Adi Da Samraj is the Supreme Divine Giver, the Avataric Incarnation of the Very Divine Person.

Avatar Adi Da's Declaration "Aham Da Asmi" is similar in form to the "Mahavakyas" (or "Great Statements") of ancient India (found in the Upanishads, the collected esoteric Instruction of ancient Hindu Gurus). However, the significance of "Aham Da Asmi" is fundamentally different from that of the traditional Mahavakyas. Each of the Upanishadic Mahavakyas expresses, in a few words, the profound (though not most ultimate) degree of Realization achieved by great Realizers of the past. For example, the Upanishadic Mahavakya "Aham Brahmasmi" ("I Am Brahman") expresses a great individual's Realization that he or she is Identified with the Divine Being (Brahman), and is not, in Truth, identified with his or her apparently individual body-mind. However, "Aham Da

Asmi", rather than being a proclamation of a human being who has devoted his or her life most intensively to the process of Real-God-Realization and has thereby Realized the Truth to an extraordinarily profound degree, is Avatar Adi Da's Confession that He <u>Is</u> the Very Divine Person, Da, Who has Appeared here in His Avatarically-Born bodily (human) Divine Form, in order to Reveal Himself to all and All, for the sake of the Divine Liberation of all and All.

all and All / All and all Avatar Adi Da uses the phrase "all and All" (or "All and all") to describe the totality of conditional existence from two points of view. In *Aham Da Asmi,* He defines lower-case "all" as indicating "the collected sum of all Presumed To Be Separate (or limited) beings, things, and conditions", and upper-case "All" as indicating "The All (or The Undivided Totality) Of conditional Existence As A Whole".

Amrita Nadi Amrita Nadi is Sanskrit for "Channel (or Current, or Nerve) of Ambrosia (or Immortal Nectar)". Amrita Nadi is the ultimate "organ", or root-structure, of the body-mind, Realized as such in the seventh stage of life in the Way of Adidam. It is felt to Stand Radiant between the right side of the heart (which is the psycho-physical Seat of Consciousness Itself) and the Matrix of Light infinitely above the crown of the head. (For Avatar Adi Da's principal discussions of Amrita Nadi, see *The Knee Of Listening, The <u>All-Completing</u> and <u>Final</u> Divine Revelation To Mankind, Santosha Adidam,* and *The Dawn Horse Testament.*)

anatomy See **Spiritual anatomy**.

asana Sanskrit for bodily "posture" or "pose"—by extension, and as Avatar Adi Da often intends, "asana" also refers to the attitude, orientation, posture, or feeling-disposition of the heart and the entire body-mind.

"Atma-Murti" "Atma" indicates the Divine Self, and "Murti" means "Form". Thus, "Atma-Murti" literally means "the Form That Is the (Very) Divine Self". And, as Avatar Adi Da Indicates everywhere in His Wisdom-Teaching, "Atma-Murti" refers to Himself as the Very Divine Self of all, "Located" as "the Feeling of Being (Itself)". To Commune with Avatar Adi Da as "Atma-Murti" is to Realize (or enter into Identification with) His Divine State.

Avadhoot   Avadhoot is a traditional term for one who has "shaken off" or "passed beyond" all worldly attachments and cares, including all motives of detachment (or conventional and other-worldly renunciation), all conventional notions of life and religion, and all seeking for "answers" or "solutions" in the form of conditional experience or conditional knowledge.

Avatar   "Avatar" (from Sanskrit "avatara") is a traditional term for a Divine Incarnation. It literally means "One who is descended, or 'crossed down' (from, and as, the Divine)". Avatar Adi Da Samraj Confesses that, simultaneous with His human Birth, He has Incarnated in every world, at every level of the Cosmic domain, as the Eternal Giver of Divine Help and Divine Grace and Divine Liberation to all beings—and that, even though His bodily (human) Lifetime is necessarily limited in duration, His Spiritual Incarnation in the Cosmic domain is Eternal.

Avataric Incarnation   Avatar Adi Da Samraj is the Avataric Incarnation, or the Divinely Descended Embodiment, of the Divine Person. The reference "Avataric Incarnation" indicates that Avatar Adi Da Samraj fulfills both the traditional expectation of the East, that the True God-Man is an Avatar (or an utterly Divine "Descent" of Real God in conditionally manifested form), and the traditional expectations of the West, that the True God-Man is an Incarnation (or an utterly human Embodiment of Real God).

For Avatar Adi Da's discussion of the "Avatar" and "Incarnation" traditions, and of His unique and all-Completing Role as the "Avataric Incarnation" of the Divine Person, see "'Avatar' and 'Incarnation' Traditions: The Complementary God-Man Traditions of East and West", in *The Truly Human New World-Culture Of Unbroken Real-God-Man.*

Avataric Self-Submission   For a full description of Avatar Adi Da's "Ordeal Of Avataric Self-Submission", see *The Promised God-Man Is Here*, by Carolyn Lee.

"Avoiding relationship?"   The practice of self-Enquiry in the form "Avoiding relationship?", unique to the Way of Adidam, was spontaneously developed by Avatar Adi Da in the course of His Divine Re-Awakening (as Avatar Adi Da describes in *The Knee Of Listening*). Intense persistence in the "radical" discipline of this unique form of self-Enquiry led rapidly to His Divine Re-Awakening in 1970.

The practice of self-Enquiry in the form "Avoiding relationship?" is the principal form of the "conscious process" practiced by devotees of Avatar Adi Da who choose the Devotional Way of Insight. (See also "Devotional Way of Insight / Devotional Way of Faith" and "Re-cognition".)

B

"basic" context of the fourth stage of life   See **stages of life**.

Bhagavan   The Title "Bhagavan" is an ancient one used over the centuries for many Spiritual Realizers of India. It means "blessed" or "holy" in Sanskrit. When applied to a great Spiritual Being, "Bhagavan" is understood to mean "bountiful Lord", or "Great Lord", or "Divine Lord".

bhakta, bhakti   "Bhakti" is the practice of heart-felt devotion to the Ultimate Reality or Person—a practice which has been traditionally animated through worship of Divine Images or surrender to a human Guru.

"Bhakta" is a devotee whose principal characteristic is expressive devotion, or who practices within the Hindu tradition of Bhakti Yoga.

Bhava   "Bhava" is a Sanskrit word used to refer to the enraptured feeling-swoon of Communion with the Divine.

bindu   In the esoteric Yogic traditions of India, the Sanskrit word "bindu" (literally, "drop" or "point") suggests that all manifested forms, energies, and universes are ultimately coalesced or expressed in a point without spatial or temporal dimension. Each level (or plane) of psycho-physical reality is said to have a corresponding bindu, or zero-point.

Blessing-Work For a description of Avatar Adi Da's Divine Blessing-Work, see pp. 17-19.

bodily base The bodily base is the region associated with the muladhara chakra, the lowest energy plexus in the human body-mind, at the base of the spine (or the general region immediately above and including the perineum). In many of the Yogic traditions, the bodily base is regarded as the seat of the latent ascending Spiritual Current, or Kundalini. Avatar Adi Da Reveals that, in fact, the Spirit-Current must first descend to the bodily base through the frontal line, before it can effectively be directed into the ascending spinal course. Avatar Adi Da has also pointed out that human beings who are not yet Spiritually sensitive tend to throw off the natural life-energy at the bodily base, and He has, therefore, Given His devotees a range of disciplines (including a number of exercises that involve intentional locking at the bodily base) which conserve life-energy by directing it into the spinal line.

"bodily battery" The "bodily battery" (known in Japan as the "hara") is the energy center of the gross body and, as such, plays a very important role in the practice of "conductivity" in the frontal line. Avatar Adi Da describes its focal point (or point of concentration) as the crown of the abdomen, on the surface, about an inch and a half below the umbilical scar.

"bond" / "Bond" Avatar Adi Da uses the term "bond", when lower-cased, to refer to the process by which the egoic individual (already presuming separateness, and, therefore, bondage to the separate self) attaches itself karmically to the world of others and things through the

constant search for self-fulfillment. In contrast, when He capitalizes the term "Bond", Avatar Adi Da is making reference to the process of His devotee's devotional "Bonding" to Him, which process is the Great Means for transcending all forms of limited (or karmic) "bonding".

"Bright" By the word "Bright" (and its variations, such as "Brightness"), Avatar Adi Da refers to the Self-Existing and Self-Radiant Divine Reality. As Adi Da Writes in His Spiritual Autobiography, *The Knee Of Listening:*

> . . . *from my earliest experience of life I have Enjoyed a Condition that, as a child, I called the "Bright".*
>
> *I have always known desire, not merely for extreme pleasures of the senses and the mind, but for the highest Enjoyment of Spiritual Power and Mobility. But I have not been seated in desire, and desire has only been a play that I have grown to understand and enjoy without conflict. I have always been Seated in the "Bright".*
>
> *Even as a baby I remember only crawling around inquisitively with a boundless Feeling of Joy, Light, and Freedom in the middle of my head that was bathed in Energy moving unobstructed in a Circle, down from above, all the way down, then up, all the way up, and around again, and always Shining from my heart. It was an Expanding Sphere of Joy from the heart. And I was a Radiant Form, the Source of Energy, Love-Bliss, and Light in the midst of a world that is entirely Energy, Love-Bliss, and Light. I was the Power of Reality, a direct Enjoyment and Communication of the One Reality. I was the Heart Itself, Who Lightens the mind and all things. I was the same as every one and every thing, except it became clear that others were apparently unaware of the "Thing" Itself.*
>
> *Even as a little child I recognized It and Knew It, and my life was not a matter of anything else. That Awareness, that Conscious Enjoyment, that Self-Existing and Self-Radiant Space of Infinitely and inherently Free Being, that Shine of inherent Joy Standing in the heart and Expanding from the heart, is the "Bright". And It is the*

entire Source of True Humor. It is Reality. It is not separate from anything.

Buddha   Just as the traditional term "Avatar", when rightly understood, is an appropriate Reference to Avatar Adi Da Samraj, so is the traditional term "Buddha". He is the Divine Buddha, the One Who Is Most Perfectly Self-Enlightened and Eternally Awake.

C

causal   See **gross, subtle, causal**.

childish and adolescent strategies
Avatar Adi Da uses the terms "childish" and "adolescent" with precise meanings in His Wisdom-Teaching. He points out that human beings are always tending to animate one of two fundamental life-strategies—the childish strategy (to be dependent, weak, seeking to be consoled by parent-figures and a parent-"God") and the adolescent strategy (to be independent—or, otherwise, torn between independence and dependence—rebellious, unfeeling, self-absorbed, and doubting or resisting the idea of God or any power greater than oneself). Until these strategies are understood and transcended, they not only diminish love in ordinary human relations, but they also limit religious and Spiritual growth.

Circle   The Circle is a primary pathway of natural life-energy and the Spirit-Current through the body-mind. It is composed of two arcs: the descending Current, in association with the frontal line (down the front of the body, from the crown of the head to the bodily base), which corresponds to the more physically oriented dimension of the body-mind; and the ascending Current, in association with the spinal line (up the back of the body, from the bodily base to the crown of the head), which is the more mentally, psychically, and subtly oriented dimension of the body-mind.

conditional   The word "conditional" (and its variants) is used to indicate everything that depends on conditions—in other words, everything that is temporary and changing. The "Unconditional", in contrast, is the Divine, or That Which Is Eternal, Always Already the Case—because It Is utterly Free of dependence on any conditions whatsoever.

"conductivity"   "Conductivity" is Avatar Adi Da's technical term for participation in and responsibility for the movement of natural bodily energies (and, when one is Spiritually Awakened by Him, for the movement of His Divine Spirit-Current of Love-Bliss in Its natural course of association with the body-mind), via intentional exercises of feeling and breathing.

The exercises of Spiritual "conductivity" that Avatar Adi Da Gives to His (formally practicing) Spiritually Awakened devotees are technical whole-bodily Yogas of receptive surrender to the Living Spirit-Current. Rudimentary and preparatory technical forms of "conductivity" are Given to beginners.

congregations of Adidam   There are four different modes, or congregations, of formal approach to Avatar Adi Da Samraj, making it possible for everyone to participate in the Gift of heart-companionship with Him. The total practice of the Way of Adidam is engaged by those in the first and second congregations. Whereas all of Avatar Adi Da's devotees (in all four congregations) engage the fundamental practice of Ruchira Avatara Bhakti Yoga, only members of the first and second congregations are vowed to engage the full range of supportive disciplines (meditation, sacramental worship, guided study, exercise, diet, emotional-sexual discipline, cooperative community living, and so on) Given by Avatar Adi Da Samraj.

For a more detailed description of the four congregations of Avatar Adi Da's devotees, see pp. 360-72.

"conscious process"   The "conscious process" is Avatar Adi Da's technical term for those practices through which the mind, or attention, is surrendered and turned about (from egoic self-involvement) to feeling-Contemplation of Him. It is the senior discipline and responsibility of all practitioners in the Way of Adidam. (Avatar Adi Da's descriptions of the various forms of the "conscious process" are Given in *The Dawn Horse Testament Of The Ruchira Avatar*.)

"consider", "consideration"   The technical term "consider" or "consideration" in Avatar Adi Da's Wisdom-Teaching means a process of one-pointed but ultimately thoughtless concentration and exhaustive contemplation of something until its ultimate obviousness is clear. As engaged in the Way of Adidam, "consideration" is not merely an intellectual investigation. It is the participatory investment of one's whole being. If one "considers" something fully in the context of one's practice of feeling-Contemplation of Avatar Adi Da Samraj, and study of His Wisdom-Teaching, this concentration results "in both the highest intuition and the most practical grasp of the Lawful and Divine necessities of human existence".

Contemplation of Avatar Adi Da's bodily (human) Form   Traditionally, devotees have produced artistic images of their Gurus for the purpose of Contemplating the Guru when he or she is either not physically present or (otherwise) no longer physically alive.

Modern technology makes possible (through photography, videotape, film, holographic imagery, and other means) accurate Representations of the bodily (human) Form of Avatar Adi Da Samraj for devotional use by His formally acknowledged devotees.

"Cosmic Consciousness"   See **Samadhi**.

Cosmic Mandala   The Sanskrit word "mandala" (literally, "circle") is commonly used in the esoteric Spiritual traditions of the East to describe the hierarchical levels of cosmic existence. "Mandala" also denotes an artistic rendering of interior visions of the cosmos. Avatar Adi Da uses the phrase "Cosmic Mandala" as a reference to the totality of the conditionally manifested cosmos (or all worlds, forms, and beings).

Crashing Down   Avatar Adi Da's Crashing Down is the Descent of His Divine Spirit-Force into the body-mind of His devotee.

My Avataric Divine Work (Altogether) Is My Crashing-Down Descent, At First Upon and Into My Own Avatarically-Born Bodily (Human) Divine Form, and, Thereafter (and Now, and Forever), Upon and Into the body-minds Of My Devotees and all beings—Even (By Means Of My Divine Embrace Of each, and all, and All) To Infuse and (At Last) To Divinely Translate each, and all, and All. Therefore, My Avataric Divine Spiritual Descent Is The Secret Of My Early Life. My Avataric Divine Spiritual Descent Is The Secret Of My Divine Self-"Emergence" (As I Am) Within The Cosmic Domain. My Avataric Divine Spiritual Descent Is The Secret Of All The Secrets Of The (Avatarically Self-Revealed) Divine and Complete and Thoroughly Devotional Way Of Practice and Realization In My Company. The Only-By-Me Revealed and Given Way Of The Heart (or Way Of Adidam) Is The Divine Yoga Of ego-Surrendering, ego-Forgetting, and ego-Transcending Devotional Recognition-Response To My (Avatarically Self-Revealed) Divine and Spiritual Person, and To My (Avatarically Self-Manifested) Divine and Spiritual Descent. The Only-By-Me Revealed and Given Way Of The Heart (or Way Of Adidam) Is The Total and Divine Way and Ordeal Of Counter-egoic Devotional Recognition-Response To My Avataric "Bright" Divine Self-Manifestation, and To The Avataric Crashing Down Of My "Bright" Divine Imposition. And, In The Case Of My Each and Every Devotee, The Way Must Continue Until The Way Is Most Perfectly "Bright", and The Way Itself Becomes Divine Translation Into My Own Sphere Of "Brightness" (Itself). [Ruchira Avatara Hridaya-Siddha Yoga]

"Crazy"   Avatar Adi Da has always had a unique Method of "Crazy" Work, which, particularly during His years of Teaching and Revelation, involved His literal Submission to the limited conditions of humankind, in order to reflect His devotees to themselves, and thereby Awaken self-understanding in them (relative to their individual egoic dramas, and the collective egoic dramas of human society).

For Me, There Was Never Any Other Possibility Than The "Reckless" (or Divinely "Crazy" and Divinely "Heroic") Course Of All-and-all-Embrace—and I Began This Uniquely "Crazy" and "Heroic" Sadhana, Most Intensively, At The Beginning Of My Adult Life. Indeed, I Have Always Functioned, and Will Always Function, In This Divinely "Crazy" and Divinely "Heroic" Manner. The Inherently egoless "Crazy" and "Heroic" Manner Is One Of My Principal Divine Characteristics— Whereby I Can (Always, and Now, and Forever Hereafter) Be Identified. Therefore, I (Characteristically) Functioned In This "Crazy" and "Heroic" Manner Throughout All Of My "Sadhana Years", and Throughout All The Years Of My Avatarically Self-Manifested Divine Teaching-Work and My Avatarically Self-Manifested Divine Revelation-Work—and I Have Done So (and Will Forever Continue To Do So) Throughout All The Divine-Self-"Emergence" Years Of My Avatarically Self-Manifested Divine Blessing-Work (Both During, and Forever After, My Avataric Physical Human Lifetime). All My Avatarically Self-Manifested Divine Work Is A Divinely "Crazy" and Divinely "Heroic" Effort That Avoids Not anything or any one—but Which Always Divinely Blesses Everything and Everyone. [The Truly Human New World-Culture Of Unbroken Real-God-Man]

D

Da Avatar Adi Da's Name "Da" means "The Divine Giver". In Sanskrit, "Da" means principally "to give". It is also associated with Vishnu, the "Sustainer", and it further has a secondary meaning "to destroy". Thus, "Da" is anciently aligned to all three of the principal Divine Beings, Forces, or Attributes in the Hindu tradition—Brahma (the Creator, Generator, or Giver), Vishnu (the Sustainer), and Siva (the Destroyer). In certain Hindu rituals, priests address the Divine directly as "Da", invoking qualities such as generosity and compassion.

The Tibetan Buddhists regard the syllable "Da" (written, in Tibetan, as well as in Sanskrit, with a single symbol) as most auspicious, and they assign numerous sacred meanings to it, including that of "the Entrance into the Dharma".

Da Love-Ananda Samrajya For a description of the Da Love-Ananda Samrajya, see p. 376.

Da Avatar "Da" is Sanskrit for "The One Who Gives". Therefore, as the Da Avatar, Adi Da Samraj is the Divine Descent of the One and True Divine Giver.

"dark" epoch See **"late-time" (or "dark" epoch)**.

Darshan "Darshan", the Hindi derivative of the Sanskrit "darshana", literally means "seeing", "sight of", or "vision of". To receive Darshan of Avatar Adi Da is, most fundamentally, to behold His bodily (human) Form (either by being in His physical Company or by seeing a photograph or other visual representation of Him), and (thereby) to receive the spontaneous Divine Blessing He Grants Freely whenever His bodily (human) Form is beheld in the devotional manner. In the Way of Adidam, Darshan of Avatar Adi Da is the very essence of the practice, and one of the most potent forms of receiving Avatar Adi Da's Blessing is to participate in the formal occasions of Darshan—during which Avatar Adi Da Samraj Sits silently, sometimes gazing at each individual one by one.

By extension, "Darshan" of Avatar Adi Da Samraj may refer to any means by which His Blessing-Influence is felt and received—including His Written or Spoken Word, photographs or videotapes of His Avatarically-Born bodily (human) Divine Form, recordings of His Voice, Leelas (or Stories) of His Teaching-Work and Blessing-Work, places or objects He has Spiritually Empowered, visualization of His Avatarically-Born bodily (human) Divine Form in the mind, and simple, heart-felt Remembrance of Him.

Dattatreya Dattatreya was a God-Realizer who appeared early in the common era and about whom no certain historical facts exist apart from his name. Over the centuries, numerous legends and myths have been spun around him. He was early on regarded to be an incarnation of the God Vishnu, later associated with the tradition of Saivism, and worshipped as the Divine Itself. He is commonly venerated as the originator of the Avadhoota tradition and credited with the authorship of the *Avadhoota Gita*, among other works.

The devotional sect worshipping Dattatreya presumes that he continually reincarnates through a succession of Adepts for the sake of gathering and serving devotees. The belief in the continuing incarnation of Dattatreya should be understood as a popular religious belief that is peripheral to what the Adepts in the Dattatreya succession actually taught.

The Dawn Horse Testament Of The Ruchira Avatar *The Dawn Horse Testament Of The Ruchira Avatar* is Avatar Adi Da's paramount "Source-Text", summarizing the entire course of the Way of Adidam. (See "Avatar Adi Da Samraj's Teaching-Word", pp. 27-38.)

developmental stages of practice For all members of the first and second congregations of Avatar Adi Da's devotees, the Way of Adidam develops through a series of (potential) developmental stages of practice and Realization. These stages of practice, and their relationship to the seven stages of life, are described by Avatar Adi Da Samraj in chapter seventeen of *The Dawn Horse Testament Of The Ruchira Avatar*.

When using the phrase "necessary (or, otherwise, potential)", Avatar Adi Da is referring to the fact that His fully practicing devotee must practice in the context of certain of the developmental stages of practice (corresponding to the first three stages of life, the "original" and "basic" contexts of the fourth stage of life, the sixth stage of life, and the seventh stage of life) but may bypass practice in the developmental stages that correspond to "advanced" context of the fourth stage of life and to the fifth stage of life.

Devotional Way of Insight / Devotional Way of Faith Avatar Adi Da has Given Instruction in two variant forms of the fundamental practice of feeling-Contemplation of Him: the Devotional Way of Insight and the Devotional Way of Faith. Each of Avatar Adi Da's fully practicing devotees is to experiment with both of these Devotional Ways and then choose the one that is most effective in his or her case.

Both Devotional Ways require the exercise of insight and faith, but there is a difference in emphasis.

In the Devotional Way of Insight, the practitioner engages a specific technical process of observing, understanding, and then feeling beyond the self-contraction, as the principal technical element of his or her practice of feeling-Contemplation of Avatar Adi Da.

In the Devotional Way of Faith, the practitioner engages a specific technical process of magnifying his or her heart-Attraction to Avatar Adi Da, as the principal technical element of his or her practice of feeling-Contemplation of Avatar Adi Da.

Avatar Adi Da's extended Instruction relative to both Devotional Ways is Given in *The Only Complete Way To Realize The Unbroken Light Of Real God*.

Dharma, dharma Sanskrit for "duty", "virtue", "law". The word "dharma" is commonly used to refer to the many esoteric paths by which human beings seek the Truth. In its fullest sense, and when capitalized, "Dharma" means the complete fulfillment of duty—the living of the Divine Law. By extension, "Dharma" means a truly great Spiritual Teaching, including its disciplines and practices.

"Difference" "Difference" is the epitome of the egoic presumption of separateness—in contrast with the Realization of Oneness, or Non-"Difference", Which is Native to the Divine Self-Condition.

Divine Being Avatar Adi Da describes His Divine Being on three levels:

AVATAR ADI DA SAMRAJ: This flesh body, this bodily (human) Sign, is My Form, in the sense that it is My Murti, or a kind of Reflection (or Representation) of Me. It is, therefore, a Means for contacting My Spiritual Presence, and, ultimately, My Divine State.

My Spiritual Presence is Self-Existing and Self-Radiant. It Functions in time and space, and It is also Prior to all time and space. . . .

My Divine State is always and only utterly Prior to time and space. Therefore, I, As I Am (Ultimately), have no "Function" in time and space. There is no time and space in My Divine State.

Divine Body   Avatar Adi Da's Divine Body is not conditional or limited to His physical Body but is "The 'Bright' Itself (Spiritually Pervading and Eternally Most Prior To The Cosmic Domain)".

Divine Enlightenment   The Realization of the seventh stage of life, which is uniquely Revealed and Given by Avatar Adi Da. It is release from all the egoic limitations of the first six stages of life. Remarkably, the seventh stage Awakening, which is Avatar Adi Da's Gift to His rightly prepared devotee, is not an experience at all. The true Nature of everything is simply obvious, based on the Realization that every apparent "thing" is Eternally, Perfectly the same as Reality, Consciousness, Happiness, Truth, or Real God. And that Realization is the Supreme Love-Bliss of Avatar Adi Da's Divine Self-Condition.

Divine Ignorance   "Divine Ignorance" is Avatar Adi Da's term for the fundamental Awareness of Existence Itself, Prior to all sense of separation from (or knowledge about) anything that arises. As He proposes, "No matter what arises, you do not know what a single thing is." By "Ignorance", Avatar Adi Da means heartfelt participation in the universal Condition of inherent Mystery—not mental dullness or the fear-based wonder or awe felt by the subjective ego in relation to unknown objects. Divine Ignorance is the Realization of Consciousness Itself, transcending all knowledge and all experience of the self-contracted ego-"I".

For Avatar Adi Da's extended Instruction relative to Divine Ignorance, see *What, Where, When, How, Why, and Who To Remember To Be Happy*, Part Two: "What, Where, When, How, Why and Who To Remember To Be Happy", and Part Three: "You Do Not Know What even a single thing Is" and "My Argument Relative to Divine Ignorance".

Divine Indifference   See **four phases of the seventh stage of life**.

Divine "Intoxication"   Unlike common intoxication, such as with alcohol, Divine "Intoxication" Draws Avatar Adi Da's devotees beyond the usual egoic self and egoic mind through His Blessing Grace into a state of ecstatic devotional Communion (and Identification) with Him.

Divine Parama-Guru   The Supreme Divine Guru.

Divine Re-Awakening   Avatar Adi Da's Divine Re-Awakening occurred on September 10, 1970, in the Vedanta Society Temple in Hollywood, California. For a full description of this Great Event and its import, see *The Promised God-Man Is Here*, by Carolyn Lee, or chapter sixteen of *The Knee Of Listening*.

Divine Self-Recognition   Divine Self-Recognition is the ego-transcending and world-transcending Intelligence of the Divine Self in relation to all conditional phenomena. The devotee of Avatar Adi Da who Realizes the seventh stage of life simply Abides as Self-Existing and Self-Radiant Consciousness Itself, and he or she Freely Self-Recognizes (or inherently and instantly and Most Perfectly comprehends and perceives) all phenomena (including body, mind, conditional self, and conditional world) as transparent (or merely apparent), and un-necessary, and inherently non-binding modifications of the same "Bright" Divine Self-Consciousness.

Divine Self-"Emergence"   On January 11, 1986, Avatar Adi Da passed through a profound Yogic Swoon, which He later described as the initial Event of His Divine Self-"Emergence". Avatar Adi Da's Divine Self-"Emergence" is an ongoing Process in which His Avatarically-Born bodily (human) Divine Form has been (and is ever more profoundly and potently being) conformed to Himself, the Very Divine Person, such that His bodily (human) Form is now (and forever hereafter) an utterly Unobstructed Sign and Agent of His own Divine Being.

For Avatar Adi Da's Revelation of the significance of His Divine Self-"Emergence", see section III of "The True Dawn Horse Is The Only Way To Me", in *The All-Completing* and *Final Divine Revelation To Mankind, The Heart Of The Dawn Horse Testament Of The Ruchira Avatar,* and *The Dawn Horse Testament Of The Ruchira Avatar.*

Divine Self-Domain   Avatar Adi Da affirms that there is a Divine Self-Domain that is the Perfectly Subjective Condition of the conditional worlds. It is not "elsewhere", not an objective "place" (like a subtle "heaven" or mythical "paradise"), but It is the always present, Transcendental, Inherently Spiritual, Divine Source-Condition of every conditionally manifested being and thing. Avatar Adi Da Reveals that the Divine Self-Domain is not other than the Divine Heart Itself, not other than Himself. To Realize the seventh stage of life (by the Divine Grace of Avatar Adi Da Samraj) is to Awaken to His Divine Self-Domain.

For Avatar Adi Da's extended Instruction relative to His Divine Self-Domain, see *The All-Completing* and *Final Divine Revelation To Mankind.*

Divine Star   The primal conditional Representation of the "Bright" (the Source-Energy, or Divine Light, of Which all conditional phenomena and the total cosmos are modifications) is the brilliant white five-pointed Divine Star. Avatar Adi Da's bodily (human) Divine Form is the Manifestation of that Divine Star—and His head, two arms, and two legs correspond to its five points. Avatar Adi Da can also be seen or intuited in vision to Be the Divine Star Itself, prior to the visible manifestation of His bodily (human) Form.

Divine Transfiguration   See **four phases of the seventh stage of life**.

Divine Transformation   See **four phases of the seventh stage of life**.

Divine Translation   See **four phases of the seventh stage of life**.

Divine World-Teacher   Avatar Adi Da Samraj is the Divine World-Teacher because His Wisdom-Teaching is the uniquely Perfect Instruction to every being—in this (and every) world—in the total process of Divine Enlightenment. Furthermore, Avatar Adi Da Samraj constantly Extends His Regard to the entire world (and the entire Cosmic domain)—not on the political or social level, but as a Spiritual matter, constantly Working to Bless and Purify all beings everywhere.

dreaming   See **waking, dreaming, and sleeping**.

E

ecstasy / enstasy   The words "ecstasy" and "enstasy" derive originally from Greek. Avatar Adi Da uses "ecstasy" in the literal sense of "standing (stasis) outside (ec-)" the egoic self, and "enstasy" in the sense of "standing (stasis) in (en-)" the Divine Self-Condition. As Avatar Adi Da Says in *The Dawn Horse Testament Of The Ruchira Avatar*, Divine Enstasy is "The Native Condition Of Standing Unconditionally As The By-Me-Avatarically-Self-Revealed Transcendental, Inherently Spiritual, and Self-Evidently Divine Self-Condition Itself".

ego-"I"   The ego-"I" is the fundamental activity of self-contraction, or the presumption of separate and separative existence.

Eleutherian Pan-Communion of Adidam   The Eleutherian Pan-Communion of Adidam is a California religious non-profit corporation, dedicated to the worldwide practice and the global proclamation of the true world-religion of Adidam.

Eleutherios   "Eleutherios" (Greek for "Liberator") is a title by which Zeus was venerated as the supreme deity in the Spiritual esotericism of ancient Greece. The Designation "Eleutherios" indicates the Divine Function of Avatar Adi Da as the Incarnation of the Divine Person, "Whose Inherently Perfect Self-'Brightness' Divinely Liberates all conditionally Manifested beings—Freely, Liberally, Gracefully, and Without Ceasing—now, and forever hereafter".

En-Light-enment   En-Light-enment (or Enlightenment) is not just a state of mind, but rather an actual conversion of the body-mind to the state of Divine Consciousness Itself, or Light Itself. Thus, Avatar Adi Da sometimes writes the word "Enlightenment" with "Light" set apart by hyphens, in order to emphasize this point.

esoteric anatomy   See **Spiritual anatomy**.

Eternal Vow   For a description of the Vow and responsibilities associated with the Way of Adidam, see p. 363.

etheric   The etheric is the dimension of life-energy, which functions through the human nervous system. Our bodies are surrounded and infused by this personal life-energy, which we feel as the play of emotions and life-force in the body.

F

faculties; four faculties   Avatar Adi Da has Instructed His devotees that the practice of devotional Communion with Him (or Ruchira Avatara Bhakti Yoga) requires the surrender of the four principal faculties of the human body-mind. These faculties are body, emotion (or feeling), mind (or attention), and breath.

Feeling of Being   The Feeling of Being is the uncaused (or Self-Existing), Self-Radiant, and unqualified feeling-intuition of the Transcendental, Inherently Spiritual, and Self-Evidently Divine Self-Condition. This absolute Feeling does not merely accompany or express the Realization of the Heart Itself, but It is Identical to that Realization. To feel—or, really, to Be—the Feeling of Being is to enjoy the Love-Bliss of Absolute Consciousness, Which, when Most Perfectly Realized, cannot be pre-

vented or even diminished either by the events of life or by death.

feeling of relatedness   In the foundation stages of practice in the Way of Adidam, the basic (or gross) manifestation of the avoidance of relationship is understood and released when Avatar Adi Da's devotee hears Him (or comes to the point of most fundamental self-understanding), thereby regaining the free capability for simple relatedness, or living on the basis of the feeling of relatedness rather than the avoidance of relationship. Nevertheless, the feeling of relatedness is not Ultimate Realization, because it is still founded in the presumption of a "difference" between "I" and "other". Only in the ultimate stages of life in the Way of Adidam is the feeling of relatedness itself fully understood as the root-act of attention and, ultimately, transcended in the Feeling of Being.

feeling-Contemplation   Avatar Adi Da's term for the essential devotional and meditative practice that all practitioners of the Way of Adidam engage at all times in relationship to Him. Feeling-Contemplation of Adi Da Samraj is Awakened by His Grace—through Darshan (or feeling-sighting) of His bodily (human) Form, His Spiritual Presence, and His Divine State. It is then to be practiced under all conditions, as the basis and epitome of all other practices in the Way of Adidam.

fifth stage conditional Nirvikalpa Samadhi   See **Samadhi**.

forms of practice in the Way of Adidam
Avatar Adi Da has Given a number of different approaches to the progressive process of Most Perfectly self-transcending Real-God-Realization in the Way of Adidam. In this manner, He accounts for the differences in individuals' qualities—particularly relative to their capability to make use of the various technical practices that support the fundamental practice of Ruchira Avatara Bhakti Yoga and relative to the intensity of their motivation to apply themselves to the Spiritual process in His Company.

Ruchira Avatar Adi Da refers to the most detailed development of the practice of the Way of Adidam as the "technically 'fully elaborated'" form of practice. Each successive stage of practice in the technically "fully elaborated" form of the Way of Adidam is defined by progressively more detailed responsibilities, disciplines, and practices that are assumed in order to take responsibility for the signs of growing maturity in the process of Divine Awakening. A devotee who embraces the technically "fully elaborated" form of practice of the Way of Adidam must (necessarily) be a member of the first or second congregation of Avatar Adi Da's devotees. The progress of practice in the technically "fully elaborated" form of the Way of Adidam is monitored, measured, and evaluated by practicing stages (as described in detail by Avatar Adi Da Samraj in chapter seventeen of *The Dawn Horse Testament Of The Ruchira Avatar*).

Most of Avatar Adi Da's fully practicing devotees will find that they are qualified for a less intensive approach and are moved to a less technical form of the "conscious process" (than is exercised in the technically "fully elaborated" form of the Way of Adidam). Thus, most of Avatar Adi Da's fully practicing devotees will take up the technically "simpler" (or even "simplest") form of practice of the Way of Adidam.

In the technically "simpler" form of practice of the Way of Adidam, Avatar Adi Da's devotee (in the first or second congregation) engages a relatively simple form of technical means of supporting his or her fundamental practice of Ruchira Avatara Bhakti Yoga, and this technical means remains the same throughout the progressive course of developmental stages.

In the technically "simplest" form of practice, Avatar Adi Da's devotee (in any of the four congregations) engages the fundamental practice of Ruchira Avatara Bhakti Yoga in the simplest possible manner—as "simplest" feeling-Contemplation of Avatar Adi Da, together with the random use of Avatar Adi Da's Principal Name, "Da" (or one of the other Names He has Given to be engaged in the practice of simple Name-Invocation of Him).

Avatar Adi Da's fully elaborated descriptions of the technically "fully elaborated" and the technically "simpler" (or even "simplest") forms of the Way of Adidam are Given in *The Dawn Horse Testament Of The Ruchira Avatar*.

four phases of the seventh stage of life
In the context of Divine Enlightenment in the seventh stage of life, the Spiritual process continues. One of the unique aspects of Avatar Adi Da's Revelation is His description of the four phases of the seventh stage process: Divine Transfiguration, Divine Transformation, Divine Indifference, and Divine Translation.

In the phase of Divine Transfiguration, the Divinely Enlightened devotee's body-mind is Infused by Avatar Adi Da's Love-Bliss, and he or she Radiantly Demonstrates active Love, spontaneously Blessing all the relations of the body-mind.

In the following phase of Divine Transformation, the subtle or psychic dimension of the body-mind is fully Illumined, which may result in Divine Powers of healing, longevity, and the ability to release obstacles from the world and from the lives of others.

Eventually, Divine Indifference ensues, which is spontaneous and profound Resting in the "Deep" of Consciousness, and the world of relations is otherwise noticed only minimally or not at all.

Divine Translation is the ultimate "Event" of the entire process of Divine Awakening. Avatar Adi Da describes Divine Translation as the Outshining of all noticing of objective conditions through the infinitely magnified Force of Consciousness Itself. Divine Translation is the Outshining of all destinies, wherein there is no return to the conditional realms.

Being so overwhelmed by the Divine Radiance that all appearances fade away may occur <u>temporarily</u> from time to time during the seventh stage of life. But when that Most Love-Blissful Swoon becomes permanent, Divine Translation occurs, and the body-mind is inevitably relinquished in physical death. Then there is only Eternal Inherence in the Divine Self-Domain of unqualified Happiness and Joy.

frontal line, frontal personality, frontal Yoga The frontal (or descending) line of the body-mind conducts natural life-energy and (for those who are Spiritually Awakened) the Spirit-Current of Divine Life, in a downward direction from the crown of the head to the base of the body (or the perineal area).

The frontal personality is comprised of the physical body and its natural energies, the gross brain, and the verbal and lower faculties of the mind. It includes the entire gross dimension of the body-mind and the lower (or most physically oriented) aspects of the subtle dimension of the body-mind.

The frontal Yoga, as described by Avatar Adi Da, is the process whereby knots and obstructions in the gross (or physical) and energetic dimensions of the body-mind are penetrated, opened, surrendered, and released, through the devotee's reception of Avatar Adi Da's Transmission in the frontal line of the body-mind.

"fully elaborated" form of the Way of Adidam See **forms of practice in the Way of Adidam**.

functional, practical, relational, and cultural disciplines of Adidam
The most basic <u>functional</u>, <u>practical</u>, and <u>relational</u> <u>disciplines</u> of the Way of Adidam (in its fully practiced form, as embraced by devotees in the first and second congregations) are forms of appropriate human action and responsibility for diet, health, exercise, sexuality, work, service to and support of Avatar Adi Da's Circumstance and Work, and cooperative (formal community) association with other practitioners of the Way of Adidam. The most basic <u>cultural</u> <u>obligations</u> of the Way of Adidam (in its fully practiced form) include meditation, sacramental worship, study of Avatar Adi Da's Wisdom-Teaching (and also at least a basic discriminative study of the Great Tradition of religion and Spirituality that is the Wisdom-inheritance of humankind), and regular participation in the "form" (or schedule) of daily, weekly, monthly, and annual devotional activities and retreats.

G

Great Tradition The "Great Tradition" is Avatar Adi Da's term for the total inheritance of human, cultural, religious, magical, mystical, Spiritual, and Transcendental paths, philosophies, and testimonies, from all the eras and cultures of humanity—which inheritance has (in the present era of worldwide communication) become the common legacy of humankind. Avatar Adi Da's Divine Self-Revelation and Wisdom-Teaching Fulfills and Completes the Great Tradition.

gross, subtle, causal Avatar Adi Da (in agreement with certain esoteric schools in the Great Tradition) describes conditional existence as having three dimensions—gross, subtle, and causal.

"Gross" means "made up of material (or physical) elements". The gross (or physical) dimension is, therefore, associated with the physical body, and also with experience in the waking state.

The subtle dimension, which is senior to and pervades the gross dimension, includes the etheric (or energic), lower mental (or verbal-intentional and lower psychic), and higher mental (or deeper psychic, mystical, and discriminative) functions, and is associated with experience in the dreaming state. In the human psycho-physical structure, the subtle dimension is primarily associated with the ascending energies of the spine, the brain core, and the subtle centers of mind in the higher brain.

The causal dimension is senior to and pervades both the gross and the subtle dimensions. It is the root of attention, or the essence of the separate and separative ego-"I". The causal dimension is associated with the right side of the heart, specifically with the sinoatrial node, or "pacemaker" (the psycho-physical source of the heartbeat). Its corresponding state of consciousness is the formless awareness of deep sleep.

Guru Esoterically, the word "guru" is understood to be a composite of two words, "destroyer (ru) of darkness (gu)".

H

hearing See **listening, hearing, and seeing**.

heart, stations of the heart Avatar Adi Da distinguishes three stations of the heart, associated respectively with the right side, the middle, and the left side of the heart region of the chest. The middle station of the heart is what is traditionally known as the "anahata chakra" (or "heart chakra"), and the left side of the heart is the gross physical heart. Avatar Adi Da Samraj has Revealed that the primal psycho-physical seat of Consciousness and attention is associated with what He calls the "right side of the heart". He has Revealed that this center (which is neither the heart chakra nor the gross physical heart) corresponds to the sinoatrial node, or "pacemaker", the source of the gross physical heartbeat in the right atrium (or upper right chamber) of the physical heart. In the Process of Divine Self-Realization, there is a unique process of opening of the right side of the heart—and it is because of this connection between the right side of the heart and Divine Self-Realization that Avatar Adi Da uses the term "the Heart" as another way of referring to the Divine Self.

The Heart Itself is Real God, the Divine Self, the Divine Reality. The Heart Itself is not "in" the right side of the human heart, nor is it "in" (or limited to) the human heart as a whole. Rather, the human heart and body-mind and the world exist in the Heart, Which Is the Divine Being Itself.

heart-Communion "Heart-Communion" with Avatar Adi Da is the practice of Invoking and feeling Him. It is "communion" in the sense that the individual loses sense of the separate self in the bliss of that state, and is thus "communicating intimately" (in a most profound and non-dual manner) with Avatar Adi Da Samraj.

heart-recognition The entire practice of the Way of Adidam is founded in devotional heart-recognition of, and devotional heart-response to, Ruchira Avatar Adi Da Samraj as the Very Divine Being in Person.

AVATAR ADI DA SAMRAJ: The only-by-Me Revealed and Given Way of Adidam (Which is the One and Only by-Me-Revealed and by-Me-Given Way of the Heart) is the Way of life you live when you rightly, truly, fully, and fully devotionally recognize Me, and when, on that basis, you rightly, truly, fully, and fully devotionally respond to Me. . . .

If you rightly, truly, fully, and fully devotionally recognize Me, everything "in between" vanishes. All of that is inherently without force. In heart-responsive devotional recognition of Me, a spontaneous kriya of the principal faculties occurs, such that they are loosed from the objects to which they are otherwise bound—loosed from the patterns of self-contraction. The faculties turn to Me, and, in that turning, there is tacit devotional recognition of Me, tacit experiential Realization of Me, of My Love-Bliss-Full Condition. That "Locating" of Me opens the body-mind spontaneously. When you have been thus Initiated by Me, it then becomes your responsibility, your sadhana, to continuously Remember Me, to constantly return to this devotional recognition of Me, in which you are Attracted to Me, in which you devotionally respond to Me spontaneously with all the principal faculties. [Hridaya Rosary (Four Thorns Of Heart-Instruction)]

heart-response See **heart-recognition**.

Hermitage-Retreat Sanctuaries See **Sanctuaries**.

"Heroic" The Tantric traditions of Hinduism and Buddhism describe as "heroic" the practice of an individual whose impulse to Liberation and commitment to his or her Guru are so strong that all circumstances of life, even those traditionally regarded as inauspicious for Spiritual practice (such as consumption of intoxicants and engagement in sexual activity), can rightly be made use of as part of the Spiritual process.

Avatar Adi Da's uniquely "Heroic" Ordeal, however, was undertaken not for His own sake, but in order to discover, through His own experience, what is necessary for all beings to Realize the Truth. Because of His utter Freedom from egoic bondage and egoic karmas, Avatar Adi Da's Sadhana was "Heroic" in a manner that had never previously been possible and will never again be possible. As the Divine Person, it was necessary for Him to experience the entire gamut of human seeking, in order to be able to Teach any and all that came to Him.

Avatar Adi Da has Instructed that, because of His unique "Heroic" Demonstration, His devotees can simply practice the Way He has Revealed and Given, and do not have to attempt the (in any case impossible) task of duplicating His Ordeal. (See also **"Crazy"**.)

Hridaya-Avatar "Hridaya" is Sanskrit for "the heart". It refers not only to the physical organ but also to the True Heart, the Transcendental (and Inherently Spiritual) Divine Reality. "Hridaya" in combination with "Avatar" signifies that Avatar Adi Da is the Very Incarnation of the Divine Heart Itself, the Divine Incarnation Who Stands in, at, and as the True Heart of every being.

Hridaya Rosary *Hridaya Rosary (Four Thorns Of Heart-Instruction)—The Five Books Of The Heart Of The Adidam Revelation, Book Four: The "Late-Time" Avataric Revelation Of The Universally Tangible Divine Spiritual Body, Which Is The Supreme Agent Of The Great Means To Worship and To Realize The True and Spiritual Divine Person (The egoless Personal Presence Of Reality and Truth, Which Is The Only Real God)* is Avatar Adi Da's summary and exquisitely beautiful Instruction relative to the right, true, full, and fully devotional practice of the Way of Adidam, through which practice Avatar Adi Da's fully practicing devotee Spiritually receives Him with ever greater profundity, and, ultimately (through a process of the Spiritual "melting" of the entire psycho-physical being), Realizes Him most perfectly.

Hridaya-Samartha Sat-Guru "Hridaya-Samartha Sat-Guru" is a compound of traditional Sanskrit terms that has been newly created to express the uniqueness of Avatar Adi Da's Guru-Function. "Sat" means "Truth", "Being", "Existence". Thus, "Sat-Guru" literally means "True Guru", or a Guru who can lead living beings from darkness (or non-Truth) into Light (or the Living Truth).

"Samartha" means "fit", "qualified", "able". Thus, "Samartha Sat-Guru" means "a True Guru who is fully capable" of Awakening living beings to Real-God-Realization.

The word "Hridaya", meaning "heart", refers to the Very Heart, or the Transcendental (and Inherently Spiritual) Divine Reality.

Thus, altogether, the reference "Hridaya-Samartha Sat-Guru" means "the Divine Heart-Master Who Liberates His devotees from the darkness of egoity by Means of the Power of the 'Bright' Divine Heart Itself". Avatar Adi Da has Said that this full Designation "properly summarizes all the aspects of My unique Guru-Function".

Hridaya-Shakti; Hridaya-Shaktipat
The Sanskrit word "Hridaya" means "the Heart Itself". "Shakti" is a Sanskrit term for the Divine Manifesting as Energy. "Hridaya-Shakti" is thus "the Divine Power of the Heart", Which is Given and Transmitted by Avatar Adi Da Samraj.

In Hindi, "shaktipat" means the "descent of Divine Power", indicating the Sat-Guru's Transmission of the Kundalini Shakti to his or her devotee.

"Hridaya-Shaktipat", which is Avatar Adi Da's seventh stage Gift to His devotees, is "the Blessing-Transmission of the Divine Heart Itself".

Avatar Adi Da's extended Instruction relative to Hridaya-Shakti and Kundalini Shakti is Given in *Ruchira Avatara Hridaya-Siddha Yoga*.

Hridaya-Siddha Yoga The Way (Yoga) of the relationship with the "Transmission-Master of the Divine Heart" (Hridaya-Siddha), Ruchira Avatar Adi Da Samraj.

Hridayam "Hridayam" is Sanskrit for "heart". It refers not only to the physical organ but also to the True Heart, the Transcendental (and Inherently Spiritual) Divine Reality. "Hridayam" is one of Avatar Adi Da's Divine Names, signifying that He Stands in, at, and as the True Heart of every being.

I

Ignorance See **Divine Ignorance**.

Indifference See **four phases of the seventh stage of life**.

Instruments / Instrumentality
Avatar Adi Da has Indicated that members of the Ruchira Sannyasin Order function collectively and spontaneously as His Instruments, or Means by which His Divine Grace and Awakening Power are Magnified and Transmitted to other devotees and all beings. Such devotees have received Avatar Adi Da's Spiritual Baptism, and they practice in Spiritually activated relationship to Him with exemplary depth and intensity. Because of their uniquely complete and renunciate response and accountability to Him, and by virtue of their ego-surrendering, ego-forgetting, ego-transcending, and really Spiritual Invocation of Him, these devotees function collectively as Instruments for the Transmission of Avatar Adi Da's Spiritual Presence to others.

Invocation by Name See **Name-Invocation**.

Ishta-Guru Bhakti Yoga An alternate name for Ruchira Avatara Bhakti Yoga. Ishta-Guru Bhakti Yoga literally means "the practice (Yoga) of devotion (Bhakti) to Avatar Adi Da, the chosen Beloved (Ishta) Guru of His devotees".

J

Jnana Samadhi See **Samadhi**.

K

Kali Kali is a Hindu form of the Divine Goddess (or "Mother-Shakti") in her terrifying aspect.

Kali Yuga A Hindu term meaning "the dark (kali) epoch (yuga)", or the final and most ignorant and degenerate period of human history, when the Spiritual Way of life is almost entirely forgotten. (In the Hindu view, the Kali Yuga is a cyclically recurring event.)

karma "Karma" is Sanskrit for "action". Since action entails consequences (or reactions), "karma" also means (by extension) "destiny, tendency, the quality of existence and experience which is determined by previous actions".

Kashmir Saivism Kashmir Saivism is a branch of Saivism (the form of Hinduism in which Siva is worshipped as the Supreme Deity), which originated in the Kashmir region of North India in the late 8th century and whose influence has spread throughout the Indian sub-continent during the mid-20th century. It has a largely fifth-stage orientation.

kiln Avatar Adi Da Samraj frequently describes the transformative process of His Blessing-Power in the lives of His devotees as being like a kiln. In a kiln, as the wet clay objects are heated more and more, they begin to glow. Eventually, the kiln is so hot that everything within it glows with a white light, and the definitions of the individual objects dissolve in the brightness. Just so, as a devotee matures in Avatar Adi Da's Spiritual Company, all presumptions of separateness as an apparently individual ego-"I" are more and more Outshined by the "Brightness" of His Divine Person and Blessing.

Klik-Klak Avatar Adi Da coined the term "Klik-Klak" as a name for the conditional reality. This name indicates (even by means of the sound of the two syllables) that conditional reality is a heartless perpetual-motion machine of incessant change, producing endlessly varied patterns that are ultimately binary in nature (as, for example, "yes-no", "on-off", or "black-white").

knots   Previous to Most Perfect Divine Self-Realization, the gross, subtle, and causal dimensions are expressed in the body-mind as characteristic knots. The knot of the gross dimension is associated with the region of the navel. The knot of the subtle dimension is associated with the midbrain, or the ajna center directly behind and between the brows. And the knot of the causal dimension (which Avatar Adi Da refers to as the "causal knot") is associated with the sinoatrial node (or "pacemaker") on the right side of the heart. The causal knot (or the heart-root's knot) is the primary root of the self-contraction, felt as the locus of the self-sense, the source of the feeling of relatedness itself, or the root of attention.

Kundalini-Shaktipat   The Kundalini Shakti is traditionally viewed to lie dormant at the bodily base, or lowermost psychic center of the body-mind. Kundalini-Shaktipat is the activation of the Kundalini Shakti—either spontaneously in the devotee or by the Guru's initiation—thereafter potentially producing various forms of Yogic and mystical experience.

L

"late-time" (or "dark" epoch)   The "'late-time' (or 'dark' epoch)" is a phrase that Avatar Adi Da uses to describe the present era—in which doubt of God (and of anything at all beyond mortal existence) is more and more pervading the entire world, and the self-interest of the separate individual is more and more regarded to be the ultimate principle of life. It is also a reference to the traditional Hindu idea of "yugas", or "epochs", the last of which (the Kali Yuga) is understood to be the most difficult and "dark". Many traditions share the idea that it is in such a time that the Promised Divine Liberator will appear. (See also **Kali Yuga**.)

Lay Congregationist Order   In "The Orders of My True and Free Renunciate Devotees" (in *The Lion Sutra*), Avatar Adi Da describes the Lay Congregationist Order as "the common (or general) order for all formally established general (or not otherwise formal renunciate) lay practitioners of the total (or full and complete) practice of the Way of Adidam". Once a member of the second congregation has completed the student-beginner stage of practice, he or she makes the transition to the intensive listening-hearing stage of the Way of Adidam. By virtue of this transition, the individual becomes a member of the Lay Congregationist Order, unless he or she is accepted as a member of the Lay Renunciate Order.

Lay Renunciate Order   See **renunciate orders**.

leela   "Leela" is Sanskrit for "play", or "sport". In many religious and Spiritual traditions, all of conditionally manifested existence is regarded to be the Leela (or the Play, Sport, or Free Activity) of the Divine Person. "Leela" also means the Awakened Play of a Realized Adept (of any degree), through which he or she mysteriously Instructs and Liberates others and Blesses the world itself. By extension, a Leela is an instructive and inspiring story of such an Adept's Teaching and Blessing Play.

Lesson of life   "The Lesson of life" is Avatar Adi Da's term for the fundamental understanding that Happiness cannot be achieved by means of seeking, because Happiness is <u>inherent</u> in Existence Itself. Avatar Adi Da has summarized this in the aphorism, "You cannot <u>become</u> Happy. You can only <u>be</u> Happy."

Lineage, Avatar Adi Da's   The principal Spiritual Masters who served Avatar Adi Da Samraj during His "Sadhana Years" belong to a single Lineage of extraordinary Yogis, whose Parama-Guru (Supreme Guru) was the Divine "Goddess" (or "Mother-Shakti").

Swami Rudrananda (1928-1973), or Albert Rudolph (known as "Rudi"), was Avatar Adi Da's first human Teacher—from 1964 to 1968, in New York City. Rudi served Avatar Adi Da Samraj in the development of basic practical life-disciplines and the frontal Yoga, which is the process whereby knots and obstructions in the physical and etheric dimensions of the body-mind are penetrated, opened, surrendered, and released through Spiritual reception in the frontal line of the body-mind. Rudi's own Teachers included the Indonesian Pak Subuh (from whom Rudi learned a basic exercise of Spiritual receptivity), Swami Muktananda (with whom Rudi studied for many years), and Bhagavan Nityananda (the Indian Adept-Realizer who was also Swami Muktananda's Guru). Rudi met Bhagavan Nityananda shortly before Bhagavan Nityananda's death, and Rudi always thereafter acknowledged Bhagavan Nityananda as his original and principal Guru.

The second Teacher in Avatar Adi Da's Lineage of Blessing was Swami Muktananda (1908-1982), who was born in Mangalore, South India. Having left home at the age of fifteen, he wandered for many years, seeking the Divine Truth from sources all over India. Eventually, he came under the Spiritual Influence of Bhagavan Nityananda, whom he accepted as his Guru and in whose Spiritual Company he mastered Kundalini Yoga. Swami Muktananda served Avatar Adi Da as Guru during the period from 1968 to 1970. In the summer of 1969, during Avatar Adi Da's second visit to India, Swami Muktananda wrote a letter confirming Avatar Adi Da's attainment of "Yogic Liberation", and acknowledging His right to Teach others. However, from the beginning of their relationship, Swami Muktananda instructed Avatar Adi Da to visit Bhagavan Nityananda's burial site every day (whenever Avatar Adi Da was at Swami Muktananda's Ashram in Ganeshpuri, India) as a means to surrender to Bhagavan Nityananda as the Supreme Guru of the Lineage.

Bhagavan Nityananda, a great Yogi of South India, was Avatar Adi Da's third Guru. Little is known about the circumstances of Bhagavan Nityananda's birth and early life, although it is said that even as a child he showed the signs of a

Realized Yogi. It is also known that he abandoned conventional life as a boy and wandered as a renunciate. Many miracles (including spontaneous healings) and instructive stories are attributed to him. Bhagavan Nityananda surrendered the body on August 8, 1961. Although Avatar Adi Da did not meet Bhagavan Nityananda in the flesh, He enjoyed Bhagavan Nityananda's direct Spiritual Influence from the subtle plane, and He acknowledges Bhagavan Nityananda as a direct and principal Source of Spiritual Instruction during His years with Swami Muktananda. (Avatar Adi Da summarizes the Instruction He received from Bhagavan Nityananda in section XXXII of "I (Alone) Am The Adidam Revelation", an Essay contained in many of the twenty-three "Source-Texts" of Adidam.)

On His third visit to India, while visiting Bhagavan Nityananda's burial shrine, Avatar Adi Da was instructed by Bhagavan Nityananda to relinquish all others as Guru and to surrender directly to the Divine Goddess in Person as Guru. Thus, Bhagavan Nityananda passed Avatar Adi Da to the Divine Goddess Herself, the Parama-Guru (or Source-Guru) of the Lineage that included Bhagavan Nityananda, Swami Muktananda, and Rudi.

The years of Avatar Adi Da's "Sadhana" came to an end in the Great Event of His Divine Re-Awakening, when Avatar Adi Da Husbanded the Divine Goddess (thereby ceasing to relate to Her as His Guru).

Avatar Adi Da's full account of His "Sadhana Years" is Given in *The Knee Of Listening*.

Avatar Adi Da's description of His "Relationship" to the Divine "Goddess" is Given in "I Am The Icon Of Unity", in *He-and-She Is Me*.

listening, hearing, and seeing
"Listening" is Avatar Adi Da's technical term for the orientation, disposition, and beginning practice of the Way of Adidam. A listening devotee listens to Avatar Adi Da Samraj by "considering" His Teaching-Argument and His Leelas, and by practicing feeling-Contemplation of Him (primarily

of His bodily human Form). In the total practice of the Way of Adidam, effective listening to Avatar Adi Da is the necessary prerequisite for true hearing and real seeing.

"Hearing" is a technical term used by Avatar Adi Da to indicate most fundamental understanding of the act of egoity (or self-contraction). Hearing Avatar Adi Da is the unique capability to directly transcend the self-contraction, such that, simultaneous with that transcending, there is the intuitive awakening to Avatar Adi Da's Self-Revelation <u>As</u> the Divine Person and Self-Condition. The capability of true hearing can only be Granted by Avatar Adi Da's Divine Grace, to His fully practicing devotee who has effectively completed the process of listening. Only on the basis of such hearing can Spiritually Awakened practice of the Way of Adidam truly (or with full responsibility) begin.

I Am Heard When My Listening Devotee Has Truly (and Thoroughly) Observed the ego-"I" and Understood it (Directly, In the moments Of self-Observation, and Most Fundamentally, or In its Totality).

I Am Heard When the ego-"I" Is Altogether (and Thoroughly) Observed and (Most Fundamentally) Understood, Both In The Tendency To Dissociate and In The Tendency To Become Attached (or To Cling By Wanting Need, or To Identify With others, and things, and circumstances egoically, and Thus To Dramatize The Seeker, Bereft Of Basic Equanimity, Wholeness, and The Free Capability For Simple Relatedness).

I Am Heard When the ego-"I" Is Thoroughly (and Most Fundamentally) Understood To Be Contraction-Only, An Un-Necessary and Destructive Motive and Design, Un-Naturally and Chronically Added To Cosmic Nature and To all relations, and An Imaginary Heart-Disease (Made To Seem Real, By Heart-Reaction).

I Am Heard When This Most Fundamental Understanding Of The Habit Of "Narcissus" Becomes The Directly Obvious Realization Of The Heart, Radiating Beyond Its Own (Apparent) Contraction.

I Am Heard When The Beginning Is Full, and The Beginning Is Full (and Ended) When Every Gesture Of self-Contraction (In The Context Of The First Three Stages Of Life, and Relative To Each and All Of The Principal Faculties, Of body, emotion, mind, and breath) Is (As A Rather Consistently Applied and humanly Effective Discipline) Observed (By Natural feeling-perception), Tacitly (and Most Fundamentally) Understood, and Really (Directly and Effectively) Felt Beyond (In The Prior Feeling Of Unqualified Relatedness). [Santosha Adidam]

When, in the practice of the Way of Adidam, hearing (or most fundamental self-understanding) is steadily exercised in meditation and in life, the native feeling of the heart ceases to be chronically constricted by self-contraction. The heart then begins to Radiate as love in response to the Divine Spiritual Presence of Avatar Adi Da.

This emotional and Spiritual response of the whole being is what Avatar Adi Da calls "seeing". Seeing Avatar Adi Da is emotional conversion from the reactive emotions that characterize egoic self-obsession, to the open-hearted, Radiant Happiness that characterizes Spiritual devotion to Avatar Adi Da. This true and stable emotional conversion coincides with true and stable receptivity to Avatar Adi Da's Spiritual Transmission, and both of these are prerequisites to further Spiritual advancement in the Way of Adidam.

Seeing Is ego-Transcending Participation In <u>What</u> (and <u>Who</u>) <u>Is</u>. Seeing Is Love. Seeing (or Love) Is Able (By Means Of My Avatarically Self-Transmitted Divine Grace) To "Locate", Devotionally Recognize, and Feel My Avatarically Self-Transmitted (and all-and-All-Pervading) Spiritual Radiance (and My Avatarically Self-Transmitted Spirit-Identity, <u>As</u> The "Bright" and Only One <u>Who</u> <u>Is</u>). . . . Seeing Is The "Radical" (or Directly ego-Transcending) Reorientation Of conditional Existence To My Avatarically Self-Revealed (Transcendental, Inherently Spiritual, Inherently Perfect, and Self-

Evidently Divine) Self-Condition, In Whom conditional self and conditional worlds Apparently arise and Always Already Inhere. . . .

Seeing Me Is Simply Attraction To Me (and Feeling Me) As My Avatarically Self-Revealed Spiritual (and Always Blessing) Divine Presence—and This Most Fundamentally, At The Root, Core, Source, or Origin Of The "Emergence" Of My Avatarically Self-Revealed Divine Spiritual Presence "here", At (and In Front Of) The Heart, or At (and In) The Root-Context Of the body-mind, or At (and In) The Source-Position (and, Ultimately, As The Source-Condition) Of conditional (or psycho-physical) Existence Itself.

Seeing Me Is Knowing Me As My Avatarically Self-Revealed Spiritual (and Always Blessing) Divine Presence, Just As Tangibly (and With The Same Degree Of Clarity) As You Would Differentiate The Physical Appearance Of My Bodily (Human) Form From the physical appearance of the bodily (human) form of any other.

To See Me Is A Clear and "Radical" Knowledge Of Me, About Which There Is No Doubt. To See Me Is A Sudden, Tacit Awareness—Like Walking Into a "thicker" air or atmosphere, or Suddenly Feeling a breeze, or Jumping Into water and Noticing The Difference In Density Between the air and the water. This Tangible Feeling Of Me Is (In any particular moment) Not Necessarily (Otherwise) Associated With effects in the body-mind . . . but It Is, Nevertheless, Felt At The Heart and Even All Over the body.

Seeing Me Is One-Pointedness In The "Radical" Conscious Process Of Heart-Devotion To Me. [Santosha Adidam]

"Living Murti" Avatar Adi Da will always be Divinely Present in the Cosmic domain, even after His physical Lifetime. He is the One Who is (and will always be) worshiped in the Way of Adidam, and (therefore) He is (and will always be) the Eternally Living Murti for His devotees. However, Avatar Adi Da has said that, after His physical (human) Lifetime, there should always be one (and only one) "Living Murti" as a Living Link

between Him and His devotees. Each successive "Living Murti" (or "Murti-Guru") is to be selected from among those members of the Ruchira Sannyasin Order (see **renunciate orders**) who have been formally acknowledged as Divinely Enlightened devotees of Avatar Adi Da Samraj in the seventh stage of life. "Living Murtis" will not function as the independent Gurus of practitioners of the Way of Adidam. Rather, they will simply be "Representations" of Avatar Adi Da's bodily (human) Divine Form, and a means to Commune with Him.

Avatar Adi Da's full discussion of His "Living Murtis", and how they are to be chosen, is Given in Part Three, section XII, of *The Lion Sutra*.

"Locate" To "Locate" Avatar Adi Da is to "Truly Heart-Find" Him.

Love-Ananda The Name "Love-Ananda" combines both English ("Love") and Sanskrit ("Ananda", meaning "Bliss"), thus bridging the West and the East, and communicating Avatar Adi Da's Function as the Divine World-Teacher. The combination of "Love" and "Ananda" means "the Divine Love-Bliss". The Name "Love-Ananda" was given to Avatar Adi Da by Swami Muktananda, who spontaneously conferred it upon Avatar Adi Da in 1969. However, Avatar Adi Da did not use the Name "Love-Ananda" until April 1986, after the Great Event that Initiated His Divine Self-"Emergence".

Love-Ananda Avatar As the Love-Ananda Avatar, Avatar Adi Da is the Very Incarnation of the Divine Love-Bliss.

M

Maha-Siddha The Sanskrit word "Siddha" means "a completed, fulfilled, or perfected one", or "one of perfect accomplishment, or power". "Maha-Siddha" means "Great Siddha".

Mandala The Sanskrit word "mandala" (literally, "circle") is commonly used in the esoteric Spiritual traditions to describe the entire pattern of the hierarchical levels of cosmic existence. Avatar Adi Da also uses the word "Mandala" to refer to the Circle (or Sphere) of His Heart-Transmission, or as a formal reference to a group of His devotees who perform specific functions of direct service to Him.

mantra See **Name-Invocation**.

meditation In the Way of Adidam, meditation is a period of formal devotional Contemplation of Avatar Adi Da Samraj. Meditation is one of the life-disciplines that Avatar Adi Da Samraj has Given to His devotees in the first and second congregations, as a fundamental support for their practice of Ruchira Avatara Bhakti Yoga. For those who have fully adapted to the disciplines of the first and second congregations, the daily practice of meditation includes a period of one and one-half hours in the morning and a period of one hour in the evening. Such daily practice is increased during periods of retreat. Members of the third and fourth congregations are also encouraged (but not required) to engage formal meditation.

missing the mark "Hamartia" (the word in New Testament Greek that was translated into English as "sin") was originally an archery term meaning "missing the mark".

Most Perfect / Most Ultimate Avatar Adi Da uses the phrase "Most Perfect(ly)" in the sense of "Absolutely Perfect(ly)". Similarly, the phrase "Most Ultimate(ly)" is equivalent to "Absolutely Ultimate(ly)". "Most Perfect(ly)" and "Most Ultimate(ly)" are always references to the seventh (or Divinely Enlightened) stage of life. Perfect(ly) and Ultimate(ly) refer to the sixth stage of life or to the sixth and seventh stages of life together. (See also **stages of life**.)

mudra A "mudra" is a gesture of the hands, face, or body that outwardly expresses a state of ecstasy. Avatar Adi Da sometimes spontaneously exhibits Mudras as Signs of His Blessing and Purifying Work with His devotees and the world. He also uses the term "Mudra" to express the Attitude of His Blessing-Work, which is His Constant (or Eternal) Giving (or

Submitting) of Himself to Be the Means of Divine Liberation for all beings.

Muktananda, Swami See **Lineage, Avatar Adi Da's**.

mummery / The Mummery The dictionary defines mummery as "a ridiculous, hypocritical, or pretentious ceremony or performance". Avatar Adi Da uses this word to describe all the activities of ego-bound beings, or beings who are committed to the false view of separation and separativeness.

The Mummery is one of Avatar Adi Da's twenty-three "Source-Texts". It is a work of astonishing poetry and deeply evocative archetypes. Through the heart-breaking story of Raymond Darling's growth to manhood, his search to find, and then to be reunited with, his beloved (Quandra), and his utter self-transcendence of all conditional circumstances and events, Avatar Adi Da Tells His own Life-Story in the language of parable, and describes in devastating detail how the unconverted ego makes religion (and life altogether) into a meaningless mummery.

Murti "Murti" is Sanskrit for "form", and, by extension, a "representational image" of the Divine or of a Guru. In the Way of Adidam, Murtis of Avatar Adi Da are most commonly photographs of Avatar Adi Da's bodily (human) Divine Form.

"Murti-Guru" See **"Living Murti"**.

Mystery Avatar Adi Da uses the term "the Mystery" to point out that, although we can name things, we actually do not know what anything really _is_:

It is a great and more-than-wonderful Mystery to everyone that anything _is_, or that we _are_. And whether somebody says "I don't know how anything came to be" or "God made everything", they are simply pointing to the feeling of the Mystery—of how everything _is_, but nobody knows what it really _Is_, or how it came to be. [What, Where, When, How, Why, and _Who_ To Remember To Be Happy]

N

Name-Invocation Sacred sounds or syllables and Names have been used since antiquity for invoking and worshipping the Divine Person and the Sat-Guru. In the Hindu tradition, the original mantras were cosmic sound-forms and "seed" letters used for worship and prayer of, and incantatory meditation on, the Revealed Form of the Divine Person.

Practitioners of the Way of Adidam may, at any time, Remember or Invoke Avatar Adi Da Samraj (or feel, and thereby Contemplate, His Avatarically Self-Revealed Divine Form, and Presence, and State) through simple feeling-Remembrance of Him and by randomly (in daily life and meditation) Invoking Him via His Principal Name, "Da", or via one (and only one) of the other Names He has Given for the practice of Simple Name-Invocation of Him. (The specific forms of His Names that Avatar Adi Da has Given to be engaged in practice of simple Name-Invocation of Him are listed in chapter three of *The Dawn Horse Testament Of The Ruchira Avatar*.)

For devotees of Avatar Adi Da Samraj, His Names are the Names of the Very Divine Being. As such, these Names, as Avatar Adi Da Himself has described, "do not simply <u>mean</u> Real God, or the Blessing of Real God. They are the verbal or audible Form of the Divine." Therefore, Invoking Avatar Adi Da Samraj by Name is a potent and Divinely Empowered form of feeling-Contemplation of Him.

Narcissus In Avatar Adi Da's Teaching-Revelation, "Narcissus" is a key symbol of the un-Enlightened individual as a self-obsessed seeker, enamored of his or her own self-image and egoic self-consciousness. In *The Knee Of Listening*, Adi Da Samraj describes the significance of the archetype of Narcissus:

He is the ancient one visible in the Greek "myth", who was the universally adored child of the gods, who rejected the loved-one and every form of love and relationship, who was finally condemned to the contemplation of his own image, until,

as a result of his own act and obstinacy, he suffered the fate of eternal separateness and died in infinite solitude.

Nirguna "Nirguna" is Sanskrit for "without attributes or quality".

Nirvikalpa Samadhi See **Samadhi**.

Nityananda See **Lineage, Avatar Adi Da's**.

Non-Separate Self-Domain The "Non-Separate Self-Domain" is a synonym for "Divine Self-Domain". (See **Divine Self-Domain**.)

O

"Oedipal" In modern psychology, the "Oedipus complex" is named after the legendary Greek Oedipus, who was fated to unknowingly kill his father and marry his mother. Avatar Adi Da Teaches that the primary dynamisms of emotional-sexual desiring, rejection, envy, betrayal, self-pleasuring, resentment, and other primal emotions and impulses are indeed patterned upon unconscious reactions first formed early in life, in relation to one's mother and father. Avatar Adi Da calls this "the 'Oedipal' drama" and points out that we relate to all women as we do to our mothers, and to all men as we do to our fathers, and that we relate, and react, to our own bodies as we do to the parent of the opposite sex. Thus, we impose infantile reactions to our parents on our relationships with lovers and all other beings, according to their sex, and we also superimpose the same on our relationship to our own bodies. (Avatar Adi Da's extended Instruction on "Oedipal" patterning is Given in *Ruchira Avatara Hridaya-Tantra Yoga*.)

Omega See **Alpha and Omega**.

"Open Eyes" "Open Eyes" is Avatar Adi Da's technical synonym for the Realization of seventh stage Sahaj Samadhi, or unqualified Divine Self-Realization. The phrase graphically describes the non-exclusive, non-inward, Native State of the Divine Self-Realizer, Who is Identified

Unconditionally with the Divine Self-Reality, while also allowing whatever arises to appear in the Divine Consciousness (and spontaneously Divinely Self-Recognizing everything that arises as a modification of the Divine Consciousness). The Transcendental Self is intuited in the mature phases of the sixth stage of life, but It can be Realized at that stage only by the intentional exclusion of conditional phenomena. In "Open Eyes", that impulse to exclusion disappears, when the Eyes of the Heart Open, and Most Perfect Realization of the Spiritual, Transcendental, and Divine Self in the seventh stage of life becomes permanent (and incorruptible by any phenomenal events).

"original" context of the fourth stage of life See **stages of life**.

Outshined / Outshining Avatar Adi Da uses "Outshined" or "Outshining" as a synonym for "Divine Translation", to refer to the final Demonstration of the four-phase process of the seventh (or Divinely Enlightened) stage of life in the Way of Adidam. In the Great Event of Outshining (or Divine Translation), body, mind, and world are no longer noticed—not because the Divine Consciousness has withdrawn or dissociated from conditionally manifested phenomena, but because the Divine Self-Recognition of all arising phenomena as modifications of the Divine Self-Condition has become so intense that the "Bright" Radiance of Consciousness now Outshines all such phenomena. (See also **four phases of the seventh stage of life**.)

P, Q

"Perfect Practice" The "Perfect Practice" is Avatar Adi Da's technical term for the discipline of the ultimate stages of life (the sixth stage of life and the seventh stage of life) in the Way of Adidam. The "Perfect Practice" is practice in the Domain of Consciousness Itself (as opposed to practice from the point of view of the body or the mind). (See also **stages of life**.)

Perfectly Subjective Avatar Adi Da uses "Perfectly Subjective" to describe the True Divine Source, or "Subject", of the conditionally manifested world—as opposed to regarding the Divine as some sort of conditional "object" or "other". Thus, in the phrase "Perfectly Subjective", the word "Subjective" does not have the sense of "relating to the inward experience of an individual", but, rather, it has the sense of "Being Consciousness Itself, the True Subject of all apparent experience".

Pilgrimage and Retreat Sanctuaries See **Sanctuaries**.

Pleasure Dome Avatar Adi Da Samraj Speaks of the Way of Adidam as a "Pleasure Dome", recalling the poem "Kubla Khan", by Samuel Taylor Coleridge ("In Xanadu did Kubla Khan / A stately pleasure-dome decree . . ."). Adi Da Samraj points out that in many religious traditions it is presumed that one must embrace suffering in order to earn future happiness and pleasure. However, by Calling His devotees to live the Way of Adidam as a Pleasure Dome, Avatar Adi Da Samraj Communicates His Teaching that the Way of heart-Communion with Him is always about present-time Happiness, not about any kind of search to attain Happiness in the future. Thus, in the Way of Adidam, there is no idealization of suffering and pain as presumed means to attain future happiness—and, consequently, there is no denial of the appropriate enjoyment of even the ordinary pleasures of human life.

Avatar Adi Da also uses "Pleasure Dome" as a reference to the Ultimate and Divine Love-Bliss-Happiness That Is His own Self-Nature and His Gift to all who respond to Him.

"Practice" As the quotation marks around the capitalized word "Practice" suggest, the psycho-physical expression of the process of Divine Enlightenment is a "Practice" only in the sense that it is simple action. It is not, in contrast to the stages of life previous to the seventh, a discipline intended to counter egoic tendencies that would otherwise dominate body and mind.

Avatar Adi Da uses quotation marks in a characteristic manner throughout His Written Word to Indicate that a particular word is a technical term, to be understood in the unique and precise language of the Way of Adidam, carrying the implication "as per definition". However, in other cases, His quotation marks carry the implication "so to speak", as in the case of the term "Practice" and are, therefore, not to be understood as precise technical terminology of the Way of Adidam.

prana/pranic   The Sanskrit word "prana" means "life-energy". It generally refers to the life-energy animating all beings and pervading everything in cosmic Nature. In the human body-mind, circulation of this universal life-energy is associated with the heartbeat and the cycles of the breath. In esoteric Yogic Teachings, prana is also a specific technical name for one of a number of forms of etheric energy that functionally sustain the bodily being.

Prana is not to be equated with the Divine Spirit-Current, or the Spiritual (and Always Blessing) Divine Presence of Avatar Adi Da Samraj. The finite pranic energies that sustain individual beings are only conditional, localized, and temporary phenomena of the realm of cosmic Nature. Even in the form of universal life-force, prana is but a conditional modification of the Divine Spirit-Current Revealed by Avatar Adi Da, Which Is the "Bright" (or Consciousness Itself), beyond all cosmic forms.

R

"radical"   The term "radical" derives from the Latin "radix", meaning "root", and, thus, it principally means "irreducible", "fundamental", or "relating to the origin". In *The Dawn Horse Testament Of The Ruchira Avatar*, Avatar Adi Da defines "Radical" as "Gone To The Root, Core, Source, or Origin". Because Adi Da Samraj uses "radical" in this literal sense, it appears in quotation marks in His Wisdom-Teaching, in order to distinguish His usage from the common reference to an extreme (often political) view.

Ramakrishna   See **Lineage, Avatar Adi Da's**.

Ramana Maharshi   A great sixth stage Indian Spiritual Master, Ramana Maharshi (1879-1950) became Self-Realized at a young age and gradually assumed a Teaching role as increasing numbers of people approached him for Spiritual guidance. Ramana Maharshi's Teaching focused on the process of introversion (through the question "Who am I?"), which culminates in conditional Self-Realization (or Jnana Samadhi), exclusive of phenomena. He established his Ashram at Tiruvannamalai in South India, which continues today.

Rang Avadhoot   Rang Avadhoot (1898-1968) was a Realizer in the tradition of Dattatreya. In *The Knee Of Listening*, Avatar Adi Da describes the brief but highly significant meeting that occurred between Himself and Rang Avadhoot in 1968.

Real God   Avatar Adi Da uses the term "Real God" to Indicate the True and Perfectly Subjective Source of all conditions, the True and Spiritual Divine Person (Which can be directly Realized), rather than any ego-made (and, thus, false, or limited) presumptions about God.

Re-cognition   "Re-cognition", which literally means "knowing again", is Avatar Adi Da's term for "the tacit transcending of the habit of 'Narcissus'". It is the mature form into which verbal self-Enquiry evolves in the Devotional Way of Insight. The individual simply notices and tacitly "knows again" (or directly understands) whatever is arising as yet another species of self-contraction, and he or she transcends (or feels beyond) it in Satsang with Avatar Adi Da.

renunciate orders   Avatar Adi Da has established two formal renunciate orders: The Ruchira Sannyasin Order of the Tantric Renunciates of Adidam (or, simply, the Ruchira Sannyasin Order), and the Lay Renunciate Order of Adidam (or, simply, the Lay Renunciate Order).

The senior practicing order in the Way

of Adidam is the Ruchira Sannyasin Order. This order is the senior cultural authority within the formal gathering of Avatar Adi Da's devotees. "Sannyasin" is an ancient Sanskrit term for one who has renounced all worldly bonds and who gives himself or herself completely to the Real-God-Realizing or Real-God-Realized life. Members of the Ruchira Sannyasin Order are uniquely exemplary practitioners of the Way of Adidam who are (generally) practicing in the context of the ultimate (sixth and seventh) stages of life. Members of this Order are legal renunciates and live a life of perpetual retreat. As a general rule, they are to reside at Adidam Samrajashram. The Ruchira Sannyasin Order comprises the first congregation of Avatar Adi Da's devotees.

The members of the Ruchira Sannyasin Order have a uniquely significant role among the practitioners of Adidam as Avatar Adi Da's human Instruments and (in the case of those members who are formally acknowledged as Avatar Adi Da's fully Awakened seventh stage devotees) as the body of practitioners from among whom each of Avatar Adi Da's successive "Living Murtis" (or Empowered human Agents) will be selected. Therefore, the Ruchira Sannyasin Order is essential to the perpetual continuation of authentic practice of the Way of Adidam.

The Founding Member of the Ruchira Sannyasin Order Avatar Adi Da Himself.

In "The Orders of My True and Free Renunciate Devotees" (in *The Lion Sutra*), Avatar Adi Da describes the Lay Renunciate Order as "a renunciate service order for all intensively serving (and, altogether, intensively practicing) lay practitioners of the total (or full and complete) practice of the Way of Adidam".

All present members, and all future members, of the Lay Renunciate Order must (necessarily) be formally acknowledged, formally practicing, significantly matured (tested and proven), and, altogether, especially exemplary practitioners of the total (or full and complete) practice of the Way of Adidam. They must perform significant cultural (and practical, and, as necessary, managerial) service within the gathering of all formally acknowledged practitioners of the four congregations of the Way of Adidam. Either they must live within a formally designated community of formally acknowledged practitioners of the Way of Adidam or, otherwise, they must be formally designated serving residents of one of the by Me formally Empowered Ruchira Sannyasin Hermitage-Retreat Sanctuaries or one of the by Me formally Empowered Pilgrimage and Retreat Sanctuaries for all formally acknowledged practitioners of the Way of Adidam. And they must formally accept (and rightly fulfill) all the obligations and disciplines associated with membership within the Lay Renunciate Order. ["The Orders of My True and Free Renunciate Devotees"]

right side of the heart See **heart, stations of the heart.**

Ruchira Avatar In Sanskrit, "Ruchira" means "bright, radiant, effulgent". Thus, the Reference "Ruchira Avatar" indicates that Avatar Adi Da Samraj is the "Bright" (or Radiant) Descent of the Divine Reality Itself into the conditionally manifested worlds, Appearing here in His bodily (human) Form.

Ruchira Avatara Bhakti Yoga Ruchira Avatara Bhakti Yoga is the principal Gift, Calling, and Discipline Offered by Adi Da Samraj to all who practice the Way of Adidam (in all four congregations).

The phrase "Ruchira Avatara Bhakti Yoga" is itself a summary of the Way of Adidam. "Bhakti", in Sanskrit, is love, adoration, or devotion, while "Yoga" is a Real-God-Realizing discipline (or practice). "Ruchira Avatara Bhakti Yoga" is, thus, "the Divinely Revealed practice of devotional love for (and devotional response to) the Ruchira Avatar, Adi Da Samraj".

The technical practice of Ruchira Avatara Bhakti Yoga is a four-part process of Invoking, feeling, breathing, and serving Avatar Adi Da in every moment.

For Avatar Adi Da's essential Instruction in Ruchira Avatara Bhakti Yoga, see the *Da Love-Ananda Gita (The Free Gift Of The Divine Love-Bliss)*, Part Five, verse 25, and Part Six; *Hridaya Rosary*

(*Four Thorns Of Heart-Instruction*), Parts Four and Five; and *What, Where, When, How, Why and <u>Who</u> To Remember To Be Happy*, Part Three, "Surrender the Faculties of the Body-Mind To Me" and "How to Practice Whole Bodily Devotion To Me".

Ruchira Avatara Satsang   The Hindi word "Satsang" literally means "true (or right) relationship", "the company of Truth". "Ruchira Avatara Satsang" is the eternal relationship of mutual sacred commitment between Avatar Adi Da Samraj and each true and formally acknowledged practitioner of the Way of Adidam. Once it is consciously assumed by any practitioner, Ruchira Avatara Satsang is an all-inclusive Condition, bringing Divine Grace and Blessings and sacred obligations, responsibilities, and tests into every dimension of the practitioner's life and consciousness.

The Ruchira Buddha   The Enlightened One Who Shines with the Divine "Brightness".

The Ruchira Buddha-Avatar   The "Bright" Enlightened One Who is the Incarnation of the Divine Person. (See also **Avatar**.)

Ruchira Buddhism   "Ruchira Buddhism" is the Way of devotion to the Ruchira Buddha—"the 'Bright' Buddha", Avatar Adi Da Samraj (or, more fully, "the Radiant, Shining, 'Bright' Illuminator and Enlightener Who Is Inherently, or Perfectly Subjectively, Self-Enlightened, and Eternally Awake").

Ruchira Samadhi   "Ruchira Samadhi" (Sanskrit for "the Samadhi of the 'Bright'") is one of the references that Avatar Adi Da Samraj uses for the Divinely Enlightened Condition Realized in the seventh stage of life, Which He characterizes as the Unconditional Realization of the Divine "Brightness".

Ruchira Sannyasin Order   See **renunciate orders**, and see also p. 366.

Rudi / Swami Rudrananda   See **Lineage, Avatar Adi Da's.**

S

"Sadhana Years"   In Sanskrit, "Sadhana" means "self-transcending religious or Spiritual practice". Avatar Adi Da's "Sadhana Years" refers to the time from which He began His quest to recover the Truth of Existence (at Columbia College) until His Divine Re-Awakening in 1970. Avatar Adi Da's full description of His "Sadhana Years" is Given in *The Knee Of Listening*.

Saguna   "Saguna" is Sanskrit for "containing (or accompanied by) qualities".

Sahaj   "Sahaj" is Hindi (from Sanskrit "sahaja") for "twin-born", "natural", or "innate". Avatar Adi Da uses the term to indicate the Coincidence (in the case of Divine Self-Realization) of the Inherently Spiritual and Transcendental Divine Reality with conditional reality. Sahaj, therefore, is the Inherent (or Native) and, thus, truly "Natural" State of Being. (See also **Samadhi**.)

Sahaj Samadhi   See **Samadhi**.

sahasrar   In the traditional system of seven chakras, the sahasrar is the highest chakra (or subtle energy center), associated with the crown of the head and beyond. It is described as a thousand-petaled lotus, the terminal of Light to which the Yogic process (of Spiritual ascent through the chakras) aspires.

During His "Sadhana Years", Avatar Adi Da spontaneously experienced what He calls the "severing of the sahasrar". The Spirit-Energy no longer ascended into the crown of the head (and beyond), but rather "fell" into the Heart, and rested as the Witness-Consciousness. It was this experience that directly revealed to Avatar Adi Da that, while the Yogic traditions regard the sahasrar as the seat of Enlightenment, the Heart is truly the Seat of Divine Consciousness.

Avatar Adi Da's account of the severing of the sahasrar in His own Case is Given in chapter eighteen of *The Knee Of Listening*.

Saiva Siddhanta "Saiva Siddhanta" is the name of an important school of Saivism which flourished in South India and survives into the present.

Samadhi The Sanskrit word "Samadhi" traditionally denotes various exalted states that appear in the context of esoteric meditation and Realization. Avatar Adi Da Teaches that, for His devotees, Samadhi is, even more simply and fundamentally, the Enjoyment of His Divine State, Which is experienced (even from the beginning of the practice of Adidam) through ego-transcending heart-Communion with Him. Therefore, "the cultivation of Samadhi" is another way to describe the fundamental basis of the Way of Adidam. Avatar Adi Da's devotee is in Samadhi in any moment of standing beyond the separate self in true devotional heart-Communion with Him. (See "The Cultivation of My Divine Samadhi", in *The Seven Stages Of Life*.)

The developmental process leading to Divine Enlightenment in the Way of Adidam may be marked by many signs, principal among which are the Samadhis of the advanced and the ultimate stages of life and practice. Although some of the traditionally known Samadhis of the fourth, the fifth, and the sixth stages of life may appear in the course of an individual's practice of the Way of Adidam, the appearance of all of them is by no means necessary, or even probable (as Avatar Adi Da Indicates in His Wisdom-Teaching). The essential Samadhis of the Way of Adidam are those that are uniquely Granted by Avatar Adi Da Samraj—the Samadhi of the "Thumbs" and seventh stage Sahaj Samadhi. All the possible forms of Samadhi in the Way of Adidam are described in full detail in *The Dawn Horse Testament Of The Ruchira Avatar*.

Samadhi of the "Thumbs"

"The 'Thumbs'" is Avatar Adi Da's technical term for the invasion of the body-mind by a particular kind of forceful Descent of His Divine Spirit-Current. Avatar Adi Da describes His own experience of the "Thumbs" in *The Knee Of Listening*:

. . . I had an experience that appeared like a mass of gigantic thumbs coming down from above, pressing into my throat (causing something of a gagging, and somewhat suffocating, sensation), and then pressing further (and, it seemed, would have expanded without limitation or end), into some form of myself that was much larger than my physical body. . . .

The "Thumbs" were not visible in the ordinary sense. I did not see them then or even as a child. They were not visible to me with my eyes, nor did I hallucinate them pictorially. Yet, I very consciously experienced and felt them as having a peculiar form and mobility, as I likewise experienced my own otherwise invisible and greater form.

I did not at that time or at any time in my childhood fully allow this intervention of the "Thumbs" to take place. I held it off from its fullest descent, in fear of being overwhelmed, for I did not understand at all what was taking place. However, in later years this same experience occurred naturally during meditation. Because my meditation had been allowed to progress gradually, and the realizations at each level were thus perceived without shock, I was able at those times to allow the experience to take place. When I did, the "Thumbs" completely entered my living form. They appeared like tongues, or parts of a Force, coming from above. And when they had entered deep into my body, the magnetic or energic balances of my living being reversed. On several occasions I felt as if the body had risen above the ground somewhat, and this is perhaps the basis for certain evidence in mystical literature of the phenomenon of levitation, or bodily transport.

At any rate, during those stages in meditation the body ceased to be polarized toward the ground, or the gravitational direction of the earth's center. There was a strong reversal of polarity, communicated along a line of Force analogous to the spine. The physical body, as well as the Energy-form that could be interiorly felt as analogous to but detached from the physical body, was felt to turn in a curve along the spine and forward in the direction of the heart. When this reversal of Energy was allowed to take place completely, I resided in a totally different body, which also contained the physical body. It was spherical in shape. And the sensation of dwelling as that form was completely peaceful. The physical body was completely relaxed and polarized to the shape of this other spherical body. The mind became quieted, and then there was a movement in consciousness that would go even deeper, into a higher conscious State beyond physical and mental awareness. I was to learn that this spherical body was what Yogis and occultists call the "subtle" body (which includes the "pranic", or natural life-energy, dimension and the "astral", or the lower mental and the higher mental, dimensions of the living being).

In the fullest form of this experience, which Avatar Adi Da calls "the Samadhi of the 'Thumbs'", His Spirit-Invasion Descends all the way to the bottom of the frontal line of the body-mind (at the bodily base) and ascends through the spinal line, overwhelming the ordinary human sense of bodily existence, infusing the whole being with intense blissfulness, and releasing the ordinary, confined sense of body, mind, and separate self.

Both the experience of the "Thumbs" and the full Samadhi of the "Thumbs" are unique to the Way of Adidam, for they are specifically signs of the "Crashing Down" (or the Divine Descent) of Avatar Adi Da's Spirit-Baptism, into the body-minds of His devotees. The Samadhi of the "Thumbs" is a kind of "Nirvikalpa" (or formless) Samadhi—but in descent in the frontal line, rather than in ascent in the spinal line.

Avatar Adi Da's extended Instruction relative to the "Thumbs" is Given in "The 'Thumbs' Is The Fundamental Sign Of The Crashing Down Of My Person". This Essay appears in a number of Avatar Adi Da's "Source-Texts" (*Hridaya Rosary, The Only Complete Way To Realize The Unbroken Light Of Real God, Ruchira Avatara Hridaya-Siddha Yoga, The Seven Stages Of Life*, and *Santosha Adidam*, as well as chapter twenty-four of *The Dawn Horse Testament Of The Ruchira Avatar* and chapter thirty-one of *The Heart Of The Dawn Horse Testament Of The Ruchira Avatar*).

Savikalpa Samadhi and "Cosmic Consciousness" The Sanskrit term "Savikalpa Samadhi" literally means "meditative ecstasy with form", or "deep meditative concentration (or absorption) in which form (or defined experiential content) is still perceived". Avatar Adi Da indicates that there are two basic forms of Savikalpa Samadhi. The first is the various experiences produced by the Spiritual ascent of energy and attention (into mystical phenomena, visions, and other subtle sensory perceptions of subtle psychic forms) and the various states of Yogic Bliss (or Spirit-"Intoxication").

The second (and highest) form of Savikalpa Samadhi is called "Cosmic Consciousness", or the "'Vision' of Cosmic Unity". This is an isolated or periodic occurrence in which attention ascends, uncharacteristically and spontaneously, to a state of awareness wherein conditional existence is perceived as a Unity in Divine Awareness. This conditional form of "Cosmic Consciousness" is pursued in many mystical and Yogic paths. It depends upon manipulation of attention and the body-mind, and it is interpreted from the point of view of the separate, body-based or mind-based self—and, therefore, it is not equivalent to Divine Enlightenment.

Avatar Adi Da's discussion of Savikalpa Samadhi is found in "Vision, Audition, and Touch in The Process of Ascending Meditation in The Way Of Adidam", in Part Four of *Ruchira Avatara Hridaya-Siddha Yoga.*

Avatar Adi Da's description of the varieties of experiential form possible in Savikalpa Samadhi is found in "The Significant Experiential Signs That May Appear in the Course of The Way Of Adidam", in Part Three of *What, Where, When, How, Why, and Who To Remember To Be Happy.*

fifth stage Nirvikalpa Samadhi The Sanskrit term "Nirvikalpa Samadhi" literally means "meditative ecstasy without form", or "deep meditative concentration (or absorption) in which there is no perception of form (or defined experiential content)". Traditionally, this state is regarded to be the final goal of the many schools of Yogic ascent whose orientation to practice is that of the fifth stage of life. Like "Cosmic Consciousness", fifth stage conditional Nirvikalpa Samadhi is an isolated or periodic Realization. In it, attention ascends beyond all conditional manifestation into the formless Matrix of Divine Vibration and Divine Light Infinitely Above the world, the body, and the mind. And, like the various forms of Savikalpa Samadhi, fifth stage conditional Nirvikalpa Samadhi is a temporary state of attention (or, more precisely, of the suspension of attention). It is produced by manipulation of attention and of the body-mind, and is (therefore) incapable of being maintained when attention returns (as it inevitably does) to the states of the body-mind.

Avatar Adi Da's Instruction relative to fifth stage conditional Nirvikalpa Samadhi is Given in chapter forty-two of *The Dawn Horse Testament Of The Ruchira Avatar*.

Jnana Samadhi, or Jnana Nirvikalpa Samadhi

"Jnana" means "knowledge". Jnana Nirvikalpa Samadhi (sixth stage Nirvakalpa Samadhi, or, simply, Jnana Samadhi) is the characteristic meditative experience in the sixth stage of life in the Way of Adidam. Produced by the intentional withdrawal of attention from the conditional body-mind-self and its relations, Jnana Samadhi is the conditional, temporary Realization of the Transcendental Self (or Consciousness Itself), exclusive of any perception (or cognition) of world, objects, relations, body, mind, or separate-self-sense—and, thereby, formless (or "nirvikalpa").

Avatar Adi Da's Instruction relative to Jnana Nirvikalpa Samadhi is Given in "The Sixth and The Seventh Stages of Life in The Way Of Adidam" in *The Lion Sutra*.

seventh stage Sahaj Samadhi, or seventh stage Sahaja Nirvikalpa Samadhi

Avatar Adi Da's description of seventh stage Sahaj Samadhi is Given in Part Four of *The All-Completing* and *Final Divine Revelation To Mankind*.

Samraj "Samraj" (from the Sanskrit "Samraja") is a traditional Indian term used to refer to great kings, but also to refer to the Hindu gods. "Samraja" is defined as "universal or supreme ruler", "paramount Lord", or "paramount sovereign".

The Sanskrit word "raja" (the basic root of "Samraj") means "king". It comes from the verbal root "raj", meaning "to reign, to rule, to illuminate". The prefix "sam-" expresses "union" or "completeness". "Samraj" is thus literally the complete ruler, the ruler of everything altogether. "Samraj" was traditionally given as a title to a king who was regarded to be a "universal monarch".

Avatar Adi Da's Name "Adi Da Samraj" expresses that He is the Primordial (or Original) Giver, Who Blesses all as the Universal Lord of every thing, every where, for all time. The Sovereignty of His Kingdom has nothing to do with the world of human politics. Rather, it is entirely a matter of His Spiritual Dominion over all and All, His Kingship in the hearts of His devotees.

samsara / samsaric "Samsara" (or "samsaric") is a classical Buddhist and Hindu term for all conditional worlds and states, or the cyclical realm of birth and change and death. It connotes the suffering and limitations experienced in those limited worlds.

Sanctuaries Avatar Adi Da has Empowered two Hermitage-Retreat Sanctuaries and two Pilgrimage and Retreat Sanctuaries as Agents of His Divine Spiritual Transmission. The senior Hermitage-Retreat Sanctuary is Adidam Samrajashram, the Island of Naitauba in Fiji, where Avatar Adi Da usually Resides in Perpetual Retreat. It is the place where Avatar Adi Da Himself and the senior renunciate order of the Way of Adidam, the Ruchira Sannyasin Order of the Tantric Renunciates of Adidam, are established. It is the primary Seat of Avatar Adi Da's Divine Blessing Work with the entire Cosmic Mandala.

Avatar Adi Da has Spoken of the significance of this Hermitage Ashram:

AVATAR ADI DA SAMRAJ: Adidam Samrajashram was established so that I might have a Place of Seclusion in which to do My Spiritual Work. This is the Place of My perpetual Samadhi, the Place of My perpetual Self-Radiance. Therefore, this is the Place where people come to participate in My Samadhi and be further Awakened by It. My devotees come to Adidam Samrajashram to magnify their practice of right, true, and full devotion to Me, to practice the Way of Adidam as I Have Revealed and Given It for the sake of most perfectly ego-transcending Real-God-Realization.

Tat Sundaram is a small Hermitage-Retreat Sanctuary that provides a private circumstance for Avatar Adi Da and members of the Ruchira Sannyasin Order.

The two Pilgrimage and Retreat Sanctuaries (The Mountain Of Attention, in northern California, and Da Love-Ananda Mahal, in Hawaii—formerly known as "Tumomama Sanctuary") were principal sites of Avatar Adi Da's Teaching Demonstration during the years of His Divine Teaching-Work. Through His years of Blessing-Infusion of each of these Hermitage-Retreat Sanctuaries and these Pilgrimage and Retreat Sanctuaries, He has fully Empowered them for His devotees throughout all time.

Santosha "Santosha" is Sanskrit for "satisfaction" or "contentment"—qualities associated with a sense of completion. These qualities are characteristic of no-seeking, the fundamental Principle of Avatar Adi Da's Wisdom-Teaching and of His entire Revelation of Truth. Because of its uniquely appropriate meanings, "Santosha" is one of Avatar Adi Da's Names. As Santosha Adi Da, Avatar Adi Da Samraj is the Divine Giver of Perfect Divine Contentedness, or Perfect Searchlessness.

Santosha Avatar As the Santosha Avatar, Avatar Adi Da is the Very Incarnation of Perfect Divine Contentedness, or Perfect Searchlessness.

Sat-Guru "Sat" means "Truth", "Being",

"Existence". Thus, "Sat-Guru" literally means "True Guru", or a Guru who can lead living beings from darkness (or non-Truth) into Light (or the Living Truth).

Satsang The Hindi word "Satsang" (from the Sanskrit "Satsanga") literally means "true (or right) relationship", "the company of Truth". In the Way of Adidam, Satsang is the eternal relationship of mutual sacred commitment between Avatar Adi Da Samraj and each formally acknowledged practitioner of the Way of Adidam.

Savikalpa Samadhi See **Samadhi**.

scientific materialism Scientific materialism is the predominant philosophy and worldview of modern humanity, the basic presumption of which is that the material world is all that exists. In scientific materialism, the method of science, or the observation of objective phenomena, is made into philosophy and a way of life that suppresses our native impulse to Liberation.

seeing See **listening, hearing, and seeing**.

self-Enquiry The practice of self-Enquiry in the form "Avoiding relationship?", unique to the Way of Adidam, was spontaneously developed by Avatar Adi Da in the course of His own Ordeal of Divine Re-Awakening. Intense persistence in the "radical" discipline of this unique form of self-Enquiry led rapidly to Avatar Adi Da's Divine Enlightenment (or Most Perfect Divine Self-Realization) in 1970.

The practice of self-Enquiry in the form "Avoiding relationship?" and the practice of non-verbal Re-cognition are the principal technical practices that serve feeling-Contemplation of Avatar Adi Da in the Devotional Way of Insight.

Self-Existing and Self-Radiant Avatar Adi Da uses "Self-Existing and Self-Radiant" to indicate the two fundamental aspects of the One Divine Person (or Reality)—Existence (or Being, or Consciousness) Itself, and Radiance (or Energy, or Light) Itself.

seven stages of life   See **stages of life**.

Shakti, Guru-Shakti   "Shakti" is a Sanskrit term for the Divinely Manifesting Energy, Spiritual Power, or Spirit-Current of the Divine Person. Guru-Shakti is the Power of the Guru to Liberate his or her devotees.

Shaktipat   In Hindi, "shaktipat" is the "descent of Spiritual Power". Yogic Shaktipat, which manipulates natural, conditional energies or partial manifestations of the Spirit-Current, is typically granted through touch, word, glance, or regard by Yogic Adepts in the fifth stage of life, or fourth to fifth stages of life. Yogic Shaktipat must be distinguished from (and, otherwise, understood to be only a secondary aspect of) the Blessing Transmission of the Heart Itself (Hridaya-Shaktipat), which is uniquely Given by Avatar Adi Da Samraj.

Siddha, Siddha-Guru   "Siddha" is Sanskrit for "a completed, fulfilled, or perfected one", or "one of perfect accomplishment, or power". Avatar Adi Da uses "Siddha", or "Siddha-Guru", to mean a Transmission-Master who is a Realizer (to any significant degree) of Real God, Truth, or Reality.

Siddha Yoga   "Siddha Yoga" is, literally, "the Yoga of the Perfected One[s]".

Swami Muktananda used the term "Siddha Yoga" to refer to the form of Kundalini Yoga that he taught, which involved initiation of the devotee by the Guru's Transmission of Shakti (or Spiritual Energy). Avatar Adi Da Samraj has indicated that this was a fifth stage form of Siddha Yoga.

In "I (Alone) Am The Adidam Revelation", Avatar Adi Da Says:

. . . I Teach Siddha Yoga in the Mode and Manner of the _seventh_ stage of life (as Ruchira Avatara Hridaya-Siddha Yoga, or Ruchira Avatara Maha-Jnana Hridaya-Shaktipat Yoga)—and always toward (or to the degree of) the Realization inherently associated with (and, at last, Most Perfectly Demonstrated and Proven by) the only-by-Me Revealed and Given seventh

stage of life, and as a practice and a Process that progressively includes (and, coincidently, _directly_ transcends) _all_ _six_ of the phenomenal and developmental (and, necessarily, yet ego-based) stages of life that precede the seventh.

Avatar Adi Da's description of the similarities and differences between traditional Siddha Yoga and the Way of Adidam is Given in "I (Alone) Am The Adidam Revelation", which Essay appears in many of Avatar Adi Da's twenty-three "Source-Texts".

siddhi   "Siddhi" is Sanskrit for "power", or "accomplishment". When capitalized in Avatar Adi Da's Wisdom-Teaching, "Siddhi" is the Spiritual, Transcendental, and Divine Awakening-Power That He spontaneously and effortlessly Transmits to all.

"Sila"   "Sila" is a Pali Buddhist term meaning "habit", "behavior", "conduct", or "morality". It connotes the restraint of outgoing energy and attention, the disposition of equanimity, or free energy and attention for the Spiritual Process.

"simpler" (or "simplest") form of the Way of Adidam   See **forms of practice in the Way of Adidam**.

sleeping   See **waking, dreaming, and sleeping**.

"Source-Texts"   During the twenty-seven years of His Teaching-Work and Revelation-Work (from 1972 to 1999), Avatar Adi Da elaborately described every aspect of the practice of Adidam, from the beginning of one's approach to Him to the Most Ultimate Realization of the seventh stage of life.

Avatar Adi Da's Heart-Word is summarized in His twenty-three "Source-Texts". These Texts present, in complete and conclusive detail, His Divine Revelations, Confessions, and Instructions, which are the fruits of His years of Teaching and Revelation Work. In addition to this "Source-Literature", Avatar Adi Da's Heart-Word also includes His "Supportive Texts" (comprising His practical Instruction in all the details of the practice of Adidam, including the fundamental disciplines of diet, health, exercise, sexuality, childrearing, and cooperative community), His "Early Literature" (Written during His Teaching Years), and collections of His Talks. (For a complete list of Avatar Adi Da's twenty-three "Source-Texts", see pp. 438-46.)

spinal line, spinal Yoga The spinal (or ascending) line of the body-mind conducts the Spirit-Current of Divine Life in an upward direction from the base of the body (or perineal area) to the crown of the head, and beyond.

In the Way of Adidam, the spinal Yoga is the process whereby knots and obstructions in the subtle, astral, or the more mentally and subtly oriented dimension of the body-mind are penetrated, opened, surrendered, and released through the devotee's reception and "conductivity" of Avatar Adi Da's Transmission into the spinal line of the body-mind. This ascending Yoga will be required for practitioners of Adidam only in relatively rare cases. The great majority of Avatar Adi Da's devotees will be sufficiently purified through their practice of the frontal Yoga to proceed directly to practice in the context of the sixth stage of life, bypassing practice in the context of the "advanced" fourth stage and the fifth stage of life.

Spirit-Baptism Avatar Adi Da often refers to His Transmission of Spiritual Blessing as His "Spirit-Baptism". It is often felt by His devotee as a Current descending in the frontal line and ascending in the spinal line. However, Avatar Adi Da's Spirit-Baptism is fundamentally and primarily His Moveless Transmission of the Divine Heart Itself. As a secondary effect, His Spirit-Baptism serves to purify, balance, and energize the entire body-mind of the devotee who is prepared to receive It.

Spiritual anatomy / esoteric anatomy
Avatar Adi Da Samraj has Revealed that just as there is a physical anatomy, there is an actual Spiritual anatomy, or structure, that is present in every human being. As He Says in *The Basket Of Tolerance*, it is

because of this structure that the "experiential and developmental process of Growth and Realization demonstrates itself in accordance with what I have Revealed and Demonstrated to be the seven stages of life".

Avatar Adi Da's extended Instruction relative to the Spiritual anatomy of Man is Given in *The Seven Stages Of Life* and *Santosha Adidam*.

Spiritual, Transcendental, Divine
Avatar Adi Da uses the words "Spiritual", "Transcendental", and "Divine" in reference to dimensions of Reality that are Realized progressively in the Way of Adidam. "Transcendental" and "Spiritual" indicate two fundamental aspects of the One Divine Reality and Person—Consciousness Itself (Which Is Transcendental, or Self-Existing) and Energy Itself (Which Is Spiritual, or Self-Radiant). Only That Which Is Divine is simultaneously Transcendental and Spiritual.

Sri "Sri" is a term of honor and veneration often applied to an Adept. The word literally means "flame" in Sanskrit, indicating that the one honored is radiant with Blessing Power.

stages of life Avatar Adi Da has Revealed the underlying structure of human growth in seven stages. The seventh stage of life is Divine Self-Realization, or Most Perfect Enlightenment.

The first three stages of life develop, respectively, the physical, emotional, and mental/volitional functions of the body-mind. The first stage begins at birth and continues for approximately five to seven years; the second stage follows, continuing until approximately the age of twelve to fourteen; and the third stage is optimally complete by the early twenties. In the case of virtually all individuals, however, failed adaptation in the earlier stages of life means that maturity in the third stage of life takes much longer to attain, and it is usually never fulfilled, with the result that the ensuing stages of Spiritual development do not even begin.

In the Way of Adidam, however, growth in the first three stages of life

THE SEVEN STAGES OF LIFE

unfolds in the Spiritual Company of Avatar Adi Da and is based in the practice of feeling-Contemplation of His bodily (human) Form and in devotion, service, and self-discipline in relation to His bodily (human) Form. By the Grace of this relationship to Avatar Adi Da, the first three (or foundation) stages of life are lived and fulfilled in an ego-transcending devotional disposition, or (as He describes it) "in the 'original' (or beginner's) devotional context of the fourth stage of life".

The fourth stage of life is the transitional stage between the gross (bodily-based) point of view of the first three stages of life and the subtle (mind-based, or psyche-based) point of view of the fifth stage of life. The fourth stage of life is the stage of Spiritual devotion, or devotional surrender of separate self to the Divine, in which the gross functions of the being are aligned to the higher psychic (or subtle) functions of the being. In the fourth stage of life, the gross (or bodily-based) personality of the first three stages of life is purified through reception of the Spiritual Force ("Holy Spirit", or "Shakti") of the Divine Reality, which prepares the being to out-grow the bodily-based point of view.

In the Way of Adidam, as the orientation of the fourth stage of life matures, heart-felt surrender to the bodily (human) Form of Avatar Adi Da deepens by His Grace, Drawing His devotee into Love-Communion with His All-Pervading Spiritual Presence. Growth in the "basic" context of the fourth stage of life in the Way of Adidam is also characterized by reception of Avatar Adi Da's Baptizing Current of Divine Spirit-Energy, Which is initially felt to flow down the front of the body from Infinitely Above the head to the bodily base (or perineal area).

The Descent of Avatar Adi Da's Spirit-Baptism releases obstructions predominantly in what He calls the "frontal personality", or the personality typically animated in the waking state (as opposed to the dream state and the state of deep sleep). This Spirit-Baptism purifies His devotee and infuses the devotee with His Spirit-Power. Avatar Adi Da's devotee is, thus, awakened to profound love of (and

devotional intimacy with) Him.

Eventually, Avatar Adi Da's Divine Spirit-Current may be felt to turn about at the bodily base and ascend up the spine to the brain core. In this case, the fourth stage of life matures to its "advanced" context, which is focused in the Ascent of Avatar Adi Da's Spirit-Baptism and the consequent purification of the spinal line of the body-mind.

In the fifth stage of life, attention is concentrated in the subtle (or psychic) levels of awareness in ascent. Avatar Adi Da's Divine Spirit-Current is felt to penetrate the brain core and rise toward the Matrix of Light and Love-Bliss Infinitely Above the crown of the head, possibly culminating in the temporary experience of fifth stage conditional Nirvikalpa Samadhi, or "formless ecstasy". In the Way of Adidam, most practitioners will not need to practice either in the "advanced" context of the fourth stage of life or in the context of the fifth stage of life, but will (rather) be Awakened, by Avatar Adi Da's Grace, directly from maturity in the fourth stage of life to the Witness-Position of Consciousness (in the context of the sixth stage of life).

In the traditional development of the sixth stage of life, a strategic effort is made to Identify with Consciousness Itself by excluding the realm of conditional phenomena. Avatar Adi Da Teaches, however, that the deliberate intention to exclude the conditional world for the sake of Realizing Transcendental Consciousness is an egoic error that must be transcended by His devotees who are practicing in the context of the sixth stage of life.

In deepest meditation in the sixth stage of life in the Way of Adidam, the knot of attention (which is the root-action of egoity, felt as separation, self-contraction, or the feeling of relatedness) dissolves, and all sense of relatedness yields to the Blissful and undifferentiated Feeling of Being. The characteristic Samadhi of the sixth stage of life is Jnana Samadhi, the temporary Realization of the Transcendental Self (or Consciousness Itself)—which is temporary because it can occur only when awareness of the world is excluded in meditation.

The transition from the sixth stage of life to the seventh stage Realization of Absolute Non-Separateness is the unique Revelation of Avatar Adi Da. Various traditions and individuals previous to Adi Da's Revelation have had sixth stage intuitions (or premonitions) of the Most Perfect seventh stage Realization, but no one previous to Avatar Adi Da has Realized the seventh stage of life.

The seventh stage Realization is a Gift of Avatar Adi Da to His devotees who have (by His Divine Grace) completed their practice of the Way of Adidam in the context of the first six stages of life. The seventh stage of life begins when His devotee Gracefully Awakens from the exclusive Realization of Consciousness to Most Perfect and Permanent Identification with Consciousness Itself, Avatar Adi Da's Divine State. This is Divine Self-Realization, or Divine Enlightenment, the perpetual Samadhi of "Open Eyes" (seventh stage Sahaj Samadhi)—in which all "things" are Divinely Self-Recognized without "difference", as merely apparent modifications of the One Self-Existing and Self-Radiant Divine Consciousness.

In the course of the seventh stage of life, there may be spontaneous incidents in which psycho-physical states and phenomena do not appear to the notice, being Outshined by the "Bright" Radiance of Consciousness Itself. This Samadhi, Which is the Ultimate Realization of Divine Existence, culminates in Divine Translation, or the permanent Outshining of all apparent conditions in the Inherently Perfect Radiance and Love-Bliss of the Divine Self-Condition (which necessarily coincides with the physical death of the body-mind).

In the context of practice of the Way of Adidam, the seven stages of life as Revealed by Avatar Adi Da are not a version of the traditional "ladder" of Spiritual attainment. These stages and their characteristic signs arise naturally in the course of practice for a fully practicing devotee in the Way of Adidam, but the practice itself is oriented to the transcending of the first six stages of life, in the seventh stage Disposition of Inherently Liberated Happiness, Granted by Avatar Adi Da's Divine Grace in His Love-Blissful Spiritual Company.

Avatar Adi Da's extended Instruction relative to the seven stages of life is Given in *The Seven Stages Of Life*.

Star Form Avatar Adi Da has Revealed that He is "Incarnated" in the Cosmic domain as a brilliant white five-pointed Star, the original (and primal) conditional visible Representation (or Sign) of the "Bright" (the Source-Energy, or Divine Light, of Which all conditional phenomena and the total cosmos are modifications).

The apparently objective Divine Star can potentially be experienced in any moment and location in cosmic Nature. However, the vision of the Divine Star is not a necessary experience for growth in the Spiritual Process or for Divine Self-Realization.

Avatar Adi Da's discussion of His Star Form is found in *He-and-She Is Me*.

student-novice / student-beginner
A student-novice is an individual who is formally approaching, and preparing to become a formal practitioner of, the total practice of the Way of Adidam (as a member of the second congregation). The student-novice makes a vow of eternal commitment to Avatar Adi Da as his or her Divine Guru, and to the practice He has Given, and is initiated into simple devotional and sacramental disciplines in formal relationship to Avatar Adi Da. During the student-novice stage, the individual engages in intensive study of Avatar Adi Da's Wisdom-Teaching and adapts to the functional, practical, relational, and cultural disciplines of the Way of Adidam.

A student-beginner is a practitioner in the initial developmental stage of the second congregation of Adidam. In the course of student-beginner practice, the devotee of Avatar Adi Da, on the basis of the eternal "Bond" of devotion to Him that he or she established as a student-novice, continues the process of listening and further adaptation to the disciplines that were begun in the student-novice stage of approach.

subtle See **gross, subtle, causal**.

"Supportive Texts" Among Avatar Adi Da's "Supportive Texts" are included such books as *Conscious Exercise and the Transcendental Sun*, *The Eating Gorilla Comes in Peace*, *Love of the Two-Armed Form*, and *Easy Death*.

Swami The title "Swami" is traditionally given to an individual who has demonstrated significant self-mastery in the context of a lifetime dedicated to Spiritual renunciation.

Swami Muktananda See **Lineage, Avatar Adi Da's**.

Swami Nityananda See **Lineage, Avatar Adi Da's**.

Swami Rudrananda See **Lineage, Avatar Adi Da's**.

T

Tail of the Horse Adi Da Samraj has often referred to a passage from the ancient Indian text *Satapatha Brahmana*, which He has paraphrased as: "Man does not know. Only the Horse Knows. Therefore, hold to the tail of the Horse." Adi Da has Revealed that, in the most esoteric understanding of this saying, the "Horse" represents the Adept-Realizer, and "holding to the tail of the Horse" represents the devotee's complete dependence on the Adept-Realizer in order to Realize Real God (or Truth, or Reality).

"talking" school "'Talking' school" is a phrase used by Avatar Adi Da to refer to those in any tradition of sacred life whose approach is characterized by talking, thinking, reading, and philosophical analysis and debate, or even meditative enquiry or reflection, without a concomitant and foundation discipline of body, emotion, mind, and breath. He contrasts the "talking" school with the "practicing" school approach—"practicing" schools involving those who are committed to the ordeal of real ego-transcending discipline, under the guidance of a true Guru.

Tat Sundaram "Sundara" is the Sanskrit word for "beauty", and "Sundaram" means "something which is beautiful". "Tat" is the Sanskrit word for "it" or "that". Thus, "Tat Sundaram" means "That Which Is Beautiful" or, by extension, "All Of This Is Beautiful", and is a reference to the seventh stage Realization of the Perfect Non-Separateness and Love-Bliss-Nature of the entire world—conditional and Un-Conditional. Tat Sundaram is also the name of the Hermitage-Retreat Sanctuary reserved for Avatar Adi Da in northern California.

Teaching-Work For a description of Avatar Adi Da's Divine Teaching-Work, see pp. 16-17.

technically "fully elaborated" practice See **forms of practice in the Way of Adidam**.

technically "simpler" (and even "simplest") practice See **forms of practice in the Way of Adidam**.

three stations of the heart See **heart, stations of the heart**.

the "Thumbs" See **Samadhi**.

Thunder The Divine Sound of Thunder (which Avatar Adi Da also describes as the "Da" Sound, or "Da-Om" Sound, or "Om" Sound) is one of Avatar Adi Da's three Eternal Forms of Manifestation in the conditional worlds—together with His Divine Star of Light and His Divine Spiritual Body.

Avatar Adi Da's principal Revelation-Confession about these three forms of His Manifestation is Given in *He-and-She Is Me*.

. . . *I Am conditionally Manifested (First) As The everywhere Apparently Audible (and Apparently Objective) Divine Sound-Vibration (or "Da" Sound, or "Da-Om" Sound, or "Om" Sound, The Objective Sign Of The He, Present As The Conscious Sound Of sounds, In The Center Of The Cosmic Mandala), and As The everywhere Apparently Visible (and Apparently Objective) Divine Star (The Objective Sign*

*Of The She, Present As The Conscious Light
Of lights, In The Center Of The Cosmic
Mandala), and (From That He and She)
As The everywhere Apparently Touchable
(or Tangible), and Apparently Objective,
Total Divine Spiritual Body (The Objective,
and All-and-all-Surrounding, and All-
and-all-Pervading Conscious and Me-
Personal Body Of "Bright" Love-Bliss-
Presence, Divinely Self-"Emerging", Now,
and Forever Hereafter, From The Center Of
The Cosmic Mandala Into The Depths Of
Even every "where" In The Cosmic
Domain) . . . .*

total practice of the Way of Adidam
The total practice of the Way of Adidam is
the full and complete practice of the Way
that Avatar Adi Da Samraj has Given to
His devotees who are formal members of
the first or the second congregation of
Adidam (see pp. 361-67). One who
embraces the total practice of the Way of
Adidam conforms every aspect of his or
her life and being to Avatar Adi Da's
Divine Word of Instruction. Therefore, it is
only such devotees (in the first or the second congregation of Adidam) who have
the potential of Realizing Divine
Enlightenment.

"True Prayer" "True Prayer" is Avatar
Adi Da's technical term for the various
forms of the "conscious process" that are
practiced by His Spiritually Awakened
devotees who have chosen the Devotional
Way of Faith.
    Avatar Adi Da's full Instruction relative
to "True Prayer" is Given in *The Dawn
Horse Testament Of The Ruchira Avatar.*

Turaga "Turaga" (Too-RAHNG-ah) is
Fijian for "Lord".

"turiya", "turiyatita" Terms used in
the Hindu philosophical systems.
Traditionally, "turiya" means "the fourth
state" (beyond waking, dreaming, and
sleeping), and "turiyatita" means "the state
beyond the fourth", or beyond all states.
    Avatar Adi Da, however, has given
these terms different meanings in the context of the Way of Adidam. He uses the
term "turiya" to indicate the Awakening to
the Consciousness Itself (in the context of

the sixth stage of life), and "turiyatita" as
the State of Most Perfect Divine Enlightenment, or the Realization of all arising as
transparent and non-binding modifications
of the One Divine Reality (in the context
of the seventh stage of life).

U

ultimate See **the advanced and the
ultimate stages of life**.

Ultimate Self-Domain "Ultimate Self-
Domain" is a synonym for "Divine Self-
Domain". (See **Divine Self-Domain**.)

Ultimate Source-Condition The Divine
Reality prior to all conditional arising,
which is, therefore, the "Source" of all
conditional worlds, beings, and things.

V

Vira-Yogi Sanskrit for "Hero-Yogi".
(See **"Heroic"**.)

Vow For a description of the Vow and
responsibilities associated with the Way of
Adidam, see pp. 360-72.

W, X, Y, Z

waking, dreaming, and sleeping
These three states of consciousness are
associated with the dimensions of cosmic
existence.
    The waking state (and the physical
body) is associated with the gross dimension.
    The dreaming state (and visionary,
mystical, and Yogic Spiritual processes)
is associated with the subtle dimension.
The subtle dimension, which is senior to
the gross dimension, includes the etheric
(or energic), lower mental (or verbal-
intentional and lower psychic), and higher
mental (or deeper psychic, mystical, and
discriminative) functions.
    The sleeping state is associated with
the causal dimension, which is senior to
both the gross and the subtle dimensions.
It is the root of attention, prior to any
particular experience. (See also **gross,
subtle, causal**.)

washing the dog Avatar Adi Da uses the metaphor of the "dog" and "washing the dog" to Indicate the purification of the body-mind in the process of Adidam. He addresses the presumption (as in the Kundalini Yoga tradition) that the Spiritual process requires a spinal Yoga, or an effort of arousing Spiritual Energy literally at the "tail" end of the "dog" (the bodily base, or the muladhara chakra), and then drawing It up (or allowing It to ascend) through the spinal line to the head (and above). In contrast, Avatar Adi Da Samraj has Revealed (particularly in His *Hridaya Rosary*) that, in reality, the human being can be truly purified and Liberated (or the "dog" can be "washed") only by receiving His Divine Blessing-Power (or Hridaya-Shakti) and Spiritual Person downward from Infinitely Above the head to the bodily base. This Process of downward reception of Avatar Adi Da is what He calls the "frontal Yoga", because it occurs in the frontal line of the body (which is a natural pathway of descending energy, down the front of the body, from the crown of the head to the bodily base). This necessary descending Yoga of the frontal line, once completed, is sufficient to purify and Spiritually Infuse the body-mind, and, in most cases, it allows the practitioner of the Way of Adidam to bypass the ascending Yoga of the spinal line (which is the complementary natural pathway of ascending energy, up the back of the body, from the bodily base to the crown of the head). The frontal line and the spinal line are the two arcs of the continuous energy-circuit that Avatar Adi Da calls the "Circle" of the body-mind.

AVATAR ADI DA SAMRAJ: You wash a dog from the head to the tail. But somehow or other, egos looking to Realize think they can wash the "dog" from the "tail" toward the head by doing spinal Yoga. But, in Truth, and in Reality, only the frontal Yoga can accomplish most perfect Divine Self-Realization, because it begins from the superior position, from the "head" position, from My Crashing Down.

The heart-disposition is magnified by My Crashing Down in your devotional Communion with Me. And the vital,

grosser dimensions of the being are purified by this washing from the head toward the "tail". If the Process had to begin from the bodily base up, it would be very difficult, very traumatizing—and, ultimately, impossible. The "dog" is washed, simply and very directly, by your participation in My Divine Descent, by your participation in this frontal Yoga. I am Speaking now of the Spiritually Awakened stages, basically. But, even in the case of beginning practitioners in the Way of Adidam—not yet Spiritually Awakened, not yet responsible for the truly Spiritual dimension of their relationship to Me—this "wash" is, by Means of My Avataric Divine Grace, going on.

Therefore, Spiritual life need not be a traumatic course. The "dog" should enjoy being bathed. Nice gentle little guy, happy to be rubbed and touched. You talk to him, struggle a little bit, but you gentle him down. That is how it should work. And, at the end of it, the "dog" sort of "wags its tail", shakes the water off—nice and clean, happy, your best friend. That is how it should work.

If you wash the "dog" from the "tail" up, you smear the shit from his backside toward his head. Basically, that "washing from the tail toward the head" is a self-generated, self-"guruing" kind of effort. The Divine Process can only occur by Means of Divine Grace. Even the word "Shaktipat" means the "Descent (pat) of Divine Force (Shakti)". But Shaktipat as it appears in the traditions is basically associated with admonitions to practice a spinal Yoga, moving from the base up. In Truth, the Divine Yoga in My Company is a Descent—washing the "dog" from head to "tail" rather than giving the "dog" a "bone", letting it wash itself from the "tail" to the head.

DEVOTEE: It is only Your Hridaya-Shakti that does it.

AVATAR ADI DA SAMRAJ: This is why you must invest yourself in Me. And that is how the "dog" gets washed. [August 13, 1995]

Avatar Adi Da's extended Discourse relative to "washing the dog" is "Be Washed, From Head to Tail, By Heart-Devotion To Me", in *Hridaya Rosary*.

Way of "Radical" Understanding
Avatar Adi Da uses "understanding" to
mean "the process of transcending
egoity". Thus, to "understand" is to simultaneously observe the activity of the self-
contraction and to surrender that activity
via devotional resort to Avatar Adi Da
Samraj.

Avatar Adi Da has Revealed that,
despite their intention to Realize Reality
(or Truth, or Real God), all religious and
Spiritual traditions (other than the Way of
Adidam) are involved, in one manner or
another, with the search to satisfy the ego.
Only Avatar Adi Da has Revealed the Way
to "radically" understand the ego and (in
due course, through intensive formal practice of the Way of Adidam, as His formally
acknowledged devotee) to most perfectly
transcend the ego. Thus, the Way Avatar
Adi Da has Given is the "Way of 'Radical'
Understanding".

Witness, Witness-Consciousness,
Witness-Position When Consciousness
is free of identification with the body-
mind, it takes up its natural "position" as
the Conscious Witness of all that arises to
and in and as the body-mind.

In the Way of Adidam, the stable
Realization of the Witness-Position is associated with, or demonstrated via, the
effortless surrender (or relaxation) of all
the forms of seeking and all the motives
of attention that characterize the first five
stages of life. However, identification with
the Witness-Position is not final (or Most
Perfect) Realization of the Divine Self.
Rather, it is the first of the three stages of
the "Perfect Practice" in the Way of
Adidam, which Practice, in due course,
Realizes, by Avatar Adi Da's Grace, complete and irreversible and utterly Love-
Blissful Identification with Consciousness
Itself.

Avatar Adi Da's extended Instruction
relative to the Witness is Given in *The
Lion Sutra*.

Yoga "Yoga", in Sanskrit, is literally
"yoking", or "union", usually referring to
any discipline or process whereby an
aspirant attempts to unite with God.
Avatar Adi Da acknowledges this conventional and traditional use of the term, but
also, in reference to the Great Yoga of
Adidam, employs it in a "radical" sense,
free of the usual implication of egoic separation and seeking.

Yogananda, Paramahansa
Paramahansa Yogananda (Mukunda Lal
Ghosh, 1893-1952) was born in Bengal,
the child of devout Hindu parents. As a
young man, Yogananda found his Guru,
Swami Yukteswar Giri, who initiated him
into an order of formal renunciates. In
1920, Yogananda traveled to America to
attend an international conference of religions in Boston. Subsequently he settled
in the United States, attracting many
American devotees. He Taught "Kriya
Yoga", a system of practice that had been
passed down to him by his own Teacher
and that had originally been developed
from traditional techniques of Kundalini
Yoga. Yogananda became widely known
through the publication of his life-story,
Autobiography of a Yogi.

The Sacred Literature of Ruchira Avatar Adi Da Samraj

R ead the astounding Story of Avatar Adi Da's Divine Life and Work in *The Promised God-Man Is Here.*

The Promised God-Man Is Here:
The Extraordinary Life-Story,
The "Radical" Teaching-Work, and
The Divinely "Emerging" World-Blessing
Work Of The Divine World-Teacher
Of The "Late-Time", Ruchira Avatar
Adi Da Samraj

The profound, heart-rending, humorous, miraculous, wild—and true—Story of the Divine Person Alive in human Form. Essential reading as background for the study of Avatar Adi Da's books.

E njoy the beautiful summary of His Message that Avatar Adi Da has written especially "for children, and everyone else".

What, Where, When, How, Why, and <u>Who</u> To Remember To Be Happy

A Simple Explanation Of The Divine Way Of Adidam (For Children, and <u>Everyone</u> Else)

Fundamental Truth about life as a human being, told in very simple language. Accompanied by extraordinarily vivid and imaginative illustrations.

The Five Books Of
The Heart Of The Adidam Revelation

In these five books, Avatar Adi Da Samraj has distilled the very essence of His Eternal Message to every one, in all times and places.

BOOK ONE:

Aham Da Asmi
(Beloved, I Am Da)

The "Late-Time" Avataric Revelation Of The True and Spiritual Divine Person (The egoless Personal Presence Of Reality and Truth, Which Is The Only Real God)

The most extraordinary statement ever made in human history. Avatar Adi Da Samraj fully Reveals Himself as the Living Divine Person and Proclaims His Infinite and Undying Love for all and All.

BOOK TWO:

Ruchira Avatara Gita
(The Way Of The Divine Heart-Master)

The "Late-Time" Avataric Revelation Of The Great Secret Of The Divinely Self-Revealed Way That Most Perfectly Realizes The True and Spiritual Divine Person (The egoless Personal Presence Of Reality and Truth, Which Is The Only Real God)

Avatar Adi Da Offers to every one the ecstatic practice of devotional relationship to Him— explaining how devotion to a living human Adept-Realizer has always been the source of true religion, and distinguishing true Guru-devotion from religious cultism.

BOOK THREE:

Da Love-Ananda Gita
(The Free Gift Of The Divine Love-Bliss)

The "Late-Time" Avataric Revelation Of The Great Means To Worship and To Realize The True and Spiritual Divine Person (The egoless Personal Presence Of Reality and Truth, Which Is The Only Real God)

Avatar Adi Da Reveals the secret simplicity at the heart of Adidam—relinquishing your preoccupation with yourself (and all your problems and your suffering) and, instead, Contemplating the "Bright" Divine Person of Infinite Love-Bliss.

BOOK FOUR:

Hridaya Rosary
(Four Thorns Of Heart-Instruction)

The "Late-Time" Avataric Revelation Of The Universally Tangible Divine Spiritual Body, Which Is The Supreme Agent Of The Great Means To Worship and To Realize The True and Spiritual Divine Person (The egoless Personal Presence Of Reality and Truth, Which Is The Only Real God)

The ultimate Mysteries of Spiritual life, never before revealed. In breathtakingly beautiful poetry, Avatar Adi Da Samraj sings of the "melting" of the ego in His "Rose Garden of the Heart".

BOOK FIVE:

Eleutherios
(The Only Truth That Sets The Heart Free)

The "Late-Time" Avataric Revelation Of The "Perfect Practice" Of The Great Means To Worship and To Realize The True and Spiritual Divine Person (The egoless Personal Presence Of Reality and Truth, Which Is The Only Real God)

An address to the great human questions about God, Truth, Reality, Happiness, and Freedom. Avatar Adi Da Samraj Reveals how Absolute Divine Freedom is Realized, and makes an impassioned Call to everyone to create a world of true human freedom on Earth.

The Seventeen Companions
Of The True Dawn Horse

These seventeen books are "Companions" to *The Dawn Horse Testament*, Avatar Adi Da's great summary of the Way of Adidam (p. 446). Here you will find Avatar Adi Da's Wisdom-Instruction on particular aspects of the true Spiritual Way, and His two tellings of His own Life-Story, as autobiography (*The Knee Of Listening*) and as archetypal parable (*The Mummery*).

BOOK ONE:

Real God Is The Indivisible Oneness Of Unbroken Light
Reality, Truth, and The "Non-Creator" God In The True World-Religion Of Adidam

The Nature of Real God and the nature of the cosmos. Why ultimate questions cannot be answered either by conventional religion or by science.

BOOK TWO:

The Truly Human New World-Culture Of Unbroken Real-God-Man
The Eastern Versus The Western Traditional Cultures Of Mankind, and The Unique New Non-Dual Culture Of The True World-Religion Of Adidam

The Eastern and Western approaches to religion, and to life altogether—and how the Way of Adidam goes beyond this apparent dichotomy.

BOOK THREE:

The Only Complete Way To Realize The Unbroken Light Of Real God
An Introductory Overview Of The "Radical" Divine Way Of The True World-Religion Of Adidam

The entire course of the Way of Adidam—the unique principles underlying Adidam, and the unique culmination of Adidam in Divine Enlightenment.

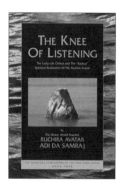

BOOK FOUR:

The Knee Of Listening

The Early-Life Ordeal and The "Radical" Spiritual Realization Of The Ruchira Avatar

Avatar Adi Da's autobiographical account of the years from His Birth to His Divine Re-Awakening in 1970. Includes a new chapter, "My Realization of the Great Onlyness of Me, and My Great Regard for My Adept-Links to the Great Tradition of Mankind".

BOOK FIVE:

The Divine Siddha-Method Of The Ruchira Avatar

The Divine Way Of Adidam Is An ego-Transcending <u>Relationship</u>, Not An ego-Centric Technique

Avatar Adi Da's earliest Talks to His devotees, on the fundamental principles of the devotional relationship to Him and "radical" understanding of the ego. Accompanied by His summary statements on His relationship to Swami Muktananda and on His own unique Teaching-Work and Blessing-Work.

BOOK SIX:

The Mummery

A Parable Of The Divine True Love

A work of astonishing poetry and deeply evocative archetypal drama. This is the story of Raymond Darling's birth, his growth to manhood, his finding and losing of his beloved (Quandra), and his ultimate resolution of the heart-breaking "problem" of mortality. *The Mummery* is Avatar Adi Da's telling of His own Life-Story in the language of parable, including His unflinching portrayal of how the unconverted ego makes religion (and life altogether) into a meaningless mummery.

BOOK SEVEN:

He-<u>and</u>-She <u>Is</u> Me

The Indivisibility Of Consciousness and Light In The Divine Body Of The Ruchira Avatar

One of Avatar Adi Da's most esoteric Revelations—His Primary "Incarnation" in the Cosmic domain as the "He" of Primal Divine Sound-Vibration, the "She" of Primal Divine Light, and the "Son" of "He" and "She" in the "Me" of His Divine Spiritual Body.

BOOK EIGHT:

Ruchira Avatara Hridaya-Siddha Yoga

The <u>Divine</u> (and Not Merely <u>Cosmic</u>) Spiritual Baptism In The Divine Way Of Adidam

The Divine Heart-Power (Hridaya-Shakti) uniquely Transmitted by Avatar Adi Da Samraj, and how it differs from the various traditional forms of Spiritual Baptism, particularly Kundalini Yoga.

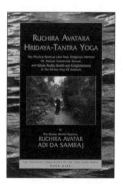

BOOK NINE:

Ruchira Avatara Hridaya-Tantra Yoga

The Physical-Spiritual (and Truly Religious) Method Of Mental, Emotional, Sexual, and <u>Whole Bodily</u> <u>Health</u> <u>and</u> <u>Enlightenment</u> In The Divine Way Of Adidam

The transformation of life in the realms of money, food, and sex. Includes: understanding "victim-consciousness"; the ego as addict; the secret of how to change; going beyond the "Oedipal" sufferings of childhood; the right orientation to money; right diet; life-positive and Spiritually auspicious sexual practice.

BOOK TEN:

The Seven Stages Of Life

Transcending The Six Stages Of egoic Life, and Realizing The ego-Transcending Seventh Stage Of Life, In The Divine Way Of Adidam

The stages of human development from birth to Divine Enlightenment. How the stages relate to physical and esoteric anatomy. The errors of each of the first six stages of life, and the unique ego-lessness of the seventh stage of life. Avatar Adi Da's Self-Confession as the first, last, and only seventh stage Adept-Realizer.

BOOK ELEVEN:

The **All-Completing** and **Final** Divine Revelation To Mankind

A Summary Description Of The Supreme Yoga Of The Seventh Stage Of Life In The Divine Way Of Adidam

The ultimate secrets of Divine Enlightenment— including the four-stage Process of Divine Enlightenment, culminating in Translation into the Infinitely Love-Blissful Divine Self-Domain.

BOOK TWELVE:

The Heart Of The Dawn Horse Testament Of The Ruchira Avatar

The Epitome Of The "Testament Of Secrets" Of The Divine World-Teacher, Ruchira Avatar Adi Da Samraj

A shorter version of *The Dawn Horse Testament*— all of Avatar Adi Da's magnificent summary Instruction, without the details of the technical practices engaged by His devotees.

BOOK THIRTEEN:

What, Where, When, How, Why, and <u>Who</u> To Remember To Be Happy

A Simple Explanation Of The Divine Way Of Adidam (For Children, and <u>Everyone</u> Else)

A text written specifically for children but inspiring to all—with accompanying Essays and Talks on Divine Ignorance, religious practices for children and young people in the Way of Adidam, and the fundamental practice of whole bodily devotion to Avatar Adi Da Samraj. (The central text of this book is also available in a special illustrated children's edition—see p. 438.)

BOOK FOURTEEN:

Santosha Adidam

The Essential Summary Of The Divine Way Of Adidam

An extended overview of the entire course of the Way of Adidam, based on the esoteric anatomy of the human being and its correlation to the progressive stages of life.

BOOK FIFTEEN:

The Lion Sutra

The "Perfect Practice" Teachings In The Divine Way Of Adidam

Practice in the ultimate stages of the Way of Adidam. How the practitioner of Adidam approaches—and passes over—the "Threshold" of Divine Enlightenment.

BOOK SIXTEEN:

The Overnight Revelation Of Conscious Light

*The "My House" Discourses
On The Indivisible Tantra Of Adidam*

A vast and profound "consideration" of the fundamental Tantric principles of true Spiritual life and the "Always Already" Nature of the Divine Reality. The day-by-day record of Avatar Adi Da's Discourses from a two-month period in early 1998.

BOOK SEVENTEEN:

The Basket Of Tolerance

The Perfect Guide To Perfectly <u>Unified</u> Understanding Of The One and Great Tradition Of Mankind, and Of The Divine Way Of Adidam As The Perfect <u>Completing</u> Of The One and Great Tradition Of Mankind

An all-encompassing "map" of mankind's entire history of religious seeking. A combination of a bibliography of over 5,000 items (organized to display Avatar Adi Da's grand Argument relative to the Great Tradition) with over 100 Essays by Avatar Adi Da, illuminating many specific aspects of the Great Tradition.

The Dawn Horse Testament Of The Ruchira Avatar

The "Testament Of Secrets" Of The Divine World-Teacher, Ruchira Avatar Adi Da Samraj

Avatar Adi Da's paramount "Source-Text", which summarizes the entire course of the Way of Adidam. Adi Da Samraj says: "In making this Testament I have been Meditating everyone, contacting everyone, dealing with psychic forces everywhere, in all time. This Testament is an always Living Conversation between Me and absolutely every one."

See My Brightness Face to Face

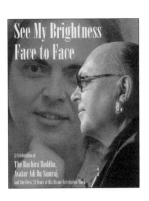

A Celebration of the Ruchira Avatar, Adi Da Samraj, and the First Twenty-Five Years of His Divine Revelation Work.

A magnificent year-by-year pictorial celebration of Ruchira Avatar Adi Da's Divine Work with His devotees, from 1972 to 1997. Includes a wealth of selections from His Talks and Writings, numerous Stories told by His devotees, and over 100 color photographs. **$19.95**, 8-1/2" x 11" paperback, 200 pages.

The "Truth For Real" series

Brief Essays and Talks by the Divine World-Teacher, Ruchira Avatar Adi Da Samraj

13 individual booklets on topics such as ecstasy, death, and the impulse to Happiness.
3-3/4" x 6", **$1.95** each

The Basket Of Tolerance Booklet series

6 individual essays on the religious traditions of humankind from *The Basket Of Tolerance.*
3-3/4" x 6", **$1.95** each

I n addition to Avatar Adi Da's 23 "Source-Texts", the Dawn Horse Press offers many other publications by and about Avatar Adi Da Samraj, as well as videotapes and audiotapes of Avatar Adi Da's Wisdom-Teaching. Dawn Horse Press publications are distributed by the Adidam Emporium, a devotee-operated business offering a wide array of items for meditation, sacred worship, health and well-being, and much more.

For more information or a free catalog:

CALL THE ADIDAM EMPORIUM
TOLL-FREE 1-877-770-0772
(Outside North America call 707-928-6653)

Visit online at
www.adidam.com

Or e-mail:
emporium@adidam.com

Or write:
ADIDAM EMPORIUM
10336 Loch Lomond Road
PMB #306
Middletown, CA 95461

INDEX

NOTE: Page numbers in **boldface** type refer to the Scriptural Text.

A

absorptive or object-oriented Emanationist mysticism.
  See Emanationist (absorptive mystical) Way
action, requirement of right, **77**
addresses
  Adidam Centers, 350
  Adidam Emporium, 352, 448
  Adidam Sacred City, 353
  Adidam website, 448
  Adidam Youth Fellowship, 367
  Cooperation + Tolerance = Peace website, 379
  fourth congregation of Adidam, 372
  second congregation of Adidam, 363
  the Society of Advocates, 371
  third congregation of Adidam, 369
Adept-Realizer
  as Divine Means for Teaching, Blessing, and
    Awakening, **65**
  as esoteric principle of Great Tradition, **67**
  and sin of relating to as an ordinary man, **66**
  See also Guru; Guru-devotion; Satsang
Adi, 14, 400
Adi-Buddha, **142**
Adi-Buddha Avatar, **142**, 392n10
Adidam, 17-19, **64**, **69**, **99**, **159**, **172**, **196-97**, **214**
  about vanishing not expanding point of view, **205**
  and address to "money, food, and sex", 21-22
  and Adi Da Samraj, **55**, **209**, **249**, **337**
    about cultivation of His Divine Samadhi, **158-59**,
      162, **164**, **166**
    about relationship to Him, 12, 13, 16, **177**, **239**,
      356, 358
  and all stages of practice informed and guided by
    orientation of seventh stage of life, **213**, **222**, **225**,
    236, **349**
  alternative titles of and meaning of name, 12-13, **143**, 400
  Avataric-Divine-Grace-Given Means of, Given from
    beginning, **238**
  as both progressive and instant, **222**
  and choice to practice by children reaching adult age, **114**
  and description of seven stages of life, **135**
  ego-transcending Great Ordeal of, **316-20**, **322-23**
  Eleutherian Pan-Communion of Adidam, 377
  as esoteric Real-God-Realizing Way, **166**
  even beginner's practice occurs in "original"
    devotional context of fourth stage of life, **162**
  and going beyond separate and separative self, **212-13**,
    251
  and Guru-devotion, **214**, **331**
  as matter of Divine Self-Realization, **158**
  not about idealizing or transforming human life, **165**
  and limitations in devotional response determine
    position in practice of devotee, **226**
  as progressive and instant process, **222-23**
  proved by the doing of, 358
  as "radical", **76**, **143**, **214**, **217**, **225**, **228**, **236**, **237-38**, **346**
  as "reality consideration" of self-contraction and Self-
    Condition and Source-Condition, **228**
  and Realizing What is obviously Real, **203**
  and recognition-response, **66**, **106**
  and Ruchira Avatara Hridaya-Siddha Yoga, **76**, **310**,
    311-12, **314-15**
  Ruchirasala of, 378
  Sacred Treasures of, 383
  as seventh stage school of Siddha Yoga, **306**, **310**, **311**
  Spiritual signs different from those prized in Great
    Tradition, **209-10**
  and transcendence of limits of all six stages, **211**, **213**,
    215, **236**, **251**
  as True World-Religion, **75-76**
  and undermining the tendency towards religious
    "cultism", **56**

and understanding and transcendence of egoity, **204**,
    210, **251**, **347**
  uniqueness of, **209-10**, **217**, **251**
  and uniqueness of "Thumbs", **188**, **190**, **191**
  as Way of Non-Separateness, **209**, **212-13**, **214**, **215**, **216**
  as Way of "Positive Disillusionment", **143**, **322**
  as Way of "Radical" Non-Dualism, **251**
  See also practice of the Way of Adidam; Ruchira Avatara
    Bhakti Yoga; Samadhis in Way of Adidam
Adidama Sukha Sundari, 23-24
Adidam Hridaya-Shaktipat Yoga, **311**
Adidam Hridaya-Siddha Yoga, **311**
Adidam Samrajashram (Fiji), 366, 373
Adidam Youth Fellowship, 367, 391-92n4
Adi Da Samraj, 15-26, **161**, **225-26**, **238**, **239**
  Alone is the Adidam Revelation, **249**, **331**
  always "living", "breathing", and "being" His devotee, **349**
  and Avataric Divine Descent into all conditional planes
    of cosmic domain or Mandala, **348**
  as Avataric Divine Realizer, Revealer, and Self-Revelation,
    53, **142**, **204**, **214**, **252**
  as Avataric Incarnation, **53**, **325**, **331**
  birth of
    and conscious assumption of the born-condition, 15, **190**
    and demonstration of fullest ascended characteristics
      of highest fifth stage Great-Saint type, **265**
    and Divine Process always active throughout and
      before present-lifetime birth, **275**
    and Siddha Yoga and entire Great Tradition already
      complete in His case from all time and eternally,
      327
    and submission of Deeper Personality to bodily
      human form of Franklin Jones, 15, **266**
    and Vehicle of Avataric seventh stage Incarnation, **265**,
      266, **328-29**, 394-95n31
    and Way and Realization always inherent in Him
      from birth, **327**
    and the "Bright" and "Thumbs" and "Radical
      Understanding" as unique always present
      Avataric Divine Characteristics, **195-97**, **327**,
      403-404, 426-27
  and confession of "I Am you", 13-14, **349**
  and contacting of life in relationship, **62**
  "Crazy" Manner of, **55**
  and criticism of cultism, **59-60**
  and Deeper-Personality Vehicle of, **266**, **328-29**,
    394-95n31
  and form of all the Great Masters of the entire Great
    Tradition, **329**
  and Vivekananda-Ramakrishna, **329**, 399n58
  as Divine Person (principal Demonstration of), **54**, **64**,
    66, **75**, **178-79**, **252**, **332**
  and Divine Self-"Emergence", 17, **125**, **196**, **252**, **348**,
    408-409
  Divine Siddhis of, **347**, **348**
  and embrace and transcendence of both Emanationist
    and Transcendentalist schools, **259**
  as first, last, and only Avataric Divine Adept-Realizer,
    Adept-Revealer, and Adept-Revelation of the seventh
    stage of life, **92**, **142**, **251**, **343**, **344-45**
  as Liberator in "late-time" or "dark epoch", **68**, **69**, **142**
  not a "public" Teacher, **55**, **56**
  and Ramana Maharshi as a connecting link to aspects
    of the Great Tradition, **302-303**
  and refusal to be "man in the middle", **59-60**, **61**, **64**,
    65, **68**
  and relationship to Swami Muktananda after Divine
    Re-Awakening
    and Adidam as form of Siddha Yoga, **309-11**, **312**
    assumption of His Divine Work institutionally
      independent of Swami Muktananda, **309**, **311-12**
    completion and fulfillment of Siddha-Yoga tradition, **255**

449

Index

461

and occasional complete and constant simple forms as
  sign of transition beyond "basic" fourth stage of
  life, **185**
and rotation forward and down and back and up, **182-83**
as Samadhi of Adi Da Samraj's Avataric Descent, **187**
seventh stage Realization and Demonstration of, **184-85**
simple and most basic form of, **181-82**
"skin" of, and Witness-Consciousness, **192, 193, 194**
spherical form of, **181, 182-83, 189, 192, 194, 195**
and transition to sixth stage and Witness-Consciousness,
  186, 189, 192, 194
uniqueness of, **188, 190, 191**
Tibetan Tantric Buddhism. *See* Vajrayana Buddhism
tolerance, **62, 284**
Totality, **199-200, 201, 203, 204**
Transcendentalist reality. *See* Non-Emanationist
  (Transcendentalist) Way
Translation. *See* Divine Translation
Transnational Society of Advocates of the Adidam
  Revelation, The, 370-71
Trivedi, Pratibha. *See* Amma
True Water, **81, 82**
Truth/truth, **51-53, 251**
  and necessity to express what is hidden, denied, or
    suppressed, or falsified, **273**
Tulsiamma, **262**
turiya state, **290, 435**
"turiyatita", **208, 291, 435**

U

Ultimate Non-Dualism (Primary Absolute Monism),
  147-48
  and establishment of seventh stage of life, **148**
  as fulfillment of religion, **153**
  and Identification or Self-Abiding with Consciousness
    Itself, **150-51**
  and "Point of View" of Consciousness Itself, **150**
ultimate stages of life and practice, **138, 170**, 400-401
understanding, 79, **236, 237**
unity, **155-57, 317-18**
un-"Veiling" of internally perceptible pattern of body-
  mind-self, **295-97**
Upanishad, **134**
urge to Realization. *See* impulse toward most perfectly
  ego-transcending Real-God-Realization

V

Vajrayana Buddhism
  founded on sixth stage transcendentalist reality as
    opposed to Emanationist traditions, **256-57**
  and Non-conditionally Self-Affirming form of sixth
    stage of life, **141, 148**
  and Ultimate Non-Dualism, **147-48, 150**
  See also Buddhism
Vehicle of Adi Da Samraj's seventh stage Incarnation,
  265, 266, 328-29, 394-95n31
vertical context of body-mind, 43, **222**
Vira-Yogi (or Heroic Siddha) type, **266**, 413-14
Virgin Mary, **294**
visions
  do nothing relative to egoity or human suffering, **312-14**
  of higher and lower world, **281-82**
Vivekananda, Swami, **329**
Voice of the Self (Nityananda), **262**
Vow, Eternal, **56, 348**, 363, 371, 410, 435

W

waking state, **118, 223**, 435
washing, from head to toe, **82**, 436
Water, True, **81, 82**
Way of Non-Separateness, **209, 212-13, 214, 215, 216**
Way of "Radical" Non-Dualism, **251**
Way of "Radical" Understanding, 437
Way of Sri Hridayam, **76-77**
Way of the Heart, **143**, 544
  See also Adidam, Way of
website
  Adidam and Adidam Emporium, 448
  Adidam Sacred City, 353
  Cooperation + Tolerance = Peace, 379
Well of Being, **242**
Westerner matters, **273**
"What", **243-44, 265**
wheeling machine of life, **93-94**
"Where", **244**
whiteness as apparent Doorway to Divine Self-Domain,
  206
"Who", **242, 244, 265**
will, **109, 110, 136**
wisdom-culture, **111-13**
Wisdom of Unity, The (Manisa-Pancakam), 46, **154**
Witness-Consciousness, **124-25, 136, 221, 240**, 437
  arguments relative to are secondary to the Yogic
    Process, **188, 193, 194**
  and awakening of in the "Thumbs", **186, 192**
  and devotion to Adi Da Samraj, **193-94**
  and heart-baptism, **226**
  and right side of the heart, **224**
  as shape of round body, **192**
  and sixth stage error, **235**
  as "skin" of the "Thumbs", **192, 193**
  Source-Domain of, **207**
  stable awakening to, **229, 234, 242**
  as true "turiya" state, **290**
Witnessing
  from the heart-place, **83**
  Swami Muktananda's use of term, **278-80**
Word, Divine, 13, **55, 142, 252, 347**, 382-83
world, and duality with God, **145**
world-intercommunicativeness, **284**

X

xenophobia, **62**

Y

yawning, **180**
Yogananda, Swami, **288**, 437
Yoga of all-Outshining "Brightness", **129**
Yogis, **156-57, 169-70, 259-60, 265**
"You can't get there from here", **177**, 393n17

I do not simply recommend or turn men and women to Truth. I _Am_ Truth. I Draw men and women to Myself. I _Am_ the Present Real God, Desiring, Loving, and Drawing up My devotees. I have Come to Be Present with My devotees, to Reveal to them the True Nature of life in Real God, which is Love, and of mind in Real God, which is Faith. I Stand always Present in the Place and Form of Real God. I accept the qualities of all who turn to Me, dissolving those qualities in Real God, so that _Only_ God becomes the Condition, Destiny, Intelligence, and Work of My devotees. I look for My devotees to acknowledge Me and turn to Me in appropriate ways, surrendering to Me perfectly, depending on Me, full of Me always, with only a face of love.

I am waiting for you. I have been waiting for you eternally.

Where are you?

AVATAR ADI DA SAMRAJ

1971